…NCE PRAISE FOR

… Messiah of Israel?

How should [illegible] think about the Church's long suppression of Jews in its midst, the recent rise of messianic Judaism, and the land of Israel? This volume is a treasure of deep reflection by some of the best thinkers among messianic Jews and Catholic and Protestant theologians. No one interested in these questions can afford to miss this book.

—Gerald McDermott
author of A New History of Redemption: The Work of Jesus the Messiah Through the Millennia

What does it mean to recognize Jesus as the Messiah of Israel–for his fellow Jews and for those drawn "from the nations"? What does it mean, in turn, for the relationship between these two communities? This volume offers learned and wise reflections from leading scholars representing both mainstream Christianity and Messianic Judaism. Readers ready to enter into this rich and complex topic will find the essays contained here to be essential reading.

—Holly Taylor Coolman
Asst. Professor, Theology Dept., Providence College

This volume is a collection of essays and responses given at an international symposium at the University of Vienna in 2022 that brings to life a rich dialogue between Messianic Judaism and Christian theology. Eminent Catholic, Protestant, and Messianic Jewish theologians exchange views on the theological significance of the emergence of Messianic Judaism and the ecclesiological implications and providential opportunities this raises for the life of the Church, as "a people made up of Jew and Gentile" (*Lumen Gentium* §9).

—Lawrence Feingold
Professor of Theology, Kenrick-Glennon Seminary, St. Louis

Few theologians have had an impact on par with Mark Kinzer, who over the past thirty years has entirely reshaped Jewish-Christian dialogue in the theological academy by focusing it on post-missionary Messianic Judaism, with crucial Christological, ecclesiological, and eschatological issues at stake. This superb book exhibits the fruits of Kinzer's longtime dialogue with German-speaking theologians led by Cardinal Christoph Schoenborn, joined by leading American theologians such as Kendall Soulen as well as the French theologian Antoine Levy, among others. To say the least, Messianic Judaism is no longer peripheral to Christian theology but has raised questions that demand answers. This book shows how far the dialogue has already advanced.

—Matthew Levering
James N. Jr. and Mary D. Perry Chair of Theology, Mundelein Seminary

Jesus—the Messiah of Israel?

JESUS—THE MESSIAH OF ISRAEL?

Messianic Judaism and Christian Theology in Conversation

edited by

MARK S. KINZER, THOMAS SCHUMACHER, AND JAN-HEINER TÜCK

with James Earle Patrick

A Herder & Herder Book
The Crossroad Publishing Company
New York

A Herder & Herder Book
The Crossroad Publishing Company
www.crossroadpublishing.com

[cip TK]

Contents

FUNDAMENTAL RELATIONS

CHRISTOLOGY—THE JEWISH JESUS

Preface

This volume documents an international symposium at the University of Vienna, which took place in July 2022 and was dedicated to the conversation between Christian theology and representatives of Messianic Judaism. Renowned theologians from the United States, Israel, and various countries throughout Europe came together to reflect on the relationship between the Messianic Jewish movement and Christian Churches and to discuss theologically controversial topics. A diversity of perspectives was planned from the outset. The assembled theologians came from different faith traditions (Messianic-Jewish, Catholic, Lutheran, Reformed, Free Church) and theological discourse cultures. Nevertheless, a decidedly academic discourse forum was chosen to explore the question of what it means when Jews confess Jesus as the Messiah of Israel and consciously adhere to a more or less Torah-observant way of life. Does this have repercussions for Christian theology? How can the constellation of Jews who believe in the Messiah and the Church be determined? How do Messianic Jewish believers situate themselves in relation to Christianity in its plural forms? What new impulses can come from this conversation? Which overhanging questions should be looked at more closely in the future? Despite all their differences, the participants of the symposium were united by their common faith in Jesus of Nazareth, the Messiah of Israel and the nations, their conviction that the Holy Spirit works in history, and their rejection of anti-Judaic substitution theologies and missionary activities toward the Jews. We look back with gratitude on the friendly atmosphere and the critical-constructive culture of discussion at the symposium.

The planning and implementation of the symposium would not have been possible without the preparatory work and support of the interdisciplinary working group moderated by Johannes Fichtenbauer on behalf of Christoph Cardinal Schönborn. The deliberations of this working group resulted in the small volume *Jesus, King of the Jews? Messianic Judaism, Jewish Christians, and Theology Beyond Supersessionism,* which was published in several languages and was intended to prepare the symposium thematically.[1] Many alert minds and helping hands contributed to the planning and realization of the symposium. Special thanks go to Dr Bernard Mallmann, who took the lead in organizing the conference, and to Dr James Earle Patrick, who played a decisive role in supervising and coordinating the printing of this volume, and also to Dr Dorothee Bauer, Michaela Feiertag, Johannes Fichtenbauer, Ann Friemel, Dr Johannes Cornides, and Florian Vorisek, who actively helped with the conference. Christoph Cardinal Schönborn hosted a generous reception for the participants of the symposium in the Archbishop's Palace and gave an impressive account of his experiences in the dialogue with Messianic Jews. We thank the Cardinal for this gesture of solidarity.

We also thank all the speakers, some of whom traveled long distances to come to Vienna and enrich the symposium with their contributions. Moreover, the English publication would not have been possible without the translation of the German-language contributions. At this point, we would like to mention John David Martin, Dr James Earle Patrick, and Dr Wayne M. Coppins, whose commitment made it possible for this volume to reach a wide audience in the English-speaking world.[2] In order to achieve a good reading flow, all non-English quotations have

1. In English, published as: James E. Patrick (ed.), *Jesus, King of the Jews? Messianic Judaism, Jewish Christians, and Theology Beyond Supersessionism* (Vienna: Toward Jerusalem Council II, 2021). For German, French, Polish, and Portuguese, contact the same publisher.

2. Articles translated from German by J.D. Martin and J.E. Patrick: Schönborn, Kasper and Tück; Rutishauser; Rucks; Schwienhorst-Schönberger; Theobald; Hoping; Mallmann; T. Schumacher; Tück; Laepple. W.M. Coppins revised all except

been translated, while the text in the original language can be found in footnotes or brackets.

We would also like to thank the team members of the Fribourg Chair of New Testament Studies, Dr Beatrice Wyss, Philemon Reinhardt, and Joëlle Wenger, for formal revisions and proofreading of the manuscript. We are also grateful for the uncomplicated and constructive cooperation with Chris Myers and Julie Boddorf from Herder&Herder (The Crossroad Publishing Company). We hope that this volume can provide valuable theological impulses for the academic conversation between the Messianic-Jewish movement and Christian theology in its various forms.

Mark S. Kinzer, Thomas Schumacher, and Jan-Heiner Tück

Rucks and T. Schumacher, who checked their own articles. U. Schumacher translated her own.

Foreword

THE SECOND VATICAN COUNCIL laid the foundation stone for a renewed relationship between Christianity and Judaism. The declaration *Nostra Aetate* reminds us that the roots of Christianity lie in Judaism. The Christian Church must never forget this rootstock that sustains her. The ecumenical dialogue with Judaism is therefore a permanent task for her. Since then, many initiatives have deepened the Jewish–Christian dialogue.

In addition, a special connection between Judaism and Christianity has grown stronger. Since the nineteenth century, there have been more and more Jews who not only see Jesus as their brother in faith or as a Jewish rabbi, but also recognize him as the expected Messiah. This Messianic Judaism lives faithful to the Torah and its commandments and believes the prophetic message that Jesus is the Messiah who is to come.

Since the year 2000, there has been a dialogue group between the Catholic Church and the Jewish Messianic movement. I am grateful to have belonged to it for several years, and to follow Cardinal Georges Cottier as leader of the Catholic side. In the many encounters, friendships have grown, as well as an understanding and a great esteem for one another.

As a fruit of the conversations, the symposium "Jesus—also the Messiah for Israel? Messianic Jewish Movement and Christianity in

Dialogue" was held in July 2022 at the University of Vienna. For the first time, the important topic of Messianic Judaism could also be illuminated academically. Scholars from all over the world came together to reflect on the subject areas of Christology, ecclesiology, and eschatology from a Christian and Messianic-Jewish perspective.

I would like to thank everyone who contributed to the success of this symposium. May these conference proceedings help advance us along the path we have begun, and deepen the dialogue between Christians and Jews, trusting in the promise that in the end "God shall be all in all" (1 Cor 15:28).

With heartfelt blessings

+ Christoph Cardinal Schönborn
Vienna, December 2022

Prologue

Already in the first centuries of Christianity, the Church rejected any positive views toward Jewish believers in Jesus as the Messiah of Israel and Savior of mankind if they chose to continue to live as Jews. During the long period since then, most Christian denominations refused to grant any special role within the Church to their Jewish members. The opposite was the case. Jewish converts suffered from prejudice, often being seen as second-class Christians.

Two relatively recent developments have changed this theological perspective dramatically. The twentieth century witnessed a growing theological interest in the Hebrew background of the Holy Scriptures, and with it a rediscovery of the Jewish foundations of the Christian faith. What had already begun earlier among the Protestants found its Catholic counterpart in the developments after the Second Vatican Council. As a result, Jewish members of historic and independent Churches were no longer forced to hide their Jewishness. Some prominent Jewish believers within even the Catholic Church and some Orthodox Churches loudly insisted that their Jewishness is foundational for the healthy self-image of the Christian Church as being comprised of Jews and Gentiles. The former Cardinal of Paris, Jean-Marie Lustiger, and the Russian Orthodox priest, Father Alexander Men, are only two among them.

The second challenge occurred in the 1970s as a new development within worldwide Judaism, namely, the Messianic Jewish movement in all its diversity. Within this phenomenon, a growing number of Jews ranging from orthodox to highly liberal backgrounds found Yeshua of Nazareth as their Messiah and as the Redeemer of humanity. Those Messianic Jews insist on their ongoing relationship with the Jewish people, having no interest in separating from the Jewish way of life and religious practice. They refuse with conviction to join any Christian denomination, and proudly associate themselves with the first "Messianic Jewish congregation of the Apostles" in Jerusalem.

Since the turn of the millennium, a rather small but growing number of theologians began to take this inner-Jewish movement more seriously, not just seeing it as another "Jewish-flavored" free-church expression. What had previously hindered the constructive interest in this phenomenon from the side of the historic Churches was the fear that any closer contact could endanger all that had been established in the flourishing Jewish–Christian dialogue.

In 1996, a group of Messianic-Jewish and Christian leaders from different Church backgrounds formed an initiative for bridging the two "worlds." Building trust was most needed; Messianic Jews share the same presuppositions as most other Jews, which result from centuries of Christian humiliation and persecution. This initiative, called Towards Jerusalem Council II (TJCII), wanted to build trust between the two camps, to invest in mutual theological understanding, and to promote the Messianic movement among Christian denominations. The driving hope is to facilitate a process to invert and thus bring full-circle what was accomplished at the "First Council of Jerusalem." According to Acts 15, the Jesus-believers from among the nations were released from any obligation toward the Jewish law, thus remaining Gentiles. TJCII labors for an agreement in which the Messianic Jews may likewise be released from pressure to assimilate with Gentile Christianity, taking up their role as the Jewish branch and expression of the Church within the united Body of Christ (Rom 11).

Parallel to TJCII, a study group consisting of theologians from the different Messianic Jewish movements and from the Catholic Church started its regular meetings in the year 2000. Their goal was to consider anew the significance of baptized Jewish members of the Church for the self-understanding of the Church, and to verify the authenticity of the Messianic Jewish phenomenon. Within this study group, many of the Catholic theologians are themselves baptized Jews. Even when the dialogue long remained as an informal gathering, it took place under the prominent guidance of the Cardinals George Cottier (Papal Household) and Christoph Schönborn (Vienna), with the approval of the Popes John Paul II, Benedict XVI, and most recently Francis.

Besides TJCII and the Messianic / Catholic Study Group, two more initiatives and their vision influenced the later Vienna Symposium. The input of "The Society for Post-Supersessionist Theology" was demonstrated by Kendall Soulen's participation in the event, as one of the Society's founders. The other influencer was "Yachad BeYeshua" (Together in Jesus), an international ecumenical fellowship of all types of Jewish disciples of Jesus—Messianic Jews, Jewish Catholics, Jewish Protestants, and Jews from the Orthodox Church—spearheaded by Mark Kinzer and Antoine Lévy, two of the main speakers in Vienna.

For all of these initiatives, two types of questions were important. The first category had to do with the relevance of Jesus Christ as the Messiah of Israel and the consequences thereof for a new perspective on Christology and ecclesiology. What were the consequences of the fact that "the Old Covenant has never been revoked" (*Catechism of the Catholic Church*, §121), and that Jesus himself, the Apostles, and the first generation of believers all laid the foundations of the Church as Jews? A new valuing of the role of baptized Jews in the Churches and in the Messianic movement has to be envisioned, including the question how the missing expression of the "Church of James" (*ecclesia ex circumcisione*) could be recovered. What would all of this reveal about the innermost identity of the Church?

The second set of questions considers the authenticity of the Messianic movement—existing structurally outside of the institutional Church boundaries. In this context, questions should be raised concerning the theological connection between the Messianic movement and the land, "Eretz Israel," and the implications of their Messianic hope as a concrete millennial perspective that challenges the classic framework of eschatology.

In the autumn of 2019, members of TJCII and of the Messianic-Jewish / Catholic Study Group and other initiatives began to prepare for a first international symposium about those questions. Such a symposium should take place within an academic setting which could awaken the interest of a wider group of biblical and systematic-theological scholars worldwide. Finally, with the great support of Vienna University Professor Jan-Heiner Tück and the Cardinal of Vienna, Christoph Schönborn, the plans were realized to hold this Symposium, "Jesus—also the Messiah of Israel?," at the Alma Mater Viennensis. Even though there were obviously major hindrances along the way, most of all surrounding the Covid pandemic, great effort was expended to bring about these symposium days, and the financial barriers were also lifted. The workload was managed through the engagement of many volunteers from both the University of Vienna and TJCII-Europe under the wise coordination of Bernard Mallmann, Ann Friemel, and James Earle Patrick.

From 11 to 13 July 2022, more than 40 scholars from different denominational Church backgrounds and from the different streams of the Messianic movement responded to the invitation and made the symposium a colorful ecumenical event. The time was ripe for such a convocation, to bring these important theological questions to the attention of the wider academic world.

Johannes Fichtenbauer
European Director of TJCII

Introductory Survey

Bernard Mallmann and Jan-Heiner Tück

"Christianity is indissolubly bound to Judaism.
If it breaks away from it, it ceases to be itself . . ."[1]

Cardinal Jean-Marie Lustiger

THE VIENNA SYMPOSIUM, which facilitated discussion between representatives of the Messianic Jewish movement and Jesus-believing Jews on the one hand and Christian theologians on the other, was entitled *Jesus—the Messiah also for Israel?* The theme of the symposium was deliberately formulated as a question rather than a thesis. Jesus is the Messiah *from* Israel, that is certain (cf. John 4:22; Matt 1:1–16; Rom 1:3), but whether he is also the Messiah *for* Israel is an open and much discussed question. In addressing this question, it cannot be ignored that there are more and more Jews who come to believe in Jesus as the Messiah of Israel without missionary activity on the part of the Church. This is no cause for Christian triumphalism. On the contrary, it would be absurd to declare Judaism in its various forms a living anachronism and to consider a Torah-pious lifestyle obsolete in terms of salvation history. Paul, a Jesus-believing Jew, already emphasizes the lasting theological significance of Israel with the words that all Israel will be

1. "Das Christentum ist unlöslich an das Judentum gebunden. Löst es sich davon ab, so hört es auf, es selbst zu sein . . ."—JeanMarie Lustiger, "Christentum unlöslich an Judentum gebunden," in Jean-Marie Lustiger, *Wagt den Glauben. Artikel, Vorträge, Predigten, Interviews 1981–1984*, trans. Hans U. v. Balthasar (Theologia romanica, 14; Einsiedeln: Johannes-Verlag, 1986): 79–86, at 84.

saved (Rom 11:26) and that the gifts of grace and the calling of God are irrevocable even during the period when Israel's mainstream identity has no place for Jesus (Rom 11:28–29). Christian theology cannot and must not overlook this. It has to reject all forms of replacement theology that declare Israel to be an obsolete quantity in the history of salvation, and must self-critically work through and eradicate anti-Jewish traces in theology, liturgy, and catechesis. Christian theology—especially after the Shoah—must defend and protect the permanent election of Israel against hostility. Pope John Paul II expressed the relationship between Judaism and Christianity in these much-quoted words in the synagogue in Rome in 1986:

> The Church of Christ discovers her "bond" with Judaism by reflecting on her own mystery [cf. *Nostra Aetate* 4]. The Jewish religion is not something "external" for us, but belongs in a certain way to the "interior" of our religion. We thus have relations with it like with no other religion. You are our privileged brothers and, one could say, our elder brothers.[2]

The Jewishness of the Church is part of her own identity. What the Second Vatican Council thus recalls was not always a matter of course in the history of the Church. Today, however, many dialogue forums are committed to this claim and, in respect for one another, they work hard to find the path that God's promises have given to his people of Jews and Gentiles. The person of Jesus Christ is not only the link, but also the point of contention in striving for the depth of God's riches, wisdom, and knowledge (Rom 11:33). Who do Jews and Christians consider this Jesus of Nazareth to be?

Jesus' Jewishness has become a fixed topos in contemporary Christology.[3] The horror of the Shoah has led to a rethinking in Christian

2. https://www.vatican.va/content/john-paul-ii/de/speeches/1986/april/documents/hf_jp-ii_spe_19860413_sinagoga-roma.html (accessed April 11, 2025).

3. Cf. Helmut Hoping, *Jesus aus Galiläa – Messias und Gottes Sohn* (Freiburg i. Br.: Herder, 2nd edn 2019); Josef Wohlmuth, *An der Schwelle zum Heiligtum. Christliche Theologie im Gespräch mit jüdischen Denkern* (Munich / Vienna / Zürich: Schöningh, 2007); Jan-Heiner Tück (ed.), *Die Beschneidung Jesu. Was sie Juden und Christen heute bedeutet* (Freiburg i. Br.: Herder, 2020); Kayko Driedger Hesselein, *Dual Citizenship: Two Natures Christologies and the Jewish Jesus* (London: T&T Clark, 2015); Barbara U. Meyer, *Jesus the Jew in Christian Memory: Theological and Philosophical Explorations* (Cambridge: Cambridge University Press, 2020); Susannah Heschel, *Der jüdische Jesus und das Christentum. Abraham Geigers Herausforderung an die christliche Theologie* (Berlin: Jüdische Verlagsanstalt, 2001); Ulrich Laepple, "Judenchristen,

theology and step by step to a *purificazione della memoria*.[4] It was mainly baptized Christians who committed the atrocities against Jewish fellow citizens under National Socialism. Not infrequently, Church dignitaries sympathized with the Nazi regime. Vienna, the venue for the conference, also provides a thought-provoking example of this in the person of Cardinal Theodor Innitzer. The Archbishop of Vienna welcomed the so-called Anschluss of Austria in the spring of 1938 and signed a greeting note with "Heil Hitler." Even though Innitzer subsequently distanced himself from Hitler and in October 1938 in St Stephen's Cathedral in Vienna called Christ "our Führer," his role remains historically controversial.[5] During the war, the Viennese cardinal founded the Archbishop's Aid Office for Non-Aryan Catholics in December 1940, which provided material, social and pastoral care for baptized Jews. Several hundred Jews were able to emigrate abroad with this support. In the decades after World War II, the Catholic Church gradually became aware of her moral debts. The Second Vatican Council in particular provided a decisive impetus with the declaration *Nostra Aetate*:

> True, the Jewish authorities and those who followed their lead pressed for the death of Christ; still, what happened in His passion cannot be charged against all the Jews, without distinction, then alive, nor against the Jews of today. Although the Church is the new people of God, the Jews should not be presented as rejected or accursed by God, as if this followed from the Holy Scriptures. All should see to it, then, that in catechetical work or in the preaching of the word of God they do not teach anything that does not conform to the truth of the Gospel and the spirit of Christ.

This short passage (in section 4)[6] may rightly be regarded as a turning point in the relationship between Judaism and the Catholic Church and is still the basis of many dialogue efforts today. However, the declaration

---

Messianische Juden und die EKD im christlich-jüdischen Gespräch von 1945 bis heute," *Theologische Beiträge* 50 (2019): 431–54.

4. Cf. Internationale Theologenkommission, *Erinnern und Versöhnen. Die Kirche und die Verfehlungen in ihrer Vergangenheit*, ed. Gerhard Ludwig Müller (Freiburg i. Br.: Johannes-Verlag, 2000).

5. Cf. Jan-Heiner Tück, *Crux. Über die Anstößigkeit des Kreuzes* (Freiburg i. Br.: Herder, 2023): 258–69.

6. On the meaning and limit of *Nostra Aetate* 4, cf. Stefan Schreiber and Thomas Schumacher (eds.), *Antijudaismen in der Exegese? Eine Diskussion 50 Jahre nach Nostra Aetate* (Freiburg i. Br.: Herder, 2015).

on Judaism was not a vote of the preparatory commission of the Council nor a wish of bishops, but it goes back to Pope John XXIII himself, who had been in personal contact with Jews since his time in Bulgaria and Turkey.[7] It is reported of the Roncalli Pope "that when he saw the pictures of the bulldozers pushing Jewish corpses into mass graves in the Nazi death camps that had just been liberated, he exclaimed: 'This is the body of Christ.'"[8] As a particular impetus, it is worth recalling here a conversation with the Jewish-French historian Jules Isaac (1877–1963) who, in the run-up to the Council, made three requests to the Pope: (1) all unjust statements about Israel in Christian doctrine should be subjected to a critical revision; (2) the erroneous legend that the Diaspora, that is, the dispersion of the Jews, was considered a punishment for the crucifixion of Jesus should be set right; and (3) the statements from the Trent Catechism should be recalled, which attributed the guilt for the death of Jesus not to the Jewish people but to "our sins." *Nostra Aetate* responded to these requests and thus gave an important impetus to post-Conciliar theology. Present-day exegesis particularly emphasizes that it is not what stands out from the Judaism of the time that is to be considered authentic to Jesus, but rather what is in continuity with the Jewish faith. Christian theology, especially of the Catholic tradition which is committed to the Second Vatican Council, is thus obliged to reject any form of substitutionary theology.

But does Jesus Christ also mean something to Jews? Or should Christology rather be left out of the Jewish–Christian conversation so as not to awaken unpleasant memories of anti-Judaic and triumphalist Christologies? Since the nineteenth century there has been a history of "bringing Jesus home" to Judaism.[9] Here, too, there is an awareness that the "brother Jesus" (Shalom Ben-Chorin) lived in and fully shared the Jewish tradition.

7. Cf. Dorothee Recker, *Die Wegbereiter der Judenerklärung des Zweiten Vatikanischen Konzils. Johannes XXIII., Kardinal Bea und Prälat Österreicher – eine Darstellung ihrer theologischen Entwicklung* (Paderborn: Bonifatius, 2007): esp. 103–200, as well as the chapter "Gottes Konsul," in Peter Hebblethwaite, *Johannes XXIII. Das Leben des Angelo Roncalli* (Zürich et al.: Benziger, 1986): 215–56.

8. ". . . daß er, als er die Bilder von den Bulldozern sah, die in den gerade befreiten Nazi-Todeslagern die jüdischen Leichen in Massengräber schoben, ausgerufen habe: 'Das ist der Leib Christi'"—Michael Wyschogrod, "Inkarnation aus jüdischer Sicht," *Evangelische Theologie* 55 (1995): 13–28, at 24.

9. Cf. Walter Homolka, *Der Jude Jesus – Eine Heimholung* (Freiburg i. Br.: Herder, 5th rev. edn 2021).

The title of the Vienna conference, *Jesus—also the Messiah for Israel?*, alluded to the thesis of the two parallel paths to salvation. That theory says that the first chosen people of Israel is saved through the Torah, but the Church from the nations through Jesus Christ! "We confess that God's covenant with the Jewish people represents a path to salvation to God—even without the recognition of Jesus Christ," it says programmatically in a document of the discussion group "Jews and Christians" at the Central Committee of German Catholics.[10] But can there be two peoples of God from a Christian perspective? Should there be two parallel paths of salvation for Israel and the nations in the one history of salvation? Would not God then be, according to a pointed remark by Robert Spaemann, a "bigamist"?[11]

The common conviction of all participants of the Vienna symposium was that God has chosen Israel and that Israel stands in the unrevoked covenant. Any form of replacement theology or supersessionism is therefore firmly rejected. The thesis of many Church Fathers that Israel has been both punished and rejected, and the old people of God replaced by the Church, the new Israel, is in need of revision. Israel is not rejected, as Paul says in Romans. God cannot be regarded as a remarried divorcee who dismisses his first wife in order to marry a new one, as the exegete Dieter Böhler SJ has noted.[12]

Another conviction of all participants in the symposium was that the widespread canonical narrative of creation, fall, redemption and consummation must be expanded by taking into account the covenant history with Israel. This covenant history is not the outdated prehistory of the Church; rather, the enduring theological dignity of Israel as the

10. "Wir bekennen, dass der Bund Gottes mit dem jüdischen Volk einen Heilsweg zu Gott darstellt – auch ohne Anerkennung Jesu Christi"—Gesprächskreis "Juden und Christen" beim Zentralkomitee der deutschen Katholiken, ed., *Nein zur Judenmission – Ja zum Dialog zwischen Juden und Christen* (on 9 March 2009): 5. Cf. Hubert Frankemölle, "Nein zur Judenmission – Ja zum Dialog: Zur Erklärung des Gesprächskreises 'Juden und Christen' beim ZdK von 2009," *Catholica (Münster)* 64 (2010): 212–29; Wilhelm Breuning, "Nein zur Judenmission – ja zum Dialog zwischen Juden und Christen," in *Im Angesicht der Anderen. Gespräche zwischen christlicher Theologie und jüdischem Denken*, ed. Florian Bruckmann and René Dausner Festschrift for Josef Wohlmuth (Paderborn: Schöningh, 2013): 125–40.

11. Robert Spaemann, "Gott ist kein Bigamist," *Frankfurter Allgemeine Zeitung*, April 20, 2009.

12. Cf. Dieter Böhler, "Durften die Christen Israel gegen die Kirche austauschen?," in *Sind Religionen austauschbar? Philosophisch-theologische Positionen aus christlicher Sicht*, ed. Johannes Arnold (Münster: Aschendorff, 2011): 1–25.

"apple of God's eye" must be recognized.[13] The history of the chosen people of Israel has theological significance for the Church.

The conviction that the Jew Jesus of Nazareth is the Messiah for Israel and for the nations also carries an aspect of promise: He has come—and he will come again to unite what has been separated and to establish the kingdom of consummation. Even if the *how* and the *when* are subject to the uncertainties of eschatology, there is hope for Jews and Christians that God's promise will be fulfilled and that he will be "all in all" (cf. 1 Cor 15:28).

Closely intertwined with this is the conviction that the Church of the beginning was a Church of Jews and Gentiles. The *ecclesia ex gentibus*, however, marginalized the *ecclesia ex circumcisione* more and more already in the first centuries and finally excluded and forgot about her. The return of the repressed Jesus-believing Jews in the nineteenth century and the Messianic Jewish movement in the twentieth century is therefore a sign in need of interpretation, which needs to be further considered in the common conversation between Messianic Jews and Christian theologians. Here again it was a common conviction of the participants that we cannot restore the Church of the beginning—*ex gentibus* and *ex circumcision*—through a theological conversation, but its original pattern calls for a fruitful togetherness that takes into account our intervening and often traumatic history. How exactly Messiah-believing Jews are to be located with regard to the Church is a controversial question that needs to be further explored.

Now, such a conversation is by no means a matter of course. When word got around that an international symposium with Messianic Jews was planned at the University of Vienna, there were frowns and critical questions among colleagues. Messianic Jews, it was objected, are no longer recognized as Jews by other varieties of Judaism, they have a reputation for proselytizing other Jews.[14] Most established Churches reject institutional mission to the Jews for theological reasons, believing

13. Cf. Jan-Heiner Tück, *Gottes Augapfel. Bruchstücke zu einer Theologie nach Auschwitz* (Freiburg i. Br.: Herder, 2nd edn 2016).

14. Cf. Peter von der Osten-Sacken, "Ein Empfehlungsbrief Christi? Zur Debatte um Judenmission, Judenchristen und messianische Juden," in *Das Heil der Anderen. Problemfeld "Judenmission,"* ed. Hubert Frankenmölle and Josef Wohlmuth, Quaestiones Disputatae, 238 (Freiburg i. Br.: Herder, 2010): 77–112.

that Israel stands fully in the saving grace of God. But there are also vehement reservations on the part of Judaism. Abraham J. Heschel's words to Augustin Cardinal Bea that the mission to the Jews is "spiritual fratricide" should be remembered. Most recently, the Vatican Commission for Religious Relations with Judaism once again underlined its rejection of a mission to the Jews in 2015:

> It is easy to understand that the so-called "mission to the Jews" is a very delicate and sensitive matter for Jews because, in their eyes, it involves the very existence of the Jewish people. This question also proves to be awkward for Christians, because for them the universal salvific significance of Jesus Christ and consequently the universal mission of the Church are of fundamental importance. The Church is therefore obliged to view evangelization to Jews, who believe in the one God, in a different manner from that to people of other religions and world views. In concrete terms this means that the Catholic Church neither conducts nor supports any specific institutional mission work directed towards Jews.[15]

All dialogue partners must therefore be aware that an official mission to the Jews cannot be justified theologically, nor Christologically. Against this background, it is not unproblematic that there are efforts within the Messianic Jewish movement to conduct formal missions to the Jews. They not only want to bear witness to Jesus as the Messiah before their fellow Jews, which is a duty for individual believers in Messiah, but they also actively advocate the turning of the whole of Judaism toward the confession of Christ. The theologian and rabbi Mark S. Kinzer stands out all the more among Messiah-believing Jews. In his book *Postmissionary Messianic Judaism*, he explains from Jewish sources why Messianic Judaism can and must see itself as a Judaism that has gone beyond the mission to the Jews.[16] Messianic Judaism should not be proselytizing its own brothers and sisters who are in fidelity to the Torah, but solely bearing witness to Messiah.

15. Commission for Religious Relations with the Jews, *"The Gifts and the Calling of God are Irrevocable" (Rom 11:29): A Reflection on Theological Questions Pertaining to Catholic–Jewish Relations on the Occasion of the 50th Anniversary of "Nostra ætate" (No. 4)*, para. 40, in http://www.christianunity.va/content/unitacristiani/en/commissione-per-i-rapporti-religiosi-con-l-ebraismo/commissione-per-i-rapporti-religiosi-con-l-ebraismo-crre/documenti-della-commissione/en.html (accessed April 11, 2025).

16. Cf. Mark S. Kinzer, *Postmissionary Messianic Judaism: Redefining Christian Engagement with the Jewish People* (Grand Rapids, MI: Brazos, 2005).

Another objection to the symposium was that Messianic Judaism is a heterogeneous group that unites different, often evangelical currents within itself. The academic exchange with them jeopardizes the state of Jewish–Christian dialogue that has been reached, and the Pontifical Council for Christian Unity and Special Relations with Judaism has not yet established official relations with Messianic Jews. The rethinking that began in the Churches after the shock of the Shoah had finally turned enemies into brothers and sisters. This must not be jeopardized.

Our response to these objections, which are understandable at first glance, was that Messianic Jews agree with us Christians in confessing Jesus as Messiah, as Christ. This is a fundamental common bond that should not be excluded or ignored for reasons of dialogue strategy. Moreover, the multifaceted Messianic Jewish movement has been growing steadily since the late 1960s and can no longer be ignored in terms of the sociology of religion alone—estimates put the number of followers at 150,000–250,000. Furthermore, with Johann Baptist Metz, the founder of the new political theology, the principle of anamnetic solidarity with the Jewish victims is to be taken seriously.[17] Messianic Jews also lost family members in the Shoah; they too are to be included in the horizon of anamnetic theology. Christians should not promote the exclusions and stigmatization that Messianic Jews often experience; it cannot be their task to duplicate the inner-Jewish conflict. A theology of exclusion and contempt has existed in the Churches for far too long! It is indeed a memorable phenomenon, even an "eschatological sign" according to Cardinal Joseph Ratzinger (1927–2022), that more and more Jews are coming to believe in Jesus, the Messiah for Israel and for the nations, without the influence of the Christian Churches. As early as 2000, therefore, Pope John Paul II (1978–2005) set up a theological study group, which first began its work under Cardinal Georges Cottier (1922–2016), then continued under Cardinal Christoph Schönborn, who was in charge until 2020. Vienna was therefore chosen as the venue for the conference, where Peter Hocken and Johannes Fichtenbauer have been doing valuable preliminary work for the dialogue with Messianic Jews for years. Finally, the Vienna symposium corresponds

17. Cf. Johann Baptist Metz, *Memoria passionis. Ein provozierendes Gedächtnis in pluralistischer Gesellschaft* (Gesammelte Schriften, 4; Freiburg i. Br.: Herder, 2017).

to the express wish of Pope Francis to deepen the conversation between Christian theology and the Messianic Jewish movement in terms of content.

The topics discussed at the symposium, as can be seen more precisely from the table of contents, after an introduction to Messianic Judaism from the different denominations,[18] touch on questions of Christology, ecclesiology, and eschatology.

(1) Jesus, the "King of the Jews," was at the same time a "servant to the circumcision," as Paul writes in Romans. What does Jesus' Jewish identity mean for Christology? The Jewishness of Jesus has long been suppressed, especially in German-speaking theology, or even explicitly denied at the time of the Third Reich, when constructions of an "Aryan Jesus" emerged. Christian theology must feel committed to the statement that Jesus became "Jewish flesh."[19] This has implications for exegetical and systematic Christology.

(2) The Church of the beginning was a Church of Jews and Gentiles. Mary, the Twelve, and Paul were Jews who lived Torah-observant lives. But the *ecclesia ex gentibus* marginalized the *ecclesia ex circumcisione* in the first centuries, even gradually excluding her with disciplinary measures. What does it mean that the Messianic Jewish movement and Jesus-believing Jews now bring back what was forgotten and lost? The disappearance of the *ecclesia ex circumcisione* is not just a phantom pain, but a gaping wound in ecclesiology. How can it be healed? The "parting of the ways" is a history of mutual disqualification and demarcation that has led to constructions of Judaism and Christianity. The historical boundary markers can be reconsidered with a view to the biblical witness. The Church's constitutive reference back to Israel must not disregard the question of the place of Jesus-believing Jews in the Church. As

18. Cf., e.g., Evangelische Kirche in Deutschland, ed., *Judenchristen – jüdische Christen – "messianische Juden." Eine Positionsbestimmung des Gemeinsamen Ausschusses "Kirche und Judentum" im Auftrag des Rates der EKD* (2017), https://www.ekd.de/ekd_de/ds_doc/Messianische_Juden.pdf (accessed April 11, 2025).

19. Karl Barth, *Kirchliche Dogmatik IV/1: Die Lehre von der Versöhnung* (Zürich: Evangelischer Verlag AG, 1953): 181. As early as 1946, Barth says, against theological efforts to deny Jesus' Jewish roots: "Jesus was necessarily Jewish" / "Jesus war notwendig Jude"—Karl Barth, *Dogmatik im Grundriß* (Lectures held in the summer semester of 1946 at the University of Bonn; Zürich: Evangelischer Verlag AG, 1947): 87.

a Church that breathes with two lungs, can it be more closely defined with Mark Kinzer as a "bilateral ecclesiology in solidarity with Israel"?[20]

(3) Finally, Messianic Jews, like charismatic Christians, live in joyful expectation that Jesus, the Messiah, will soon return. They interpret the return of many Jews to the land of Israel and the growing presence of Messianic Jews in Jerusalem as portents of the Parousia. Without slipping into a political messianism that thinks it can spell out the final scenario of salvation history, the newly emerging expectation of Parousia is a productive irritation for the Christian Churches, where the cry of "Maranatha" has almost fallen silent. Augustine taught that the thousand-year kingdom was the time of the Church between the first and second coming of Christ. With this thesis he domesticated chiliasm, and his position has found its way into magisterial statements. But is Christian theology not called upon to reconsider this position? Are historical events such as the founding of the State of Israel and the return of many Jews to the land of Israel not also significant in terms of historical theology? Can they be interpreted as God's faithfulness to Israel?

The contributions presented at the symposium are preceded by an in-depth conversation with Cardinal Walter Kasper. The long-time President of the Council for Promoting Christian Unity was intensively involved in the conversation with Judaism. He is recognized as a specialist in Jewish–Christian dialogue and has dealt intensively with questions of Christology and ecclesiology in his theological works.[21] From this perspective, he illuminates the controversial topics that were addressed at the symposium.

The symposium *Jesus—also the Messiah for Israel?* was the first academic forum in Europe to address the multifaceted phenomenon of Messianic Judaism on an interdenominational basis. Naturally, it was not possible to reap the harvest of a discussion process, but rather to draw attention to the importance of the discussion between Jesus-believing

20. Kinzer, *Postmissionary Messianic Judaism* (see note 16), ch. 4; Antoine Lévy, *Jewish Church: A Catholic Approach to Messianic Judaism* (Lanham, MD: Lexington, 2021).

21. Cf. Walter Kasper, *Jesus der Christus* (Walter Kasper – Gesammelte Schriften, 3; Freiburg i. Br.: Herder, 2007); Walter Kasper, *Kirche und Gesellschaft* (Walter Kasper – Gesammelte Schriften, 16.1–2; Freiburg i. Br.: Herder, 2019); Walter Kasper, *Juden und Christen – das eine Volk Gottes* (Freiburg i. Br.: Herder, 2020).

Jews and Christians and to survey the thematic fields of theological discourse. The present volume, an interim result of these dialogue efforts, offers an opportunity for further consideration of the authors' contributions. A next step will be to institutionalize the dialogue format. For the Christian Churches, dialogue with Judaism in its various forms is not a variety of interreligious dialogue, but has an ecumenical dimension. The engagement with those Jews who confess Jesus as the Messiah of Israel can enrich this conversation and even unlock the hope that the "original schism," of which Erich Przywara spoke, can possibly be overcome. What all Jews and Christians have in common is their belief in the one and true God, in whom true unity is found (cf. Deut 6:4–6; Zeph 3:9).

The Messianic Jews—A "Sign Pointing Forward"

An Interview

Cardinal Walter Kasper / Jan-Heiner Tück

A conference on the dialogue between Christian theology and Messianic Judaism has just taken place at the University of Vienna. The dialogue is delicate, since there is a sense in which Messianic Jews fall between the chairs. Official representatives of Judaism deny that they are Jews because they believe in Jesus the Messiah. The Christian Churches remain guarded because they do not wish to jeopardize the achievements of the Jewish–Christian dialogue. Even the Pontifical Commission for Special Relations with Judaism, if I understand correctly, has until now made no official contacts. Why is this?

Cardinal Kasper: It is as you rightly say. In the decade from 1999 to 2010 I was president of the Pontifical Commission for Religious Relations with the Jews. It was the most exciting and most challenging time of my entire professional life.[1] After much debate, the Second Vatican Council (1962–1965) with the declaration *Nostra Aetate* (1965) had achieved one of the most astounding new orientations in relations between Jews and Christians in the 2,000-year history of the Church and had condemned all forms of antisemitism past and present.

According to Erich Przywara, the separation between Jews and Christians is the "original schism" of Church history; in the words of Cardinal Christoph Schönborn, it is "the deepest wound in the body of Christ." The schism became a centuries-long estrangement, even

1. More detail on this in: Walter Kasper, *Juden und Christen – das eine Volk Gottes* (Freiburg i. Br.: Herder, 2020): 13–19.

contempt, oppression, and persecution. They reached their lowest point during the Second World War (1939–1945) in the Shoah, the attempt to annihilate European Jewry that was planned, organized, and carried out in cold blood by the National Socialist state, in which some six million Jews fell victim. After 1945, the shock over this egregious crime led to a fundamental change of thinking (*metanoia*) and to a deep repentance (*teshuva*) in almost all Churches.[2]

The Commission for Religious Relations with the Jews, founded in 1974 by Pope Paul VI, was tasked with coming to terms with the burden of a centuries-long, largely dark history, and with promoting a new cooperation between Jews and Christians on the foundation laid by the Council. The construction of a new, sincere dialogue and a trustful collaboration required, especially from us Christians, consideration and sensitivity for the Jewish partners. We agreed to respect each other's differences but in the discussions to start from what we have in common: belief in the one God and Creator as well as the Ten Words (Ten Commandments) and their significance for the joint engagement for a better and more humane world. Despite certain difficulties, we made good progress overall. From Pope John Paul II, who was on April 13, 1986, the first pope to visit the Great Synagogue of Rome, we found powerful support. Friendly encounters and dialogues between Jews and Christians at all levels worldwide are now part of everyday life in most Christian Churches. Enemies became friends.

One can only be thankful for this development—and after the history of "befriending" and alienation, the recollection of common ground continues to be important. Nonetheless, the real conversation begins to falter when differences remain bracketed out for the sake of peace. The Jewish hesitance to tackle theological questions of doctrine and the Christian vote for a "forgoing of Christological possessions" are challenged by Messianic Jews who openly confess Christ. This is indeed a theological provocation for the ongoing conversation, is it not?

Cardinal Kasper: Yes, the fundamental question that divides us was not touched with the focus on what is held in common. For the

2. An exception are some of the newer, evangelical congregations, which surely cannot be considered as Reformational Churches. The attitude among the Orthodox Churches is different and unfortunately sometimes has antisemitic traits.

Orthodox and Conservative Jewish partners close to the Jewish World Congress, the "no" to the messiahship of Jesus belonged to Jewish identity; for Christians by contrast, the faith conviction that Jesus is the Christ—that is, the expected Messiah, the Son of God, and the salvation of the world—was and remains constitutive. For the Jewish self-understanding, a Messianic Judaism therefore could not exist. Even more, since the memory of earlier compulsory catechesis is still fresh in Jewish consciousness, many Jews suspected that the dialogue might be nothing more than missionizing or proselytizing using other methods. This danger seemed to many Jews even more dangerous than the Shoah. The Shoah threatened to extinguish the physical existence of the Jewish people; the dialogue over Jesus' messiahship and even more so Messianic Judaism was and still is, in part, perceived by many Jews as a danger to the religious and cultural identity of the Jewish people as the chosen people of God and thus as a danger of a new type of Holocaust.

Because of the very pronounced sensitivity of Judaism, the Papal Commission for the dialogue with the Jews was not able to have direct contact with Messianic Jews. But that could not mean a general ban on conversation. Since I knew that Cardinal Christoph Schönborn was carrying on an informal dialogue with Messianic Jews, I kept myself informed about this younger branch of Judaism through one of his coworkers without in any way being active myself. Everything has and needs its time.

How would you position the dialogue with Messianic Jews today within the panorama of the changed relations with Judaism? Should the Catholic Church consider setting up an official dialogue format?

Cardinal Kasper: As I now know, it is a relatively small, but growing, internally pluralistic group of Jews who are to be taken seriously. They are convinced of the special election of the Jewish people and hold fast to the Torah, the Jewish law, but believe in Jesus as the expected Messiah and Savior of the world. Statistically it is not easy to compute their numbers, but it is estimated that there are between 150,000 and 250,000 members.[3]

3. In addition to the standard surveys on this topic, I found the volume by James E. Patrick (ed.), *Jesus, King of the Jews? Messianic Judaism, Jewish Christians, and*

At all times there have been Jews who have let themselves be baptized and become Christians. But this type of convert is not what is happening with Messianic Jews. They adhere to the Jewish Sabbath and holy day praxis as well as to Jewish law. Nor should they be equated with the Jewish Christianity of the first centuries, who are usually referred to as Ebionites (literally: the poor) and who were opposed by the Church Fathers because of their adoptionist Christology and their legalistic way of life that was oriented to the Jewish Torah. Messianic Christians emerged first in the nineteenth century from the evangelical mission to the Jews, and after the Second World War mostly in an evangelical context or as "newborns" from a secular context.

Through the Second Vatican Council and the declaration *Nostra Aetate* (*NA* 4), which was already prepared for by the constitution on the Church (*Lumen Gentium [LG]* 16), the dialogue situation from the Catholic side has improved considerably. The Catholic Church recognizes the election and the special salvation-historical position of the Jewish people. Although the majority of Jews did not accept the gospel of Jesus as the Christ, that is, the Messiah, Israel is still God's chosen and loved people: "His gifts of grace and his calling are irrevocable." The majority of theologians have abandoned the theory of supersessionism developed by the Church Fathers, according to which Israel, because of its unbelief in Jesus as the Messiah, lost her original election, which then passed over to the Church, making the Church the new Israel, the new people of God.

Thus, there is a broad foundation for dialogue about the fundamental concerns of Messianic Christians. Joseph Ratzinger and Christoph Schönborn recall the word of the Apostle Paul that in the end all Israel will come to faith and be saved (Rom 11:12, 26), and place the Messianic Jews in an eschatological context. They view them as a creative work of the Holy Spirit. So are they, as it were, a vanguard of the eschatological pilgrimage of the nations to Zion promised by the prophets (cf. Isa 2:2–5; Mic 4:1–3)? Even if one should be careful with such historical-theological interpretations, one will regard the Messianic Jews as a pleasing sign of the time, which is worth further reflection.

Theology Beyond Supersessionism (Vienna: Toward Jerusalem Council II, 2021), particularly appealing. A comprehensive overview is offered by the former President of the Messianic Jewish Alliance, Richard Harvey, *Mapping Messianic Jewish Theology: A Constructive Approach* (Milton Keynes: Paternoster, 2009).

The growing movement of Messianic Jews is pluriform. Despite all of its diversity, though, Messianic Jews are united by their profession of Jesus as the Messiah. The question is, of course, what they mean by "messianic"? Quite different things are associated with terms like "Messiah," "messianic," "messianic movement."

Cardinal Kasper: Indeed, the crucial question is: What does "messianic" mean to the Messianic Jews? "Messiah" and "messianic" are multilayered terms both in the Bible and in today's parlance, terms that promise good things but that can also give rise to fears of bad things. There are false prophets, about whom Jesus explicitly warns. They come across as harmless sheep, but in reality they are ravening wolves (Matt 7:15). Messiah figures appear mostly in crisis situations. They have visionary ideas and are seen as charismatic leaders and deliverers. They inspire enthusiasm and carry along the masses. But to where? As history shows, unfortunately often into the abyss. But they can also show a way out of the crisis.

Above all, the Bible is regarded as a messianic book, and Judaism as a messianic religion. But the biblical messiah theology is multilayered; it is a theology in the making. Early on appear the still-obscure saying of Balaam (Num 24:17) and the prophecy of Nathan which foretells the eternal continuance of the House of David (2 Sam 7:12–16). The writing prophets and the Psalms take up this hope. The prophets harshly criticize David's failure and even more so the unfaithfulness of his successors, and announce God's judgment. In the Babylonian exile it became reality. The messianic hope seemed to have failed. But God is faithful. He had to start again, and bestowed a new Exodus, a joyful return to Jerusalem (cf. Isa 40–41, 43ff.). After the return, the restoration of the House of David and the coming of the form of a new, Spirit-anointed Messiah figure became one of the many Messiah hopes of that time.

And these multifaceted Messiah hopes then form the pattern for Christology . . .

Cardinal Kasper: Yes, the proclamation of the birth of Jesus and of the birthplace, the city of David, Bethlehem, are shaped entirely by this hope (cf. Luke 1:32–33; 2:4). Jesus himself in his public appearances did not claim the Messiah title for himself. He distanced himself from all affectations of power and rulership and understood his appearance and fate in the sense of the song by the suffering servant of God in the second book of Isaiah (Isa 53). He did not come to be served but to serve and to give his life as a ransom for many (cf. Mark 10:42–45). Accordingly, Jesus immediately corrected Peter's confession of Messiah (Matt 16:16) with reference to his impending suffering and resurrection (Matt 16:21). Only in the trial before the High Council and Pontius Pilate is the Messiah question explicitly posed. His opponents use it to be able to position Jesus as the alleged royal pretender against Caesar (Matt 27:11; John 18:33; 19:12, 14, 19). Pilate sees through the game, turns the tables, and like his band of soldiers makes fun of this king of the Jews. The cross titulus, "Jesus of Nazareth, King of the Jews" (Mark 15:26 par.; John 19:19) is meant by Pilate as a mockery, and yet it captures the essence of Jesus' kingship. Jesus is the king on the cross; the cross is his throne. In the Fourth Gospel, the exaltation on the cross becomes his exaltation to the right hand of God and his installation as the Son of God in power (Rom 1:3–4). He has descended and is as such exalted (Phil 2:6–11). The New Testament title of Messiah includes the descent, the kenosis into lowliness, it includes the resurrection and the exaltation and Jesus' divine sonship. The Gospel according to Mark begins and ends with this confession (Mark 1:1; 15:39).

Jewish research on Jesus has "brought home" Jesus into the semantic universe of Israel as "Galilean Hasid" and "brother," but at the same time asserts reservations against concepts of New Testament Christology such as pre-existence, incarnation, kenosis, and exaltation. Here Messianic Judaism takes a clearly different path . . .

Cardinal Kasper: If we look at the different positions, then we find forms there of adoptionist Christology but also statements, and they seem to be the majority, that are based on Catholic, Orthodox, and Reformational theology. The majority of Messianic Jews oppose the views of modern liberal and postmodern life-of-Jesus research, for which Jesus is only the Galilean itinerant preacher or the elder brother. They affirm the resurrection and the deity of Jesus. One of their leading theologians speaks clearly and unequivocally for the compatibility of his understanding of Messiah with the Council of Nicaea (325),[4] whose 1700th anniversary will be celebrated in a few years by all Churches standing in the tradition of the early Church.

4. Mark S. Kinzer, "Is Jesus of Nazareth Still King of the Jews? New Testament Christology and the Jewish People," in Patrick, (ed.), *Jesus, King of the Jews?* (see note 3), 43–55, at 53.

At first glance it is a paradox: It is the Jews, of all people, who remind us of the core of Christian confession and of our common Christian tradition. But one key difference remains. The reason for Jesus' controversy with his opponents was not initially the Messiah claim but Jesus' authoritative interpretation of the Torah, specifically the Sabbath commandment and the purity regulations. Particularly in Paul's epistle to the Galatians, it is again about this dispute and about the freedom of the Christian from Jewish law: "For freedom Christ has set us free. Stand firm, therefore, and do not let yourself be subjected again to the yoke of slavery." And: "For in Christ it no longer depends on being circumcised or uncircumcised" (Gal 5:1, 6). Neither for Jesus nor for Paul did freedom mean individualistic arbitrariness. It becomes effective in love (Gal 5:6). The fulfillment of the law of Christ consists in carrying one another's burdens (Gal 6:2). Love for God and for neighbor is the all-encompassing commandment (Mark 12:28–32) and the fulfillment of the Law (Rom 13:10). This understanding of Christian freedom is the crucial and all-determining point of distinction with respect to Messianic Jews.

You have mentioned the Council of Nicaea (325), which defined the relationship of Father and Son via the non-biblical term "homo-ousios" in order to take a position against Arian subordinationism. In the Messianic Jewish movement there are reservations about the Hellenistic terminology of the early Church councils. They would obscure the biblical heritage. On the other hand, Messianic Jews agree with Karl Barth's dictum that the Word of God did not become man in a general sense but rather became "Jewish flesh," and they emphasize the Jewish root of Christology. What does the Jewishness of Jesus mean for Christology today?

Cardinal Kasper: Not only Messianic Jews but also Christian theologians today criticize the Hellenistic terminology of the early Church councils, especially in the doctrine of the Trinity, and many Christians can do little with it. Of course, if one criticizes the Hellenization of Christianity, one must not overlook the fact that Jerusalem was already a Hellenistic city at the time of Jesus, Galilee was largely bilingual, and among the first Christians, as the example of the protomartyr Stephen shows, conflicts already broke out early on between the Hellenists and the Hebrews (Acts 6:1).

Paul himself came from Tarsus in Asia Minor, at that time a center of Hellenistic culture. Thus, it should come as no surprise that Paul also made use of Hellenistic terminology when he says that the law is written by nature (*physei*) into the hearts of Gentiles, that is, into their conscience (*syneidesis*) (Rom 2:14–15). In his speech at the Areopagus in Athens he speaks of Gentiles who seek God, who can grope for him and find him, and appeals for this to the Gentile poet Aratus of Soli (cf. Acts 17:27–28).

It is especially important that the Hebrew Old Testament was translated into Greek between 250 and 100 BC and became widespread through the Septuagint. The New Testament is written in the Greek language. It is true that Jesus himself spoke in Aramaic, but we only have his words in the Greek language. Already Philo of Alexandria (14/10 BC–AD 40) who sought to explain Jewish thought with the help of Hellenic philosophy, was valued by the early Greek Church Fathers.

Today, the Hellenistic terminology is no longer comprehensible for many. For this reason, some theologians today are again taking up elements of Hebrew language or ideas offered by Jewish philosophers in order to make the Christian faith understandable in a new way.[5] Christian theologians as well as Messianic Jews stand here, I think, before the same hermeneutic problem of retranslating the biblical language and the Hellenistic language world of the tradition.

Behind the hermeneutical problem, which is at the same time an eminently pastoral problem, lies the deeper problem of substance that Karl Barth rightly pointed out. God did not become man in a general sense; he became *sarx*, that is, weak flesh (John 1:14), a Jewish man, and thus joined a people that was hated and despised even before the Christianization of antiquity. Antisemitism already had, after all, pre-Christian roots. As a Jew, Jesus belonged to a people on the edges of the Roman Empire that was partly esteemed but also partly despised. The Jewishness of Jesus is not a secondary and ultimately indifferent matter, as Karl Rahner falsely believed. By being a Jew, Jesus entered into the salvation history of God with Abraham and Moses and into the lineage of David. In his person Jesus connects Jews and Christians. The antisemitism that is unfortunately resurgent today, which must actually be designated as anti-Judaism, thus affects not only the Jews, but also the Christians.

5. Examples include: Martin Buber, Franz Rosenzweig, Hermann Cohen, Walter Benjamin, Max Horkheimer, Theodor W. Adorno, Hannah Arendt, Hans Jonas, Emmanuel Levinas, Jacques Derrida, etc.

If one isolates Jesus from his Jewishness and speaks of Jesus' humanity only in a general, abstract way, then one disincarnates him. One then falls into the gnostic danger of an ahistorical spiritualization of Christology and with this of Christianity as a whole.[6] The Church took action against this temptation early on. She has held fast to the salvation-historical Jewish anchoring of Jesus and of the Christian faith in Jesus the Christ, by incorporating into the creed the *natus ex Maria virgine* ["born of the virgin Mary"] from the line of David (Luke 1:27; Rom 1:2) and by making the circumcision of Jesus on the eighth day after his birth (Luke 2:21), as prescribed by the Jewish law, a Christian liturgical feast, which was observed on the eighth day of Christmas until the post-Conciliar liturgical reform.[7]

Jesus is the son of a "virgo israelitica" *(Augustine). By circumcision on the eighth day, he is marked as a Jew in Barth's sense. This is reminiscent of the Jewish root of Christology. At the same time, however, the work of Jesus already reaches well beyond the borders of Israel, indeed Christians ascribe universal significance to Christ . . .*

Cardinal Kasper: Christianity is enduringly rooted in the concrete history of salvation and is therefore constitutively connected with Judaism. And yet Jesus as a man, like all humans, is a *concretum universale,* whose family tree Luke traces back to Adam (Luke 3:37) and whom Paul calls the "new Adam" (1 Cor 15:22). Already during his earthly life, Jesus crossed the border to the non-Jews and turned to the centurion of Capernaum (Matt 8:5–13), the Syro-Phoenician woman (Mark 7:24–30), and the Samaritan woman at Jacob's Well (John 4:1–26). At the end, he sent out his disciples to all the nations of the world (Matt 28:19–20; Luke 24:47; Acts 1:8) and to all creatures (Mark 16:15–18).

On his missionary journeys, Paul respectively went first to the Jews (Rom 1:16) but regarded himself as the apostle to the Gentiles or to the

6. Cf. Johannes Cornides, "The Cost to the Church of Losing the Jews: Christian Doctrine as a History of Forgetting," in Patrick, ed., *Jesus, King of the Jews?* (see note 3), 33–42, at 39–40.

7. On the re-introduction of this feast, cf. Jan-Heiner Tück, "Beschneidung Jesu. Ein Zeichen gegen die latente Israelvergessenheit der Kirche," in *Beschneidung Jesus. Was sie Juden und Christen heute bedeutet*, ed. Jan-Heiner Tück (Freiburg i. Br.: Herder, 2019): 27–60.

nations (Acts 9:15; Rom 1:6; Gal 2:7–9), who was to the Jews a Jew, and to those without the law as one without the law. He knew that he was bound to the law of Christ and became all things to all men for the sake of the gospel (1 Cor 9:20–23). This is Christian freedom: rooted in the history of the first covenant people and yet open to all peoples. The distinction between Jews and non-Jews as well as the ethnic, social, and gender distinctions are relativized by baptism in Christ (Gal 3:28; 1 Cor 12:13; Rom 1:14). This means for us that we are not chained to the Hellenistic-Latin culture, and Christians cannot, pointedly, be German Christians either. Christian concreteness and—understood in the original sense of the word—catholic universality belong inseparably together.

The Church is "Church of Jews and Gentiles." But, to put it briefly, the ecclesia ex gentibus *marginalized the* ecclesia ex circumcisione *more and more in the first centuries and finally suppressed her. Now since the 1960s there have been more and more Jesus-believing Jews who have come to faith in Jesus the Messiah without the influence of the Church. Would you view it as a return of the* ecclesia ex circumcisione*?*

Cardinal Kasper: This question can only be answered in a larger context of salvation history. According to Augustine, the Church has existed since the righteous Abel (*ecclesia ab Abel iusto*). Vatican II adopted this viewpoint (*LG* 2). The Church Fathers therefore spoke of "holy Gentiles" such as Abel, Enoch, and others. According to the testimony of the New Testament, God wills the salvation of all men, and he wills it in Jesus Christ, who is the mediator between God and men (1 Tim 2:4). Adam already points forward typologically to the new Adam, who is Jesus Christ (Rom 5:14; cf. 1 Cor 15:22). Christ is the firstborn of all creation; in him, through him, and for him were all things created (Col 1:15–16); he is the key, focal point, and goal of all human history (*Gaudium et Spes* 10).

Everything that is good and true in the world is valued by the Church as preparation for the good news and as a gift from him who enlightens every human being (*LG* 16; cf. *NA* 1–2). Therefore, in the non-Christian religions, even if they distort the image of God (Rom 1:21–23), one can speak of a hidden anonymous presence of Christ, of his light and his power. Thus, the Council can say: "Those also can attain to salvation who through no fault of their own do not know the Gospel of Christ or His Church, yet sincerely seek God and moved by grace strive by their deeds to do His will as it is known to them through the dictates of conscience" (*LG* 16).

With Abraham a new epoch of salvation history begins. God steps out of his anonymity and addresses people like Abraham (Isa 41:8; James 2:23) and Moses (Exod 33:11) as his friends (*Dei Verbum* 2).[8] Abraham is called out from his people and from his ancestral homeland. He is given the promise to be father of a great people; in him all families of the earth will be blessed (Gen 12:1–3 and elsewhere). Abraham is thus called to be a nomad of faith and to walk with God. Thus, knowledge of God from the cosmic order is joined by historical revelation and faith as a journey with God in hope, which is often hope against all hope (Rom 4:18).

This hope applies especially to the covenant people of Israel, whom God, through Moses at the burning bush, promised to lead and accompany out of slavery in Egypt into a land flowing with milk and honey (Exod 3:4–12). At Sinai, God chooses Israel to be his own people, a kingdom of priests and a holy people (Exod 19:6). The making of the covenant takes place through the sprinkling with the blood of the covenant (Exod 24), which in the New Testament becomes a foresign of the blood of the new covenant shed on the cross (Luke 22:20; 1 Cor 11:25). With Moses and with Abraham, the sign of the covenant should be circumcision (Exod 12:48–49).

In the New Testament, the history of Israel and its journey through the wilderness typologically points forward to Christ and the Church (1 Cor 10:1–6). This led in the Church Fathers to typological exegesis, which interprets the Old Testament as a prefiguration of the new covenant and understands the new covenant from the old covenant as its surpassing fulfillment.[9] The Old Testament people of God thus becomes the prefiguration of the New Testament *ecclesia ex circumcisione*. Through

8. The Muslims are also counted among the Abrahamic religions. They derive their Abrahamic descent from Ishmael, the son of Hagar, Sarah's handmaid (cf. Gen 16), they are acquainted with circumcision, and they expect the Day of Judgment, when God resurrects all people and repays them. They revere God through prayer, alms, and fasting (cf. *NA* 3).

9. Typological exegesis was rediscovered and renewed especially by Jean Daniélou, *Sacramentum futuri* (Paris: Beauchesne, 1950), Henri de Lubac, *Der geistige*

its function as a pointer to Christ, it has a constitutive, unique significance for Christianity that cannot be replaced by other religions such as Hinduism or Buddhism.

To be sure, one must not make the mistake of reducing post-biblical and thus contemporary Judaism to the Old Testament. One must distinguish between pre-Christian Old Testament Judaism, to which the New Testament refers, and the Judaism that was contemporaneous with Jesus and his time, whose leaders decided against Jesus as the Christ, and finally the post-biblical Rabbinic and Talmudic Judaism, which, independent of the Church and in a critical stance toward her, developed beyond biblical Judaism. Today Judaism understands itself as either Ashkenazi or Sephardic, and depending on the case, among others, as orthodox, conservative, or as reform-oriented liberal, or also as secular Judaism.

Ecclesia ex circumcisione is the term used to designate Jewish Christianity, which consists of Jews who, coming from the circumcision, converted to Jesus Christ, were baptized, and became the Church of Jesus Christ. Paul is talking about them when he says that the distinction between Jews and Greeks has lost its meaning in Christ, that is, with baptism (Gal 3:3, 26–29; 5:6; 1 Cor 12:13; Col 3:11). The Epistle to the Ephesians reflects the relationship of the Gentile Christians (*ecclesia ex gentibus*) to the Jewish Christians. Christ "made both one and through his death broke down the dividing wall of enmity. He abolished the law with its commandments and ordinances, to make the two into one person and into the one new man. He established peace and reconciled both through the cross with God in one body. In his person he killed the enmity . . . So then you are no longer strangers without citizenship but rather fellow citizens with the holy ones and members of the household of God" (Eph 2:14–16, 19).[10]

Sinn der Schrift (Einsiedeln: Johannes-Verlag, 1952), and others. Hans Urs von Balthasar, Joseph Ratzinger. and others have taken up this concern.

10. ". . . vereinigte die beiden Teile und riss durch sein Sterben die trennende Wand der Feindschaft nieder. Er hob das Gesetz samt seinen Geboten und Forderungen auf, um die zwei zu einer Person und zu dem einen neuen Menschen zu machen. Er stiftete Frieden und versöhnte die beiden durch das Kreuz mit Gott in einem einzigen Leib. Er hat in seiner Person die Feindschaft getötet. . . . Ihr seid jetzt also nicht mehr Fremde ohne Bürgerrecht, sondern Mitbürger der Heiligen und Hausgenossen Gottes"—Rudolf Schnackenburg, *Der Brief an die Epheser*

But against the background of this important passage from Ephesians, how would you evaluate the phenomenon of the Messianic Jews? Can one see in them a kind of return of the ecclesia ex circumcisione *lost in history?*

Cardinal Kasper: It is obvious that these statements cannot be transferred to the relationship of today's Church with today's Jews outside the Church, a Church which—as *ecclesia ex gentibus*—emerged almost exclusively from the old as well as from the new Gentiles. Nor can they be transferred to the relationship of the Church to the Messianic Jews. They are a new phenomenon that did not exist at that time. They confess Jesus as the Messiah, but hold fast to the binding nature of the Old Testament–Jewish law and thus have not taken the step from Judaism to Christianity and to the Church. That is why they are also not to be confused with the Christians whom Paul criticizes harshly in Galatians because they have backslid and are again living according to the Torah (Gal 1:6–8; 2).

The Messianic Jews fall in a sense between all these chairs. They cannot be co-opted, and one should not try to do so either. They make their own contribution as a new variant of Judaism. They show that Judaism is also not just a finished entity. If I understand them correctly, they do not want to be the historical restoration of the old Jewish Christianity but rather understand themselves as witnesses to the eschatological hope proclaimed by Paul of the reconciliation of Jews and Christians at the end of time (Rom 11:12, 25–26).[11] It is exclusively an act of God and therefore excludes every form of active Church mission to Jews and proselytism.[12] It is true that there will always be individual

(Evangelisch–katholischer Kommentar, 10; Neukirchen-Vluyn: Benziger / Neukirchener, 1982): 104–27, 332–39.

11. For interpretation, Michael Theobald, *Der Römerbrief* (Darmstadt: Wissenschaftliche Buchgesellschaft, 2000): 276–82.

12. The question of mission to the Jews became acute when Pope Benedict XVI in 2007 allowed the pre-Conciliar rite of the form of celebration of the Eucharist under certain conditions. The pre-Conciliar Good Friday liturgy included intercession for the *perfidi Iudaei*, which was no longer appropriate since the Council. The Pope proposed a new formula, which caused among the Jews the misunderstanding that the proposed prayer was a call to mission to the Jews, or could at least be understood as such (on this, see Helmut Hoping, *Jesus aus Galiläa. Messias und Gottes Sohn* [Freiburg i. Br.: Herder, 2019]: 358–63). The result of an extensive discussion with the Pope, during which he referred to the position of Bernard of Clairvaux

Jews who become Christians of their own free decision. These are personal decisions that both sides must recognize on the grounds of religious freedom. They cannot and do not want to lead to a restoration of Jewish Christianity.

But should not the loss of the ecclesia ex circumcisione *be further considered? Has not the driving out of the Jewish Christians from the* ecclesia ex gentibus *wounded the Catholic Church? Does not the "original schism" between Israel and Church bring into question the Council's teaching that the Church of Jesus Christ is concretely realized in the Catholic Church and is precisely not broken up into fragments (cf.* LG *8:* "subsistit in*")?*

Cardinal Kasper: The end of the Church from the Jewish people is undoubtedly a deep, painful wound in the body of Christ. The Church was alienated from her root (Rom 11:16–24), and thus weakened in her life force. I would not speak of fragmentation. The coming of the kingdom of God proclaimed by Jesus is in its completed form only in "coming," but in the Holy Spirit it is already a reality in its beginnings (cf. *LG* 3). Thus, the Church of Christ, even though she is deeply wounded and her full realization is still pending until the reconciliation with the Jewish people, is already really there.[13]

We cannot bring about the eschatological coming of the kingdom of God through our own actions; we can only humbly hope and pray for it as an eschatological act reserved for God. But we can "work away"

(cf. Kasper, *Juden und Christen* [see note 1]: 43–44), was that while the individual Christian must testify to his faith before Jews, there can be no Church-authorized mission among the Jews. The Pope asked me to write an article along these lines for the *Osservatore Romano*. Although Benedict XVI confirmed that the article faithfully reflected our discussion, there was initially some back and forth with the publication in the Curia. In 2015, on the occasion of the 50-year anniversary of *Nostra Aetate*, the Commission for Religious Relations with the Jews was able to publish, on the foundation of this text, the declaration, *"The Gifts and the Calling of God Are Irrevocable" (Rom 11:29)*. In principle, therefore, the question of mission to the Jews can be considered settled.

13. The official German translation of *subsistit in* (*LG* 8) with *realized* is problematic, because the word *realized* assumes that the Church is really completed and finished. It would be more accurate to say: "the Church of Jesus Christ is concretely real in the Catholic Church," i.e., she is really there and yet with regard to the fully realized kingdom of God is still on the way.

at the healing of the wound by becoming aware of the Jewish root, endeavoring to concretely live out our common rootedness, and drawing strength for renewal from the Jewish root. The Church needs the Jewish people; they are by their very existence a reminder not to be arrogant: "For we do not support the root, but the root supports us" (cf. Rom 11:18).

For Messianic Jews, the hope is historically concrete. They see the return of many Jews to the land of their fathers as a sign of God's faithfulness to his people, and expect Christian dialogue partners to respond accordingly. Whoever says that Israel stands in an irrevocable covenant must actually also recognize the land promise given with this covenant, thus the expectation. Without advocating a political messianism, one could understand the land as a sacramental reality, and, in the sense of the threefold distinction of Aquinas, say:[14] *As a* signum rememorativum, *the gathering of the dispersed children of the house of Israel is a reminder of the manifold land promises of the old covenant. As a* signum demonstrativum, *the homecoming of the exiles to the land is at the same time a sign of God's covenant faithfulness to Israel. Finally, there would also be a* signum prognosticum *in this noteworthy process, insofar as a surplus is connected with the initial realization of the land promise, which points to the home in heaven. How would you assess this sacramental interpretation of the land of Israel?*

Cardinal Kasper: With this question we run up against a difficult and conflict-laden problem, in which theological controversies are closely linked to highly political disputes.[15] Even if one must distinguish between the promised land, *eretz Israel*, and the statehood, the national territory, the constitution and politics of the State of Israel, one must recognize that the Jews, after the bitter experiences of the Shoah, understandably expect us Christians to show solidarity with their land, also in political questions, and that we vigorously resist all new forms of antisemitism.

The land promise in the Old Testament is fundamental (cf. Gen 15:18–21; 17:8; Exod 3:8, etc.), and for the Jewish people it is important for survival. Also among Christians, the land which was earlier called

14. Cf. Thomas Aquinas, *Summa Theologica* III, Q. 6, art. 3.

15. Cf. for the following, the summary presentation of Hoping, *Jesus aus Galiläa* (see note 12), 348–58.

Palestine and now largely comprises the State of Israel, arouses deep religious feelings. For Christians it is the "holy land," where already Abraham was on the way, which was promised to Moses and his people, where the prophets worked and David was king; for Christians it is the land where Jesus was born, was publicly active, died and rose again, and the land where the original Christian community was at home. For every Christian visitor it is impressive to return to one's own roots, to walk in the footsteps of Jesus, and to read and meditate on the biblical texts in the places where it all happened. Thus, the holy land is also for Christians a *signum rememorativum par excellence.* It keeps awake the consciousness of the common heritage of Jews and Christians and the enduring bond of Christians with the first covenant people.

The return and homecoming of many Jewish exiles to the land of their fathers is a consequence of the Shoah and should for this very reason give us Germans reason for reflection. After the dreadful experience of the Shoah, many Jews sought in the land of their fathers a land in which they could live in peace according to their own laws and customs and where they could also defend themselves. They regard the fact that they survived and were permitted to return to and settle in the land of their fathers as a sign of God's covenantal faithfulness to his people. For us Christians, the Shoah and the return of many Jews to their land opened our eyes anew to the unbreakable validity of God's covenant with his people and the enduring importance that it also has for Christians. We too are heirs of this covenant and therefore advocates of the people of this covenant and of its land promised to it. That includes respect vis-à-vis the observance of the Torah, the Jewish religious festivals, rites and customs. Paul: "The law is holy and the commandment is holy, righteous and good" (Rom 7:12).

One who is familiar with the concrete circumstances of the taking possession of the land, who is familiar moreover with the serious conflicts, the unresolved problems, not least the great suffering experienced by non-Jews who had to leave the land, even if he sees the return of the Jews to the land of their fathers as a noteworthy sign of God's providence and faithfulness, will see it as an ambiguous sign and will therefore be cautious with a *demonstrative* sacramental interpretation. The Holy See has for this reason recognized the State of Israel under international law but has not provided any theological, let alone sacramental, interpretation. The designation "sacramental" belongs theologically only to a few very specific salvation-mediating ecclesiastical symbolic actions accompanied by effective words that were instituted by Jesus Christ. Even of the Church, the Second Vatican Council carefully says only that she is "as it were, a sacrament" (*veluti sacramentum*; *LG* 1). The homecoming of many Jewish exiles can therefore at most be described as sacramental in a very analogous sense, in which the difference is greater than the similarity.

In the case of pre-Christian cultic Jewish rites, the New Testament and the Christian tradition speak of a *praefiguratio* of the coming of Christ and the sacraments of the Church. This applies above all to Old Testament sacrifices in relation to the sacrifice of the cross, to circumcision in relation to baptism, and to the Jewish Passover meal in relation to the Eucharist; they are all accorded a prognostic meaning toward Christ. With the coming of Jesus, the Old Testament sacrifices lost their significance for salvation.[16] However, since the sacraments, for their part, have a prognostic significance with regard to the eschatological arrival (Parousia) of Jesus Christ in glory, the circumcision and the Passover meal in particular still have a prognostic significance related to the Parousia.

The Parousia is an important topic. Messianic Jews are moved by a joyful expectation of the coming of the Lord, which stands in conspicuous contrast to the "expectation fatigue" of many Christians today. They are thus an incarnated contradiction of the thesis that the Messiah is no longer expected by Jews either,[17] *and raise the question of whether Jewish expectation of Messiah and Christian hope for the Parousia come together at the end.*

Cardinal Kasper: I think that the Bible gives an utter "No" to this postmodern expectation fatigue. It is a single *Adieu tristesse* [farewell to sadness]! It was liberal theology that hung a "closed" sign at the office of eschatology for Jews and Christians alike, and thought it could be replaced by intraworldly humanist, pacifist, socialist, existentialist, and other future utopias. In the meantime, we have been rudely awakened

16. It is in this sense that one has to understand the statements in Heb 8:6–7 and 8:13.

17. Cf. Walter Homolka, Juni Hoppe, and Daniel Krochmalnik, *Der Messias kommt nicht. Abschied vom jüdischen Erlöser* (Freiburg i. Br.: Herder, 2022).

from this dance of dreams. We cannot pull ourselves out by our own hair from the swamp in which we are stuck.

Jews and Christians, for whom the Bible is, after all, the book of life, place their hope in God and expect the Messiah at the end of time as the Savior who establishes peace (*shalom*) between the nations and in the cosmos. This universal, cosmic peace also includes the reconciliation of Jews and Christians. According to Paul, when the Gentiles in full number have obtained salvation, all Israel (*pâs Israel*) will come to faith and be saved (Rom 11:12, 26). The Christians believe they know the coming Messiah in Jesus and will then recognize him again. The Jews, in the eschatological Parousia, will for the first time recognize and acknowledge Jesus of Nazareth as Messiah, who already came but was not recognized by them.

This does not mean that there is a second way of salvation for Jews apart from or alongside Jesus Christ. In him alone is salvation (Acts 4:12; 1 Tim 2:5). *Solus Christus!* He is our peace (Eph 2:14). Yet, on the basis of the will of God, inscrutable to us (Rom 11:33), Jews and Christians walk this one eschatological way of salvation in different manners, or as the Council says, "shoulder to shoulder" (*NA* 4). They are, so to speak, our siblings in faith, and form the one people of God as different "communities on the way." It is an important contribution of the Messianic Jews to have drawn attention to this again. In doing so, they remind us that we too as Church are still on the way and are only heading toward the consummation in the eternal homeland. The Church is not the goal of our journey. It is never finished and not definitive. That rightly contradicts a number of ecclesial triumphalisms.

We can form no concrete idea of the eschatological reality that surpasses all comprehension, and can speak of it only in pictures. Basically, we can only say that in the end God will be all in all (1 Cor 15:28). That does not mean spiritualizing our hope. For it says that in the end, all reality—the history of each individual as well as that of the peoples, in a special way that of the chosen people—will reach consummation. They will be purified by the judgment of God in a transfigured way and will enter into the final reality.

This universal peace cannot be anticipated or brought about by force, neither by the Jews nor by the Church, and certainly not by any intra-worldly powers. That is why Paul concludes his reflections with the following statement, with which I would also like to conclude:

"Everything is from God, and through him, and to him is the whole creation" (Rom 11:36). We may, without ever being finished, find God in all things and we with our Jewish brothers and sisters together make our way to God.

(Translated by John David Martin, James Earle Patrick, and Wayne Coppins from the German: "Die messianischen Juden – ein 'nach vorne weisendes Zeichen.' Ein Gespräch mit Walter Kardinal Kasper")

Ecclesia ex circumcisione and *ex gentibus*

The Church as a Trinitarian Ecosystem of Praise

R. Kendall Soulen

"Rejoice, O gentiles, with his people"

(Rom 15:10)

"IN THE EARLY YEARS OF THE CHURCH . . . there were the so-called Jewish Christians and the Gentile Christians, the *ecclesia ex circumcisione* and the *ecclesia ex gentibus*, one Church originating from Judaism, the other from the Gentiles, who however together constituted the one and only Church of Jesus Christ." This affirmation appears in the Roman Catholic document "The Gifts and Calling of God Are Irrevocable."[1] The fact that the affirmation appears in the past tense may seem to suggest that the ecclesial distinction between Jew and Gentile belongs exclusively to the Church's past. But that is not the document's own point of view. This becomes clear when it later states, "It is and remains a qualitative definition of the Church of the New Covenant that it consists of Jews and Gentiles, even if the quantitative proportions of Jewish and Gentile Christians may initially give a different impression."[2] According to "The Gifts and Calling of God Are Irrevocable," then, the "one and only Church of Jesus Christ" not only *was*

1. Commission for Religious Relations with the Jews, *"The Gifts and the Calling of God Are Irrevocable" (Rom 11:29)—A Reflection on Theological Questions Pertaining to Catholic–Jewish Relations on the Occasion of the 50th Anniversary of "Nostra Aetate" (no. 4)* (Vatican, 2015): 15.

2. *Ibid.*, 42.

but *is* the *ecclesia ex circumcisione* and the *ecclesia ex gentibus*. That is an extremely important affirmation with which I wholeheartedly agree. But the challenging question is this. Why should this be the case? What is it about the essence of the Church that makes the distinction between Jew and Gentile an aspect of its "qualitative definition," rather than merely a contingent expression of its historical origins?

In this lecture, I want to propose a possible answer to this question: the Church exists perpetually as the *ecclesia ex circumcisione* and the *ecclesia ex gentibus* because it is the eschatological first fruits of a global *ecosystem of praise* rooted in the life of the Holy Trinity. To elaborate this answer, I will make use of a contemporary characterization of the Church that has become prominent in recent ecumenical theology, according to which the Church is "the People of God," "the Body of Christ," and "the Temple of the Holy Spirit."[3] Since Vatican II's groundbreaking discussion of *De populo Dei* in *Lumen Gentium*, the rubric "the People of God" has provided Christians with a context in which to reflect on the Church's rootedness in God's election of the Jewish people. In a complementary fashion, I wish to suggest that "the Temple of the Holy Spirit" prompts us to reflect on the Church's character as the in-gathering of all the nations of the earth. Finally, the image of "the Body of Christ" prompts us to conceive of the Church as a *differentiated unity* of Jews and Gentiles, where the modes of doxology that are characteristic of Israel and the nations are united into a single corporate whole under the headship of Christ.

1. The Church as an ecosystem of praise

Let me begin my account by considering a passage from Irenaeus of Lyon. In the *Apostolic Preaching*, Irenaeus proposes that the One God who made and fashioned all things relates to humankind in different ways:

> To the faithful He is as Father, since "in the last times" He opened the testament of the adoption as sons; while to the Jews He is as Lord and Lawgiver, since in the intervening period, when mankind had forgotten, abandoned and rebelled against God, He brought them into slavery

3. See, e.g., the World Council of Churches, *The Nature and Mission of the Church, A Stage on the Way to a Common Statement* (Geneva, 1998), and its predecessor statements.

> by means of the Law, that they might learn that they have [as] Lord the Maker and Fashioner . . . ; and to the Gentiles He is as Creator and Almighty.[4]

According to Irenaeus, the one God relates to humankind in three different ways that are characterized by the special "name" or "face" that God presents to that portion of humanity. To "the faithful" God is "as Father," to the Jews as "Lord and Lawgiver," and to the Gentiles "as Creator and Almighty."

A casual reading of the passage might suggest that Irenaeus thinks that God's different postures toward humanity result in three non-overlapping experiences of God. If that were the case, then a person who came to know God "as Father" by entering "the covenant of adoption" would cease to know and experience God as they had formerly done as a Jew or as a Gentile. Moreover, Jews and Gentiles themselves would know God in ways that were unconnected to each other. However, a careful reading shows that this is not what Irenaeus thinks. Immediately prior to the passage above Irenaeus writes:

> And the Father is called by the Spirit "Most High" and "Almighty" and "Lord of Hosts" that we may learn [that] the God, this one Himself, He is the Maker of heaven and earth and the whole world, the Creator of angels and men, and the Lord of all, by whom all things exist, and from whom all things are nourished—merciful, compassionate, good, righteous, the God of all—both of the Jews and of the Gentiles and of the faithful.[5]

This passage makes clear that Irenaeus understands the Father's identity to include the "names" or "faces" that God presents to both Jews and Gentiles. Irenaeus' opponent Marcion had understood the Father's self-revelation to be the announcement of a hitherto completely unknown God. In contrast, Irenaeus understands it to incorporate what Jews and Gentiles already truly know about God based on God's goodness toward all. This knowledge includes belief in God as creator, which is common to Jew and Gentile, although in our first passage Irenaeus used slightly different vocabularies to express the belief in each case. But it also includes the distinctive names that Scripture associates

4. Irenaeus of Lyon, *On the Apostolic Preaching*, trans. John Behr (Crestwood, NY: St. Vladimir's Seminary Press, 1997): 44.

5. *Ibid.*, 44.

with God's "face" as made known to the Jews, such as "Most High" and "Lord of Hosts." (Like most patristic theologians, Irenaeus appears to have been ignorant of God's personal proper name, the unspoken Tetragrammaton, but he is aware of the special significance of its common biblical "Lord.") In sum, Irenaeus and Marcion would agree that addressing God as "the Father" is a distinguishing mark of the Church, but they would disagree about the significance of the term itself. For Marcion, the very fatherhood of the Father, as it were, depends on the name's exclusion of characteristically Jewish and Gentile beliefs about God, whereas for Irenaeus the opposite is true. For Irenaeus, the fatherhood of the Father is displayed by the fact that he is with equal propriety the bearer of names that are already known and praised by Israel and the nations.

There is an elegant simplicity, I think, to Irenaeus' understanding of the Church's relationship to Jews and Gentiles. The Church stands in critical solidarity with both groups, sharing their distinctive vantage points on God's names and goodness while also joining these together in light of its own. The Church is a kind of ecosystem of praise, as it were, made up of different fields of doxology that overlap in the "covenant of adoption" while extending outward in ways that are shared by all humankind.

While my proposal lacks the elegance of Irenaeus, I do intend it to be similarly simple in its basic outline. I propose that when we describe the Church as the People of God, the Body of Christ, and the Temple of the Spirit, we illuminate from different angles its character as an "ecosystem of praise" rooted in the life of the Trinity whose persons bear a fullness of divine name(s) in characteristically different ways.

- As the People of *God*, the Church is united in a special way to the First Person of the Trinity, commonly identified as the Father. But precisely as the First Person, the Father is also the Primordial Bearer of the Tetragrammaton, the *personal proper name* that the LORD revealed to Moses at the burning bush (Exod 3:15). Viewed from this perspective, the Church's ecosystem of praise is shaped by its critical solidarity with the Jewish people and the "field of doxology" that belongs originally and irrevocably to it. For of all the peoples of the earth, the Jewish people alone has been called *by its own proper name* for the purpose of living as a corporate witness to the glory of the

Father's proper name. With corporate Israel as a whole, the Church joins in the confession, "Hear O Israel, the LORD our God, the LORD is one" (Deut 6:4). Beginning with the *ecclesia ex circumcisione,* the Church also confesses that Jesus of Nazareth shares in the dignity of the Divine Name: "For us there is one God the Father . . . and one Lord Jesus Christ" (1 Cor 8:6). Because the Church confesses that Jesus Christ is the Primordial Receiver of the Father's name (John 17:11–12; Phil 2:9), a humanly unbridgeable chasm separates its confession from that of normative Judaism. Despite this chasm, the Church lives in confidence that the LORD's fidelity to the Divine Name will ultimately redound, through Jesus Christ, not only to the salvation of the *ecclesia ex circumcisione,* but to that of "all Israel" (Rom 11:26).

- As the Temple of the *Holy Spirit,* the Church is united in a special way to the Third Person of the Trinity, the person whose unique hypostatic identity is signified by *common nouns* (e.g., "Holy," "Spirit," "Love," "Gift," etc.). Viewed from this perspective, the Church's ecosystem of praise is shaped by its critical solidarity with the incipient fields of doxology that are already present amid all the nations of the earth. Unlike Israel, the nations are *not* called by personal proper name; nevertheless, their sacred and secular life provides the *common nouns* that the Church re-purposes and employs in praise of the Holy Trinity. This re-purposing is especially manifest in the *ecclesia ex gentibus,* which is the eschatological in-gathering of the nations in the midst of the nations. United to the *ecclesia ex circumcisione,* the *ecclesia ex gentibus* assumes special responsibility for executing the commission to preach the gospel so that all peoples may confess, "*in our languages* we hear them speaking about God's deeds of power" (Acts 2:11).
- As the Body of Christ, the Church is united in a special way to the Second Person of the Trinity, whom the Church's liturgy of baptism identifies by using the *kinship term* "Son" (Matt 28:19). Like the metaphor of the body, the vocabulary of kinship emphasizes the essential relatedness of those who are and remain *different.* As the Son of the Father and the head of his body the Church (Eph 5:23), Jesus Christ's own characteristic speech is itself a differentiated "ecosystem of praise." Jesus speaks to and about the One to whom he prays using kinship terms, proper name, and common nouns

("Our *Father*, hallowed be your *name*, your *kingdom* come!"). Just so, Christ's body the Church takes shape as a corporate ecosystem of praise which consists of both Jews and Gentiles, both the *ecclesia ex circumcisione* and the *ecclesia ex gentibus* (cf. 1 Cor 12:12–13). What makes Christ's body a luminous sign of the new creation is that it incorporates Jews and Gentiles into Christ's filial address to God as "Father" in such a way that their distinctive modes of praise are perfected but not destroyed (Luke 2:32; Rom 15:9–12).

Let me develop this outline in greater detail.

2. The Church as People of God: Solidarity with Israel in praise of the name of the LORD

"All the peoples of the earth shall see that you [Israel] are called by the name of the LORD."
(Deut 28:10)

Since Augustine it has been a commonplace of Western theology to say that only the Son and the Holy Spirit have missions. The Father has no mission because he is not sent. What the tradition then sometimes fails to note, however, is that the "missionless" Father does have a *purpose* for the sake of which he sent the Son and Spirit in "the fullness of time" (Gal 4:4). We must describe that purpose as the rescue of fallen humanity from sin and death, of course. But to describe the Father's purpose solely as a rescue mission is not enough. We ascend a good stretch higher if we affirm, with Augustine, that the purpose of the Father's sending of the Son and Spirit in time is to reveal their origins in eternity. The Son's mission reveals his eternal generation from the Father, just as the Spirit's mission reveals his eternal procession from the Father and the Son. But even this stops short of the Bible's highest peaks as Augustine sees them. For the revelation of the eternal processions serves the revelation of the eternal identity of the Father, the Unoriginate Origin of the divine life, knowledge of whom constitutes the eternal beatitude of creatures. Vatican II's decree *Ad Gentes* makes this point beautifully when it states:

> And so at last, there will be realized the plan of our Creator who formed man to His own image and likeness, when all who share one human nature, regenerated in Christ through the Holy Spirit and beholding the glory of God, will be able to say with one accord: "Our Father." (*Ad Gentes* 7)

When we understand the Father's purpose in this way, we see salvation history at the largest scale as a majestic unity that runs *a Patre ad Patrem*, from the Father as the Unoriginate Origin of the divine life to the Father as the final goal of creaturely doxology.[6]

I find this a compelling account of the unity of salvation history at the largest scale. Nevertheless, I have a bone to pick with it. Precisely when we describe salvation history at the largest scale, we are led astray by a monochromatic use of the kinship vocabulary of "Father, Son, and Spirit." For according to the consistent testimony of both testaments, it is simply not possible to say *who* the Father is apart from the Father's *personal proper name*. And the Father's proper name is not "Father." It is the sacred Tetragrammaton. It is because the Father is the Primordial Bearer of this name that the Scriptures ubiquitously praise him as the LORD, or, in the periphrastic speech that is characteristic of Judaism and the New Testament, as "the Blessed" (Mark 14:61), "the Power" (Mark 14:62), "the Majestic Glory" (2 Pet 1:17), and so on. If creation's goal is knowledge of the First Person in the ineffable uniqueness of his hypostatic identity, then we must say that the paternal purpose that underlies salvation history is the glorification of God the Father *as bearer of the unspoken Tetragrammaton*. The Conciliar document *Ad Gentes* would have made its point with even greater scriptural precision if it had concluded with the words,

> And so at last, there will be realized the plan of our Creator . . . when all who share one human nature . . . will be able to say with one accord: "Our Father, *hallowed be your name!*"

This refinement of our understanding of the goal of salvation history has important implications for understanding the purpose of God's election of Israel. According to Maimonides, the Tetragrammaton belongs on God's side of the distinction between eternity and time: It signifies who God is in a manner that is independent of God's relation to creation.[7] At the same time, the Bible makes clear on page after page that a singular relationship exists between God as the bearer of this name and the people known by the proper name "Israel." This relation

6. On the revelation of the Father as the purpose of the divine missions, see Lewis Ayres, *Augustine and the Trinity* (Cambridge: Cambridge University Press, 2010): 181–88.

7. Cf. Moses Maimonides, *Guide for the Perplexed* (Chicago, IL: University of Chicago Press, 1969): I.60–62.

exists not by necessity but by grace. God's free election of Israel is the outworking of God's desire to be known by name. For the sake of this name, God fashions a people out of the barren womb of Sarah and out of the chaos of bondage, so that by works of steadfast love and faithfulness, God might be glorified by name not only in the heavens but also by men and women on the earth. The promises, the exodus, the giving of the Torah, the festivals—all of these gifts (cf. Rom 9:4) stand in service of shaping Israel as a people whose corporate life testifies to the glory of the LORD (cf. Rom 15:9–10).

When Christians imagine salvation history as running *a Patre ad Patrem* in absence of the Tetragrammaton, they often pass quickly through the Old Testament on the way to the New. The Old Testament "people of God" becomes an amorphous, vaporous quantity that lacks defining features and a proper name of its own. On this view, the *ecclesia ex circumcisione* (if it is remembered at all) appears as a historical contingency without any deep foundation in the counsels of God. Karl Barth recognized the dangers of overlooking the Old Testament. He attempted to correct the problem by arguing that God elected Israel for specific purpose of witnessing to God's "No!" against sinful humanity.[8] But here Barth's reach is far too short. The purpose of Israel's election was originally *positive*, not negative: to live to the glory of the Father's name, the Tetragrammaton. That is why God's covenant with Israel comes with no "expiration date." For unlike God's "No!," the Father's identity as the primordial bearer of the Tetragrammaton is never-ending (cf. Rev 22:6). The Church of Jesus Christ can therefore be "the people of God" only insofar as it participates in the "field of doxology" that God has already established between himself and the whole Jewish people, irrespective of its posture toward the gospel (cf. Rom 9–11).

For this reason, too, the *ecclesia ex circumcisione* has a permanent place of priority within the ecosystem of praise that constitutes the life of the Church of Jesus Christ. This priority is one of sequence, not rank. Jesus Christ fulfills God's covenant with Israel, not in the sense that he brings it to an end, but in the sense that he perfects its offering of praise in his own person. The Gospel of John portrays Jesus as the one who

8. On the strengths and limitations of Barth's doctrine of Israel, see Bertold Klappert, *Israel und die Kirche: Erwägungen zur Israellehre Karl Barths* (Munich: Chr. Kaiser Verlag, 1980).

reveals the deepest mystery of the Tetragrammaton by disclosing it as "your name that you have given me" (John 17:11–12). This confession separates the *ecclesia ex circumcisione* from mainstream Judaism and the greater part of the Jewish people. But from a Christian point of view, this separation cannot sever the bond that unites the *ecclesia ex circumcisione* with the Jewish people or cancel the vocation that belongs to it. Baptism "eschatologically re-orders" (Matthew Levering) Israel's vocation around Jesus Christ, the eternal receiver of the Father's unspoken name.[9] But in this way, baptism *confirms* rather than *cancels* Israel's primordial vocation to glorify the name of the LORD. Because baptism confirms Jews in their vocation to praise the Father's name, they remain constitutionally best suited to lead the whole Church in offering praise to the Father in the name of Jesus that takes the form "the *LORD* is God!" (cf. Rom 15:9). Here the *ecclesia ex circumcisione* properly takes the lead in the antiphonal "call and response" that characterizes the life of the Church as an ecosystem of praise.[10]

At the same time, I believe that there is another dimension of the Church's ecosystem of praise in which the *ecclesia ex gentibus* is constitutionally best suited to take the lead. This brings me to a consideration of the Church as the Temple of the Holy Spirit.

3. The Church as the Temple of the Spirit: Solidarity with the nations in praise of "our God"

"The LORD of hosts is his name . . .
the God of the whole earth he is called."
(Isa 54:5)

If according to Augustine the Father is "Alpha" and "Omega" of salvation history, its center is the Father's visible sending of the Son and the Spirit in the "fullness of time" (Gal 4:4–6). These two events constitute the "novum" of the New Covenant, as it were, but according to

9. Cf. Matthew Levering, "Thomas Aquinas on Law and Love," *Angelicum* 94.2 (2017): 413–42.

10. On the antiphonal pattern of "call and response" as a distinctively African and African-American mode of praise and cultural production, see by Patricia Liggins Hill, *Call and Response: The Riverside Anthology of the African American Literary Tradition* (Boston, MA: Houghton Mifflin, 1997).

Augustine they possess different degrees of novelty. While the novelty of the incarnation is *absolute* (for prior to the incarnation the Son was not "sent"), the Spirit's sending on the day of Pentecost manifests a novelty that is *relative* to sendings that had previously occurred in the history of salvation. As Augustine observes, "If the Holy Spirit had not been given at all before, what were the prophets filled with when they spoke?"[11] Augustine identifies the novelty of the Spirit's sending with his use of the languages of "all nations" to proclaim the gospel:

> Nowhere else do we read that men had spoken languages they did not know as the Holy Spirit came upon them, in the way that occurred at Pentecost. For then his coming needed to be demonstrated by perceptible signs, to show that the whole world and all nations with their variety of languages were going to believe in Christ by the gift of the Holy Spirit.[12]

Augustine makes clear in the same passage that the Pentecostal *novum* stands in continuity with what the Spirit had previously proclaimed about the nation's languages in the "prophetic song" of Psalm 19:

> There are no languages or dialects whose voices are not heard; their sound has gone out to all the earth, and their words to the end of the world. (cf. Ps 19:3–4)[13]

On the day of Pentecost, the Spirit realized the "doxological destiny" that the languages of the nations already possessed prior to Pentecost. "All the nations" were pre-ordained to hear and proclaim the gospel in their own languages, and in this way to glorify the Holy Trinity.

Patristic theologians such as Eusebius characterized God's work among the nations prior to the incarnation as a *praeparatio evangelica*. Taking our cue from Augustine, however, I think we might speak more appropriately of that work as a *"praeparatio Pentecostae."* In the light *of* Pentecost, the Christian imagination discerns signs of God's gracious ordering of the life of the nations in preparation *for* Pentecost. God inaugurates the *praeparatio Pentecostae* prior to the fall with the blessing "Be fruitful, multiply, and *fill the earth*" (Gen 1:28), and reaffirms it in the postlapsarian world in the table of nations (Gen 10) and the story of Babel (Gen 11). Viewed from this "gentile-centric" perspective, even

11. Augustine, *The Trinity (de Trinitate)*, trans. Edmund Hill (Hyde Park, NY: New City Press, 2nd edn 2005): 183.

12. *Ibid.*, 183.

13. *Ibid.*, 183; citation of the psalm is as Augustine renders it, wherever the Hebrew differs.

God's calling of Abraham concerns the blessing of the nations (Gen 12:3; cf. Isa 19:24–25). In the New Testament, a key text that represents this perspective is Paul's sermon to the Athenians.

> From one ancestor he made all nations to inhabit the whole earth, and he allotted the times of their existence and the boundaries of the places where they would live, so that they would search for God and perhaps grope for him and find him—though indeed he is not far from each one of us. For "In him we live and move and have our being"; as even some of your own poets have said, "For we too are his offspring." (Acts 17:26–28)

Here Paul illuminates the whole of salvation-history from creation to Christ in a way that foregrounds God's saving work among the Gentiles, even to the point that God's people Israel *disappears* into the history of God's generous and even-handed (if also hidden and mysterious) providence among God's *peoples*. Finally, the Book of Revelation incorporates this same perspective into its vision of the new creation when it foretells, "a great multitude that no one could count, from every nation, from all tribes and peoples and languages . . . and they cry with a loud voice, saying, 'Salvation belongs to *our God* [!] who is seated on the throne, and to the Lamb!'" (Rev 7:9–10).

An important theme of the Christian canon read in a "gentile-forward" way is that of the eschatological temple of God. For our purposes, the crucial thing to observe is that it is precisely the presence of *Gentiles* that marks out God's temple as *eschatological*. The Old Testament introduces this theme (Ps 96:7–8; Isa 2:2–3; 25:6; 56:6–7; 66:23; Jer 3:17; Mic 4:1–2; Zec 14:16) and it is further developed in the New. At the Council of Jerusalem (Acts 15), James provides the clinching rationale for admitting Gentiles *as Gentiles* into the fellowship of Jesus by recalling prophecy that "the dwelling of David" will be rebuilt (i.e., the tabernacle) and will be open to "all other people . . . even all the gentiles" (Acts 15:17).[14] We find the same association of ideas in Ephesians 2:11–22 and 1 Peter 2:4–10, both key passages for the theme of the Church as the Temple of God, built up in the power of the Spirit.

Surely, if the presence of Gentiles *as* Gentiles is the *sine qua non* of the Church as the eschatological temple of God, then they cannot

14. Richard Bauckham, "James and the Gentiles (Acts 15.13–21)," in *History, Literature and Society in the Book of Acts*, ed. Ben Witherington, III (Cambridge: Cambridge University Press, 1996): 154–84.

be without some distinctive contribution to the Church's sacrifice of praise and thanksgiving. In the previous section, I proposed that we discern the deepest foundation of Israel's election in its vocation to glorify the First Person of the Trinity, the Primordial Bearer of the divine name. Now I wish to propose something similar with respect to the Gentiles gathered into the Church from all the peoples under heaven. Consider that whereas the Tetragrammaton and "Israel" are untranslatable proper names, "God" and "the nations" are translatable common nouns that take a unique linguistic form in every culture in which they appear. Gentiles adorn the eschatological temple with praise as only they can do, by offering up to "our God" (cf. Rev 7:10) the riches of language, culture, and concept that the Spirit has prepared beforehand in the lives of all peoples, tribes, and nations. If Israel's vocation comes to fruition when it calls out to the nations, "*The LORD* is God!," the Spirit's hidden work among the nations bears fruit when Gentile followers of Jesus shout out in response, "The LORD *is God*!" Here we may understand "God" as a placeholder for an inexhaustible plenitude of common nouns repurposed as praise names of the Trinity, such as "*Sat, Cit,* and *Ananda*" (Abhishiktananda); "*Dao, De, Qi*" (Paul S. Chung); "Parent Ancestor, Brother Ancestor, Holy Spirit" (Charles Nyamiti), "Mountain Peak, Cool Air, Freshness" (Lam Thien Loc), and so on.

4. The Church as the Body of Christ: The solidarity of Jew and Gentile in praise of God the Father

"Blessed be the God and Father of our Lord Jesus Christ, who . . . destined us for adoption as his children through Jesus Christ . . . God has put all things under his feet and has made him the head over all things for the church, which is his body . . . He is our peace; in his flesh he has made both groups ['the circumcision' and the 'uncircumcision'] into one and has broken down the dividing wall, that is, the hostility between us."
(Eph 1:3, 5, 22–23; 2:14)

The phrase "the Body of Christ" differs in an important way from the two ecclesial motifs we have already considered. Prior to the incarnation there was already a "People of God" set aside for the praise of God's proper name, namely, the Jews—a people uniquely set apart for this purpose by name. Similarly, I have suggested that prior to the Spirit's outpouring in Acts 2, the Spirit was already secretly at work among the nations, preparing them to adorn the eschatological "Temple of the Spirit" with praise by using common nouns indigenous to their languages. In contrast, there was no "Body of Christ" prior to the incarnation. The incarnation itself is the way the Second Person of the Trinity acquires a human body around which the Church can first be formed as his corporate body in the world. When we designate the Church as "the Body of Christ," we imply that the unprecedented novelty and mystery that belongs in the first instance to the incarnation belongs in a secondary and derivative way to the Church. As the corporate body gathered and nourished by Christ's body and blood, the Church exists as an extension of the incarnation and manifests it—however imperfectly—to the world.

The special place of "the Body of Christ" among the three ecclesial images is mirrored to some extent by the special place that "the Father and the Son and the Holy Spirit" (Matt 28:19) occupies in the Church's trinitarian language. As is well known, the vocabulary of divine kinship figures more prominently in the New Testament than in the Old. This fact has led some theologians to argue that the new Christian name for God is "Father, Son, and Holy Spirit." They suppose that this "new" name supersedes the Tetragrammaton and takes precedence before doxological triads from the life of the nations such as "*Sat, Cit,* and *Ananda*" and "*Dao, De, Qi.*" In effect, this position imagines "the Body of Christ" as a doxological monoculture, a kinship community comprised exclusively of "Christians" who worship "the Father, Son, and Holy Spirit" as the name of their God. Such a view has no place for an abiding distinction between the *ecclesia ex circumcisione* and *ex gentibus* in the Body of Christ.

To forestall this danger, it is necessary to cultivate an appreciation for the full "breadth and length and height and depth" of the mystery of the incarnation (Eph 3:18). An important way that we can do that is by orienting ourselves on Jesus Christ's own characteristic ways of speaking to and about God. As the Word made flesh, Jesus of Nazareth addresses the One to whom he prays using a panoply of different kinds of words:

"Our *Father*!" (kinship term)
"Hallowed be your *name*!" (the Tetragrammaton, an untranslatable proper name)
"Your *kingdom* come!" (translatable common noun)

As Irenaeus recognized and Marcion did not, Jesus' filial address to God as "Father" opens a capacious space that *includes* the kinds of names that God has used to express God's goodness toward Jew and toward Gentile. Jesus' filial address is not a monoculture but one element in a differentiated ecosystem of doxology whose roots extend to eternity and whose range encompasses all human beings of every time and place (John 1:4, 9). The incarnation is the divine lexical ecosystem made flesh, as it were, for the purpose of gathering all of humanity in a differentiated ecosystem of praise.

I propose that this understanding of the incarnation should inform our understanding of what it means for the Church to be the Body of Christ, the prolongation of the incarnation in the world. As the Body of Christ, the Church is the temporal and spatial extension in the medium of frail human flesh of Jesus Christ its head, the incarnation of the Word of God. Just as Jesus' filial address to God as "Father" opens a capacious space that includes the names that God has used to express God's goodness toward Jew and Gentile, so the Church itself is not a monoculture but a differentiated ecosystem of praise that incorporates the forms of praise that Jews and Gentiles are providentially equipped to provide. The Church is the People of God as the *ecclesia ex circumcisione,* in critical solidarity with the people Israel as a whole, and takes the lead in proclaiming, on behalf of the whole Church, "*The LORD* is God!" The Church is the Temple of the Spirit as the *ecclesia ex gentibus,* in critical solidarity with the nations of the world, and responds on behalf of the whole Church, "The LORD is *God*!" The Church is the Body of Christ as the *ecclesia ex circumcisione* and the *ecclesia ex gentibus* and offers this the antiphonal call and response to the praise of "the Father of lights" (James 1:17). The distinction between Jew and Gentile is not a passing feature of the Church's life but the luminous sign of its messianic identity both in time (Acts 15) and eternity (Rev 7:1–17, 21).[15]

15. For a fuller account of the trinitarian basis of this proposal and its systematic implications, see R. Kendall Soulen, *Irrevocable, The Name of God and Unity of the Christian Bible* (Minneapolis, MN: Fortress Press, 2022).

Introducing the Messianic Jewish Reality[1]

Richard Harvey

If reality is "the state of things as they actually exist, as opposed to an idealistic or notional idea of them,"[2] what kind of reality are we dealing with when it comes to Messianic Jews and Messianic Judaism, and how are we to appropriately describe the nature and quality of its existence?

The Messianic Jewish reality can be viewed through a variety of lenses, all of which contribute to our understanding of this unusual "state of things." The existence of Messianic Jews today poses questions for both social identity theory and theological ontology and anthropology. Religious identity is socially constructed and can be viewed using social scientific approaches, such as phenomenology, anthropology, and social psychology. Messianic Judaism can also be described as a historical phenomenon, emerging from the history of the interaction of what became Judaism and Christianity. And it can be understood as a

1. This chapter is a revised version of the presentation given in Vienna. The accompanying video and powerpoint slides and video are available at www.youtube.com/watch?v=qfyacXMLbSA&ab_channel=Psalm133 and www.dropbox.com/s/kl978a76elnz9tg/Messianic%20f%20Jewish%20Reality%20VIenna%20110722.pptx?dl=0 (both accessed April 11, 2025).

2. "Reality," *Oxford English Dictionary Online*, www.lexico.com/definition/reality (accessed May 2022).

theological reality, a sign of God's ongoing election of Israel (the Jewish people) and a prophetic pointer to God's purposes for Israel and all nations through the Messiah Yeshua as evidenced by the "remnant saved by grace."

For those of us interested in the theological significance of Messianic Judaism as a reality that is relevant to (i) our understanding of the Jewishness of Christianity, (ii) the relationship between the Church and the Jewish people, and (iii) the impact of Messianic Judaism on Jewish–Christian relations, on post-supersessionist theology, and on contemporary understandings of the interface between Jewish and Christian identities, Messianic Judaism presents a challenge to our categories and ways of understanding.

In this presentation, we limit ourselves to an overview of the modern phenomenon of Messianic Judaism, with the guiding questions as presented on the program. I leave to others in the program to address the further questions that arise.

1. Who are the Messianic Jews?

Messianic Judaism is the religion of Jewish people who believe in Jesus (Yeshua) as the promised Messiah. It is a Jewish form of Christianity and a Christian form of Judaism, challenging the boundaries and beliefs of both. The Messianic Jewish Movement refers to the contemporary movement, a renewed expression of the Jewish Christianity of the early Church. Messianic Jews construct a new social and religious identity that they express communally in Messianic Jewish congregations and synagogues, and in their individual beliefs and practices. Since the early 1970s, the significant numbers of Jewish people coming to believe in Jesus and the phenomenon of Messianic Judaism have raised several questions concerning Jewish and Christian identity and theology.[3]

Using the terms "Messianic" and "Jew" raises a plethora of definitional challenges and methodological questions.[4] For the purposes of this paper the terms "Messianic" and "Jewish" are understood to refer to Jewish people who accept Jesus (Yeshua) as their Messiah. I follow

3. Cf. Richard Harvey, *Mapping Messianic Jewish Theology: A Constructive Approach* (Milton Keynes: Paternoster, 2009): 1–2.

4. Cf. Harvey, *Mapping Messianic Jewish Theology* (see note 3), 8–12.

the demographer Sergio DellaPergola's understanding of Jewish identity. He distinguishes between core, connected, enlarged, and eligible Jewish populations.

- *Core Jewish population* means those who consider themselves Jews to the exclusion of all else.
- *Connected Jewish population* includes the core Jewish population and additionally those who say they are partly Jewish or that have Jewish background from at least one Jewish parent.
- *Enlarged Jewish population* includes the Jewish connected population and those who say they have Jewish background but not a Jewish parent, and all non-Jews living in households with Jews.
- *Eligible Jewish population* means eligible for immigration to Israel under its Law of Return (LRP).[5]

There is no agreed terminology for describing Jewish believers in Jesus, or on how to differentiate them from others similarly associated with both Jewish and Christian communities. As Gershon Nerel has observed, the entry for *meshichi* / *yehudi meshichi* in the 2003 edition of the Even-Shoshan Dictionary reads: "Jews who have pronounced themselves to be Jewish in their nationality and loyalty to the State of Israel while being Christians in their religion."[6] Kerry Warchawsky refers to three possible meanings of the term "Messianic Jew":

5. Cf. Sergio DellaPergola, "World Jewish Population, 2019," in *The American Jewish Year Book, 2019, vol. 119*, ed. Arnold Dashefsky and Ira M. Sheskin (Cham, Switzerland: Springer, 2019): 263–353 (as found at the Berman Jewish DataBank, www.jewishdatabank.org [accessed April 11, 2025]): 11. DellaPergola also uses a further category, "Jews of another religion," by which he means those who are Jewish but have joined another religious community; he includes Messianic Jews in this category.

6. Quoted in Gershon Nerel, "The Identity of Jewish Yeshua-Disciples in the State of Israel According to their Written Declarations of Faith," *Kesher* 27 (Summer/Fall 2013): 1–11, 3. For further information on terms for Jewish disciples of Yeshua, see Harvey, *Mapping Messianic Jewish Theology* (see note 3), 8–12. Stokes summarizes: "Finding agreement on definitions in the Messianic Jewish movement is problematic because of the decentralised and fluid nature of the movement. There are, at present, no agreed upon definitions, although some have attempted to suggest specific taxonomies"—Bruce Stokes, *Messianic Judaism: Ethnicity in Revitalization* (Riverside, CA: University of California, 1994): 7. Kinzer similarly observes, "After a quarter century of existence, one might have hoped that Messianic Judaism would have progressed beyond matters of fundamental self-definition.

1. A believer in a messiah, to include the Chabad followers of the Rabbi Menachem Schneerson, the followers of Rabbi Nachman of Braslav, and some settler groups.
2. A Jewish person who believes in Yeshua as Messiah.
3. A Jewish person who believes in Yeshua as Messiah and affirms the significance of and seeks to maintain a Jewish identity and lifestyle. (Non-Jews who fit this description are referred to as "Messianic gentiles.")[7]

As Cynthia Baker has observed and scholars working in the field of Jewish studies are well aware, there are significant definitional, methodological, orthographic, and semantic issues associated with the nouns *Jew, the Jews,* and the adjective *Jewish,* let alone with the additional narrowed use of the adjective *Messianic* to refer to the Christian *Christ,* capitalized even.[8] For the purposes of this paper, the terms Messianic Jew / Judaism will generally be used, as well as some other alternatives such as Jewish disciples of Yeshua (JDY) or Jewish believers in Yeshua / Yeshua-believing Jews (JBY).

The term "Messianic Jew" can thus refer to several different groups:

- Christians with a Jewish background who may not identify as Jewish—a general term[9]
- all self-identifying Jewish followers of Jesus in mainstream Churches with varying degrees of Jewish identity and expression[10]

Unfortunately, such is not the case. Our movement still struggles with basic identity questions."—Mark Kinzer, *The Nature of Messianic Judaism: Judaism as Genus, Messianic as Species* (West Hartford, CT: Hashivenu Archives, 2001): 1.

7. Cf. Keri Warshawsky, *Returning To Their Own Borders: A Social Anthropological Study of Contemporary Messianic Jewish Identity in Israel* (PhD dissertation, Hebrew University of Jerusalem, 2008): 48.

8. Cf. Cynthia M. Baker, *Jew* (Key Words in Jewish Studies, 13; New Brunswick, NJ: Rutgers University Press, 2017).

9. This might include Israeli Christians of uncertain Jewish status such as post-1989 former Soviet Union (FSU) migrants in Israel, refugees, and others those who prefer to keep their Christian religion distinctively "Christian" in a country with an explicitly Jewish character.

10. Recent surveys confirm that the term "Messianic Jew" is now the most popular term used by Jewish disciples of Jesus to describe themselves. See Richard Harvey, *Jewish Followers of Jesus in the UK*, 2023 (forthcoming); survey available at

- self-identifying members of Messianic Jewish congregations / denominations who are Torah-observant (UMJC definition)
- Jewish followers of Jesus in synagogues and Jewish communities—secret believers or those constituting an "insider movement" within other Jewish religious identities

The Union of Messianic Jewish Congregations (UMJC) defines Messianic Judaism as:

> [A] movement of Jewish congregations and groups committed to Yeshua the Messiah that embrace the covenantal responsibility of Jewish life and identity rooted in Torah, expressed in tradition, and renewed and applied in the context of the New Covenant. Messianic Jewish groups may also include those from non-Jewish backgrounds who have a confirmed call to participate fully in the life and destiny of the Jewish people. We are committed to embodying this definition in our constituent congregations and in our shared institutions.[11]

Messianic Judaism is a Jewish form of Christianity and a Christian form of Judaism, a form of cultural, religious, and theological expression adopted in recent years by an increasing number of Jewish people worldwide who believe in Yeshua (Jesus) as the promised Messiah. Messianic Judaism finds its expression in Messianic congregations and synagogues, and in the individual lifestyle of Messianic Jews, who combine Jewish identity with faith in Jesus. Whilst they are not uniform in their beliefs and expression, the majority adhere to orthodox Christian beliefs on the uniqueness and deity of Christ, the Trinity, the authority of Scripture, and so on, whilst expressing their beliefs in a Jewish cultural and religious context which affirms the continuing election of Israel (the Jewish people) and the ongoing purposes of God for his people.[12]

---

https://www.academia.edu/116275835/UK_JB_Survey (accessed April 11, 2025). For the purposes of this paper, this term does not differentiate those who self-identify as, e.g., Hebrew Catholics, Jews in the Orthodox Churches, or Jews in other Christian New Religious Movements. See Richard Harvey, "Jew, Jews. New Christian Movements," in *Encyclopedia of the Bible and Its Reception Online*, 179–180.

11. UMJC Theology Committee 2005, "Defining Messianic Judaism," https://www.umjc.org/defining-messianic-judaism (accessed May 2022).

12. Cf. Harvey, *Mapping Messianic Jewish Theology* (see note 3), 1ff. This section summarizes the Introduction, 1–13.

2. When did the Messianic Jewish Movement begin?

There have always been Jewish believers in Jesus, from the time of the early Church. These "followers of the way" or Nazarenes were known and accepted by the Church Fathers (Jerome, Justin Martyr, Epiphanius) but as Judaism and Christianity emerged as separate ways in the fourth century (cf. Boyarin) it became increasingly unacceptable to ecclesiastical and rabbinic authorities to allow the legitimacy of Jewish expressions of faith in Christ. Excluded from the Synagogue for their belief in the Trinity and divinity of Christ and anathematized by the Church for continued practice of Jewish customs, they were known as Ebionites ("the poor ones") and suspected of legalism and an adoptionist Christology.

Small groups of Jewish Christians continued in the East, and Jewish converts to Christianity were afforded protection in the midst of an antisemitic European Church by institutions such as the *Domus Conversorum* (House of Converts) which was maintained by royal patronage. But it was not until the modern missionary movement and an interest in mission to the Jewish people that a "community of testimony" of Jewish Christians re-appeared.

In 1809, Joseph Samuel Christian Frey, son of a rabbi from Posen, Hungary, encouraged the formation of the London Society for the Promotion of Christianity Among the Jews, which became the Church's Ministry Among Jewish People (CMJ). In 1813, Frey gathered forty-one Hebrew Christians to form the Benei Abraham (Children of Abraham), the first independent Hebrew Christian association. Encouraged by CMJ and other Jewish missions, the growing number of "Hebrew Christians," as they called themselves, formed their own Hebrew Christian Alliance of Great Britain (1866), Hebrew Christian Prayer Union (1882), and International Hebrew Christian Alliance (1925).

In 1883, Joseph Rabinowitz founded the "Israelites of the New Covenant" in Kishinev, Bessarabia. He held services in Hebrew and Yiddish, and word of his activities encouraged the growth of Hebrew Christian congregations worldwide. Mark John Levy worked tirelessly for the formation of the International Hebrew Christian Alliance. He was successful in his attempt to gain approval from the Episcopalian Church in the United States for Jewish Christians to continue to observe Jewish customs such as Sabbath, circumcision, and *kashrut*, but was widely rejected by his fellow Hebrew Christians who saw this as Judaizing and going back under the Law. They developed their own liturgies and Hebrew Christian congregations in Europe, Palestine, and the United States. In the United Kingdom in the 1920s, Paul Levertoff, a Hasidic Jew who became an Anglican minister, officiated at the "Meal of the Holy King," a combination of Jewish and Christian liturgy.

By the end of the nineteenth century, it was estimated on the basis of baptismal statistics that over a million Jewish people had become Christians, many for reasons of assimilation and emancipation from the ghettos into European society with access to commerce, education, and secular society.[13] Nevertheless a recognizable number, such as Alfred Edersheim, Adolph Saphir, Augustus Neander, and Bishop Samuel Schereschewsky, wished to retain aspects of their Jewish identity alongside faith in Christ and were both influential in the Church and a testimony to their people.

After the Second World War, the Holocaust, and the establishment of the State of Israel, Jewish believers in Jesus from a new generation were concerned to rediscover their ethnic roots and express their faith from a Jewish perspective. In the wake of the Jesus movement of the 1970s, "Jews for Jesus" moved from a slogan used on the streets of San Francisco to an organization of Jewish missionaries to their people. At the same time, the Messianic Jewish Alliance of America encouraged the establishment of Messianic congregations and synagogues. In Israel, a new generation of native-born Israelis (*sabras*) were finding the Messiah and starting Hebrew-speaking congregations. At the beginning of the twenty-first century an international network of Messianic groups exists, expressing denominational, theological, and cultural diversity, but united by belief in Yeshua, hence its name Yachad BeYeshua.[14]

Messianic Jews, to varying degrees, observe the Sabbath, keep kosher food laws, circumcise their sons, and celebrate the Jewish festivals, seeing Jesus and the Church in Acts as their model and example. They celebrate Passover showing how Yeshua came as the Passover Lamb, and practice baptism, linking to the Jewish *mikveh* (ritual bath). They worship with their own liturgies, based on the synagogue service, with readings from the Torah and New Testament. Pointing to Paul's teaching in Romans 9–11 and his practice on his missionary journeys, their

13. The Jewish mission historian De le Roi reported 224,000 baptisms on the basis of church records. Johannes De le Roi, *Judentaufen im 19. Jahrhundert: ein statistischer Versuch* (Leipzig: Hinrichs, 1899): 56.

14. https://www.yachad-beyeshua.org/ (accessed April 11, 2025).

hermeneutic of Scripture repudiates traditional Christian anti-Judaism ("the Jews killed Christ") and supersessionism (the Church replaces Israel as the "new Israel"), arguing for forms of Torah observance that testify to the presence of the believing remnant in the midst of unbelieving Israel as a witness to the Messiah.

3. What do Messianic Jews have in common and what are their differences?

Messianic Jewish Theology (MJT) has developed in the light of its Protestant evangelical background and its engagement with Jewish concerns. The doctrinal statements of Messianic Jewish organizations are uniformly orthodox but are often expressed in Jewish rather than Hellenistic thought forms and are more closely linked to Jewish concepts and readings of Scripture. Many Messianic Jews are influenced by the Charismatic Movement, although an increasing number are opting for more formal styles of worship using the resources of the Jewish prayer book, and standard liturgical features such as the wearing of the prayer-shawl *(tallit)* and the use of Torah scrolls.

Messianic Jews are generally united in their acceptance of Yeshua (Jesus) as Messiah, Lord, Savior, and incarnate Son of God. They affirm the authority of the Scriptures. They have varying views on the place of the sacraments and the role and authority of Jewish and Christian tradition. In the Diaspora, their Jewish identity is expressed through Jewish cultural and religious practice, whereas in Israel a more secular and civil Israeli identity is more observed. They differ on the role of Torah, their relationship with the wider Jewish and Christian communities, and on the nature of their witness. Their eschatologies vary, but tend to be premillennialist with a strong loyalty to the State of Israel both politically and prophetically.

Mark Kinzer defines Messianic Jewish Theology (MJT) according to its shape and main concerns:

> Messianic Jewish theology is disciplined reflection about God's character, will, and works, and about God's relationship to Israel, the Nations, and all creation, in the light of God's irrevocable election of Israel to be a kingdom of priests and a holy nation, and God's creative, revelatory, and redemptive work in Messiah Yeshua. Messianic Jewish theology is rooted in divine revelation (Torah), pursued in the context of Jewish communal life and tradition and in respectful conversation with the entire Christian theological tradition, and informed by prayer, by

> experience of the world, and by all available sources of human knowledge and understanding.[15]

Richard Harvey describes MJT as

> [A] theology constructed in dialogue with Judaism and Christianity, refined in discussion between reflective practitioners engaged with Messianic Judaism, and developed into a new theological tradition based on the twin epistemic priorities of the continuing election of the Jewish people and the recognition of Jesus as the risen Messiah and incarnate Son of God.[16]

As with Jewish theologies in general, MJT focuses on the traditional organizing categories of God, Torah, and Israel, which are further expanded to include the doctrine of God and the doctrine of Yeshua, the role of Torah in theory and in practice, and the nature and destiny of Israel (the Jewish people).

The Messianic movement represents a classic example of the contextualization of theology and ethnotheological formation. As the movement matures, it provides an object lesson of the challenges and possibilities of mission in a gospel-resistant culture with 2,000 years of misperception of the Christian message. Some Messianic Jews would advocate Messianic congregations as the most effective missionary tool, but this is not borne out by the evidence of the majority of Jewish believers in Jesus, who come to faith through the witness of their Christian friends in mainstream Churches. Some would argue that all Jewish believers in Jesus should remain (or become) Torah-observant, or they will be lost to their people, but this view also has not been accepted by the majority of Messianic Jews, who are happy in their membership of the universal Church. They see their freedom in the Messiah as allowing them to choose how much they identify with different forms of Judaism and Jewish identity. In terms of witness, Messianic Jews vary in their styles and strategy. An unknown number, often "secret believers," retain active membership in non-messianic synagogues, but this option is not typical. Others are highly visible in high-profile witness on the streets in major cities, stalls at New Age festivals in Israel and elsewhere, and meeting Israeli tourists on the hippy trail in India. Others prefer a

15. Mark S. Kinzer, "The Shape of Messianic Jewish Theology (Session 1): What Is Messianic Jewish Theology?" (MJTI Lecture, Fuller Theological Seminary, 2005): 1; cited in Harvey, *Mapping Messianic Jewish Theology* (see note 3), 46.

16. Harvey, *Mapping Messianic Jewish Theology* (see note 3), 262.

less overt engagement within the Jewish community through joining communal organizations, and through day-to-day contact with friends and family. A growing number of Messianic Jews recognize their missionary calling to be a "light to the nations" and a blessing to the whole Church, and seek ways to educate and challenge the Church as to the riches of its heritage and the Jewish roots of its faith.

MJT is an emerging theology. Reform Jewish theologian Byron Sherwin's categories of authenticity, coherence, contemporaneity, and communal acceptance that "characterize a valid Jewish theology" are applicable to it and serve as guidelines for its development.[17] The *authenticity* of MJT is evident in that whilst it draws from both Jewish and Christian theological traditions, it is in the process of articulating its own position. It is beginning to speak with its own "inner voice." Its claim to authenticity will only be recognized as it responds effectively to the louder voices of the two larger theological traditions amongst which it clamors for a hearing. By finding and articulating its own authentic "theological voice" it will challenge the boundary lines that have traditionally separated Judaism from Christianity.

The *coherence* of MJT around the two epistemic priorities of the Messiahship of Jesus and the election of Israel (the Jewish people) has yet to be stated systematically and comprehensively. These two key affirmations, if held together in creative tension, provide fruitful ground for the elaboration of a coherent theology. The methodological issues to be addressed pose a considerable challenge to such a project. Questions of the nature of the sources, norms, methods, content, and results of such a systematic MJT await the production of a comprehensive work at a level that has thus far been beyond any one individual within the Messianic movement. Since 2009, a number of attempts have been made to organize the theological discussions within the Messianic Jewish world, such as the Borough Park Symposium and the Helsinki Consultation,[18] and a number of journals and books published by single and multiple authors on the subjects germane to MJT.[19]

17. Byron L. Sherwin, *Toward a Jewish Theology: Methods, Problems, and Possibilities* (Lampeter / Queenston, Ontario / Lewiston, NY: Edwin Mellen, 1991): 9.

18. http://helsinkiconsultation.squarespace.com/helsinki-consultation/ (accessed March 14, 2024).

19. See, e.g., David Rudolph, ed., *The Borough Park Papers: Symposium I: The Gospel and the Jewish People* (New York: Messianic Jewish Publishers, 2012); David Rudolph, ed., *The Borough Park Papers: Symposium II: The Deity of Messiah and the Mystery*

The *contemporaneity* of MJT is also a concern. The writings of the formative period in the 1970s and 1980s are not as relevant in the new millennium, when they expressed the thinking of those pioneering the movement. The postformative positions proposed by Mark Kinzer and the Hashivenu[20] group have yet to gain general support. The issues that concern the contemporary Jewish community and its Messianic contingent are as pressing as ever. Jewish identity, the survival of the Jewish people, the question of Israel, and the coming of the Messiah are issues that MJT must address appropriately, constructively, and persuasively in a contemporary context.

The *communal acceptance* of MJT is vital, as the growth and maturity of the Messianic movement is dependent on its acceptance of MJT in the light of changing needs and contexts. For MJT to be accepted by the Messianic community and the wider Jewish and Christian communities with which it interacts, it must provide answers that are satisfying, relevant, and applicable to future generations. With such concerns for authenticity, coherence, contemporaneity, and communal acceptance in view, the present state of MJT is now examined through a characterization of the various theological streams within the Messianic movement.

4. A typology of Messianic Jewish theologies

In my doctoral thesis, *Mapping Messianic Jewish Theology*,[21] I attempted to map the contours and varieties of theological understandings within the modern Messianic Jewish movement on these topics, and proposed an eightfold typology of differing theological streams within a developing theological tradition.

---

of God (New York: Messianic Jewish Publishers, 2012); David Rudolph, ed., *The Borough Park Papers: Symposium III: How Jewish Should the Messianic Jewish Community Be?* (New York: Messianic Jewish Publishers, 2012); David Rudolph, ed., *The Borough Park Papers Symposium IV: Messianic Jewish Perspectives on the Israeli-Palestinian Conflict* (New York: Messianic Jewish Publishers, 2020); David Rudolph and Joel Willetts, *Introduction to Messianic Judaism: Its Ecclesial Context and Biblical Foundations* (Grand Rapids, MI: Zondervan Academic, 2013); *Kesher: A Journal of Messianic Judaism*, available online at https://www.kesherjournal.com/ (accessed October 10, 2019); David Rudolph, "What is Messianic Judaism?," https://www.messianicjudaism.net/ (accessed October 10, 2019).

20. http://hashivenu.org/ (accessed October 10, 2019).

21. Harvey, *Mapping Messianic Jewish Theology* (see note 3), 264–76.

At present there is no consensus or unitary theology of Messianic Judaism. Here we propose a typology to describe the plurality of MJT. Previous studies have observed different strands within the Messianic movement, and these are briefly discussed.

David Stern described a series of future options for Messianic Jews, based on "ideal types" of Messianic Judaism and Hebrew Christianity.[22] His options are "Ultimate Messianic Jew" (UMJ), "Ultimate Hebrew Christian" (UHC), and a range of more limited possibilities within these two main categories; "Ultimately Jewish but Limited Messianic possibilities" (UJLM); "Ultimate Hebrew Christianity of Today" (UHCT); "Present Limit of Hebrew Christianity" (PLHC); "Present Limit of Messianic Judaism" (PLMJ). He poses the question "if you are a Messianic Jew, in which direction are you headed?" The discussion is unsatisfactory, limited as it was by the then incipient nature of the Messianic movement and its lack of theological development at the time. Stern's grid constructs a dualistic and antithetical relationship between "Hebrew Christianity" and "Messianic Judaism." As one of the leaders of Messianic Judaism in the 1970s, he is at pains to distance Messianic Judaism from Hebrew Christianity, and his use of the metaphor of parent and child oversimplifies the questions and polarizes the alternatives, without articulating the nature of the theological questions involved.

Mark Kinzer distinguishes between "Missionary" and "Postmissionary" Messianic Judaism.[23] "Missionary Messianic Judaism" developed from Hebrew Christianity and the Jewish Missions. It was formulated by individuals like Joseph Rabinowitz and organizations such as "Jews for Jesus." It was then expressed in the 1970s and 1980s by the MJAA and the UMJC. Kinzer articulates five principles that Postmissionary Messianic Judaism affirms and assesses to what degree they are held by others.[24] These are: (i) Israel's irrevocable election and covenant; (ii) the normative force of basic Jewish practice (Torah observance); (iii) the validity of rabbinic tradition; (iv) "a bilateral ecclesiology" that accepts the continuing position of the Jewish people as the people of God in

22. David Stern, *Messianic Jewish Manifesto* (Jerusalem: Jewish New Testament Publications, 1988): 234–38.

23. Mark S. Kinzer, *Postmissionary Messianic Judaism: Redefining Christian Engagement with the Jewish People* (Grand Rapids, MI: Brazos Press, 2005).

24. *Ibid.*, 293.

partnership with the *ecclesia* of the nations; and (v) national solidarity with Israel. This enables Kinzer to distinguish between the new "Postmissionary" paradigm he proposes, and other previous forms.

Both Stern and Kinzer use dualist conceptual schemes, of Hebrew Christianity and Messianic Judaism (Stern) and more recently of "Missionary" and "Postmissionary" Messianic Judaism (Kinzer). Stern's aim is to argue for "Messianic Judaism" over against "Hebrew Christianity," and Kinzer favors "Postmissionary Messianic Judaism" against "Missionary Messianic Judaism." Both oversimplify the complexity of MJT for their own purposes, and without further detailing of the considerable theological variation found within MJT. Therefore, a new typology is needed.

The eightfold typology proposed here is more tentative and less dualist than those of Stern and Kinzer, tracing developing "streams" rather than clearly defined "schools" of theology within Messianic Judaism. The groupings are somewhat arbitrary and there are some overlaps, but leading voices are identified that speak representatively for each stream. My book describes their characteristic methods, criteria, and assumptions used; the structure and organization of their thought; their key concerns and emphases; the influences and the resources they draw from in Jewish and Christian theology; the degree to which they are reflective and self-aware of the process of theologizing; the contexts and constituencies to which they are linked; and the possible future for their thought.

In what follows, the views of each stream on the nature of God, the Messiah, the Torah in theory and in practice, and the future of Israel will be summarized where they have been addressed. The types of MJT begin with those closest to the Protestant evangelicalism from which the Messianic movement has emerged, at the one end of the spectrum, to those who locate their core identity within "Jewish social space" and Jewish religious and theological norms.

Type 1—Jewish Christianity, Christocentric and Reformed (Maoz)

This type of MJT may be characterized as Christian proclamation, with limited cultural and linguistic translation into a Jewish frame of reference. Baruch Maoz identifies himself as an ethno-cultural "Jewish" Christian in dialogue with those in the Messianic movement who advocate a return to a religious "Judaism."[25] Maoz works with the presuppositions of Reformed Protestantism and is highly critical of rabbinic Judaism. His theology is shaped to correct what he sees as the error of Messianic Judaism of compromise on Christian essentials by acceptance of rabbinic Judaism.

Maoz's doctrine of God reflects Christian orthodoxy with little engagement with Jewish theological concerns. His Christology is expressed in the creeds, and expounded as Reformed Dogmatics. The Law is fulfilled in Christ, with Jewish observance permitted only when in conformity with New Testament practice. The key theological concern is the elevation of Jesus as Messiah, the uniqueness of his saving work, and the challenge to Rabbinic Judaism that this poses. Judaism and Jewish identity cannot be allowed to diminish the authority of Christ as revealed in Scripture. The hermeneutical system is that of the Protestant Reformation and conservative evangelicalism.

Maoz has a strong political loyalty to the State of Israel, but justifies this on the grounds of national and cultural identity. He is critical of premillennialism and studiedly agnostic on eschatology. Maoz's thought, with its Christian Reformed theological emphasis, its non-charismatic and anti-rabbinic attitude, appeals to those with a focus on Scripture as interpreted through the Reformation tradition. Within the land of Israel such views are popular with those disaffected with the more superficial elements of the Messianic movement and unimpressed with more engaged forms of Torah-observance. The challenge for Maoz's approach will be to develop an appropriate, coherent doctrine of Israel, and a theology of culture that does not artificially separate an ethnocultural "Jewishness" from religious "Judaism." Maoz's arbitrary distinction between the two is problematic, and has not met with general acceptance.[26]

Type 2—Dispensationalist Hebrew Christianity (Fruchtenbaum)

Arnold Fruchtenbaum is the leading theologian in this group, whose expression of Jewishness and Jewish identity are defined within the

25. Baruch Maoz, *Judaism Is Not Jewish: A Friendly Critique of the Messianic Movement* (Fearn, UK: Christian Focus Publications, 2003). Others include Stan Telchin, *Messianic Judaism Is Not Christianity: A Loving Call to Unity* (Grand Rapids, MI: Mentor, 2004).

26. Cf. Richard Harvey, "Judaism Is Not Jewish [by Baruch Maoz]: A Review," *CWI Herald* (Summer 2003), https://banneroftruth.org/us/resources/articles/2003/judaism-not-jewish/ (accessed February 13, 2025).

parameters of dispensationalism.[27] The shape of Fruchtenbaum's theology is determined by a systematic and programmatic application of dispensationalist teaching and method to existential questions of Jewish identity and faith in Jesus.

Fruchtenbaum's God is the God of Protestant evangelicalism, articulated in the mode of "revised dispensationalism," with little room for speculative thought or contextualization.[28] There is no use for rabbinic or Jewish tradition unless it confirms and illustrates biblical revelation as reflected through a dispensationalist hermeneutic. Orthodox Christology is viewed through a conservative evangelical lens. There are some attempts at translation into Jewish cultural contexts, but a literal rather than dynamic equivalence is sought. The Abrahamic covenant is fulfilled in the Messiah, and the Torah seen as the dispensation of the Mosaic Law has come to an end. Practice of those national and cultural Jewish elements that do not go against the NT is permitted, but the rabbinic re-interpretation of the Torah and its claims to authority are false.

Fruchtenbaum's concern is an effective rooting of gospel proclamation within a Jewish context, and with a strong eschatological agenda of dispensationalism, which looks forward with certainty to the imminent return of Christ, the rapture, tribulation, and millennial kingdom. This is the focus and center of his system.

With this clearly defined theological base, hermeneutical method, and eschatological scheme, Fruchtenbaum's articulate exposition appeals to those looking for a clear theological system. The combination of political support for Israel and a strong eschatological emphasis will continue to influence the Messianic movement. However, it also contains the weaknesses of dispensationalism: its hermeneutical methods; its nineteenth-century amalgam of rationalism, romanticism, and historical consciousness; and the problem of Israel and the Church as two peoples of God. These will not gain acceptance with the majority of Messianic Jews, and they will look for alternatives.

27. Arnold Fruchtenbaum, *Hebrew Christianity: Its Theology, History and Philosophy* (Tustin, CA: Ariel Ministries Inc, 1983). Others include Barry Leventhal, Louis Goldberg, and Louis Lapides.

28. For distinctions between Classical, Revised, and Progressive Dispensational, see Craig Blaising and Darrell Bock, *Progressive Dispensationalism* (Grand Rapids, MI: Baker Academic, 2000).

Type 3—Israeli National and Restorationist (Nerel)

Gershon Nerel's theology is observable in his historical studies of Jewish believers in the early Church, and in the nineteenth and early twentieth centuries. His theological system is implicit rather than explicit in his narrative of the histories of Jewish believers in Yeshua (JBYs). He has yet to produce a systematic exposition of his theology. Nevertheless, he is representative of many Israeli Messianic Jews, who express their proximity to Christianity in solid creedal affirmations, and practice a form of Messianic Judaism which is Hebrew-speaking, rooted in modern Israeli society and culture, but with little regard for rabbinic orthodoxy as a religious system. Culturally, ethnically, and nationally, like the majority of secular Israelis, they identify with Israel and its aspirations as a State, serving in the army, living in kibbutz or moshav, and putting their children through the Israeli school system.

The heart of Nerel's theology is the eschatological significance not just of the modern Zionist movement and the return to the land, but also the re-establishment of JBYs in Israel to renew the original apostolic Church of Peter and James. For Nerel, this has significant implications for the shape and unity of the Church, challenging it to repent of supersessionism and anti-Judaism. JBYs bear a special "eschatological spiritual authority." This challenges Israel to recognize the imminent return of her Messiah, and calls Jewish people worldwide to make *aliyah,* in preparation for the end times. In the light of antisemitism and supersessionism, Nerel's Messianic Judaism is a powerful prophetic call to Israel and the nations to see what God is doing today. His theological system is not concerned with minutiae of doctrinal formulas, but with a clear pragmatic involvement in a Restorationist program. The fact that Messianic Judaism does not have twenty centuries of tradition to look to is a distinct advantage as it develops its theology.

> The very fact that *congregations of JBY lack a two-millennia tradition* helps them to easily find the bridge between themselves and the first-century model of JBY as portrayed in the New Testament.[29]

29. Gershon Nerel, "Modern Assemblies of Jewish Yeshua-Believers between Church and Synagogue," in *How Jewish is Christianity? Two Views on the Messianic Movement,* ed. Stanley Gundry and Louis Goldberg (Grand Rapids, MI: Zondervan Academic, 2003): 92–107, at 106 (italics his).

> There exists a clear resemblance between the messianic movement of Jewish believers in Jesus and the modern Zionist movement. Basically, both movements highlight the idea of bridging a historical gap between modern times and biblical times. Namely, they consciously reject allegations that they maintain anachronistic approaches. On the contrary, contemporary Jewish Jesus-believers and mainstream Zionists raise the opposite argument that they still possess a natural right to bypass the last two millennia and directly relate to the pre-exilic period in Israel's history.[30]

Nerel's theological method and shape blends the independent evangelical stream of the previous generation of Messianic Jews who made *aliyah* in the 1950s with the establishment of the State of Israel and the Zionist movement, combining Jewish political action and Christian eschatology. His eschatology is premillennial, but he avoids the systematization of dispensationalism. His realized eschatology stresses the significance of the re-emergence of Messianic Jews in the Land. This could become an important factor in the future, as the Messianic movement grows in Israel and takes on greater political and prophetic relevance.

Type 4—New Testament Halakha, *Charismatic and Evangelical (Juster, Stern)*

The most popular type of MJT found within the Messianic movement is that of David Stern and Daniel Juster, who advocate "New Testament *halakha*" within a Jewish expression of faith that is evangelical and charismatic.[31] It is the dominant influence within the UMJC and integrates belief in Jesus as Messiah with Jewish tradition. It expresses Christian orthodoxy within a Jewish cultural and religious matrix, seeing a prophetic and restorative role for Messianic Judaism in the renewal of both Judaism and Christianity. Its theological system is an eclectic combination of evangelical innovation and traditional Jewish observance.

30. Gershon Nerel, "Primitive Jewish Christians in the Modern Thought of Messianic Jews," in *Le Judéo-Christianisme Dans Tous Ses États: Actes Du Colloque De Jérusalem 6–10 Juillet 1998*, ed. Simon Mimouni and Stanley Jones (Paris: CERF, 2001): 399–425.

31. Daniel Juster, *Jewish Roots: A Foundation of Biblical Theology for Messianic Judaism* (Rockville, MD: Davar, 2013). Other key practitioners are Burt Yellin, Barney Kasdan, and the majority of UMJC (Union of Messianic Jewish Congregations) and MJAA (Messianic Jewish Alliance of America) leaders.

Belief in God and the Trinity follows Christian orthodoxy, but this is translated into Jewish forms of thought and expression. Nicene Christology is recontextualized and expressed in Jewish terms. The doctrine of the incarnation is expressed apologetically and in dynamically equivalent Jewish terms. The Torah is re-defined in the light of Yeshua, and the Oral Torah is critically evaluated in the light of the New Testament. The Messianic movement belongs to the movement of restoration of the whole Church, and is part of Israel. Historic premillennialist eschatology brings urgent expectation of what God is doing in the land and among the people of Israel.

Salvation is only by faith in Yeshua. Yet Israel is still the people of God, and her future salvation is assured. Until this happens, evangelistic witness is imperative, but must be done in ways that are culturally sensitive, showing how the Messianic movement is part of the Jewish community, not separate from it or outside it. Scripture is the supreme authority, but must be interpreted and applied contextually, following the "Fuller School of World Mission" approach developed by Glasser, Goble, and Hutchens. The Oral Torah can help to understand and interpret New Testament *halakha*. The Torah to be observed is that of Yeshua and his followers, with some appropriate adjustments for today.

The future of this stream within the movement is bright, as it occupies the middle ground between Jewish and Christian spheres of influence. It has found popular expression in many Messianic congregations, especially in the United States, combining a vibrant charismatic expression of faith with a "Torah-positive" attitude to Jewish tradition. However, its theological integrity and authenticity has yet to be made explicit, and the tension between tradition and innovation reconciled. The pioneering statements made by Juster and Stern in the formative period of the 1970s and 1980s have yet to be consolidated. It remains to be seen how the combination of charismatic evangelicalism and "New Covenant Torah observance" will be accepted by the next generation in Israel and the United States.

Type 5—Traditional Judaism and the Messiah (Schiffman, Fischer, Berkowitz)

Several independent thinkers can be situated between Stern and Juster on one side and Kinzer and Hashivenu on the other. They cannot be easily aligned, as their thinking has not fully emerged and it is difficult to locate their contribution precisely. Nevertheless, in the United States—John Fischer and Michael Schiffman, and in Israel—Ariel Berkowitz, David Friedman and Arieh Powlison, bring perspectives which are both "Torah-positive" and appreciative of rabbinic tradition without the full affirmation given them by Kinzer and the Hashivenu group.[32] The systematization of their views is incomplete, and their theological reflection has yet to be abstracted. They practice a halachic orthopraxy informed by faith in Jesus. It is possible that new streams of MJT may emerge more fully from this as yet disparate group. Whilst they remain close to Jewish orthodoxy, their doctrine of revelation does not see rabbinic tradition as the inspired, God-given means for the preservation of the Jewish people (as does Kinzer), but their observance of rabbinic *halakha* is stronger than that of Juster and Stern.

Powlison brings a new spirituality to his thinking, and Friedman and Berkowitz bring a new orientation to the Torah, making it available, in principle if not in practice, to the nations.[33] Fischer approaches Torah from his own orthodox Jewish background, but with the eyes of a New Testament follower of Yeshua. This group have maintained orthodox Christian beliefs, whilst interacting with Jewish traditional views and objections, on the nature of God, the Messiah, and the Torah. Their eschatology is premillennial. Their observance of Torah follows orthodoxy, whilst allowing for re-statement where appropriate. Scripture is read in the light of rabbinic tradition, but is still supreme as authoritative revelation. The emerging shape of this theology is not clear, but could result in "Messianic Hasidism" with a possibly more orthodox Jewish expression.

Type 6—"Postmissionary Messianic Judaism" (Kinzer, Nichol, Sadan)

Mark Kinzer's "Postmissionary Messianic Judaism" presents the potential for a programmatic theological system. Combatting supersessionist

32. E.g., David Friedman, *The Relationship of Yeshua and the First Century CE Messianic Jewish Community to the Mitzvot of the Mosaic Covenant* (PhD dissertation, California Graduate School of Theology, 1992).

33. Cf. Arye Powlinson, "Rabbinic Judaism as a Background to Scripture," in *Tishrei* 32.2 (May 2003)—under "Yeshua and Limits of Rabbinic Authority."

readings of Scripture to argue for the ongoing election of Israel and the legitimacy of a Torah-observant Messianic Judaism, Kinzer employs postliberal[34] and postcritical Jewish and Christian theological resources. His understanding of the revelation of God through the Scriptures and Jewish tradition acknowledges the significance of the Jewish and Christian faith communities through which such revelation is mediated. Ecclesiology and soteriology cohere around his bilateral understanding (reflecting Karl Barth) of the community of God made up of both "unbelieving" Israel and the Church, with Jesus present in both, visible to the *ekklesia* but only partially recognized by Israel. This "mature Messianic Judaism" is summarized by the Hashivenu statement of purpose:

> Hashivenu envisions mature Messianic Judaism to be an authentic expression of Jewish life that maintains substantial continuity with Jewish tradition. But this is a Judaism that is energized by faith in Yeshua of Nazareth, whom we honor as both the promised Messiah and the fullness of Torah. Mature Messianic Judaism is not simply Judaism plus Yeshua, or Yeshua plus Judaism, but an integrated and seamless whole in which discipleship to Yeshua is expressed in traditional Jewish forms, and in which the contemporary practice of Judaism is renewed in Yeshua and by the power of the Spirit.[35]

It is clear that Kinzer's influences and assumptions place him outside the mainstream of Protestant evangelicalism, especially the conservative variety often found within previous forms of Messianic Judaism. His view of the authority and inspiration of Scripture is tempered by

34. Postliberalism began as a reaction to theological liberalism. Karl Barth's reaction against Protestant liberal theology of the nineteenth and early twentieth centuries was taken up by some of his followers in the United States to produce a new engagement with the Bible, Church tradition and contemporary culture. This sat in-between the "liberal" and "conservative" labels. Key postliberal theologians include George Lindbeck, Hans Frei, and Stanley Hauerwas, and the academic journals *First Things* and *Pro Ecclesia* are representative of postliberal thought. Postliberalism reacts against the relativism and rationalism of theological liberalism, with a more sympathetic reading of the Bible and Church tradition, but with an openness to theological ecumenism, the existence and impact of other faiths, and engagement with contemporary culture. Cf. Richard Harvey, "Shaping the Aims and Aspirations of Jewish Believers (Review of Mark S. Kinzer's Postmissionary Messianic Judaism)," *Mishkan* 48 (2006): 18–21.

35. https://hashivenu.org (accessed February 14, 2023).

respect for Jewish traditions of interpretation, and the influence of critical and postcritical biblical scholarship and postliberal theology.

Kinzer advocates solidarity with the Jewish community.[36] He encourages sympathetic identification with the religious and cultural concerns of Judaism, as found in the North American context. The primary location of identity is "within the Jewish community" in order that Messianic Jews will "have Jewish grandchildren." One purpose is to refute the accusation of assimilation that is levelled at JBYs by the Jewish community.

"Postmissionary Messianic Judaism" arises as one way of negotiating the tension between proclamation of Jesus as Messiah and the preservation of Jewish belief, practice, and identity. Such concerns reflect the challenges facing the Messianic movement worldwide as it grows in theological, spiritual, communal, and personal maturity. Kinzer's response is a Messianic Judaism that echoes Conservative Judaism in its liturgy and practice, and integrates belief in Yeshua in the context of loyalties and identity to "Jewish space."

Kinzer sees Jesus as divine, but within a Judaism not inhospitable to the possibility of the divinity and incarnation of the Son of God. The historic Christian formulations of the Trinity are inadequate in Jewish contexts because they are steeped in Hellenism. New postcritical formulations are required that emerge from Jewish tradition and are recognized as possible understandings of the nature of God. The Scriptures of Judaism and Christianity are both inspired, and to be interpreted within a non-supersessionist appreciation of the canonical and communal contexts in which they arose.

Torah is observed in the light of Orthodox and Conservative *halakha*, with some modifications. Jewish believers thus integrate Messianic beliefs within traditional synagogal life, and witness to the Messiah through the presence of a community within the Jewish community rather than through overt appeal to individuals from without.

Kinzer's approach is the most theologically creative proposal to have emerged within Messianic Judaism in recent years, but it remains to be

36. Others in this group include Stuart Dauermann, Paul Saal, Rich Nichol, Jason Sobel, and the New England Halachic Council.

seen how much communal acceptance it will receive. It builds on North American Conservative Judaism in its method and expression, and departs significantly from the evangelical foundations to which much of Messianic Judaism still adheres. Its theological articulation, whilst profound, may not find popular appeal.[37]

Type 7—Rabbinic Halakha *in the Light of the New Testament (Shulam)*

Joseph Shulam expresses an Israeli form of Messianic Judaism using the resources of Orthodox Judaism. Shulam makes the call to 'do Messianic Jewish *halakha*' and to cut the 'umbilical cord' that connects Messianic Judaism to Christian denominations. He reads the Scriptures within the controlling hermeneutical framework of the Jewish tradition. His aim is to teach the Church the Jewish roots of its faith by a series of commentaries on the Jewish sources of the New Testament writings.[38]

The project is incomplete, and it is not clear how such a theology will be formulated. Shulam's main concern is to clear away the preliminary barriers of twenty centuries of non-Jewish reading of the Scriptures. His call for Messianic *halakha* is in reaction to the 'gentilization' of Messianic Judaism. Whilst he advocates a return to *halakha*, it is not clear in what form this will emerge. However, his is a genuine and Israeli-based expression of a Jewish orthodoxy linked to orthodox Christian beliefs about Jesus. His perspective is one that should be recognized within the spectrum of MJT, and it is possible that others will follow in his emphases.

Shulam disassociates himself from mainstream (and 'gentilized') Christianity, situating himself within Jewish social and religious space. He combines Messianic Judaism with mystical traditions in Judaism that lead to affirmations of his faith. Rabbinic, and even mystical traditions are part of the revelatory process, and to be held in balance with Scripture. Shulam's theological system is based on a midrashic approach to Scripture, a reading of the New Testament influenced by David Flusser, and some expression of the Jewish mystical tradition (Kabbalah) factored in to his overall approach.

37. Kinzer's work *Postmissionary Messianic Judaism* (see note 23) has been the subject of major discussions and reviews in *Mishkan* 48 (2006)—"Reactions to Postmissionary Messianic Judaism," and in *Kesher* 20 (Winter/Spring 2006).

38. E.g., Joseph Shulam with Hilary Le Cornu, *A Commentary on the Jewish Roots of Romans* (Baltimore, MD: Lederer Messianic Publications, 1997).

Type 8—Messianic Rabbinic Orthodoxy (Brandt, Marcus)

Elazar Brandt advocates a form of Messianic Judaism that is close to rabbinic orthodoxy, but is a minority position within the Messianic movement. He is convinced that Messianic Jews must

> make every effort to remain committed to the 4 pillars of Jewish existence that have always held us together—G-d,[39] land, people and Torah. History repeatedly shows that groups who have abandoned any of these commitments have quickly disappeared from the scene.[40]

His advocacy of Torah observance is so strong that:

> I dare say that it is less dangerous to follow the wrong messiah than to follow the wrong Torah.[41]

The authority of Torah, which for him is interpreted through rabbinic tradition, influences his Christology:

> The rightful Messiah will come to Jerusalem where his throne will be established and where he will rule Israel and the nations with justice according to the Torah. There is no such thing as a Messiah who does not keep Torah and teach his people to do so. If Yeshua does not do and teach Torah, then he is not the Messiah—not for Israel, and not for anybody else.[42]

This leads him to oppose all forms of supersessionism.

> There is no such thing as a Messiah who is not the Messiah of Israel. A Messiah who rejects Israel and chooses another people group is not the Messiah promised in the Bible.[43]

Messianic Jews have no special status among their people as the "faithful remnant" of Romans 9–11, but rather take their stand within the faithful found within all Israel. They cannot claim special status as the "remnant" because of their belief in Yeshua, as this would disenfranchise others who do not believe in him.

39. Brandt follows an orthodox Jewish custom of not writing the word "God" in full.

40. Elazar Brandt, email message to author, February 26, 2007. This has been referred to at length to ensure accurate representation of Brandt's views, and because he has published few statements of his position on these questions.

41. *Ibid.*

42. *Ibid.*

43. *Ibid.*

> Jews who claim to follow Yeshua and to know and do his Torah more perfectly than other Jews, and on such a basis claim to be the "true Israel," or the "true remnant of Israel," or other such language, are no less in the replacement camp than Christians who believe G-d has rejected Israel and chosen them instead.[44]

Brandt's soteriology includes all Israel.

> The "Israel" who today walks the streets of Jerusalem and the cities throughout the land, and the Jews who are identifiable outside of the land, are the Israel that G-d is going to see through to redemption. He staked his name on this by an oath. This includes Haredis and secular, Conservative and Reform as well as Zionist and uncommitted. "All Israel shall be saved," said Paul. If G-d does not keep this promise, then he is not G-d. He said so Himself.[45]

Brandt's hermeneutics call for a return to halachic orthodoxy. To Brandt this means abandoning a "spiritualizing and fantasizing" approach to the Bible, and returning to "literal interpretation and obedience." Jews who believe in Yeshua remain Jews. They are called to repent, not by being "sorry for personal sins," but by returning to the covenant, and remaining "faithful to our G-d, land, people and Torah." As regards the witness of Messianic Jews to their people:

> Our best testimony to our own people will be if we can show that we are doing this because we met Yeshua. Instead, we have been doing our best to show that we have broken our covenant with the four pillars [God, Land, People and Torah] since we have met Yeshua. What reason is there today or in the past for our people to see us otherwise?[46]

This type is at the far end of the continuum and expresses a tendency to move back into Judaism at the expense of Christian affirmations and distinctives. Elazar Brandt is more comfortable within Jewish Orthodoxy, and likewise, there are ultra-orthodox Hasidim who come to believe in Jesus and remain in their communities, practicing as "secret believers," invisible to outsiders, as part of an "insider movement." Uri Marcus even goes so far as to put forward a revised adoptionist Christology.

Like Brandt, Marcus distances himself from "Hellenistic" and "Gentile" Christianity. Marcus subscribes to Orthodox Jewish views on the

44. *Ibid.*
45. *Ibid.*
46. *Ibid.*

indivisibility and singularity of the Divine nature which rules out the possibility of the Trinity. However, his dispensational premillennial eschatology and its charismatic expression relate closely to Christian Zionism, and his denial of the Trinity and incarnation has caused controversy in Christian Zionist and Messianic Jewish circles.

For Marcus, Jesus is the human Messiah, who did not claim deity and is not divine. Scripture is read in context of rabbinic tradition, which informs and controls the results of such reading. Rabbinic *halakha* is accepted, and there is little overt proclamation. Whilst the theology of this stream has yet to be comprehensively or systematically articulated, it is an influential if heterodox group within the Messianic movement. Without clearer definition of the significance of Yeshua, it is likely that for some it will be a means back into Jewish orthodoxy, and that an increasing number of Messianic Jews will take up the label of "Orthodox" or "Just Jewish."

5. What are the actual facts and numbers?

There are some 150,000 Jewish believers in Jesus worldwide, according to conservative estimates of 100,000 in the United States, approximately 15,000–30,000 in Israel, the remainder being found throughout the approximately 14 million worldwide Jewish population. There are over 200 Messianic groups in the United States, and some 280 in Israel.

The numbers and demographics of Messianic Jews and Messianic congregations worldwide have yet to be systematically compiled. The table below uses a variety of methods for estimating these, with varying degrees of reliability. Following the methods of demographer Sergio DellaPergola for estimating the world Jewish population, we use the estimates for those with one Jewish grandparent, eligible to become Israeli citizens under the Law of Return (LRP). A proportion of LRP Jews are in churches, and we estimate those. We then estimate the number of self-identifying Jewish disciples of Jesus in the mainstream churches. We then use the data available from national surveys of Messianic congregations, giving their general attendance and the number of individual Jewish disciples of Jesus in them. Whilst these figures are compiled in various ways, there are reasonable grounds for presenting them as an estimate of the number of Messianic Jews in Messianic congregations globally.

Global Population Estimate of Jewish Believers in Yeshua (2020)

Country	Total	Core Jewish Population	Law of Return Population[47]	*LRPJBY*[48]	*Self-Identifying JBYs Estimate*[49]	MJCs	MJC Attendance	JBYs known (incl. in MJCs)
World (100%)[50]	7,691m	14,787,200	23,809,100 (0.3% of total pop)	*476,180*	*150,000*	674	37,408	15,486
Americas	**1,011m**	**6,466,900**	**13,416,700 (1.3%)**	***268,330***	***120,000***	**181**	**10,185**	**3,001**
United States (39% of total CJP)	329m	5,700,000	12,000,000 (3.6%)	*240,000/ (870,771[51])*	*100,000*	166	9,535	2,851
UMJC 65 congregations / 3,000 attendance / 1,000 JBYs MJAA 101 congregations / 6,535 attendance / 1,851 JBYs								

47. Sergio DellaPergola (2020). "World Jewish Population, 2020," in *The American Jewish Year Book, 2020, vol. 120* (Cham, Switzerland: Springer, 2020): 273–370. https://link.springer.com/chapter/10.1007/978-3-030-78706-6_7/tables/14 (accessed April 11, 2025).

48. Estimates are in *italics*. For Jewish-background believers in churches, we use a conservative estimate of 2% of LRP, since apart from Israel the wider population in these countries is traditionally Christian, but other estimates exist such as that of the Glaser/Lifeway survey 2018 (below). For Israel, some estimates are more than twice the figure here.

49. Usually 10–30% of LRPJBY estimate.

50. DellaPergola, "World Jewish Population, 2020" (see note 47), 273–370.

51. Mitch Glaser writes "This number, by projection, is 870,771, reflecting a Lifeway formula which avers that 16% of the U.S. adult population hold evangelical beliefs—almost 40 million people (as of July 2016; https://www.census.gov/popclock/). The Lifeway analysts then multiplied this population group by the percentage of those who claimed to have at least one Jewish parent or grandparent which was more precisely 2.1817%, in order to project the 870,771 number. By using the broader Pew estimate of 7.8 million US Jewish adults, both by ethnicity and religion (to be further explained), the percentage of adult American Jews with evangelical beliefs would be approximately 12%." Mitch Glaser, "How Many Jewish Believers in Yeshua are there in the World Today? Paper given at Messianic Leaders Roundtable November 12–14, 2018 Phoenix, AZ," available online at https://www.academia.edu/39721916/How_Many_Jewish_Believers_in_Yeshua_are_there_in_the_World_Today (accessed May 2022), 12.

Country	Total	Core Jewish Population	Law of Return Population	*LRPJBY*	*Self-Identifying JBYs Estimate*	MJCs	MJC Attendance	JBYs known (incl. in MJCs)
Canada (2.7%)	37m	393,000	700,000 (1.9%)	*14,000*	*2,000*	10	400	100[52]
Central & South America, incl. Caribbean[53]	644.5m	373,800	716,300 (0.1%)	*14,330*	*2,000*	5	*250*	*50*[54]
Israel[55] (46%)	**9.1m**	**6,773,400**	**7,220,700 (79%)**	***144,410***	***15,000***	**284**	**15,323**	**8,125**[56]

52. Andrew Barron estimates.

53. Countries with large LRP are Argentina (360,000), Brazil (180,000), Mexico (65,000), Uruguay (28,000), Chile (28,000), Panama (13,000), and Venezuela (14,000), but these have no known MJCs.

54. International Alliance of Messianic Congregations and Synagogues. For UMJC and MJAA abbreviations, see n.31.

55. State of Israel (de jure), including Judea–Samaria, for completeness of Jewish population figures.

56. David Serner and Alex Goldberg, *Jesus-Believing Israelis: Exploring Messianic Fellowships* (Jerusalem, 2022). See also Erez Soref, "Findings of New Research on the Messianic Movement in Israel" in https://www.oneforisrael.org/bible-based-teaching-from-israel/findings-of-new-research-on-the-messianic-movement-in-israel/ (accessed April 11, 2025); Erez Soref, "The Messianic Jewish Movement in Modern Israel," in *Israel, the Church and the Middle East*, ed. Mitch Glaser and Darrell Bock (Grand Rapids, MI: Kregel, 2018): 144–48. Soref estimates 30,000–60,000 Messianic Jews in 300 congregations. Only in Israel do JBYs outnumber Gentiles in MJCs, with 53% JBYs among MJC attenders. In Russia the estimate is 50%, in the United States 28.5%, and in France a mere 7.5%. Jewish members being a minority in MJCs may have implications for their development of authentically Jewish congregational life and theology.

Country	Total	Core Jewish Population	Law of Return Population	*LRPJBY*	*Self-Identifying JBYs Estimate*	MJCs	MJC Attendance	JBYs known (incl. in MJCs)
Europe[57] (9%)	**829m**	**1,329,400**	**2,820,800 (0.3%)**	***56,420***	***10,000***	**205**	**11,700**	**4,300**
France[58] (3%)	64.8m	448,000	750,000 (1.2%)	*15,000*	*1,500*	10	800	60
Russia (1%)	146.7m	155,000	600,000	*12,000*	*1,500*	20	2,000	1,000[59]
United Kingdom (2%)	66.8m	292,000	410,000	10,649[60] *8,200*	*1,200*	15	600	60
Germany (0.8%)	83.1m	118,000	275,000[61]	*5,500*	*750*	25	1500	500[62]
Ukraine	42m	45,000	200,000	*4,000*	*2,000*	*100*	*5000*	2,000[63]
Hungary	9.8m	47,200	130,000 (1.3%)	*2,600*	*300*	*1*	*30*	10[64]

57. EU 28 member states plus FSU (incl. all of Russia) plus other Europe. Turkey has a LRP of 23,000, but no known MJCs. Countries with LRP below 9,500 are not itemized (e.g., in descending order: Czechia, Bulgaria, Greece, Ireland, Slovakia, Portugal); those with 500 Jews or less include Channel Islands, North Macedonia, Malta, Slovenia.

58. Joshua Turnil, personal email correspondence, June 20, 2022.

59. Paula Juntilla, "Europe and Messianic Congregations: A brief summary," in *Euroopan juutalaisten kutsu*, ed. Paula Juntilla and Harri Kröger (Keuruu: Aikamedia, 2013). Personal email from Maxim Ammosov (Moscow); Patmos; Keymedia staff (2013).

60. Juntilla, "Europe" (see note 59).

61. "Germany's *core* Jewish population at 118,000 in 2013, of which all but about 5,000–6,000 are post-Soviet immigrants; the community numbers about 250,000 if non-Halachic-Jewish relatives are included."—Sergio DellaPergola, "World Jewish Population, 2013," in *The American Jewish Year Book, 2013, vol. 113*, ed. Arnold Dashefsky and Ira M. Sheskin (Dordrecht: Springer, 2013): 279–358.

62. Vladimir Pikman, personal email, June 25, 2022.

63. Roger Finch, Messianic Bible Institute, Odessa, 2013, via Paula Juntilla.

64. Kata Tar, Budapest, August 10, 2022.

Country	Total	Core Jewish Population	Law of Return Population	*LRPJBY*	*Self-Identifying JBYs Estimate*	MJCs	MJC Attendance	JBYs known (incl. in MJCs)
Netherlands	17.3m	29,800	63,000	*1,260*	*200*	*15*	*500*	50[65]
Italy	60.3m	27,300	48,000	*960*	*100*	*1*	30	10[66]
Belgium	11.5m	29,000	45,000	*900*	*100*	*2*	*30*	50[67]
Belarus	9.5m	8,500	33,000	*660*	*250*	10	1000	200[68]
Sweden	10.3m	15,000	30,000	*600*	*70*	0	0	50
Switzerland	8.6m	18,500	28,000	*560*	*60*	*1*	*30*	*10*[69]
Spain	47.1m	13,000	22,000	*440*	*60*	0	0	50
Austria	8.9m	10,300	20,000	*400*	*50*	1	50	10
Romania	19.4m	8,900	20,000	*400*	*200*	0	0	200
Latvia	1.9m	4,500	16,000 (0.8%)	*320*	*40*	3	100	30[70]
Poland	38.4m	4,500	13,000	*260*	*30*	0	0	0
Lithuania	2.8m	2,400	10,500	*210*	*25*	1	30	10[71]
Denmark	5.8m	6,400	9,500	*190*	*20*[72]	0	0	0

65. Paula Juntilla email from Renaldo van de Schuur (Israel and the Bible).
66. Juntilla, *ibid.*; Dr. Ron Diprose; Anja Kolehmainen (Finnish Lutheran Folksmission).
67. Juntilla email (see note 65).
68. *Ibid.*
69. Stephen Pacht, Swiss Messianic Jewish Alliance.
70. Juntilla email (see note 65).
71. *Ibid.*
72. *Ibid.*

Country	Total	Core Jewish Population	Law of Return Population	*LRPJBY*	*Self-Identifying JBYs Estimate*	MJCs	MJC Attendance	JBYs known (incl. in MJCs)
Africa, Asia, Oceania[73] (1.5%)	**5,842m**	**217,500**	**350,900**	***7,010***	***700***	**4**	**200**	**60**
Australia (0.8%)	25m	118,000	160,000	*3,200*	*350*	2	100	30
South Africa	58.6m	52,300	85,000	*1,700*	*200*	2	100	30
World (100%)	**7,691m**	**14,787,200**	**23,809,100**	***476,180***	***150,000***	**674**	**37,408**	**15,486**[74]

73. Not incl. Russia or Turkey, and Israel is listed independently. Others with large LRP are Azerbaijan (20,500), Iran (13,000), New Zealand (10,500), Uzbekistan (10,000), and Kazakhstan (9,500), but these have no known MJCs. All others have LRP below 9,500, incl. India and China.

74. Table developed with the help of James Earle Patrick and Andrew Smith.

Conclusion

The Messianic Jewish reality comprises less than 2% of the world Jewish population of fifteen million, which is itself less than 0.02% of the world population of 7.6 billion. And yet it is a reality today after two thousand years, because of one Jewish man, the Messiah Yeshua. It was Samuel Taylor Coleridge who said that the symbol "partakes of the reality which it renders intelligible."[75]

We exist—to represent to Israel and all nations the reality of Yeshua, the Messiah of Israel and Savior of all nations. For this contributor, the Messianic Jewish reality is a deeply personal one. I belong to a group who identify as Jewish followers of the Messiah Jesus. The elements of my own personal background, upbringing, and religious education as an assimilated, liberal, British Jew of German and Russian-Polish ancestry, combined with my experience of and belief in Yeshua (Jesus) as the Messiah of Israel and Savior of all nations, challenge me to live out and express this sense of calling—an unusual gift to be received from the Almighty.[76] The modern Messianic Jewish movement is a recent one, but it seeks to answer in today's world the age-old question of "What does it mean to be Jewish and believe in Jesus?"

75. William Shedd (ed.), *The Complete Works of Samuel Taylor Coleridge*, vol. 1 (New York: Harper & Brothers, 1853): 437; cited by Mary Rahme, "Coleridge's Concept of Symbolism," *Studies in English Literature, 1500–1900*, vol. 9.4 (1969): 619–32, at 621.

76. Richard Harvey, *But I'm Jewish!* (San Francisco, CA: Purple Pomegranate Productions, 1996). https://www.dropbox.com/s/khpam9p1xgqnrz5/BIJ.pdf?dl=0 (accessed May 2022).

Hebrew-Speaking Catholics, Hebrew Catholics, and Jewish Catholics

David M. Neuhaus, SJ

I AM HAPPY TO BE HERE in order to address you, although the title of the conference is a little ambiguous for people like me. The two partners in dialogue here seem to be Messianic Jews and Christians. As someone who defines himself as a Jewish Catholic, I am not sure where I fit in. But I suppose that is an important part of a theological, theoretical discussion and not just a personal question of identity. One other preliminary comment is that I am aware that speaking about Catholics might give a wrong impression: that all Jewish Christian believers in the Body of Christ are Catholics and that would be to ignore the important individuals and communities that do exist within the Orthodox and Eastern Churches as well as the other ecclesial communities issuing from the Reformation and those that are evangelical.

1. Definitions

Among the many aspects of the reorientation of the Catholic Church's discourse with regard to Jews and Judaism after the Second Vatican Council in the 1960s, one might also mention the change that has taken place in past decades with regard to the Catholic Church's position on the Jewish identity of those who have become Catholic. In former times, a baptized Jew was characterized as an ex-Jew, having given up his or her Jewish identity at the baptismal font. Jews had become Catholics and Jewish identity was to be discarded. However, in our times, Jews who are baptized into the Catholic Church can not only retain their Jewish identity, but indeed celebrate it. Pope John Paul II described emblematic Jewish Catholic Edith Stein in 1987 in his address to the Jewish community in Cologne as "a daughter of Israel who remained faithful, as a Jew, to the Jewish people, and, as a Catholic, to our crucified Lord Jesus Christ."[1] In his homily pronounced for Stein's canonization in 1998, John Paul II declared, "She understood that it was very important for her 'to be a daughter of the chosen people and to belong to Christ not only spiritually, but also through blood.'"[2]

Although Catholics who are Jews are few in number, the group is a very diverse one. From an institutional point of view, the two best known structures that regroup Jews who are Catholics are the Saint James Vicariate for Hebrew-Speaking Catholics in Israel (known popularly as the "*kehilla*"), and the Association of Hebrew Catholics (henceforth AHC), active predominantly in the Anglophone Jewish Diaspora. Interestingly, among the founding figures of both structures are two Jewish Catholics who lived as Carmelites in the Monastery of Stella Maris in Haifa, Daniel (Oswald) Rufeisen and Elias (John) Friedman. The differences in perspective that characterized these two emblematic figures reveal the great diversity to be found among Jewish Catholics. This diversity imposes itself even on the choice of terminology: Hebrew-speaking Catholic or Hebrew Catholic. I myself will prefer the use of the term "Jewish Catholic" and I hope the distinctions will become clear in what follows.

Whereas today, the Catholic Church celebrates the Jewish identity of Jewish Catholics, like all other Jews, they themselves are constantly dealing with the dilemma of what it means to be Jewish today. A Jew according to religious law is the child of a Jewish mother or someone who converts to Judaism. Is being Jewish today primarily a religious reality or is it a national / cultural / ethnic one? It would be undoubtedly true to speak of the Jewish people as a religious reality up to the beginning of modernity. Then *halakha* (Jewish religious law) defined Jewish

1. Pope John Paul II, *Address to Members of the Jewish Central Council of Cologne* (1.5.1987).

2. Pope John Paul II, *Homily for the Canonization of Edith Stein* (11.10.1998).

identity. However, modernity not only shattered the unity of practice at the heart of traditional Jewish identity through the emergence of different streams of Judaism (ultra-Orthodoxy, modern Orthodoxy, Conservative Judaism, Reform Judaism, etc.) but also gave birth to a Jewish secular rejection of traditional religious practice altogether. However, can one claim to be Jewish when one practices another religion? This was the claim of Rufeisen in his process brought before the Supreme Court in Israel in the early 1960s.

Whereas there is little agreement among Jews today as to what constitutes a Jew, I suggest that two important elements in the identity of the contemporary Jew have emerged: a sense of peoplehood and a sense of shared history. These two elements are more decisive than religion in unifying Jews today, when the majority of Jews do not practice any form of traditional religion. Whereas the element of Torah was at the core of identity in former times, today the concepts of *'Am* (People) and *Eretz* (Land) have largely overshadowed Torah. Among Jewish Catholics there are a few who keep aspects of *halakhic* Jewish life (*shabbat*, dietary laws, etc.), however, the vast majority of those who claim their Jewish identity do so in a modern sense: If a secular Jew, who practices little or nothing of Jewish tradition, can be Jewish, why can't I?

2. *Jewish in the Church*

Be this as it may, what does it mean to be Jewish in the Church today? What is the status of the Jewish Catholic as a Jew? I would assume that no Catholic would have a problem with a Jewish Catholic who insists on his or her national, ethnic, sociological, or cultural Jewish identity. Both Rufeisen and Friedman were strongly Zionist, seeing the State of Israel as inaugurating a new period in Jewish history that could open Jews, secure in their state, to Christians and Christianity. They did have different readings though of what it meant to be Jewish in the Church.

On the one hand, Rufeisen and other founders of the *kehilla* believed that they were reestablishing the ancient Church of the Circumcision, the community of Saint James in Jerusalem, a community of Jews who believe in Jesus without ceasing to be Jews. For example, Rufeisen commented, "For me the acceptance of Christianity was a Jewish step."[3] He

3. Nehama Tec, *In the Lion's Den: The Life of Oswald Rufeisen* (Oxford: Oxford University Press, 1990): 168.

would insist that his move toward Jesus as Messiah was steeped in his Jewish identity, a move similar to the earliest Jewish disciples of Jesus. From a theological point of view, the founders of the *kehilla* wanted the expression of their faith in Jesus as Messiah to be Jewish, not only deeply rooted in the Scriptures of Israel, but also formulated in the expressions of the Jewish people throughout the centuries and thus at home in the Hebrew language, in a society in which the majority were Jews and in a state that defined itself as Jewish. What brings the faithful of the *kehilla* together is their shared use of the Hebrew language and their being at home in Jewish society. This is a rather secular and modern sense of being Jewish.

On the other hand, Friedman insisted that the Hebrew Catholic was an Israelite, a member of the people of Israel, however Jewish tradition, practice, and belief, based on Jewish religion and unenlightened by the revelation of Christ, were no longer appropriate for the Hebrew Catholic. He wrote in his 1987 opus *Jewish Identity*: "An Israelite who today accedes to the Christian faith is not a Judeo-Christian. Not only did Judeo-Christians frequent the synagogue until their expulsion from it around the year 80 of the Christian era, they believed that the Law of Moses was still valid."[4] Vestiges of Jewish culture should only be retained in order to encourage Jews to convert without the fear of losing their specific national identity. Sabbath observance or the Passover meal might be practiced within the Catholic context by Catholics of Jewish origin in order to express their Israelite identity. In a 2010 interview conducted by David Moss, president of the AHC, with the patron of the association, Roman Catholic Cardinal Archbishop Raymond Burke, Burke clarified that traditional Jewish practices are permitted because they are carried out in the light of Christ.[5] The interview strongly underlines that baptized Hebrew Catholics remain part of God's elect, holding a special place as heirs of historical Israel. There is, however, no word in the long interview on the status of Jews who do not believe in Christ. However, the flyer that describes the Association of Hebrew Catholics on their website states: "The tragic exile of post-Christic [*sic!*] Jewry was due to their incredulity, their refusal to

4. Elias Friedman, *Jewish Identity* (New York, NY: Miriam Press, 1987): 65.

5. David Moss, "An Interview with Archbishop Raymond Burke on the Occasion of the AHC Conference of October 1–3, 2010," *The Hebrew Catholic* 88 (2010–2011): 34–35.

acknowledge the divinity of Jesus. This thought should prompt Hebrew Catholics to redress the situation by their exemplary orthodoxy"[6]—orthodoxy in Catholic faith and practice.

3. *Catholic in Israel*

When Jewish Catholics live in the midst of Jewish society, whether in Israel or in the Diaspora, what is their relationship with their Jewish brothers and sisters who do not accept Jesus as Messiah? Again, our emblematic use of the two Stella Maris Carmelites characterizes (or perhaps caricaturizes) diversity.

Rufeisen and the founders of the *kehilla* encouraged a relationship of dialogue with Jews, including religious Jews, and did not engage in any form of missionary activity. In this spirit, in recent years, a twinning has taken place between the *kehilla* and a synagogue community in Jerusalem, *Kehillat Zion*, that includes not only social action together but also study. Members of the two *kehillot* frequent each other's liturgical worship without syncretism but in a spirit of respect and dialogue. A similar fraternizing, although less frequent, was established between the *kehilla* in Beer Sheba and a local synagogue. Undoubtedly this dialogue is facilitated by the fact that the *kehilla* presents itself as a Catholic community that speaks Hebrew rather than as a Jewish Catholic community.

The *kehilla* has underlined the traumatic relations between Jews and Christians through the centuries, recognizing that mission in any form is part of the problem. It seeks to incarnate a loving presence of Church in the midst of the people of Israel. On its website, the *kehilla* is described as working "to strengthen the relationship between Jews and Christians, sharpening the Church's awareness of its Jewish roots and of the Jewish identity of Jesus and his apostles" and seeking "to sharpen the awareness of Jews in Israel with regard to the history, teaching and contribution of the Church to society. Our faithful are engaged fully in the life of Israeli Jewish society and in the life of the Catholic Church."[7]

6. https://www.hebrewcatholic.net/wp-content/uploads/2013/07/Presenting-AHC.pdf (accessed March 14, 2024).

7. https://www.catholic.co.il/?cat=sjv&view=article&id=10171 (accessed March 14, 2024).

This loving presence is one in which ideally Jews would not feel threatened by proselytizing efforts but feel at home and recognize the Jewish, Hebrew, and Israeli contours of the *kehilla*. As formulated in the pastoral letter published to mark the 60th anniversary of the *kehilla*, "When questioned about our faith, the words of Peter can serve us as a guide: 'Reverence the Lord Christ in your hearts and always have your answer ready for people who ask the reason for the hope that you all have, yet do it with gentleness and reverence' (1 Peter 3:15)."[8] Witness replaces mission and implies dialogue within the *kehilla*.

The AHC, although avoiding the word "mission," uses the word "witness" as a synonym for mission. The opening statement on its website states: "If you are a Catholic, we hope that you will be motivated to learn more and to collaborate with us in this work. If you are of Jewish origin, we hope you will join us in providing a collective witness of Jewish people to Jesus and His Church."[9] The collective witness is that of Jews speaking to Jews about Christ and encouraging them to join the fold, a traditionally missionary attitude.

A new voice has appeared in this debate: Antoine Lévy with his magnum opus *Jewish Church: A Catholic Approach to Messianic Judaism*.[10] In this volume, Lévy engages with the Messianic Jewish theologian Mark Kinzer, arguing for the integration of Messianic Judaism into the Catholic Church in order to gain not only catholicity for the Church (not only Gentiles but Jews too) but universality for the Jews (not only Jews but Gentiles too). As Lévy writes: "A Messianic Jew in the denominational sense of the term is a member of a movement that will not find its fully Catholic realization as long as this movement subsists independently from the wider Church. A Catholic Jew—or a (Christian-)Orthodox Jew for that matter—is a member of a Church that is still far from her fully Messianic accomplishment because its Jewish component is still insufficiently manifested."[11] Lévy's description of the Jewish Church he envisages resonates to some degree with the ideas of

8. https://www.catholic.co.il/?cat=docs&view=article&id=1136&m=Vicariate (accessed March 14, 2024).

9. https://www.hebrewcatholic.net/about-the-ach/welcome-message/ (accessed March 7, 2023).

10. Cf. Antoine Lévy, *Jewish Church: A Catholic Approach to Messianic Judaism* (Lanham, MD: Lexington Books, 2021).

11. *Ibid.*, 5.

the AHC, reserved about rabbinic tradition even if rooted in the Jewish people, particularly defined by nationalism. He writes, "The qualitative leap that proceeds from the revelation of Christ cannot but draw Messianic Judaism outside of the traditional setting of the Synagogue. The truth is that if Jewish disciples cannot be disciples of Yeshua in the same manner as their Gentile brethren because they are Jewish, they cannot either be religiously Jewish in the same manner as their Jewish brethren because they are disciples of Yeshua."[12]

4. Conclusion

At the end of this paper, I offer a personal reflection. As a Jewish Catholic I cultivate a dual belonging, to the Church and to the Jewish people. I am not satisfied with simply being a Hebrew-speaking Catholic. I love the Hebrew language that I have intentionally adopted and made my own. However, I am not a Zionist, and Jewish nationalism neither corresponds to how I understand the vocation of the Jewish people nor to the teaching of the Catholic Church. At the same time, I am not a Hebrew Catholic, as I seek to understand Judaism from the perspective of religious Jews who do not believe in Jesus, believing that they have much to teach the Church religiously and spiritually.

I am a Jewish Catholic, affirming that my identity is a double one. I feel at home not only among the Jewish people but in their synagogues too. The religious language, liturgy, and feasts are part of my heritage, a heritage I ignored before becoming Catholic and which I rediscovered as a Catholic. I feel at home in the Catholic Church, where I discovered not only Jesus the Messiah but also his Father, the God of Israel. It is clear that feeling at home in the Church and in the Synagogue means I am sometimes suspect in both but that is a privilege rather than a burden. Perhaps I would have been burnt at the stake as a Judaizer in centuries gone by or expelled from the Synagogue as belonging to one of the *minim*.[13] In this vocation, I know I am not alone.

I do not seek to combine Judaism and Christianity into a comfortable syncretism. Rather, I seek to preserve communion with my people

12. *Ibid.*, 195.
13. Rabbinic term for heretics.

in their vocation and destiny. At the same time, I seek to follow Jesus within the Catholic Church. In the post-Conciliar Church, Catholic teaching seems to propose that we are called to await the day, known to God alone, when Jews and Christians will converge, becoming one united people of God. I believe that we who are Jewish Catholics are invited to be signs of that long awaited eschatological convergence. I completely affirm the words in *Nostra Aetate* paragraph 4, "In company with the Prophets and the same Apostle [i.e., Paul], the Church awaits that day, known to God alone, on which all peoples will address the Lord in a single voice and 'serve him shoulder to shoulder' (Zephaniah 3:9)."[14]

14. Second Vatican Council, *Nostra Aetate*, paragraph 4 (1965).

The Place of Encounter with Jesus-Believing Jews in the History of Jewish–Catholic Dialogue

Christian M. Rutishauser, SJ

When one first looks at the Jewish–Catholic dialogue, as it developed in the twentieth century, one observes that Jesus-believing Jews or messianic Judaism are not a topic in it. Exceptions are the Hebrew-speaking churches in Israel, though they can hardly be said to be internationally known, and the double identity of Edith Stein who was murdered by the Nazis as a baptized Jew.[1] The conversion of Israel to Christ as an end-time event was also not a topic in this dialogue, although the Roman Catholic Church made recourse to Romans 9–11 in the renewal of her Israel theology, that is, to the text in which Paul speaks of the salvation of Israel at the end of time (11:26). In contrast to evangelical circles which interpret the Zionistic return to Eretz Israel eschatologically and in this context expect a conversion of the Jewish

1. https://www.lpj.org/en/the-patriarchate/diocese/vicariates/saint-james-vicariate-1 (accessed April 11, 2025); Waltraud Herbstrith, *Edith Stein – ihr wahres Gesicht? Jüdisches Selbstverständnis – Christliches Engagement – Opfer der Shoa, Forum Religionsphilosophie*, vol. 3 (Münster: LIT, 2006); Elisabeth Endres, *Edith Stein. Christliche Philosophin und jüdische Märtyrerin* (Munich: Piper, 1987); Susanne Gottlöber, "Das Fremde im Eigenen – die Auseinandersetzung mit der jüdischen Identität. Edith Stein und Simone Weil im Vergleich," in *Europa und seine Anderen. Emmanuel Levinas. Edith Stein. Józef Tischner, Religionsphilosophie. Diskurse und Orientierungen*, vol. 5, ed. Hanna-Barbara Gerl-Falkovitz, René Kaufmann, and Hans Rainer Sepp (Dresden: Thelem, 2010): 179–89.

people to Christ, Catholic theology, in accord with "Notes on the Correct Way to Present the Jews and Judaism in Preaching and Catechesis in the Roman Catholic Church" (1985),[2] looks with a secular view of the Middle East conflict. Instead, the questions of the dialogue were the question of the significance of Judaism post Christum and the question of the baptism of Jews, insofar as they are addressees of Christ's universal claim to salvation. A deeper look, however, reveals that Catholic-baptized Jews made a significant contribution to the establishment of Jewish–Catholic dialogue. A few, also since the Council, have given thought to the question of what their place could be in the renewed theology of Judaism. With the Vatican document for the 50-year anniversary of *Nostra Aetate*, "'The Gifts and the Calling of God Are Irrevocable' (Rom 11:29)," official Catholic theology says explicitly and for the first time that the Church consists of Jews and Gentiles.[3] From these observations there emerges a tripartite structure for my essay: (1) First we will look at the Catholic-baptized Jews who got the Jewish–Catholic dialogue off the ground. (2) Then we will ask how the conviction of the enduring significance of Israel and the question of the mission to the Jews, which emerges from the universal claim to salvation of Jesus, developed in Jewish–Catholic dialogue. (3) Finally, we will take a look at the aforementioned Vatican document and at Daniel Rufeisen and Cardinal Lustiger, who, as Catholic-baptized Jews, saw the beginnings of an *ecclesia ex circumcisione* in the Hebrew-speaking churches of Israel.

1. Catholic-baptized Jews as catalysts of the Jewish–Christian dialogue

It is widely known that since the Middle Ages via the early modern period and into the nineteenth century, Catholic-baptized Jews played a significant role, whether in Christian anti-Judaism or in the attempts at converting Jews, which ranged from peaceful to aggressive. For the thirteenth century, one thinks, for example, of the burnings of the

2. http://www.christianunity.va/content/unitacristiani/en/commissione-per-i-rapporti-religiosi-con-l-ebraismo/commissione-per-i-rapporti-religiosi-con-l-ebraismo-crre/documenti-della-commissione/en2.html (accessed April 11, 2025), (VI.1).

3. http://www.christianunity.va/content/unitacristiani/en/commissione-per-i-rapporti-religiosi-con-l-ebraismo/commissione-per-i-rapporti-religiosi-con-l-ebraismo-crre/documenti-della-commissione/en.html (accessed April 11, 2025) (No. 43).

Talmud in Paris and the forced disputations in Barcelona in July of 1263.[4] In Paris, the convert Nicholas Donin, a French Jew, made thirty-five charges against the Talmud, which supposedly denigrated the Christian faith. After that event, he organized in 1240, with papal authority, a disputation between Christian theologians and four rabbis who were required to stand as witnesses to the proceedings. In the years that followed, there were burnings of the Talmud. In another example from Barcelona, a baptized Jew by the name of Paul, who had become a Dominican, was the principal actor when Rabbi ben Nachman was forced to defend himself against the proposition that the Talmud itself proved that Jesus is Messiah. The defense must have turned out well for Nachmanides, but two years later he was forced to leave Aragon because the Dominicans accused him of circulating false accounts of the proceedings. In yet another example from the sixteenth century, the Jewish convert Anthonius Margaritha had a marked influence on Martin Luther with his work, "Der gantz jüdisch Glaub,"[5] published in 1530. His portrayal of Jewish customs and of the synagogue liturgy as blasphemous strengthened the reformer's anti-Judaism. The Jesuit Order founded in 1540, supported the ghettoizing of Jews in the Holy City, a step that Pope Paul VI implemented from the year 1555.[6] Spanish *conversos*—Jews who had converted to Catholicism—streamed into this order; up to one-fourth of the Society of Jesus may have been of Jewish heritage in the first decades, which led to difficult internal tensions. In the nineteenth century, the brothers Theodore and Alphonse Ratisbonne, who came from an assimilated Jewish banking family in Strasbourg, founded the *Congrégation de Notre-Dame de Sion* for the conversion of Jews, after their own conversion to the Catholic Church. Only after the First World War and later after the Shoah did members of this

4. Robert Chazan, *From Anti-Judaism to Anti-Semitism. Ancient and Medieval Christian Constructions of Jewish History* (Cambridge: Cambridge University Press, 2016): 136–39.

5. ["The entire Jewish faith"]; Thomas Kaufmann, *Luthers "Judenschriften"* (Tübingen: Mohr Siebeck, 2011): 130, 175–76.

6. Robert Maryks, *The Jesuit Order as a Synagogue of Jews. Jesuits of Jewish Ancestry and Purity-of-Blood Laws in the Early Society of Jesus* (Leiden / Boston, MA: Brill, 2010): 41–156; Marc Rastoin, *Du même sang que Notre Seigneur. Juifs et Jésuites aux débuts de la Compagnie* (Montarouge: Bayard, 2011): 63–128, 275–300.

religious order become more and more pioneers of Jewish–Christian dialogue.[7]

In the societal context of racially based antisemitism, as it had spread since the late nineteenth century, Catholic-baptized Jews began to view the Jewish people differently. Although baptized, they were themselves threatened by antisemitism and wanted to help their fellow Jews. They also learned to understand Judaism theologically in a new way, as I wish to show with three examples.

Paul Démann,[8] born into an assimilated family in Budapest on July 18, 1912, began to study architecture, turned soon to Christianity, and let himself be baptized in 1934. In 1937, he became a member of the *Congrégation de Notre-Dame de Sion* and a student at the Jesuit high school St Albert in Leuven. This was followed by eleven years of theology with an emphasis on exegesis, and he was ordained to the priesthood in 1944. During the war years, he participated in the Belgian resistance, hiding and rescuing Jews. After the war, he began his doctoral work on Romans 9–11, a work that he would never finish. In his thinking, he connected the mystery of the salvation of Israel at the end of time with three ecclesiological reflections: First, with the ecclesiology of Yves Congar, who understood the Church as the people of God. Second, with the Church as *mysterium*, as she is portrayed in the encyclical *Mystici corporis* by Pius XII. And third, with the ecumenical insight that the one Church of Christ is divided into confessional Churches.[9] Thus, he specified the relationship of the Church to the Jewish people no longer in terms of mission but rather as a primordial schism that preceded all Church divisions, while at the end of time the Jewish people restores the catholicity of the Church that is being rediscovered. In 1952, Démann wrote on the occasion of the *Week of Christian Unity*:

> Now the Jews are not Christians. And yet they are not a people for mission either, a people still alienated from the people of God. If they are not separate Christians, they will be separate members of the people of God, but members separated from it by a rupture which did not occur,

7. Olivier Rota, "Les Pères de Sion. Une vocation spécifique assume avec difficulté (1925–1970)," *Sens* 3 (2009): 184–96.

8. Cf. "Hommage à Paul Démann" (topic booklet), *Sens* 2 (2006).

9. Olivier Rota, "Dépasser les cadres du philosémitisme: La vision œcuménique de Paul Démann," *Les Archives Juives* 40 (2007): 117–30, at 121–23.

like the others, in the Church already formed, but at the very moment of its birth within the ancient People of God.[10]

He explained the connection of the Jewish–Christian relationship with the Church's ecumenism in many articles appearing in *Cahiers Sioniens*, a journal that he himself edited from 1951 to 1955. It is his genuine theological contribution. The *Cahiers* were published by the Center for the Study and Documentation for the Renewal of Jewish–Christian Relations in Paris, which he founded. The Center can be viewed as a predecessor of the *Service d'information et de documentation judéo-chrétien* (SIDIC) that the *Congrégation de Notre-Dame de Sion* founded in November of 1965 in Rome in connection with the declaration *Nostra Aetate*. Additionally, Démann's contributions in the *Freiburger Rundbrief*, which was founded in 1948 by Gertrud Luckner, are characterized by "his affirmation of the Jewish roots of Christianity, on the one hand, and his belief in the inseparable unity of the ecumenical faith community, on the other hand."[11] Together with his friend Jules Isaac, whom he had met at the Emergency Conference on Antisemitism at Seelisberg in 1947, Démann thus worked continually on a new Christian view of the Jewish people. Both men were convinced that the Church must fundamentally renew her teaching on Israel, and thus became forerunners for *Nostra Aetate*.

Another forerunner is Johannes Österreicher.[12] Born in 1904 into a Moravian Jewish family, he was influenced by the local Zionist youth

10. "Or les juives ne sont pas des chrétiens. Et pourtant, ils ne sont pas non plus un peuple de mission, un peuple encore étrangé au peuple de Dieu. S'ils ne sont pas des chrétiens séparés, ils seront bien des membres séparés du peuple de Dieu; mais des membres séparés de lui par une rupture qui ne s'est pas produit comme les autres, dans l'Eglise déjà formée, mais au moment même de sa naissance au sein de l'ancien Peuple de Dieu"—Rota, "Dépasser les cadres du philosémitisme" (see note 9), 124.

11. ". . . sein Bekenntnis zur jüdischen Wurzel des Christentums und damit zur tragenden Bedeutung der Bundesschrift des Judentums für die Bibel des Christentums einerseits und seine Überzeugung von der untrennbaren Einheit der Glaubensgemeinschaft, der Ökumene, andererseits"—Petrus Bsteh, "Paul Démann und Jules Isaac – zwei Freunde im jüdisch-christlichen Dialog," *Religionen unterwegs* 22 (2016): 24–28, at 25.

12. In detail: Dorothee Recker, *Die Wegbereiter der Judenerklärung des Zweiten Vatikanischen Konzils. Johannes XXIII., Kardinal Bea und Prälat Österreicher – eine Darstellung ihrer theologischen Entwicklung* (Paderborn: Bonifatius, 2007): 310–99.

movement. Through his meeting with Max Josef Metzger, who was murdered by Nazis in 1944, he began to become interested in Christianity. In 1924, he was baptized into the Roman Catholic Church. For his parents, this was a heavy blow. After theological training in Graz and Vienna, he was ordained as a priest in 1927 and carried out pastoral care duties in Lower Austria and Vienna. In 1934, he was a co-founder of the Vienna Pauluswerk and the first editor of its journal, *Die Erfüllung*. The goals were to fight antisemitism and to improve mutual understanding between Jews and Christians. The conversion of Jews was also included in this. When Österreicher later spoke out against the conversion of Jews and for a Jewish–Christian dialogue, he experienced mistrust from the Jewish side because of this.[13] In 1938, he fled via Switzerland to Paris, but he spoke out through the radio against National Socialism. In his book, *Rassenhass ist Christushass*, he advanced the thesis that Hitler's extermination of the Jews was ultimately directed also against the Church, since antisemitism opposed the Judaeo-Christian image and conception of humanity.[14] In 1940, he ultimately went into exile in the United States. After the war, he became a pioneer of Jewish–Christian dialogue. In 1953, he founded the Institute for Judeo-Christian Studies at Seton Hall University in Newark, New Jersey. In the years from 1955 to 1970, he edited five volumes of *The Bridge. A Yearbook of Judeo-Christian Studies*. As a co-worker of Cardinal Bea, he had considerable influence on the textual development of *Nostra Aetate*. He attempted to arbitrate in the conflict that arose around it, principally with the bishops from the Arab world, who assumed a Jewish infiltration of the council. Beginning with his "Bittschrift" ["Petition"] from the year 1960, he argued for the unity of salvation history, according to which the Church already has her beginning with Abraham and thus can be understood only in close connection with the Jewish people.[15] He argued that the patriarchs and the prophets of the Old Testament should be celebrated in the Church as saints in the liturgy as they are

13. Johannes Österreicher, *The Apostolate to the Jews* (New York: America Press, 1948); in *Freiburger Rundbrief* I 1/2 (1949): 42–43.

14. [*"Racial Hatred is Christ-Hatred"*]; Recker, *Die Wegbereiter der Judenerklärung* (see note 12), 370–80.

15. Clemens Thoma, "Johannes M. Österreicher. Prediger gegen den Nationalsozialismus und Wegbereiter von *Nostra aetate*," *Freiburger Rundbrief. Neue Folge*, 4 (2004): 261–67.

in the Jerusalem Patriarchate. As "new" Israel, the Church joins the old Israel: "Not only for the well-being of the Jews, but also for the sake of the spiritual progress of the faithful and as a witness of perfect unity that the Church of Jews and gentiles was, is, and ever shall be, we ask you to affirm our votes."[16]

The conversion to the Church of the Dutch Jew, Sophie van Leer, born in 1872, was quite different in its effects.[17] Her mother taught her to keep a good Orthodox Jewish house. Her father modeled a religious-utopian brand of socialism to her that combined Jewish, Freemasonic, and Christian elements. Starting in 1914, van Leer sought contacts in the expressionist art scene of Berlin. Unsettled by the First World War, she nevertheless became an ascetic anarchist and was imprisoned in the Munich Soviet Republic. When she was in danger of being executed, she vowed to convert to the Catholic faith if she survived. Shortly after being released, she let herself be baptized, taking the Christian name Franziska, and experienced a strengthening of her Jewish self-consciousness. She connected the Catholic faith with a Zionistic hope for redemption. In 1924, she visited her younger sister Clara in the kibbutz Beth Alpha, but had to leave the kibbutz after a half year because she had started missionizing the kibbutz residents. But the dream of a Catholic kibbutz stayed with her for all her life. In 1926, with the support of Cardinal Faulhaber, she succeeded in founding the *Opus sacerdotale Amici Israel*, together with the priest who baptized her, the Franciscan Laetus Himmelreich, who in the meantime had become secretary of *Propaganda Fidei* in the Vatican, and with the Crosier Father Anton van Asseldonk.[18] In the two years of its existence, the organization had 3,000 priests, 328 bishops, and 19 cardinals. They were to pray

16. "Nicht nur um des Wohls der Juden willen, sondern auch wegen des geistlichen Fortschritts der Gläubigen und der Bezeugung der vollkommenen Einheit, die die Kirche aus Juden und Heiden war, ist und stets sein wird, erbitten wir die Zustimmung zu unseren Voten."—Johannes Österreicher, "Kommentierende Einleitung zu *Nostra aetate*," in *Lexikon für Theologie und Kirche: das zweite Vatikanische Konzil;* II (Freiburg i. Br.: Herder, 1967), 416.

17. In detail: Theo Salemink, "Katholische Identität und das Bild der jüdisch 'Anderen.' Die Bewegung *Amici Israel* und ihre Aufhebung durch das Heilige Offizium im Jahre 1928," *Zeitschrift für Theologie und Kulturgeschichte* 1 (2006): 91–105.

18. Thomas Brechenmacher, *Der Vatikan und die Juden. Geschichte einer unheiligen Beziehung vom 16. Jahrhundert bis zur Gegenwart* (Munich: Beck, 2005): 154–63.

for the conversion of the Jews. Like other philosemitic circles that grew up in France and Germany in the face of raging antisemitism,[19] *Amici Israel* was concerned "not merely with a conversion offensive or even a prayer confraternity, but rather it also represented an initiative that wanted to fight Catholic antisemitism, change the liturgy, and provide a real support for Jews and Jewry—and even for Zionism."[20] The initiative of *Amici Israel* to remove the word "perfidis" from the intercession for the Jews on Good Friday ultimately led to the condemnation of her writing, *Pax super Israel*, and is alleged to have led to the dissolution of the association, as historian Hubert Wolf has described in detail.[21] In the 1930s, Sophie van Leer developed a Catholic-millenarian form of thought. Influenced and nourished by mysticism, she saw herself as "Jesus' twin sister," believed she had to live, together with van Asseldonk, as new Eve and new Adam in the land of Israel and interpreted the Zionist return to the land now explicitly as an end-time event in which Israel was finally to be saved as a whole. A Pauline-eschatological interpretation of history, as is still influential in many evangelical circles up to the present, let her refrain from the mission to the Jews during the time of history.[22]

From the three examples presented here, the following observations can be drawn:

(1) The phenomenon of baptized Jews who no longer turn against the Jewish people but rather assign it a positive value in salvation history and increasingly refrain from active conversion efforts is a new phenomenon of the modern period.

19. Jim Bernauer, *Jesuit Kaddish. Jesuits, Jews and the Holocaust Remembrance* (Notre Dame, IN: University of Notre Dame Press, 2020): 78–96.

20. ". . . nicht nur um eine Bekehrungsoffensive oder lediglich eine Gebetsvereinigung, sondern [sie] stellte zugleich eine Initiative dar, die den katholischen Antisemitismus bekämpfen, die Liturgie verändern und eine reale Unterstützung für die Juden und das Judentum – und sogar für den Zionismus – erreichen wollte," Salemink, "Katholische Identität" (see note 17), 94.

21. Hubert Wolf, *Papst und Teufel. Die Archive des Vatikans und das dritte Reich* (Munich: Beck, 2008): 95–143.

22. Marcel Poorthuis, "Eine Jüdin und ein Priester als neuer Adam und neue Eva im Heiligen Land. Die Mystik der Sophie (Francisca) van Leer (1892–1953)," in *Mystikerinnen der Neuzeit und Gegenwart*, ed. Anja Middelbeck-Varwick and Markus Thurau (Frankfurt a. M.: Lang, 2009): 102–3.

(2) It is striking that in these biographies of conversion to Catholicism, not one shows a deepened Jewish-Orthodox life conduct. Conversion was not a turning away from Rabbinic Judaism. Conversion meant finding faith for the first time and leaving a secular, nationalistic, or utopian-ideological worldview behind. Van Leer's worldview was nourished by an eclectic utopian-mystical hope for redemption. Démann came from an assimilated family. Österreicher's youth was shaped by a Zionism that read the Hebrew Bible as a history book and as a national library. Something similar could be said for Daniel Rufeisen and Cardinal Lustiger, about whom we will be speaking next. Lustiger emphasized that his baptism was not an abandonment of his Jewish identity but rather that he grasped this for the first time in its significance through the Christian catechesis.[23]

(3) It was not just secularized Jewry but also modern antisemitism that shaped the lives of Jewish converts to the Church. After their conversions, they continued advocating for their fellow Jews and showed solidarity with them. They knew that antisemitic hatred was a racial ideology against which baptism would offer no protection. In this way Catholic-baptized Jews raised their voice not only against antisemites but against anti-Judaism in the Church.

(4) The conviction that they should refrain from mission to the Jews establishes itself only slowly among baptized Jews. With respect to attitudes toward the mission to the Jews, Thérèse Andrevon-Gottstein distinguishes between two groups of converts that can be designated as forerunners of Jewish–Christian dialogue:[24] first, the converts of the nineteenth century up to the First World War who took part in the missionary movements of their time and who wanted to honor the Jewish people and lead it to its consummation. Then the second generation, who, in light of the pervasive antisemitism in society and informed by historical research on New Testament Judaism and by the ecumenical movement, learned to appreciate Judaism in a new way.

23. Jean Marie Cardinal Lustiger, *Choix de Dieu: Entretiens avec Jean-Louis Missika et Dominique Wolton* (Paris: Éditions de Fallois, 1987): 57–59. For an English translation, see: Jean-Marie Cardinal Lustiger, Jean Louis Missika, and Dominique Wolton, *Choosing God, Chosen By God: Conversations with Jean-Marie Cardinal Lustiger*, trans. Rebecca Howell Balinski (San Fancisco, CA: Ignatius Press, 1991).

24. Thérèse Andrevon-Gottstein, *Les précurseurs catholiques d'une pensée nouvelle face à Israël dans sa permanence* (unpublished).

Also, as baptized Catholics, they continued to understand themselves to be Jewish.

(5) In any case, they helped Catholics to understand Jews in terms of their own self-understanding and made the Church increasingly aware of the Jewish character of the New Testament. In this way, they prepared the way for the Jewish–Catholic dialogue. This should be remembered above all in the face of the fact that baptized Jews and Messianic Judaism scarcely play a role any longer in the post-Conciliar dialogue and are also excluded.

2. The enduring election of Israel and the question of the mission to the Jews

Neither in the pre-Conciliar theology nor in the Jewish–Catholic dialogue that developed after the Council was the question ever raised about a special place for Jews who believe in Christ in the Church. In pre-Conciliar thinking, baptized Jews were deemed exactly equal to baptized Gentiles. Regardless of a person's original nationality or religion, after baptism each one was in the same way Roman Catholic. Theologically, Jewish identity no longer played a role. If baptized Jews were disadvantaged in the history of the Church, as, for example, the *conversos* in Spain were in the early modern period, this was sociologically and psychologically grounded. Since the Jewish Christians of late antiquity had died out, there were, from the Church's point of view, only Jews and Christians remaining. Moreover, the Jewish–Catholic dialogue since *Nostra Aetate* is a dialogue between two communities of faith. Baptized Jews are not specifically mentioned. For pragmatic reasons, missionizing activity was, for the most part, refrained from, and the Jewish people were given a new classification as the "people of God." Cardinal Lustiger, for example, was according to the rite and ethical duty a Catholic like any other, even if he explicitly emphasized his Jewish ancestry.[25] In its historical retrospective, *Nostra Aetate* identifies

25. The commemorative inscription to him in the Cathedral of Notre Dame says "I was born Jewish. I received the name of my paternal grandfather, Aaron. Having become Christian by faith and by baptism, I have remained Jewish, as did the Apostles. I have as my patron saints: Aaron the high priest, Saint John the Apostle, Holy Mary full of grace. Named 139th archbishop of Paris by His Holiness the pope

the Apostles and disciples of Jesus not as Jesus-believing Jews, but instead correctly states that they came from the Jewish people and thus are Jews: "She also recalls that the Apostles, the Church's mainstay and pillars, as well as most of the early disciples who proclaimed Christ's gospel to the world, sprang from the Jewish people." After the promulgation of *Nostra Aetate*, two fundamental presuppositions had to be established and expressed with theological nuance before Jewish–Catholic dialogue could develop at all: on the one hand, the establishment of an enduring positive specification of the Jewish people in the Christian narrative of salvation, and on the other hand, the forgoing of traditional, active mission or evangelization among Jews. Both questions are decisive for positioning Jesus-believing Jews and Messianic Judaism today in the horizon of Jewish–Christian dialogue.

As for the first question, *Nostra Aetate* 4 is no longer oriented to patristic theology, which encompasses different forms of the doctrine of substitution (replacement theology), but to Romans 9–11. As is well known, Paul speaks there of the enduring election of Israel and of the fact that at the end of time, when all the nations have found their way to God, Israel will be saved as a whole in a mysterious way (Rom 11:25–32). This theology finds expression in the new formulation of the intercessory prayers for the Jews on Good Friday: "Hear the prayers of your Church, that the people you first made your own may attain the fullness of redemption." In Catholic theology since the 1980s, the enduring election of Israel has been positively formulated with the phrase "the irrevocable covenant." Pope John Paul II coined this phrase, and this language found its way into the Roman Catholic catechism (No. 121). This gave rise to the much-discussed question of how the covenants within the Hebrew Bible on the one hand and the Old and New Covenants on the other hand, which Christians see as based on their double Bible, relate to one another.[26] In this discussion, which cannot

---

John-Paul II, I was enthroned in this cathedral on 27 February 1981, and here I exercised my entire ministry. Passers-by, pray for me." https://cardinals.fiu.edu/bios1983.htm#Lustiger (accessed April 11, 2025).

26. Hubert Frankemölle, *Der ungekündigte Bund? Antworten des Neuen Testaments* (Quaestiones disputatae, 172; Freiburg i. Br. / Basel / Vienna: Herder, 1998); John T. Pawlikowski and Hayim G. Perelmuter, eds., *Reinterpreting Revelation and Tradition. Jews and Christians in Conversation* (Franklin, WI: Sheed & Ward, 2000).

be presented here, two Catholic basic positions developed.[27] The first is that of the Jewish–Catholic dialogue committees, which the *Vatican's Commission for Religious Relations with the Jews* also represents with their document, "'The Gifts and the Calling of God Are Irrevocable' (Rom 11:29)." There is, admittedly, only one single covenant of God, to which all other covenants are subordinated (No. 32). The Jewish people nevertheless represents at the time of history a salvation entity of its own, even though not a way of salvation that is independent from the Church (No. 35). On the other side, a position developed among dogmaticians who oriented themselves more strongly to the continuity of tradition. The article of Pope emeritus Benedict from 2018 is a prominent representative of this position. Benedict speaks of the substitution of individual elements of the Old Testament order by the New Testament order,[28] orients himself again to the Augustinian variation of salvation-historical narratives, and designates the term "irrevocable covenant" as unsuitable or inadequate for a theology of the Jewish people.[29] I must leave both positions free of comment here. However, the enduring meaning of Israel and the value of the "irrevocable covenant" that gives the Jewish people its theological dignity and identity also *post Christum* will be decisive factors in determining what status is to be assigned to Jesus-believing Jews both on the horizon of the Jewish–Catholic relationship and in the Church.

As to the second question, that of the mission to the Jews, it is more relevant to the Jewish–Catholic dialogue insofar as it directly affects Jewish existence. Just as baptized Jews were nothing more than Christians for Catholics, it is the same from a Jewish perspective—a *meshummad*, a Jew who has fallen away into the Christian faith, is actually no longer a Jew. While a Jew, from a *halakhic* perspective, always remains Jewish, even if he presents himself as an atheist or adheres to

27. Didier Pollefeyt, "Unrevoked Covenant—Revoked Covenant—Indestructible Love? The Reception of Nostra Aetate 4 in Jewish–Catholic Relations," in *"Res opportunae nostrae aetatis." Studies on the Second Vatican Council offered to Mathijs Lamberigts*, ed. Dries Bosschaert and Johan Leemans (Leuven / Paris / Bristol: Peeters Publishers, 2020): 483–98.

28. Joseph Ratzinger / Benedict XVI, "Grace and Vocation Without Remorse. Comments on the Treatise *De Iudaeis*," *Communio: International Catholic Review* 45 (2018): 163–84, at 170–80.

29. *Ibid.*, 184.

Buddhism, he is lost to his people if he lets himself be baptized. In light of the painful history of the forced missionizing of the Jews by the Church, this is understandable from a psychological point of view. The drama of conversion can be read off all family histories, even in the families of twentieth-century converts who maintained a positive relationship to their origins.[30]

For this reason, at the birth of the official Jewish–Catholic dialogue through the Council, the forgoing of the mission to the Jews was a *conditio sine qua non* of the Jewish dialogue partners. As an example, let us recall Abraham J. Heschel who responded to the Church's offer of dialogue, but clearly emphasized in his article "No Religion Is an Island" that mission to the Jews offends against the personal dignity of Jews and makes interreligious dialogue impossible.[31] Equally well-known is his statement to Cardinal Bea—Christian mission to the Jews, as he found it in a draft of the Council for a declaration on the Jews, is "spiritual fratricide." He himself would prefer the gas chambers of Auschwitz to conversion to Christianity.[32] Josef Dov Soloveitchik argued in his pamphlet from February 1964, following the debates on the Council's declaration on the Jews, that truths of faith would contain absolute obligations toward God, for which reason a dialogue that negotiates theological positions could not be carried out.[33] Above all, he did not trust the Church to meet Jews as equals and recognize them as an independent, living faith community, a stance which he also had every reason to hold prior to the emergence of *Nostra Aetate*.

The debates about the mission to the Jews in the Jewish–Catholic dialogue since *Nostra Aetate* cannot be laid out here. However, it should be remembered that the question came up for discussion for the first time in 1977 at the International Liaison Committee (ILC), and that a public debate was first sparked off in 2002 in relation to the document "Reflections on Covenant and Mission" by the American National Council

30. Shalom Goldman, *Jewish–Christian Difference and Modern Jewish Identity. Seven Twentieth-Century Converts* (New York, NY / London: Lexington Books, 2015).

31. Abraham J. Heschel, "No Religion Is an Island," *Union Seminary Quarterly Review* 2 (1966): 117–34.

32. Reuven Kimelman, "Rabbis Joseph B. Soloveitchik and Abraham Joshua Heschel on Jewish–Christian Relations," *The Edah Journal* 4:2 (2004): 2–21, at 6. Also published in *Modern Judaism* 24.3 (2004): 251–71, at 255.

33. Joseph D. Soloveitchik, "Confrontation," *Tradition* 2 (1964): 5–28.

of Synagogues and the Committee on Ecumenical and Interreligious *Affairs* of the United States Catholic bishops. There, a decisive passage reads: "The term mission, in its proper sense, refers to conversion from false gods and idols to the true and one God, who revealed himself in the salvation history with his elected people. Thus mission, in this strict sense, cannot be used with regard to Jews, who believe in the true and one God."[34] Not mission, but dialogue must therefore determine Jewish–Christian relations. When Pope Benedict reformulated the Good Friday intercession for the Jews for use in the Tridentine rite, which he had extraordinarily allowed again, in 2009, the Discussion Group "Jews and Christians" of the Central Committee of German Catholics argued similarly in its position paper, "Nein zur Judenmission, Ja zum Dialogue zwischen Juden und Christen" ("No to Jewish Mission, Yes to Dialogue Between Jews and Christians").[35] Cardinal Walter Kasper took up the discussion, saying that Jews should be led into the New Covenant even though this meant something different for them than it would for non-Jews.[36] Cardinal Lehmann also commented on the topic, organizing his reflections in ten points.[37] He wrote that a specific mission to the Jews did not belong to the missionary theology of the Roman Catholic Church, since the separation of Israel from salvation is only partial and temporary. Israel's redemption is anchored in the covenant which has never been revoked, even though Judaism does not represent an independent

34. "Reflections on Covenant and Mission," *Origins* 32:13 (September 5, 2002): 218–24, at 220. Online at both https://nationalcouncilofsynagogues.org/wp-content/uploads/docs/Reflections-on-Covenant-and-Mission.pdf, and https://www.usccb.org/resources/Reflections-on-Covenant-and-Mission.pdf (both accessed April 11, 2025)—"Roman-Catholic Reflections," section: "Evangelization and the Jewish People."

35. For the German position paper, see https://www.zdk.de/positionen/2009/nein-zur-judenmission-ja-zum-dialog-zwischen-juden-und-christen. For an English translation, see https://ccjr.us/dialogika-resources/themes-in-today-s-dialogue/conversion/zdk09mar9 (both accessed March 18, 2024).

36. Adam Gregerman, "The Desirability of Jewish Conversion to Christianity in Contemporary Catholic Thought," *Horizons* 45 (2018): 4–24.

37. Karl Cardinal Lehmann, "Judenmission. Hermeneutische und theologische Überlegungen zu einer Problemanzeige im jüdisch-christlichen Gespräch," in *Das Heil der Anderen. Problemfeld: "Judenmission,"* ed. Hubert Frankemölle and Josef Wohlmuth (Quaestiones Disputatae, 238; Freiburg i. Br./ Basel / Vienna: Herder, 2010): 142–67, at 165–67.

path to salvation. In 2015, the Vatican document, "'The Gifts and the Calling of God Are Irrevocable' (Rom 11:29),"[38] formulated:

> From the Christian confession that there can be only one path to salvation, however, it does not in any way follow that the Jews are excluded from God's salvation. . . . The Church is therefore obliged to view evangelisation to Jews, who believe in the one God, in a different manner from that to people of other religions and world views. In concrete terms this means that the Catholic Church neither conducts nor supports any specific institutional mission work directed towards Jews. (Nos. 36, 40)

In defense of his 2018 article mentioned above, Pope emeritus Benedict ultimately adopts the interpretation of Matthew 28 according to which the risen one, as Jewish Messiah, spoke with a view to the world of the nations when he gave his command to baptize. From this, he reasons that "What applied and applies for Israel is therefore not mission but rather the dialogue about whether Jesus of Nazareth is the 'Son of God, the Logos.'"[39]

Amidst differing theological emphases and the differentiated debate, we can say by way of summary: Catholic theology holds fast to Christ's universal claim to salvation, but recognizes the special status of the Jewish people, since it already stands in covenant with God. Israel has until the end of time a mysterious calling of its own. The traditional missionary task to lead people through Christ to the God of the Bible is aimed at the Gentiles. The Jewish–Christian relationship is defined by commitment to dialogue, not mission. How this dialogue is to be shaped, however, is an open question. Moreover, there remains a tension between dialogue and evangelization. Reflection on what a Christian claim vis-à-vis the Jewish people consists in has continued in the last five years.[40] For Jesus-believing Jews who are Catholic today, this certainly means recognizing the enduring theological significance

38. http://www.christianunity.va/content/unitacristiani/en/commissione-per-i-rapporti-religiosi-con-l-ebraismo/commissione-per-i-rapporti-religiosi-con-l-ebraismo-crre/documenti-della-commissione/en.html (accessed April 11, 2025).

39. "Für Israel galt und gilt daher nicht Mission, sondern der Dialog darüber, ob Jesus von Nazareth der' Sohn Gottes, der Logos' ist."—Joseph Ratzinger / Benedict XVI, "Nicht Mission, sondern Dialog," *Herder Korrespondenz* 12 (2018): 13–14, at 14.

40. Cf. Christian M. Rutishauser, "Christliche Mission gegenüber Juden neu überdacht. Weiterführende Reflexionen zum vatikanischen Dokument 'Denn

of Israel and refraining from active traditional mission among the Jews. *Post-supersessionist* and *post-missionary* are the two conditions for Jesus-believing Jews in the horizon of Jewish–Catholic dialogue.

3. Ecclesia ex circumcisione

The Vatican document "The Gifts and the Calling" aims to provide an answer to the tension that arises within the structure of Catholic teaching: that, on one hand, the Old Covenant of God with Israel is believed to be still significant for salvation and irrevocable, and, on the other hand, the central confession of faith in Christ as the only and universal mediator of salvation cannot be relativized. It therefore extensively addresses the relationship between the Old and New Covenants and between Judaism and Christianity. In Section 6 (No. 43) of "The Gifts and the Calling," the last paragraph of the systematic text section, it states, for the first time in an official Church text on the dialogue, that the Church constitutively consists of Jews and Gentiles. With this, Jesus-believing Jews are explicitly addressed. If we examine the paragraph, it becomes clear that the statement, however, applies less to them than to the specification of the relationship between Jews and Christians. Nevertheless, we can draw some conclusions from it:

> It is and remains a qualitative definition of the Church of the New Covenant that it consists of Jews and Gentiles, even if the quantitative proportions of Jewish and Gentile Christians may initially give a different impression. Just as after the death and resurrection of Jesus Christ there were not two unrelated covenants, so too the people of the covenant of Israel are not disconnected from "the people of God drawn from the Gentiles." Rather, the enduring role of the covenant people of Israel in God's plan of salvation is to relate dynamically to the "people of God of Jews and Gentiles, united in Christ," he whom the Church confesses as the universal mediator of creation and salvation. In the context of God's universal will of salvation, all people who have not yet received the gospel are aligned with the people of God of the New Covenant. "In the first place there is the people to whom the covenants and promises were given and from whom Christ was born according to the flesh (cf. Rom 9:4–5). On account of their fathers this people remains most dear

---

unwiderruflich sind Gnade und Berufung, die Gott gewährt' (Röm 11,29)," *Kirche und Israel* 36 (2021): 13–29, at 23–26.

to God, for he does not repent of the gifts he makes nor of the calls he issues (cf. Rom 11:28–29)" (*Lumen Gentium*, 16).

The Jewish people is therefore not only set in relationship to the Church of the Gentiles but to a Church that essentially consists "of Jews and Gentiles." The text does not go further in explaining how Jews and Gentiles stand in relationship to each other in the Church. The language takes its orientation from Ephesians 2 and uses this qualitative specification of the Church to designate the relationship of the Jewish people and Christianity. Since, however, the latter is in any case bordering and demarcating as well as "aligned with," it can be inferred that Gentiles and Jews are not absorbed without distinction as individuals into the one Catholic Church, as was the case in the pre-Conciliar period, but rather preserve their own respective positions as groups. Jesus-believing Jews are aligned in the Church to the other, the Gentile Christians, and vice versa. This would correspond to the direction of the New Testament impetus, according to which Jewish and Gentile Christians share table fellowship with each other, while also remaining different. Not only does the confrontation in Acts 15:1–29 testify to this, but also the Gospels, which place the bread stories for the nations (Matt 15—seven baskets are left over) and for the Jews (Matt 14—twelve baskets are left over) next to one another. In addition to the sending of the disciples to all nations by the risen one (Matt 28), Matthew is also aware of a sending of the disciples exclusively to the house of Israel (Matt 10).[41]

Put another way, it is true that the Vatican document does not speak of an *ecclesia ex circumcisione* and an *ecclesia ex gentibus* in this qualitative specification of the Church. However, since it does use these terms in its historical section (Sec. 2, No. 15) and recognizes in its systematic section the enduring and special status of the Jewish people also *post Christum*, which is one of the foundations of the Jewish–Catholic relationship, one may conclude that Jesus-believing Jews possess a status of their own in the Church as a community. The covenant with Israel is not a covenant with individual Jews but with the collective Israel,

41. Cf. Christian Rutishauser, "'The Old Unrevoked Covenant' and 'Salvation for All Nations in Christ': Catholic Doctrines in Contradiction?" in *Christ Jesus and the Jewish People Today: New Explorations of Theological Interrelationships*, ed. Philip A. Cunningham, Joseph Sievers, Mary Boys, and Hans Hermann Hendrix (Grand Rapids, MI / Cambridge, UK: Eerdmans, 2011): 229–50.

which also retains its significance in the Church, in the new covenant. A speculative but visionary proposal of what a "Jewish Church" in communion with the Roman Catholic Church could look like has been recently put forth by Antoine Lévy.[42] One consequence for Jewish–Catholic dialogue is that Jews are not only to be found on the Jewish side but also on the Catholic side, not in the spirit in which we have historically encountered them, but as it has been described in the course of this article. The dialogue situation grows ever more complex.

For my own part, I close with a look at the self-understanding and the theology of Daniel Rufeisen (1922–1998) and Cardinal Lustiger (1926–2007). After the Council, both began to work on a "Jewish Church" within the Catholic Church. They saw its seed as having been sown in the Hebrew parishes in Israel. Father Daniel identified himself as a Jewish person of Catholic faith.[43] The development of the Hebrew-speaking Church in the young state of Israel came for him from the impulse of the *ad fontes* movement and the inculturation of faith, as the Council demanded.[44] Moreover, for him the discovery of Jewish Christians in New Testament and early Church research did not remain only an historical insight. Rather, he saw himself and his churches as standing in continuity with them, even though he was aware that not all of his church members were of Jewish heritage. The celebration of the liturgy in a Hebrew that had much in common with the Hebrew of the Rabbinic tradition was consciously chosen as a bridge to the Jewish people. In his parish work, Father Daniel clearly demarcated himself from Messianic Jewish movements, as they were coming from the United States to Israel. He was neither American nor Protestant. He wanted to return to the Catholic Church her universality and free her from the corset of the Roman imperial Church. The semitic element of being Christian must once again find a place in the Roman Catholic

42. Antoine Lévy, *Jewish Church. A Catholic Approach to Messianic Judaism* (Lanham, MD / Boulder, CO / New York, NY / London: Lexington, 2021).

43. For more about his biography and his fight for citizenship in Israel as a baptized Jew, see: Christian Rutishauser, "Daniel Rufeisen und die Frage nach jüdisch-christlicher Identität," in *Religion zwischen Mystik und Politik. "Ich lege mein Gesetz in sie hinein und schreibe es auf ihr Herz." (Jer 31,33)*, ed. Ulrich Winkler (Jerusalemer Theologisches Forum, 35; Münster: Aschendorff, 2020): 295–316.

44. Nechama Tec, *In the Lion's Den: The Life of Oswald Rufeisen* (Oxford: Oxford University Press, 1990): 235.

Church.[45] He brought this request before Pope John Paul II in 1984 in an audience in Rome,[46] and also lobbied for the recognition of the state of Israel by the Vatican.

Since that time the Hebrew / Roman Catholic parishes have grown. Today, they are under the governance of the St. James Vicariate, which is part of the Latin Patriarchate of Jerusalem. Their self-description says: "Our Vicariate gathers the Hebrew-speaking Catholics who live in Israel, those belonging to the Jewish people together with those coming from the nations, including a number of local Christians and migrants."[47] Alongside passing on the faith in a non-Christian society, taking a stand for peace and justice, and the dialogue with Jews and Muslims, a fourth challenge is mentioned:

> Serving as a bridge between the Universal Church and the people of Israel: the Vicariate works to strengthen the relationship between Jews and Christians, sharpening the Church's awareness of its Jewish roots and of the Jewish identity of Jesus and his apostles. The Vicariate seeks to sharpen the awareness of Jews in Israel with regard to the history, teaching and contribution of the Church to society. Our faithful are engaged fully in the life of Israeli Jewish society and in the life of the Catholic Church.[48]

Cardinal Lustiger unfolded his view of the Jewish presence in the Roman Catholic Church in similar terms, albeit on an international level. He developed a Catholic–Jewish dialogue activity between France and North America. His initiatives were not always coordinated with the Vatican. He had as a goal the promotion of mutual understanding and coming to terms with the suffering of the Shoah. He drew Father Patrick Desbois into this work, who has, since then, carried out pioneering work in the Ukraine.[49] Lustiger saw antisemitism arising from the spirit of the Enlightenment, and less from Christian anti-Judaism.[50] While the latter competed for a spiritual inheritance, any theological legacy was in itself unbearable for modernity. The continuity between

45. *Ibid.*, 240.

46. *Ibid.*, 244.

47. https://catholic.co.il/?cat=sjv&view=article&id=10171 (accessed September 5, 2022).

48. *Ibid.*

49. Patrick Desbois, *La Shoah par balles: La mort en plein jour* (Paris: Plon, 2019).

50. Lustiger, *Choix de Dieu* (see note 23), 100–108.

Old and New Testament tradition, which he emphasized in the Jewish–Catholic dialogue, was something that he also saw as first rupturing through Enlightenment belief in linear progress.[51] Beginning in 1951, Lustiger visited Israel every year and followed the growth of the Hebrew churches. Like Rufeisen, he placed them in continuity with the Jewish Christianity of antiquity. In his view, it would be wrong to suggest that the Jews had not recognized Jesus as the Messiah, since Jews formed the original Church, though this was destroyed later by the Byzantines and ultimately by Islam.[52] Christ, however, opened the Jewish faith to all of humanity, for which a Jewish original Church was necessary—and is also necessary today: "The pagans can only believe in the Messiah of Israel if there is at least a part of Israel that has recognized by faith its own Messiah, the Messiah of God."[53] In the Hebrew churches, Lustiger sees therefore a mustard seed type of new beginning of the *ecclesia ex circumcisione*. "Because if God permits it to regain its identity within the Church, it will be an inestimable blessing for the faith of all."[54]

(Translated by John David Martin, James Earle Patrick, and Wayne Coppins from the German: "Der Ort der Begegnung mit Jesus-gläubigen Juden in der Geschichte des katholisch-jüdischen Dialogs")

51. Cf. Jean-Marie Cardinal Lustiger, *The Promise*, trans. Rebecca Howell Balinski, Msgr. Richard Malone, Jean Duchesne, and Rivka Karplus (Grand Rapids, MI: Eerdmans, 2007): e.g., 148. From the original French: Lustiger, *La Promesse* (Paris: Éditions Parole et Silence, 2002).

52. Lustiger, *Choix de Dieu* (see note 23), 112–13.

53. "les païens ne peuvent croire au Messie d'Israël que s'il y a au moins une partie d'Israël qui a reconnu par la foi son propre Messie, le Messie de Dieu."—Lustiger, *Choix de Dieu* (see note 23), 126.

54. Lustiger, *The Promise* (see note 51), 129.

The Place of Encounter with Messianic Jews in the History of Jewish–Protestant Dialogue

Hanna Rucks

1. Introduction

THE TITLE OF THIS ARTICLE poses the question: What do we mean by "Jewish–Protestant dialogue"? Which Jewish–Protestant conversations do we mean when we speak of "Jewish–Protestant" dialogue?

In this article, I will focus exclusively on the official dialogue—how it is constituted in working groups and other platforms within the institutional *Landeskirchen* [regional state-churches] in Germany, and on how it finds expression in Church statements, writings, and books written by "dialogue-theologians." In terms of regional and historical frameworks, this article examines the Jewish–Protestant dialogue as it developed in Germany after the Second World War.

2. The Jewish–Protestant dialogue after 1945 and the effect of the participation of Jesus-believing Jews on this dialogue

Stirred into consciousness by the events of the Shoah, German theology after the Second World War began afresh to think through and to describe the relationship of the Church to the Jewish people. Jesus-believing Jews played an important role in this process in several respects. Immediately after the war, they made the theme of ecclesiastic antisemitism apparent to the churches in a unique way.

This came about because, in the first two or three years after the war, Christian aid organizations, missions to Jews, and the *Ökumenische Rat der Kirchen* (ÖRK [Ecumenical Council of Churches])—among them Adolf Freudenberg—repeatedly posed the question of aid to so-called "Jewish Christians."[1] Adolf Freudenberg was secretary of the Refugee Commission of ÖRK and was himself married to a Jesus-believing Jewish woman.[2] While Jews who were members of synagogues received support from the Jewish side, Jesus-believing Jews received no aid from those sources. Facing pressure from abroad about this matter, the aid organization of the *Evangelische Kirche in Deutschland* (EKD [Protestant Church in Germany]) and its affiliated church aid agencies who were considering the very practical question of how to distribute donations, found themselves having to deal with their own attitudes toward Jesus-believing Jews and their own antisemitism. An intra-Church conflict that had been building over several years led to a stronger awareness of the Church's special responsibility toward Jesus-believing Jews and to being made aware for the first time of their own antisemitism. But it was not only in this respect that Jesus-believing Jews played an important role in intra-Church developments to work through ecclesial antisemitism and to find a new relationship with Israel. They also played an active role as co-shapers of this process. The Jewish–Protestant dialogue in Germany is rooted in impulses that came from missionary organizations for Jews after the Shoah and the end of the Second World War.[3] In response to pressure from abroad, the EKD set up a department for Israel issues in 1947—Otto von Harling, who was rooted in the Jewish mission field, was appointed as department head. But far more pioneering was another impulse that came from the circles of Jewish mission: At the request of the International Committee on the Christian Approach to the Jews, Karl-Heinrich Rengstorf founded a German branch in 1948 under the title *Deutscher Evangelischer Ausschuss für den Dienst an Israel* [German Protestant Committee for Ministry to Israel].

1. Cf. Siegfried Hermle, *Evangelische Kirche und Judentum – Stationen nach 1945* (Göttingen: Vandenhoeck & Ruprecht, 1990): 70–96. So also in the following when not otherwise indicated.

2. Cf. Uta Gerdes, *Ökumenische Solidarität mit Christlichen und jüdischen Verfolgten. Die CIMADE in Vichy-Frankreich 1940–1944* (Göttingen: Vandenhoeck & Ruprecht, 2005): 59.

3. Cf. Hermle, *Evangelische Kirche und Judentum* (see note 1), 195 ff.

Soon, the beginnings of a new orientation with respect to the Church and Israel would come from this committee that gained the support of the EKD and stood under its auspices. At its founding, Karl-Heinrich Rengstorf first gathered organizations dedicated to the mission to the Jews.[4] Since many Jesus-believing Jews were active in these organizations, Christians of Jewish ancestry naturally belonged to the extended circle of those who shaped the principal work of the committee. Within the first months, the committee dropped its specific orientation toward mission to the Jews; since representatives of charity organizations for non-Christian Jews were also invited, the missional theme was set aside.[5] Even practical questions such as support for refugees receded into the background; the committee became, in the coming years, the most important committee for the development of a new German theology of Israel in the regional state-churches.

Such internal developments of the committee did not lead to any disruption in the cooperation of Jesus-believing Jews: At the first large assembly in October 1948, we hear of nine Jewish Christians among the eighty participants.[6] At the second large assembly, a Jesus-believing Jew served with Hans Ehrenberg among the speakers.[7] Rengstorf, who led the German committee, added another wide-reaching innovation: He invited Rabbi Leo Baeck, a Jewish speaker, to attend the October 1948 assembly—thus establishing the approach of cooperating with representatives of the Jewish side. This led to the committee having conversations *with* Jewish people instead of *about* them. The dominant spirit of these meetings was one in which participants could listen to each other, address their differences, and re-think their attitudes. At least, this is how it was described by Heinz David Leuner, the European Secretary of the International Hebrew-Christian Alliance who likewise soon began to attend the assemblies.[8] If one reads the reports in the periodical *Der Zeuge* [*The Witness*], a paper published by Leuner for the Hebrew-Christian Alliance, the view prevailed—not only with him but also among the central Jewish figures in the dialogue—that

4. *Ibid.*, 205–6.
5. *Ibid.*, 214–15.
6. *Ibid.*, 221.
7. *Ibid.*, 228–29.
8. Cf. Heinz D. Leuner, "Studientagung," *Der Zeuge* 12 (1954): 19–20; cf. also Heinz D. Leuner, "Kirche und Judentum," *Der Zeuge* 10 (1953): 16–17.

Jewish-Christians act as a kind of bridge, that is, a mediating role in the rediscovery of the relationship between Christians and Jews.[9]

At the insistence of one particular Jesus-believing Jew, the Pastor Fritz Majer-Leonhard, as well as from Adolf Freudenberg, requests from the German committee were presented to the *Deutscher Evangelischer Kirchentag* [German Protestant Church Congress].[10] In 1952, Freudenberg offered a first Israel theology event at this church congress. From 1953 onwards, the *Deutscher Evangelischer Ausschuss für den Dienst an Israel* [German Protestant Committee for Ministry to Israel] organized events four times at different church congresses, which took a look at the subject of the Church and Israel. However, the organizers never invited speakers from the Jewish side to these events as part of the church congress. In 1956, the committee's commitment to the church congresses ceased—however the congress leadership decided shortly thereafter to take the subject into their own hands. Among other things, they founded with Freudenberg's participation the working group of the Jewish–Protestant dialogue, which is still the best-known official dialogue platform in Germany: the *Arbeitsgemeinschaft Juden und Christen beim Deutschen Evangelischen Kirchentag* [Working Group for Jews and Christians at the German Protestant Church Congress].[11] Representatives of the Synagogue were part of this group from the beginning—as well as Heinz David Leuner. He was a close friend of Rabbi Robert Rafael Geis, who was also a member of the working group.[12] In 1961, this working group concluded a trailblazing declaration for Jewish–Protestant dialogue. Among other things, the declaration states:

> Jews and Christians are indissolubly linked. The denial of this togetherness gave rise to hatred of Jews among Christians. The denial has become a *chief cause* [emphasis in the original and in the following] of the persecution of Jews. Jesus of Nazareth is betrayed when the members of the Jewish people as one of whom he came into the world, are despised

9. Cf. Heinz D. Leuner, "Judenchristen als Brücke zwischen Israel und Ökumene," *Der Zeuge* 13 (1954): 3; cf. Alfred Rueff, "Judenchristen im Lichte jüdischen Schrifttums des 20. Jahrhunderts," *Der Zeuge* 25 (1961): 14–18, at 17.

10. Cf. Hermle, *Evangelische Kirche und Judentum* (see note 1), 251–62. So also in the following.

11. Cf. *Ibid.*, 11.

12. Cf. Ulrich Laepple, "'Nicht nur den Juden die Kirche, sondern der Kirchen die Juden erklären': Heinz David Leuner – Judenchrist und Brückenbauer (1906 bis 1977)," *Theologische Beiträge* 38.4/5 (2007): 223–38, at 231, 238.

> because they are Jews. Every form of Jew hatred is *Godlessness* and leads to self-annihilation. . . . Where Jews live among us, it is our duty to provide for their lives and for their flourishing to the highest possible degree. As Germans, we must do everything possible for the development of Israel and whatever serves peace for the State of Israel and for her Arab neighbors. We wish that compensation proceedings with regard to those formerly "persecuted due to race" be carried out and concluded with the particular urgency and generosity. Any material compensation however must bespeak an entirely *new attitude.* In Germany, the so-called Jewish question today is above all a question about the future of the German people. . . . Contrary to the false assertion, widespread in the Church for centuries, that God rejected the Jewish people, let us reflect again on the Apostle's word: "God has not abandoned his people, whom he has chosen from ages past" (Romans 11:2). A new encounter with the God of the chosen people will either confirm or awake anew the insight that Jews and Christians live together out of *God's faithfulness,* that they might praise him and serve him in light of biblical hope everywhere and among all peoples.[13]

3. Encounter with Messianic Jews in theological proposals from the German dialogue-theologians

In the early days of Jewish–Protestant dialogue in Germany, however, Jesus-believing Jews were not only met physically within these

13. "Juden und Christen sind unlösbar verbunden. Aus der Leugnung dieser Zusammengehörigkeit entstand die Judenfeindschaft in der Christenheit. Sie wurde zu einer *Hauptursache* der Judenverfolgung. Jesus von Nazareth wird verraten, wenn Glieder des jüdischen Volkes, in dem er zur Welt kam, als Juden mißachtet werden. Jede Form von Judenfeindschaft ist *Gottlosigkeit* und führt zur Selbstvernichtung. . . . Wo Juden unter uns leben, sind wir verpflichtet, ihr Leben und Wohlergehen nach *bestem Vermögen* zu fördern. Auch muß von uns Deutschen alles getan werden, was dem Aufbau und dem Frieden des *Staates Israel* und seiner arabischen Nachbarn dient. Wir wünschen, daß Entschädigungsverfahren gegenüber ehemals 'Rasseverfolgten' mit besonderer Dringlichkeit und Großzügigkeit aufgenommen bzw. beendet werden. Der materiellen Entschädigung muß aber auch eine *neue Gesinnung* entsprechen. In Deutschland ist die sogenannte Judenfrage heute vor allem eine Frage nach der Zukunft der Deutschen. . . . Gegenüber der falschen, in der Kirche jahrhundertelang verbreiteten Behauptung, Gott habe das Volk der Juden verworfen, besinnen wir uns neu auf das Apostelwort: 'Gott hat sein Volk nicht verstoßen, das er zuvor ersehen hat' (Röm 11,2). Eine neue Begegnung mit dem von Gott erwählten Volk wird die Einsicht bestätigen oder neu erwecken, daß Juden und Christen gemeinsam aus der *Treue Gottes* leben, daß sie ihn preisen und ihm im Lichte der biblischen Hoffnung überall unter den Menschen dienen."—cited according to Heinz D. Leuner, "Juden und Christen gehören zusammen," *Der Zeuge* 26 (1961): 13–14.

dialogue platforms and heard with their own contributions. One could also encounter them in theological projects. One in particular should be named here, that of the German theologian Peter von der Osten-Sacken. He accepted the existence of Jesus-believing Jews in his theological thought, and ascribed to them a central role. In 1982, Peter von der Osten-Sacken wrote in his work *Grundzüge einer Theologie im christlich–jüdischen Gespräch* [*Fundamental Characteristics of Theology in Christian–Jewish Dialogue*] about the impact of Messianic Jews, and asked the question if the statement in John 4:22—"salvation comes from the Jews"—might not also have an ecclesiological meaning for the present.[14] This, because "the multitude of Jews who believe in the Gospels, that is, the Jewish Christians or—as those belonging to the growing Protestant confession are called—Messianic Jews, in unity with the suffering of the Jewish people, have emerged for the Church in our century as a reality with unmistakable contours."[15] And: the Church had, "regardless of the current situation and dispute, for the sake of herself and her gospel, every reason to understand the fundamental meaning of her Jewish-Christian part in the Diaspora as well as in the land of Israel."[16] There are three reasons for this: First, they are "ecclesiologically the indispensable bridge between Israel and the gentiles, with the specific task to give witness to the indissoluble unity between the two in light of the gospels and to nurture it."[17] Secondly, the New Testament texts are of importance in view of Jewish Christianity, because

14. Cf. Hanna Rucks, *Messianische Juden. Geschichte und Theologie der Bewegung in Israel* (Neukirchen-Vluyn: Neukirchener Theologie, 2014): 487–90. So also in the following.

15. "die Schar der Juden, die ans Evangelium glaubt, d. h. der Judenchristen oder – wie sich diejenigen protestantischer Konfession zunehmend nennen – der Messianischen Juden, in unserem Jahrhundert in Einheit mit dem Leidensweg des jüdischen Volkes für die Kirche zu einer Realität mit unverwechselbaren Konturen geworden ist."—Peter von der Osten-Sacken, *Grundzüge einer Theologie im christlichen-jüdischen Gespräch* (Munich: Chr. Kaiser, 1982): 144.

16. "ungeachtet der jeweils aktuellen Situation und Auseinandersetzung, um ihrer selbst und ihres Evangeliums willen allen Grund, sich der fundamentalen Bedeutung ihres judenchristlichen Teils in der Diaspora wie im Land Israel bewußt zu warden."—*Ibid.*, 148.

17. "ekklesiologisch nicht wegdenkbare Brücke zwischen Israel und den Völkern mit dem spezifischen Auftrag, jene unlösliche Zusammengehörigkeit zwischen beiden gerade auch angesichts des Evangeliums zu bezeugen und einzuprägen."—*Ibid.*, 149–50.

it is not simply a historical relic, but a present-day reality.[18] Finally, the Jewish Christians are Paul's first argument against the casting off of the Jewish people—and with it against supersessionist theology; von der Osten-Sacken identifies them with the chosen "remnant" out of Israel from Romans 11. The Gentile churches should for this reason be thankful that the Jewish-Christian groups exist "as a sign of God's faithfulness—and first of all his faithfulness toward themselves."[19] It is the task of the Church to help bear the burden of the loneliness of Jewish Christians—expelled from the Jewish side as apostate, they are often branded as "heretics" and "Judaizers" from the Christian side. It is the ". . . task of the churches of the nations . . . , not to abolish the Jewish-Christian identity, but rather to help the disputed, contested and, in the sense described, isolated representatives of Israel in the congregation of Jesus Christ precisely in the shaping of their identity . . ."[20]

4. The change: The disappearance of Jesus-believing Jews from Jewish–Protestant dialogue in Germany

But these statements from the 1980s did not remain von der Osten-Sacken's last word on the Messianic Jews. In his publications it is possible to observe a remarkable change that took place not only in his case, but within the Jewish–Protestant dialogue generally. In 2010, von der Osten-Sacken published an article with the title, *Ein Empfehlungsbrief Christi?* [*A Letter of Recommendation from Christ?*]. Here, he takes on the topic of the mission to the Jews. He demonstrates how the Jewish mission is perceived from the Jewish side and how mission activity directed at Jews puts the Christian–Jewish relationship—built up over decades—in jeopardy.[21] In doing so, he emphasizes that the phenomenon of the

18. Cf. *Ibid.*, 150–51.

19. "als Zeichen für die Treue Gottes – in erster Linie seiner Treue ihr selbst gegenüber"—*Ibid.*, 153–54.

20. ". . . Aufgabe der Völkerkirchen . . . , nicht etwa die judenchristliche Identität aufzuheben, vielmehr den umstrittenen, angefochtenen und im dargelegten Sinne vereinsamten Repräsentanten Israels in der Gemeinde Jesu Christi gerade bei der Ausprägung ihrer Identität zu helfen . . ."—*Ibid.*, 155.

21. Cf. Peter von der Osten-Sacken, "Ein Empfehlungsbrief Christi? Zur Debatte um Judenmission, Judenchristen und messianische Juden," *Quaestiones Disputatae* 238 (2010): 77–112, at 77–81.

Messianic Jews could not be separated from that of the Jewish mission, because among other reasons, the Messianic Jews in Germany (whom von der Osten-Sacken has in mind above all) were "still to a noteworthy extent recruited in the states of the former Soviet Union by evangelical Jewish mission organizations from home and abroad."[22] After a look at the history,[23] von der Osten-Sacken goes into the present-day Messianic Jewish movement and shows how Michael Wyschogrod classifies the movement.[24] Wyschogrod was of the opinion that a Jewish-Christian way would not be acceptable for the Jewish side, because the Jesus-believing Jews most often feel themselves distanced from Jewish identity within two to three generations. Only when the Church is ready for Jesus-believing Jews to be able to maintain their Jewish identity in perpetuity—which for Wyschogrod meant Torah observance, an element he understood in New Testament terms as a duty for Jesus-believing Jews—would there be meaningful change. Wyschogrod's approach conflicts with that of von der Osten-Sacken in the point that von der Osten-Sacken saw no Torah duty for Jesus-believing Jews in Scripture, but certainly he saw there the possibility of upholding the commands of Torah. Beside this, there remained one problem that Wyschogrod did not address: The New Testament left open what the common life of Jews and non-Jews in one congregation could or should look like—when each kept their own identity. Von der Osten-Sacken poses the question of whether a common life of this kind is even possible. This problem as well as Wyschogrod's observation that Jesus-believing Jews over the short or long term would be assimilated into the Church, led von der Osten-Sacken to the insight that "for the churches, the question of Jewish-Christian or Messianic Jewish congregations might seriously, or at least primarily, be framed in connection with the State of Israel."[25] Only in this context would it appear possible for Jesus-believing Jews to maintain a Jewish identity. For that reason, he did not deem the life

22. "zu einem nennenswerten Teil noch in den Staaten der ehemaligen Sowjetunion durch evangelikale judenmissionarische Organisationen aus dem In- und Ausland angeworben"—*Ibid.*, 80.

23. Cf. *Ibid.*, 81–88.

24. Cf. *Ibid.*, 88–92. So also in the following.

25. "sich die Frage judenchristlicher oder messianisch-jüdischer Gemeinden für die Kirchen ernsthaft überhaupt nur oder zumindest in erster Linie in Verbindung mit dem Staat Israel"—*Ibid.*, 92. So also in the following.

of Messianic Jews in Germany, which he addresses in the next section, as having a viable future.[26] As a side note, von der Osten-Sacken mentioned on the margins the liturgical aspects of the Messianic congregation of Vladimir Pikman in Berlin, and a Messianic Jewish creed, which states among others: "We believe that Messianic Judaism today is the continuation of biblical, orthodox Judaism."[27] He commented on this statement as follows:

> It may be left an open question what this excessive claim of Messianic Jews is based on, with which they position themselves as a replacement of the Jewish life which has grown and been proven over 2000 years, while at the same time they liturgically and ritually exploit it. One thing, however, seems inevitable: After rejections of every possible form of destructive replacement theology have been issued all over the country over the last decades—that is, the alleged replacement of Israel by the Church—the churches can, here at the latest, only distance themselves in the clearest possible terms from the Messianic Jews.[28]

Confronted with this type of commentary, the surprised reader might naturally ask: What happened between 1982 and 2010 to cause such a fundamental change in the classification of and response to Jesus-believing Jews in the Jewish–Protestant dialogue? By way of a thesis, I would like to offer the following interpretive framework: The circles of the official Jewish–Protestant dialogue in Germany have not managed to keep up with the theological and ecclesiological changes that have taken place among Jesus-believing Jews in the last fifty years. Programmatic for the types of changes among Jesus-believing Jews that are meant here is the name change from International Hebrew Christian Alliance into International Messianic Jewish Alliance. Central to understanding the development in Jewish–Protestant dialogue is

26. Cf. *Ibid.*, 92–97. So also in the following.

27. "Wir glauben, dass messianisches Judentum heute die Fortsetzung des biblischen, rechtmäßigen Judentums ist"—*Ibid.*, 96.

28. "Es mag dahingestellt sein, worauf sich dieser maßlose Anspruch messianischer Juden gründet, mit dem sie sich an die Stelle des in 2000 Jahren gewachsenen und bewährten jüdischen Lebens setzen, während sie es gleichzeitig liturgisch und rituell ausbeuten. Eins jedoch scheint unabweislich: Nach den in den letzten Jahrzehnten kirchlicherseits landauf, landab erfolgten ausdrücklichen Absagen an jede Form des zerstörerischen Substitutionsanspruchs (die angebliche Ersetzung Israels durch die Kirche) können sich die Kirchen spätestens hier nur aufs Deutlichste von den messianischen Juden distanzieren."—*Ibid.*, 96–97.

this: In Germany no inner transformation process had ever taken place by which "Hebrew Christians" would gradually identify themselves as "Messianic Jews," or by which the children of Hebrew Christians suddenly wanted to live a Messianic Jewish identity. The Hebrew-Christian movement that had helped to found the Jewish–Protestant dialogue in Germany, died out—due to the age of its members and emigration[29]—and thereby lost its place in the Jewish–Protestant dialogue circles. The transformation from "Hebrew Christian" to "Messianic Jewish" took place abroad, and when Messianic Jews from the former Soviet Union suddenly appeared in Germany in the 1990s, worlds collided. Because now the Jesus-believing Jews presently living in Germany suddenly were not "Hebrew Christians" any more but "Messianic Jews," and moreover, they were Soviet Jews and not German Jews, this fact posed an additional intercultural challenge. What kind of tensions were generated in dialogue circles by the change from Hebrew Christians to Messianic Jews can be seen from von der Osten-Sacken's remarks.

On the one hand, there is the issue of separate Jewish-Christian congregations, an idea that von der Osten-Sacken does not theologically question, but he does express serious concerns about the concrete form of such an identity and the possibility of such an approach in Germany and in other places in the Diaspora. About the issue of "separate congregations," he probably had concerns as early as 1982 as to whether this could be realized in the Diaspora. In his book, *Grundzüge,* he points to an internal discussion of the International Hebrew Christian Alliance in 1937. The Alliance at that time had rejected the founding of its own "Jewish-Christian" congregations, but advocated it for the land of Israel in the sense of a yet-to-be-founded native Church.[30] Additionally, not only the *I*nternational Hebrew Christian Alliance, but also the German Jesus-believing Jews in Jewish–Protestant dialogue after the Second World War, distanced themselves from the idea of founding their own congregations. The experience of twelve years of National Socialism was enough to make them want to steer clear away from it. For example, there is a letter addressed from Majer-Leonhard to the "First Hebrew Christian Synagogue" in Los Angeles, a body that had donated

29. Cf. Laepple, "Heinz David Leuner" (see note 12), 238, fn. 44.
30. Cf. von der Osten-Sacken, *Grundzüge* (see note 15), 146.

money for Jewish Christians in the post-war years to found their own congregations. Majer-Leonhard reacted to these donations with the comment that such a plan made no sense in the German context because one had to work in the opposite direction. After Jesus-believing Jews had been excluded from the German churches, one sought to emphasize the unity of the Jesus-believing Jews and Gentile Christians. The experience of the twelve years of National Socialism had shown that if Jesus-believing Jews received help from anywhere during these years, then it had come from the churches.[31] But it was not only these life experiences that Majer-Leonhard had experienced himself, but also the Church's own antisemitism during the Nazi years, which had made the idea of having a dedicated "Jewish-Christian" congregation "impossible." After "non-Aryan Christians" had been excluded from the Gentile Christian churches during the Nazi years, such a move would have been understood as an approval of the Church's antisemitic policy during those years. The fact that "the new Jesus-believing Jews," namely the "Messianic Jews," started their own congregations, was certainly a theological challenge for Jesus-believing Jews within the Jewish–Protestant dialogue circles in Germany in the first decades.[32]

All of this may have left an imprint that is felt today in the way that Messianic Jews are perceived within the dialogue circles. Doubt remains about the appropriateness of Messianics forming their own "Jewish-Christian" congregations—at least in the Diaspora. And the attitude and experiences of the Hebrew Christians who were part of the early Jewish–Protestant dialogue in Germany may be the reason that even today questions about the "Messianic Jewish congregations" keep arising in the context of such dialogue, similar to those expressed here by von der Osten-Sacken.

A further point that emerges from von der Osten-Sacken's remarks is that the "new" Messianic Jewish movement that established itself in the seventies in America and Israel and which later energized the Messianic Jewish movement in the former Soviet Union was theologically influenced by Christian movements that were categorized in the German regional state-church context as "free-church." For

31. Cf. Hermle, *Evangelische Kirche und Judentum* (see note 1), 149–50.

32. Cf. Heinz D. Leuner, "Die Idee der Allianz," *Der Zeuge* 3–4 (1951): 1–5, at 3–5.

some dialogue-theologians in the regional state-churches, this called up an almost reflexive defensiveness. To exaggerate just a little, one might express it as the following: The "Hebrew Christians" from the initial dialogue were "state-churchers," but the "Messianic Jews" are "free-churchers." To put the expression in von Osten-Sacken's words: "[E]vangelical organizations which missionize Jews" are backing the Messianic Jewish movement in Germany.[33] This means that patterns of conflict that run between state and free churches in Germany and which are evident when distinguishing the terms *evangelisch* [Protestant] and *evangelikal* [evangelical], now suddenly stand between Christian ("state-church," Protestant) dialogue-theologians and ("free-church," evangelical) Messianic Jews.

A third point becomes clear from von der Osten-Sacken's remarks. Not only among the Jesus-believing Jews did changes occur over the decades. The Jewish–Protestant dialogue has also developed. The rejection of "Jewish mission" has become a very central issue. Already in 1982, von der Osten-Sacken had voiced reservations about some forms of the Messianic Jewish mission. He wrote: "Nor can it be an aim to applaud when Jewish-Christian groups, as apparently here and there in the USA, display a missionary zeal bordering on fanaticism which destroys more than it builds up, as the missionizing of gentile Christians once did and sometimes still does today."[34] But simultaneously, he spoke positively at that time of "Jewish Christians" as having the responsibility to bear witness.[35] In 2010, he identified the Messianic Jewish movement completely with the mission to the Jews. This identification burdens the encounter between Messianic Jews and Jewish–Protestant dialogue circles today.

A further point can be made: When reading von der Osten-Sacken, but also in other statements, one often senses fear of the social consequences of bringing Messianic Jews into the dialogue. There is the danger that one might lose a Jewish dialogue partner or put a

33. Von der Osten-Sacken, "Empfehlungsbrief" (see note 21), 80.

34. "Noch auch kann es Ziel sein, zu applaudieren, wo judenchristliche Gruppen, wie anscheinend hier und da in den United States, einen ans Fanatische grenzenden Missionseifer an den Tag legen, der – wie einst und manchmal auch noch heute der heidenchristliche – mehr zerstört als aufbaut."—von der Osten-Sacken, *Grundzüge* (see note 15), 148.

35. Cf. *Ibid.*, 155–56.

well-developed trust at risk through contact with the Messianic Jews.[36] In other words, Messianic Jews posed not only theological challenges, but also social difficulties.

The practical result is that Messianic Jews—who have made their home in Germany since the 1990s—have not yet been included in official Jewish–Protestant dialogue. Nevertheless, it should be noted: How much interest there actually is among German Messianic Jews in getting a place within the dialogue platforms and being invited to talks, is another matter—conversations this author has had testify to the fact that there is also sometimes very little interest on the part of the Messianic Jews.

5. The rapprochement in Jewish–Protestant dialogue with Messianic Jews

Nevertheless, there has been movement: At the church congress in Stuttgart in 2015, there occurred for the first time a "trialogue" between the Jewish journalist Micha Brumlik, the Messianic Jew Richard Harvey, and a representative of the regional state-churches, Bishop Ralf Meister. The theme was also taken up at the level of the EKD. After the EKD in their three declarations, "Christians and Jews" from the years 1975, 1991, and 2000, respectively had touched only marginally on the theme of Messianic Jews,[37] in 2017 the *Gemeinsame Ausschuss für "Kirche und Judentum"* [Joint Committee for "Church and the Jewish people"] worked out a position paper in the framework of the EKD advisory board. It was published under the title "Christian Jews—Jewish Christians—'Messianic Jews.'"[38]

36. Cf. von der Osten-Sacken, "Empfehlungsbrief" (see note 21), 78–79, which describes the ecclesial "no" to the mission to the Jews (and for him therefore also to the Messianic Jews, as they present themselves in the present day) as a precondition for any dialogue from the Jewish side. Cf. also Evangelische Kirche in Deutschland [EKD], ed., *Judenchristen – jüdische Christen – 'messianische Juden'. Eine Positionsbestimmung des gemeinsamen Ausschusses 'Kirche und Judentum' im Auftrag des Rates der EKD* (Hannover, 2017; downloaded from https://www.ekd.de/ekd_de/ds_doc/Messianische_Juden.pdf), 22–23.

37. The EKD devotes some thought to the topic in the appendix to the third declaration, or rather presents mainly the history of the Messianic Jewish movement, cf. Kirchenamt der EKD, ed., *Christen und Juden I–III. Die Studien der Evangelischen Kirche in Deutschland 1975–2000* (Gütersloh: Gütersloher Verlagshaus, 2002): 169–72.

38. EKD (ed.), *Judenchristen* (see note 36).

The paper lays out the Messianic Jewish movement in four steps. The history of the movement is presented, with a focus on Germany, and then its distinguishing features are outlined which include such things as divine service practices, celebration of the sacraments, or the festivals in the annual cycle. In the next step, the paper summarizes theological aspects, particularly the special relationship between Israel, Jesus-believing Jews, and the Church, as they had been previously analyzed in two separate Messianic Jewish proposals—those by Mark Kinzer ("Postmissionary Judaism") and Alex Jacob ("Enlargement Theology"). Then the paper describes which circles support the Messianic Jewish movement, among which the organizations Chosen People Ministries, *Evangeliumsdienst für Israel* (EDI [Gospel Ministry for Israel]) and *Arbeitsgemeinschaft für das messianische Zeugnis an Israel* (AMZI [Working Group for the Messianic Testimony to Israel]) are mentioned by name. It is in this connection that a theological criticism appears for the first time. The paper cites a book published by AMZI and authored by Tuvay Zaretzky, who writes: "Jews as well as non-Jews . . . only come into the full enjoyment of the promised blessings . . . through belief in Jesus."[39] The position paper makes the following comment:

> The supporters, like most Messianic Jewish congregations themselves, consider non-Christ-believing Judaism to be deficient and accuse it of not having recognized the Messiah Jesus. Herein lies a fundamental difference from the declarations of most regional state-churches, which emphasize the faithfulness of God to his people Israel, in that they do not tie it fundamentally to the agreement of Jews to the confession of Christ. This explains the high sensitivity and concern of Jewish congregations in the face of missionary activities. They expect the churches to distance themselves clearly from Messianic Jewish groups and their evangelical Christian supporters, if they cast into doubt the legitimacy of Jewish existence when it is not accompanied by a confession of Christ.[40]

39. "In den vollen Genuss des verheißenen Segens . . . kommen Juden wie auch Nichtjuden . . . nur durch den Glauben an Jesus."—cited according to EKD, ed., *Judenchristen* (see note 36), 15.

40. "Die Unterstützer wie die meisten messianisch-jüdischen Gemeinden selbst halten demnach das nicht-christusgläubige Judentum für defizitär und werfen ihm vor, den Messias Jesus nicht erkannt zu haben. Hierin liegt ein grundlegender Unterschied zu den Erklärungen der meisten Landeskirchen, die die Treue Gottes zu seinem Volk Israel betonen, indem sie diese nicht grundsätzlich an die Zustimmung

The "position paper" continues after this commentary with an interpretation of the phenomenon "Messianic Jews," in which two questions in particular are pursued: namely, whether Messianic Jewish groups and congregations could count as Jewish, and whether one could consider them from an ecclesial perspective as part of the Congregation of Christ. For the latter, questions are formulated that can provide answers, for example, whether there is a common understanding in the sense of the Leuenberg Church Fellowship with respect to the sacraments, and whether the Trinity—not in the dogmatic wording but in factual content—would be affirmed from the side of Messianic Jews. On that point it states: "When, on the cross, the eternal being of God and the truth of God manifests itself, the factual content of the Trinitarian formula is known at its core."[41] With regard to the question if one could recognize Messianic Jewish groups in dialogue as Jewish dialogue partners, this paper declines to offer an opinion. It is not the role of Christian theology to decide who can be counted as Jewish and who not.

In its four closing points, the position paper makes statements that are very important for our context. That is:

> In the last decades, a relationship of trust has grown in Germany, not least because of the willingness of Jewish interlocutors (both women and men) to engage in dialogue in the encounter between Christians and Jews, for which we are thankful. Wherever in this country "Messianic Jewish" congregations and groups are accepted as Jewish dialogue partners, irritations have occurred at every level of Christian–Jewish encounter and the cultivated trust is destroyed. Not least because of this, the Protestant Church will exercise the utmost reservation with regard to claims formulated by "Messianic Jewish" congregations.[42]

---

von Juden zum Christusbekenntnis binden. Dies erklärt die hohe Sensibilität und Sorge jüdischer Gemeinden angesichts missionarischer Aktivitäten. Sie erwarten von den Kirchen eine deutliche Distanzierung von messianisch-jüdischen Gruppen und ihren christlich-evangelikalen Unterstützern, sofern diese die Legitimität der jüdischen Existenz in Zweifel ziehen, wenn diese nicht von einem Christusbekenntnis begleitet wird."—*Ibid.*, 16.

41. "Wenn sich im Kreuz das ewiggültige Wesen und die Wahrheit Gottes manifestiert, ist der Sachgehalt der trinitarischen Formeln im Zentrum bekannt."—*Ibid.*, 18.

42. "In den letzten Jahrzehnten ist in Deutschland nicht zuletzt durch die Gesprächsbereitschaft jüdischer Partnerinnen und Partner in der Begegnung von Christen und Juden ein Vertrauensverhältnis gewachsen, für das wir dankbar sind. Wo hierzulande 'messianisch-jüdische' Gemeinden und Gruppen als jüdische

This has been the most comprehensive position determination that has been issued by the EKD so far. And it must be positively noted that Messianic Jews were also invited to participate in the antecedent discussions.[43] The position paper opens the doors a crack wide for the conversation with Messianic Jews. Nevertheless, four points of criticism should be mentioned at this point, which then lead to a final vote on "the place of encounter with Messianic Jews in Jewish–Protestant dialogue."

First, despite all efforts at objectivity, one nevertheless sees a slightly tendentious portrait of the "phenomenon of Messianic Jews" emerge. "Messianic Jews" are once more represented in a very close connection with the theme of "Jewish mission"—as it were, in a way that stretches the bounds of factual correctness. Thus the foreword begins with the statement that "'Jews for Jesus' or also 'Messianic Jews' is the self-identifying name of a movement that has been active in the United States since the 1970s and in Germany since the beginning of the 1990s."[44] That is patently a false statement, since "Jews for Jesus" is the name of an organization known for their energetic and even provocative missionary activities in the field, and is in no way a widely used term of self-identification; but it is a foreign and negative term historically used by Jewish critics for the whole movement.[45] Such an identification of "Jews for Jesus" with "Messianic Jews" creates the impression in half-informed people that Messianic Jews should be identified with "mission to the Jews." To name a second example, the historical overview states the following: "In the nineteenth century, Christian mission organizations began to found 'Jewish-Christian' congregations in areas

---

Dialogpartner in Anspruch genommen werden, entstehen auf allen Ebenen christlich-jüdischer Begegnung Irritationen, und gewachsenes Vertrauen wird zerstört. Nicht zuletzt deshalb wird die Evangelische Kirche im Blick auf durch 'messianisch-jüdische' Gemeinden formulierte Ansprüche äußerste Zurückhaltung üben."—*Ibid.*, 22–23.

43. Cf. Ulrich Laepple, "Judenchristen, Messianische Juden und die EKD im christlich-jüdischen Gespräch von 1945 bis heute," *Theologische Beiträge* 50 (2019): 431–54, at 450.

44. "'Jews for Jesus' ('Juden für Jesus') oder auch 'Messianische Juden' ist die Selbstbezeichnung einer Bewegung, die seit den 70er Jahren in den United States und in Deutschland etwa seit Anfang der 90er Jahre aktiv ist."—EKD, ed., *Judenchristen* (see note 36), 6.

45. Cf. Rucks, *Messianische Juden* (see note 14), 249.

with large Jewish populations (Hungary, Galicia, and Southern Russia). The congregation of 'Israelites of the New Covenant' associated with Joseph Rabinowitz was active from 1884 until the Shoah in Kishinev (today Moldova)."[46] Further on, the text takes up the founding of the mission organization, Chosen People Ministries. In this context, the sentence describing Rabinowitz's congregation reads as if it had to do with a congregation founded by a Jewish missionizing organization—or a congregation that saw itself as such an organization. Rabinowitz's congregation, however, was a "Messianic Jewish 'shooting star'" that had as good as no contact with mission organizations. Here, the context invokes "missionary" images as if they were things that played out in reality. One final remark on this point of critique: In the EKD study from the year 2000, the history of the Messianic Jewish movement is told without ever once mentioning the words "mission" or "mission organization."[47] One can undoubtedly present the history of Messianic Judaism in different ways, various factors leading to the awakening of the movement. The position paper, however, tells little of the breadth of these factors, but instead seems determined to stress the missionary element.

The second point of critique has to do with the above-cited commentary about the attitude of Messianic Jews toward non-Jesus-believing Jews.

> The supporters, like most Messianic Jewish congregations themselves, consider non-Christ-believing Judaism to be deficient and accuse it of not having recognized the Messiah Jesus. Herein lies a fundamental difference from the declarations of most regional state-churches, which emphasize the faithfulness of God to his people Israel, in that they do not tie it fundamentally to the agreement of Jews to the confession of Christ.[48]

46. "Im 19. Jahrhundert begannen zugleich christliche Missionsgesellschaften, in Gebieten mit starker jüdischer Bevölkerung (Galizien, Ungarn und Südrussland) 'judenchristliche' Gemeinden zu gründen. Die Gemeinde der 'Israeliten des Neuen Bundes' von Joseph Rabinowitsch war von 1884 bis zur Shoah in Kischinew (heute Moldawien) tätig."—EKD, ed., *Judenchristen* (see note 36), 10.

47. Cf. Kirchenamt der EKD, ed., *Christen und Juden I–III* (see note 37), 170–71.

48. "Die Unterstützer wie die meisten messianisch-jüdischen Gemeinden selbst halten demnach das nicht-christusgläubige Judentum für defizitär und werfen ihm vor, den Messias Jesus nicht erkannt zu haben. Hierin liegt ein grundlegender

It is precisely the above-cited statements in the position paper that make clear that these evangelical supporters of Messianic Jews did not make the faithfulness of God to His people contingent on agreeing to the confession of Christ. The statement says explicitly that they endorse the call of Israel as chosen and reject any supersessionist theology. *That* is not the point. Neither, as the following formulation expresses, is it the point that the legitimacy of Jewish existence is cast into doubt by Messianic Jews, when it is not accompanied by a confession of Christ. The disturbing, disparaging elements toward rabbinic Judaism lie somehow elsewhere; "full enjoyment of the blessings" is lacking—what could this mean? At this point it would also be not so far-fetched to point out that intra-Jewish "deficiency descriptions" of various types are not abnormal in and of themselves (Messianic Jews are themselves often subjected to deficiency descriptions from the side of other Jews, but putting that aside for the moment, one has only to follow the use of the phrase "*yehudi amiti*" ["true Jew"] to accurately grasp intra-Jewish deficiency descriptions). What distinguishes the attitude of Messianic Jews from that of the Orthodox, who also classify Liberal Jews as deficient? In such questions, a more nuanced and precise presentation of the problematic in Messianic Jewish statements about non-Jesus-believing Judaism would have been helpful.

The third critique is in reference to the historical overview. It is striking that any reference to the German Hebrew Christian Alliance, to other Jewish-Christian initiatives in Germany before the Second World War (e.g., the Jerusalem Church in Hamburg), and any reference to the Shoah, is lacking. That is especially remarkable, since the paper sets out specifically to deal with the situation in Germany. Today's Messianic Judaism in Germany would look very different if the Shoah had not wiped out most of the Hebrew Christian alliances in Europe and weakened the German alliance so much that it later collapsed. The paper unfortunately skips over ecclesiastical failures at the time toward Jesus-believing Jews and the resulting burden of responsibility for it in

Unterschied zu den Erklärungen der meisten Landeskirchen, die die Treue Gottes zu seinem Volk Israel betonen, indem sie diese nicht grundsätzlich an die Zustimmung von Juden zum Christusbekenntnis binden."—EKD, ed., *Judenchristen* (see note 36), 16.

the encounter with Messianic Jews. Neither does it say even a single word about the contribution made by "Hebrew Christians" in the first decades of the Jewish–Protestant dialogue in Germany.

Finally, the paper lacks any distinction between "Messianic Jews" and "Messianic non-Jews." It speaks of whole "Messianic Jewish groups" and "Messianic Jewish congregations," for example, in the formulation: "Wherever in this country 'Messianic Jewish' congregations and groups are accepted as Jewish dialogue partners, irritations have occurred at every level of Christian–Jewish encounter and the cultivated trust is destroyed. Not least because of this, the Protestant Church will exercise the utmost reservation with regard to claims formulated by 'Messianic Jewish' congregations."[49] Naturally, in the present-day order of Messianic Jewish congregations in Germany it is difficult to classify these congregations unequivocally as "Jewish" congregations because they are composed of a mixture of Jesus-believing Jews and Jesus-believing non-Jews. But it would not be necessary always to speak of "groups." Dialogue partners are, as a rule, individuals. For when someone claims to speak as a "Jew" with Church representatives, it is precisely then that his Jewish heritage becomes most relevant. The consequence of the non-differentiation is that, according to the position paper, both groups should be treated the same way. In my opinion, the position paper tempts members of the German regional state-churches who relied on the paper for their information about Messianic Jews to deny the Jewishness of Jesus-believing Jews if in doubt, because the proven Jewish interlocutors in the dialogue (usually members of synagogue congregations) advise them to do so. That would be a highly problematic step for both historical and theological reasons.

The above-cited lines from the position paper make one thing very clear: If the "Hebrew Christians" after 1945 were for many a bridge in Jewish–Protestant dialogue in Germany, and were themselves involved in bringing about that dialogue, Messianic Jews of the present day do just the opposite. They appear to be a danger for the dialogue. They are therefore not only missing in the dialogue, but are deliberately "kept outside." Nevertheless, the door to conversation with Messianic Jews

49. *Ibid.*, 22–23.

has been opened a little bit through the EKD position determination of 2017.

(Translated by John David Martin and James Earle Patrick, with input from Hanna Rucks, from the German: "Der Ort der Begegnung mit Messianischen Juden in der Geschichte des jüdisch-protestantischen Dialogs")

Messianic Judaism and the Hermeneutic of Canonical Discourse

Ludger Schwienhorst-Schönberger

1. Introduction

IN THE LAST FIFTY YEARS, the exegesis of the Old Testament has, by and large, left the model of replacement theology (supersessionism) behind. At least one can say this for large parts of Old Testament biblical scholarship taught at universities and seminaries in Europe and in the United States and of the academic institutions influenced by them.

One encounters replacement theology in biblical hermeneutics above all in connection with the specification of the relationship between the Old and New Testaments. In this field, it asserts that the Old Testament is replaced by the New Testament. This basic statement can be given varied expressions. The narrated history that is told in the Old Testament can be viewed as a prehistory to the history narrated in the New Testament; as historical material it might be interesting, but it is theologically largely irrelevant.[1] A broader, sharper variation

1. In this context, reference is made to the discussions following the theses of Notger Slenczka, *Vom Alten Testament und vom Neuen. Beiträge zur Neuvermessung ihres Verhältnisses* (Leipzig: Evangelische Verlagsanstalt, 2017). Cf. Bernard Mallmann, *Dekanonisierung des Alten Testaments? Rückfragen an Notger Slenczka aus Sicht katholischer Theologie* (Studien zur systematischen und spirituellen Theologie, 57; Würzburg: Echter, 2021).

of this model is the so-called contrast model. According to it, what is narrated in the Old Testament is not only to be viewed as a provisional history vis-à-vis the New Testament but as a failed history in relation to it. In this view, the theological content that is to be derived from the Old Testament would stand in contrast to what is revealed in the New Testament. As a classical representative of this direction, it would be good to mention Marcion, who famously viewed the Old Testament Scriptures as not belonging to the Christian canon and accepted from the New Testament only those pieces that are to be understood as being in—apparently—clear opposition to the Old Testament.

Since the 1970s, much effort has been made to overcome this and other similar positions in biblical scholarship focused on the Old Testament. In German-language Catholic exegesis, my teacher Erich Zenger was significantly involved in this effort. To undercut every form of marginalization of the Old Testament already in the approach, he argued that the term "Old Testament" should be replaced by the designation "First Testament." His tombstone in the Central Cemetery in Münster is inscribed in the following way: "Erich Zenger (1939–2010)—Teacher of the First Testament."

In what follows, I would like to show how a post-supersessionist model for specifying the relationship between Old and New Testaments could change again through the dialogue with Messianic Jews. In what follows, I will introduce three models for determining the relationship between the Old and New Testaments:

(1) The replacement theology model
(2) The post-replacement theology model (Erich Zenger, Christoph Dohmen)
(3) A proposed new model that is appropriate for the dialogue between the Messianic Jewish movement and Christian theology

2. The unity of the Scriptures: Hermeneutic of canonical discourse

For our purposes, it is not necessary to introduce all three models extensively. As a student of Erich Zenger and a close colleague of Christoph Dohmen, I have immense sympathy for the second model, which, to put it simply, emphasizes the independence of the Old Testament in the framework of biblical theology and rejects every form of marginalization and relativizing. Still, there is a point in relation to which I do not agree with this model. And it is precisely this point that impacts the—in my view justified—concern that underlies the dialogue between Messianic Jews and Christian theologians and that is to be strengthened theologically and presented for discussion within the context of our symposium "Jesus—also the Messiah for Israel? Messianic Jewish Movement and Christianity in Dialogue."

In the volume that he wrote together with the Viennese Jewish studies scholar Günter Stemberger, *Hermeneutik der Jüdischen Bibel und des Alten Testaments*, Christoph Dohmen developed the model of the "double way of reading the Old Testament" (*doppelten Leseweise des Alten Testaments*). It is primarily directed against those models that, in the context of Christian theology, require the Old Testament to be read from the outset and exclusively in a Christian way. In contrast, Dohmen speaks of a "*prae-position* of the Bible of Israel,"[2] which is to be understood both with respect to the subject matter and with respect to time. According to Dohmen, it is

> [p]recisely the canonical order of the Old and New Testament that summons . . . Christians to a double way of reading the Old Testament. . . . It enables and also requires one to read the Old Testament *also* without Christian interpretation. . . . Since the Bible of Israel as the Old Testament was placed before the New Testament without Christian interpretation or change, it requires and allows the first reading of the Old Testament to blend out the Christian context, which is possible primarily through a perception of the original (Hebrew and Aramaic) texts. Only the second reading, which places these texts in a Christian interpretive context, must take into account the text that the authors of the New Testament used. That text, however, is the Greek text of the LXX.[3]

2. "*Prae-Position* der Bibel Israels"—Christoph Dohmen and Günter Stemberger, *Hermeneutik der Jüdischen Bibel und des Alten Testaments* (Kohlhammer Studienbücher Theologie, 1.2; Stuttgart: Kohlhammer, 2nd edn 2019): 171–75. Cf. also my review in *Theologische Revue* 117 (Jan 2021): 3 pages.

3. "[g]erade die kanonische Anordnung von Altem und Neuem Testament . . . die Christen zu einer doppelten Leseweise des Alten Testaments auf. . . . Sie ermöglicht und verlangt, das Alte Testament auch ohne christliche Interpretation zu lesen. . . . Da die Bibel Israels als Altes Testament ohne christliche Interpretation oder Änderung dem Neuen Testament vorangestellt wurde, verlangt und erlaubt das erste Lesen des Alten Testaments den christlichen Kontext auszublenden, was vornehmlich durch ein Wahrnehmen der ursprünglichen (hebräischen und

According to Dohmen, while the Christian understanding of the Old Testament is, of course, possible, it represents only "one—not the only—possibility of interpretation for the Bible of Israel."[4] Dohmen ascribes a highly problematic "forgetting of Israel" to traditional Christian exegesis. In its place, the Regensburg Old Testament scholar sets a hermeneutic of remembering Israel: "A hermeneutic of the Old Testament *is* remembering Israel."[5] Dohmen regards a "hermeneutic of the Old Testament that is *remembering Israel*" as "*the* opportunity for Christian theology in the twenty-first century."[6]

Dohmen emphasizes that the Old Testament was not expanded, shortened, or revised in a Christian way, which certainly would have been possible in the context of the emergence and continuation of biblical writings, but rather that "it was placed before the New Testament without any Christian interpretation or change."[7] And precisely this fact requires—thus Dohmen—that it be read also by Christians in a first act *without* Christian interpretation.

At this point, I would like to raise an objection or at least note my reservations. Is it really necessary, in a strictly theological sense, that the Christian understanding of the Old Testament *must* go through the Jewish understanding of these texts, that is, that the Christian understanding must pass through two levels of understanding—a Jewish and a Christian? With a view to the theme of our symposium, the question becomes sharper: *Which* Jewish understanding of the Old Testament must Christian theology pass through before it may come to the genuine Christian understanding? An orthodox-rabbinic, a Jewish-liberal, or perhaps a Jewish-messianic understanding? The position that Dohmen represents basically excludes the Messianic-Jewish understanding as the

---

aramäischen) Texte möglich ist. Erst das zweite Lesen, das diese Texte in einen christlichen Interpretationszusammenhang stellt, muss den Text berücksichtigen, den die Autoren des Neuen Testaments benutzt haben. Das aber ist der griechische Text der LXX."—Dohmen and Stemberger, *Hermeneutik* (see note 2), 236.

4. "eine – nicht die einzige – Interpretationsmöglichkeit der Bibel Israels dar"—*Ibid.*, 237.

5. "Hermeneutik des Alten Testaments *ist* Israelerinnerung"—*Ibid.*, 233.

6. "Hermeneutik des Alten Testaments, die *Israelerinnerung* ist" . . . "*die* Chance christlicher Theologie im 21. Jahrhundert"—*Ibid.*, 233.

7. "ohne christliche Interpretation oder Änderung dem Neuen Testament vorangestellt wurde"—*Ibid.*, 236.

horizon for the first reading from the outset, because it is not a reading without the New Testament. Messianic Judaism reads the TaNaK—the "Old Testament" consisting of Torah, Nevi'im (Prophets), and Ketuvim (Writings)—messianically, which means in light of the *Yeshua haMashiach* attested in the New Testament, his life, teachings, deeds, death and resurrection. Characteristic of this is *The Complete Jewish Study Bible*,[8] which is typical for the self-understanding of Messianic Judaism. It completely rejects the division of the Bible into Old and New Testaments. Its guiding principle is the unity of the Scriptures ("the Bible's unity"):

> The *Complete Jewish Bible* graphically presents this unity by eliminating all separation between the *Tanakh* and *B'rit Hadashah*. Most Christian translations insert a special title page to divide the Old Testament from the New and even number the pages separately, so that the book *Mattityahu* (Matthew) starts on the New Testament's own page 1. The *Complete Jewish Bible* divides the entire Bible into seven major sections: the *Torah*, the Prophets, the Writings, the Gospels, the Acts of the Emissaries (Apostles), the Letters, and the book of Revelation. Pagination is continuous. There is no need to collect the first three-quarters of the Bible into the "Old Testament" and the last quarter into the "New." Rather, the Bible is presented as a seamless whole, a unified word of God, a complete Jewish bible for all humanity.[9]

If one uses this division and its associated hermeneutic as a basis, the thesis of the *prae*-position of the Bible of Israel makes no sense. For Messianic Judaism, there is no Bible of Israel separated from the New Testament: "Thus the New Testament apart from the Old is heretical, and the Old Testament apart from the New is incomplete—two testaments, one Bible."[10] For Messianic Judaism, the so-called Old Testament is "incomplete." This is presumably also the reason for the provocative title: *The Complete Jewish Study Bible (CJB)*—probably with a critical allusion to *The Jewish Study Bible (JSB)*.[11]

In Messianic Judaism, a central element of Catholic biblical hermeneutics returns to the fore in pointed form—the unity of Scripture.

8. The full title is: David Stern (trans.), *The Complete Jewish Study Bible. Insights for Jews and Christians. Illuminating the Jewishness of God's Word*, ed. Barry Rubin (Peabody, MA: Hendrickson, 2016 / 2021).

9. *Ibid.*, xxx.

10. *Ibid.*, xxx.

11. Cf. Adele Berlin and Marc Brettler (eds.), *The Jewish Study Bible. Torah—Nevi'im—Kethuvim* (Oxford: Oxford University Press, 2004 / 2014).

Under the influence of some trends in historical-critical exegesis, this concept has largely been forgotten or even rejected as something that is no longer plausible exegetically. In recent years, however, the theme has become an object of constructive discussions.[12]

Against this background, Dohmen's hermeneutical model requires an update, since without taking into account the questions raised from the side of Messianic Judaism, it leads to the view—which is problematic in my opinion—that the Jewish-rabbinic, or to put it more precisely, the Jewish-non-messianic understanding is closer to the meaning of the Old Testament texts than the Jewish-messianic understanding. This, in turn, would mean that the Messianic Jews fall between the chairs: Either they stop with the non-Christian first reading of the Old Testament and remain Jewish, or they go over to the Christian second reading and become Christians. *Tertium non datur* [The third is not given]. Thus, I would like us to consider whether this well-intended post-supersessionist model of the specification of the relationship between Old and New Testaments, as represented by Dohmen, marginalizes the Messianic-Jewish understanding of the Old Testament. Therefore, I am suggesting that we not operate with an opposition between two fixed ways of reading—one Jewish and one Christian—but rather approach the subject matter in a more open way, by reading and meditating on the Scriptures of the Old Testament with an open mind and then doing the same with the New Testament. This would basically be the model of *hermeneutical dialogicity*,[13] or to use Zenger's language: the *hermeneutic of canonical discourse*: "Concretely, this program means that there is no *predetermined* priority of meaning or significance placing the New Testament ahead of the Old Testament and thus also that there can be no superiority of Christianity in relation to Judaism, as Christian theology has decreed for centuries . . ." Vis-à-vis Zenger, I would like to add here: *et vice versa*! This applies also in the opposite direction! ". . . Rather, it is about bringing Old Testament and New Testament voices into a

12. Cf. Rudolph Voderholzer, *Die Einheit der Schrift und ihr geistiger Sinn. Der Beitrag Henri de Lubacs zur Erforschung von Geschichte und Systematik christlicher Bibelhermeneutik* (Freiburg i. Br.: Johannes Verlag, 1998). Ludger Schwienhorst-Schönberger, "Die Einheit der Schrift ist ihr geistiger Sinn. Ein Beitrag in der Reihe 'Die Bibel unter neuen Blickwinkeln,'" *Bibel und Kirche* (3/2008): 179–83.

13. "Dialogicity" can be defined roughly as a state of being in constant dialogue.

two-way discourse with one another in such a way that they mutually illuminate each other."[14]

With respect to the specification of the relationship between Judaism and Christianity, I am thus arguing for a model of symmetry. Dohmen, by contrast, advocates the model of asymmetry. He speaks of the temporal and material priority ("temporal and material precedence") of the Bible of Israel.[15] But whether the historical reconstructions to support this claim are correct or not is disputed in the research. Did Christianity emerge from Judaism, or are they both religions siblings of a common mother? In his famous address in the synagogue in Rome in 1986, Pope John Paul II named the Jewish people "our older brothers." The Jewish studies scholar Peter Schäfer no longer speaks only of the emergence of Christianity from Judaism but rather also of the "birth of Judaism out of the spirit of Christianity."[16] Günter Stemberger lists a number of examples that show that rabbinical scriptural exegesis also from time to time reacts to Christianity:[17]

> There are quite a number of rabbinical texts that with greater or lesser clarity can be understood as being in dialogue with the Christian

14. "Konkret bedeutet dieses Programm, dass es keine vorgegebene Sinn- und Bedeutungspriorität des Neuen Testaments vor dem Alten Testament gibt und demnach auch keine Superiorität des Christentums gegenüber dem Judentum geben kann, wie christliche Theologie dies jahrhundertelang dekretiert hat. Vielmehr geht es darum, die alttestamentlichen und die neutestamentlichen Stimmen so in einen wechselseitigen Diskurs zu bringen, dass sie sich gegenseitig erhellen"—Erich Zenger and Christian Frevel, "Heilige Schrift der Juden und der Christen," in *Einleitung in das Alte Testament*, ed. Christian Frevel (Stuttgart: Kohlhammer, 9th updated edn 2016): 21.

15. "zeitliches und sachliches Voraus"—Dohmen and Stemberger, *Hermeneutik* (see note 2), 149.

16. Peter Schäfer, *Die Geburt des Judentums aus dem Geist des Christentums. Fünf Vorlesungen zur Entstehung des rabbinischen Judentums* (Tübingen: Mohr Siebeck, 2010). According to Christoph Dohmen, "Der vierteilige Kanon der Heiligen Schrift. Eine Spurensuche mit Gregor dem Grossen," in *Dein Wort ist meinem Fuss eine Leuchte.* FS Schwienhorst-Schönberger, ed. Georg Braulik, Agnethe Siquans, and Jan-Heiner Tück (Freiburg i. Br.: Herder, 2022): 158–66, at 159: "this thought is meaningful and correct exclusively with respect to the emergence of rabbinic Judaism; by contrast, detached from this concrete historical situation, this idea makes no sense." ["ist dieser Gedanke ausschließlich im Blick auf die Entstehung des rabbinischen Judentums sinnvoll und richtig, losgelöst von dieser konkreten historischen Situation ergibt dieser Gedanke hingegen keinen Sinn."]

17. Günter Stemberger, "Hermeneutik der jüdischen Bibel," in Dohmen and Stemberger, *Hermeneutik* (see note 2), 29–141, at 117–119.

> tradition. . . . Just as Christian biblical exegesis also already drew upon rabbinic traditions very early on . . . , Jewish interpretation of the Holy Scriptures should also not be viewed as wholly isolated but rather time and again attests the dialogue with Christianity.[18]

Neither the Jewish nor the Christian understanding of the Old Testament or TaNaK has priority *in principle*, in such a way that the one would be directed to the other. Both can learn a great deal from each other and can meet one another in mutual respect. Neither one is required to relativize the normative claim to validity of its understanding, let alone give it up. The Jewish and the Christian understanding are interpretations of the Holy Scriptures that stand on an equal footing and wrestle with each other for the truth.[19]

18. "Es gibt eine Vielzahl von rabbinischen Texten, die mehr oder weniger deutlich als im Dialog mit christlichen Traditionen verstanden werden können . . . So wie christliche Bibelauslegung schon sehr früh auch rabbinische Traditionen aufgenommen hat . . . , ist auch die jüdische Auslegung der heiligen Schriften nicht völlig isoliert zu sehen, sondern bezeugt immer wieder den Dialog mit dem Christentum."—Stemberger, "Hermeneutik" (see note 17), 119.

19. This is also the view of the document prepared by the Pontifical Biblical Commission: "The Jewish People and their Sacred Scriptures in the Christian Bible" from the year 2001—https://www.vatican.va/roman_curia/congregations/cfaith/pcb_documents/rc_con_cfaith_doc_20020212_popolo-ebraico_en.html (accessed April 11, 2025). It states "that the Jewish reading of the Bible is a possible one, in continuity with the Jewish Sacred Scriptures from the Second Temple period, a reading analogous to the Christian reading which developed in parallel fashion. Both readings are bound up with the vision of their respective faiths, of which the readings are the result and expression. Consequently, both are irreducible. On the practical level of exegesis, Christians can, nonetheless, learn much from Jewish exegesis practiced for more than two thousand years, and, in fact, they have learned much in the course of history. For their part, it is to be hoped that Jews themselves can derive profit from Christian exegetical research" (No. 22). Dohmen appreciates the document from the Biblical Commission but sees the danger that it loses sight of the "notion of asymmetry" ("Asymmetriegedanken")—Dohmen and Stemberger, *Hermeneutik* (see note 2), 202. To me, by contrast, the document seems to get it right when it superordinates or subordinates neither the Christian understanding of the Scriptures to the Jewish understanding, nor the Jewish to the Christian. It would probably also benefit the Christian–Jewish dialogue if they met each other as equals. The model of the "double way of reading" that Dohmen developed has the advantage of protecting the Old Testament against Christological appropriation. But one may not overlook the fact that for Christians there cannot be any "pre-Jesus" way of reading. The demand that the Old Testament be read "purely and without admixture" ("rein und unvermischt") which Dohmen makes with an allusion to the Creed of Chalcedon (p. 220), must be supplemented by the phrase "without separation and undivided." And that is exactly the position expressed by Messianic Judaism.

3. Transformations and transitions

The *hermeneutic of canonical discourse* can be realized in the context of two different reading models that do not contradict each other but rather complement each other. Using an image, this can be expressed in the model of a stream and in the model of a cathedral. The stream model is oriented toward the reading flow and toward narrated history, the cathedral model toward the building that emerged through the history of its building, toward the completed form, in which all the parts are constitutive for the structure of the whole.

Applying the stream model to the Bible, one can say: The stream flows with varying speeds, sometimes it becomes broader, sometimes narrower and deeper; there are rapids and cataracts, but it is ultimately the same stream that comes from a single source. From a Christian point of view, this applies to both the Old Testament and the New Testament. With the New Testament, no new stream begins, but the stream that comes out of the depths of history takes on a very specific course in the New Testament, while remaining the same stream, into which, as it were, all that precedes flows together. Expressed in terms of the reading model, the New Testament tells the story (of the revelation of God) to the end.

With the aid of this model, I would like to show, using three selected themes, that the changes that begin with the New Testament are not principally different in kind from those that the stream experienced in its Old Testament course. In other words, the religious symbol system attested in Holy Scripture has undergone far-reaching changes in the course of its history. They do not apply only to the transition from Old to New Testament but rather run throughout the whole history of biblically attested faith.

3.1. Kingship and state

Beginning with the Davidic kingdom and the (so-called) Divided Kingdom that soon followed it, the faith of Israel was basically a kind of state religion. Religion and state were very closely bound to each other both in the northern kingdom of Israel and in the southern kingdom of Judah. The sanctuaries in Bethel and Jerusalem were state sanctuaries. This symbiosis of state and religion broke down in 722 for the northern kingdom and in 586 for the southern kingdom. Except for a short episode during the Maccabean era, it was not taken up again in the history of Judaism. Modern Zionism with the founding of the State of Israel represents a special case, which I do not wish to discuss further now. What is important to me here is the following: The theology of kingship bound up with the symbiosis of state and religion underwent a far-reaching revision after the downfall of the state. This process was prepared for by the pre-exilic prophets of judgment, especially Jeremiah. In this respect, Israel differed fundamentally from its neighboring peoples, who were much more powerful politically. In those cases, the existing close connection between state and religion led to the downfall of religion with the downfall of states. The development in Israel (Judah) took a different course. To put it concisely: the state collapsed; the religion survived. From the kingship theology in the pre-exilic era, the Messiah idea emerged in the postexilic era, the theology of a messianic kingship. Within the Old Testament, a constructive dialogue developed between kingship theology that went in the direction of a theology of the messianic kingship, and a theology of the kingship of God. In recent scholarship on the Psalms, these two directions are usually connected with two successive redactional phases of the Psalter, the messianic psalter (Psalms 2–72) and the theocratic psalter (Psalms 2–100, or Psalms 1–150). Erich Zenger speaks of a messianic and a theocratic horizon of the book of psalms.[20] The *messianic* perspective is marked above all by the macro-structurally intentional positioning of Psalm 2 (the beginning of the first book of Psalms), 72 (the end of the second book of Psalms), 89 (the end of the third book of Psalms) 101 (the beginning of the Davidic compositions after the YHWH-Kingship-Composition, Psalms 93–100), 110 (the end of the small Davidic composition, Psalms 108–110), and 144 (the end of the small Davidic composition, Psalms 138–144); to these can be added the royal psalms 122, 127, 132, which revolve around the promise to David. The king-theological line of the Psalter is interwoven with a *theocratic* perspective, which especially includes Psalms 8, 19, 29, 45–48, 93–100, and 145. This process of transformation and dialogue already starts in the Old Testament's history of emergence. In light of new historical events, it is updated and expanded in the New Testament. *A hermeneutic of canonical discourse now says* that themes that have arisen in tension

20. Cf. Erich Zenger, "Das Buch der Psalmen," in *Einleitung* (see note 14), 431–55, at 437.

with one another, and stand in tension with one another in the form of the canon are not to be played off against one another but rather are to be set into relation with one another in the framework of a theological reflection. If one wishes to describe the separation of Judaism and Christianity in a very simplified way against this background, then one could say that the Christians place themselves more strongly in the tradition of the messianic psalter ("Jesus is the Messiah, the Anointed of God, the King of Israel") and the Jews more strongly in the tradition of the theocratic psalter ("YHWH is King").

3.2. Sanctuary and sacrifice

The religion that is attested in the Old Testament belonged to the widespread sacrifice religions of antiquity for a good thousand years. Sacrifices were made at the temple in Jerusalem. The book of Leviticus with its many prescriptions for sacrifice and priestly laws is in the middle of the Torah. The ritual of the great day of atonement is found at the center of the book of Leviticus (Lev 16–17). After a caesura of about seventy years, the temple in Jerusalem was rebuilt after the end of exile, and the sacrificial service was started up again. Despite a critique of the sacrificial cult that appeared time and again primarily in prophetic circles, Judaism was a religion in which the sacrificial cult played a central role. The late post-exilic book of the prophet Malachi endeavors to provide a theological deepened understanding of sacrifice. With the destruction of the second temple in 70 AD, this tradition ended definitively. Once again, a far-reaching transformational process took place. In place of (animal) offerings in the temple, came the "sacrifice of the lips." The theology of sacrifice and cult, which was deeply anchored in the history of religion and literary history of Israel, had to be fundamentally reconceived; it found a place in the synagogue liturgy in modified form. The New Testament also stands squarely in the tradition of a fundamental reconfiguration of the Old Testament sacrificial cult, in particular the book of Hebrews and yet also the narratives of the cleansing of the temple and the interpretation of the death of Jesus in the Gospels, as well as the soteriology of the Pauline letters. Thus, here too we encounter a far-reaching transformation, both within post-biblical Jewish literature and in the New Testament. Both traditions participate in the religious mutations of late antiquity, as the religious studies scholar Guy G.

Stroumsa has described them.[21] Except for small splinter groups, there are, to my knowledge, no more efforts in Judaism to rebuild the temple and to resume the sacrificial cult—a clear difference, for example, from the taking up again of the project "Jewish State" in modern Zionism.

3.3. Land promise and homecoming

A highly sensitive and controversial theme in today's Jewish–Christian dialogue is the promise of the land. That the land promise has played a significant role in the history of Judaism should be beyond dispute.[22] After the exile there have always been groups who returned to the land. It is, however, theologically significant that the Torah does not end with the entrance of Israel into the land of promise but abruptly breaks off with the death of Moses. YHWH showed Moses the whole land, but he was not allowed to set foot in it (Deut 34:1–9).

Right before his death, Tobit sees in a vision a time when Jerusalem will be rebuilt "from sapphire and emerald, its walls from precious stones, its towers and battlements from pure gold" (Tobit 13:17). For Tobit, the time of the exile is no longer only the time when Israel was disciplined by the Lord for all its sins (Tobit 13:5) but also the time when Israel bears witness to the true God "before all peoples" in "the land of exile" (Tobit 13:3, 6). The prospect of a still future taking possession of the land, in the sense of a gathering and return of Israel, shapes the theology of the land, as it is to be understood on the basis of the final form of the Pentateuch. There may once have been an original literary connection ("Hexateuch") between the (older) promise of a (first-time) taking possession of the land, as it was promised to the patriarchs in the book of Genesis, and the narratives of the (first-time) fulfillment of this promise in the book of Joshua. It is theologically significant, however, that this literary unity was broken through the redaction of the Pentateuch. The Jewish order of readings from the Torah ends in the book of Deuteronomy with the viewing of the land of the promise (Deut

21. Cf. Guy G. Stroumsa, *Das Ende des Opferkultes. Die religiösen Mutationen der Spätantike* (Berlin: Verlag der Weltreligionen, 2nd edn 2012).

22. On this point and the following, cf. Ludger Schwienhorst-Schönberger, "Land," in *Wörterbuch alttestamentlicher Motive*, ed. Michael Fieger, Jutta Krispenz, and Jörg Lanckau (Darmstadt: wbg Academic, 2013): 299–305.

34:1–4) and then begins again with the creation narrative in the book of Genesis. The gift of the land is thus pushed into a still outstanding future in the "founding myth" of Israel. The taking of the land that occurred under Joshua did not last. The actual and enduring taking possession of the land by Israel is still outstanding (see also Amos 9:15; Jer 31:40; Ezek 37:25). With this, the Torah is directly oriented to the gathering of Israel and the return to the promised land (see also 2 Chron 36:22 ff.). This is viewed as an event that is set in motion by God, in which Israel will use no violence. The third beatitude from the Sermon on the Mount falls along the line of this understanding: "Blessed are those who use no violence, for they will inherit the land" (Matt 5:5).

In this context, the question of what is meant by "land" here and in some other texts that speak of the return and gathering of Israel is open. Is a concrete land in view, as is clearly the case in the older texts, or can tendencies toward a shift in meaning in the direction of the metaphorical—similarly to what we find with "sacrifice" and "king"—be discerned in the late land promise texts? Frank-Lothar Hossfeld was able to show that a process of metaphorizing the land had already started in the Psalter (Psalms 16, 73, 142) and in early Jewish literature.[23] This process is intensified in the Christian tradition (cf. Heb 4:1–11; 6:13–20; 11:8–10). Not the land, but the closeness to God takes precedence here (see also Ezek 11:16). Cornelis J. de Vos has written a comprehensive monograph on the subject.[24] He writes: "The land is frequently replaced by the other, newly conceptualized 'spaces' in which this very closeness to God can occur, without it being necessary for one to be in the land or in the temple."[25] Joseph Ratzinger / Benedict XVI expressed himself in this vein in his article titled, "Grace and Calling Without Remorse:

23. Frank-Lothar Hossfeld, "Die Metaphorisierung der Beziehung Israels zum Land im Frühjudentum und im Christentum," in *Zion. Ort der Begegnung*, FS Laurentius Klein, ed. Ferdinand Hahn et al. (Bodenheim: Athenäum Hain Hanstein, 1993): 19–33.

24. Cornelis J. de Vos, *Heiliges Land und Nähe Gottes. Wandlungen alttestamentlicher Landvorstellungen in frühjüdischen und neutestamentlichen Schriften* (Göttingen: Vandenhoeck & Ruprecht, 2012).

25. "Das Land wird des Öfteren durch andere, neu konzipierte 'Räume' ersetzt, in denen sich eben diese Gottesnähe ereignen kann, ohne dass der Mensch im Land oder Tempel sein muss."—Cornelis J. de Vos, "Die Bedeutung des Landes Israel in den jüdischen Schriften der hellenistisch-römischen Zeit," *Jahrbuch für biblische Theologie* 23 (2008): 75–99, at 98.

Comments on the Treatise *De Iudaeis*." As the destruction of the Second Temple was viewed as final within Judaism, so Christian faith has given a new meaning to the Old Testament land promise. According to this, so the emeritus pope, "a theologically-understood acquisition of land in the sense of a new political messianism was unacceptable" for the Catholic Church.[26] The Church's position that the Jewish people like every other people has a claim to their own land in terms of natural law remains untouched thereby. This and other positions advocated in the article have provoked a lively discussion, in which some of the colleagues involved in this symposium have participated.

The following alternatives thus present themselves for discussion: (1) With the return of Jews to the land beginning in the twentieth century and the accompanying emergence of the State of Israel, the promise with which the Torah ends realizes itself in history. The return of Jews into the land would then be assigned a genuine theological meaning. (2) Like other institutions (state, kingship, temple, or sacrificial cult), the land promise is after the exile no longer to be understood in a historical-concrete but rather in a spiritual-metaphorical sense (land as place of God's presence). This understanding is found already in Hellenistic Judaism (Philo) and is theologically normative in Christianity. This means that the process of (final) redemption is no longer to be connected to the return of Israel (and/or of a Messianic Judaism that believes in Jesus as the Messiah). The return of Jews and the emergence of the State of Israel in the twentieth century is assigned no genuine theological meaning, even if they are to be appreciated and recognized in terms of natural law as an expression of divine blessing (Pope Benedict XVI). If I see it correctly, this is a controversial theme in the diverse spectrum of Messianic Judaism. Between the two positions sketched above, there are intermediary forms which, however, cannot be discussed further here. In closing, it should be remembered that a distinction must be made between the return to the land of promise and the establishment of a state.

26. Joseph Ratzinger / Benedict XVI, "Gnade und Berufung ohne Reue. Anmerkungen zum Traktat 'De Iudaeis,'" *Communio: Internationale Katholische Zeitschrift* 47 (2018): 387–406, at 401; cf. Joseph Ratzinger / Benedict XVI, "Grace and Vocation Without Remorse: Comments on the Treatise *De Iudaeis*," *Communio: International Catholic Review* 45 (2018): 163–84, at 178.

4. "Un-Jewishness" in the message of Jesus? On Joseph Klausner's interpretation of Jesus

In my view, dialogue between Messianic Jews and Christian theologians depends on taking to heart two fundamental principles of Catholic biblical hermeneutics: (1) the unity of Scripture consisting of the Old and New Testaments; and closely connected with this: (2) the inspiration of Holy Scripture, namely—and this is very important!—of all of its parts, both of the Old and of the New Testament.

With some theologians, one comes away with the impression that they have replaced the first article of the Apostolic Creed with the teaching of Marcion, when they formulate their creed in the words: "I believe in the God of Love." But the Apostolic Creed does not begin with the statement, "I believe in the God of Love" but with: "I believe in God, the Father, the Almighty, the Creator of Heaven and Earth." And with this we are referred to the beginning of the Bible, to Genesis 1:1. Origen already pointed out that one must begin with the Old Testament in the Christian instruction in the faith. To understand the becoming human of the divine Word, one must first get to know the becoming Scripture of the divine Word, as it is told and attested in the first part of the Bible.

Ignoring this principle leads to a decontextualized Christology. It is not difficult to see why such an approach is rejected by Judaism. It should also be rejected by Christian theology. In the last section of my presentation, I would like to elucidate these thoughts with reference to the Jesus book of the great Jewish scholar Joseph Klausner. In my view, his work *Jesus of Nazareth: His Time, His Life and His Teaching*, which was originally published in Hebrew in Jerusalem in the year 1922, belongs among the most important engagements with Jesus and his teaching from the perspective of a Jewish scholar.[27] Joseph Klausner (1874–1958) came from Lithuania, grew up in Odessa, and studied in Heidelberg with Max Weber, among others. He was a passionate cultural Zionist and emigrated in 1919 to Palestine, where he obtained a position first as Professor of Jewish Literature and later as Professor of the Second Temple Period at Hebrew University, which he had helped to found. The

27. The quotations that follow, with page numbers in parentheses, are cited according to Joseph Klausner, *Jesus of Nazareth: His Life, Times, and Teaching* (trans. H. Danby; New York: Macmillan, 1925).

writer Amos Oz impressively memorialized his great uncle in his novel *Judas*. The critical reaction from both the Jewish and the Christian sides toward Klausner's book remind one of similar reactions to the concerns of Messianic Jews. In one address, held on May 25, 2017 in Berlin, Amos Oz described the reaction to his great uncle's book:

> The Jews reproached Joseph Klausner for dealing with Jesus at all again—after all the evil that has been done to the Jewish people in the name of Jesus. But many Christians were also incensed. They were so upset that they insisted that the English Anglican priest Herbert Danby (1889–1953)—the English missionary who had translated Joseph Klausner's book into English—be fired; for Klausner portrays the Savior as a nonconformist, rebellious Jewish rabbi. But uncle Joseph smiled under his moustache and said to himself: "If Jews and Christians are equally unsatisfied, I probably did everything right."[28]

Klausner wanted to show that Jesus was a Jew and remained so "until his last breath" (368), but that at the same time there were good reasons why the Jewish people rejected his teaching. Had the Jewish people accepted his teaching, it would have destroyed itself and thereby missed its mission in the world, according to Klausner.

My thesis is that Klausner's critique of the teaching of Jesus is justified when that teaching is separated from the Old Testament. Since this separation has often taken place in the history of Christianity and even persists today—despite all assertions to the contrary—Klausner's critique has lost none of its relevance. I can imagine that this might even be one of the reasons for the new edition of the book.[29] Here a theological clarification is necessary. If I understand the concerns of Messianic

28. "Die Juden warfen Joseph Klausner vor, dass er sich überhaupt wieder mit Jesus befasste – nach all dem Bösen, das den Juden im Namen Jesu zugefügt worden war. Aber auch viele Christen waren aufgebracht. So aufgebracht, dass sie darauf bestanden, den anglikanischen Priester Herbert Danby (1889–1953) – den englischen Missionar, der Joseph Klausners Bücher ins Englische übersetzt hatte – zu entlassen; denn Klausner zeichnet den Erlöser als nonkonformistischen, rebellischen jüdischen Rabbi. Onkel Joseph aber lächelte unter seinem Schnurbart und sagte sich: 'Wenn Juden und Christen gleichermaßen unzufrieden sind, habe ich wahrscheinlich alles richtig gemacht.'"—Amos Oz, *Jesus und Judas. Ein Zwischenruf*, German trans. Susanne Naumann; afterword by Rabbi Walter Homolka (Ostfildern: Patmos Verlag, 2022; cited according to: https://shop.verlagsgruppe-patmos.de/media/pdf/978-3-8436-1051-3.pdf, accessed June 5, 2022).

29. The German translation of the third, revised edition from 1952 (Jerusalem: The Jewish Publishing House Ltd. / Berlin: Jüdischer Verlag GmbH.) was reissued in 2021 with an afterword by the Jewish studies scholar Christian Wiese.

Jews correctly, then it has to do with placing Jesus' life and teaching (once again) in the overall matrix of Jewish tradition, as it is attested through the "Holy Scriptures" in Jesus' lifetime, and understanding it from that perspective. When that happens, so I would like to submit for discussion in what follows, the objections that Klausner raises against Jesus and his teaching in a very understandable way, largely disappear.

Klausner's decisive accusation against Jesus' teaching is that it breaks up the sociopolitical unity of the Jewish religion through its pointed statements and one-sided emphases, making it into a religion for a few chosen ones and thereby depriving the religion of its ability to place all of concrete daily life under the governance of God. The problematic development, which Christianity adopted, is connected to the fact that the seeds of the dissolution of Jewishness were based already in the person and teaching of Jesus. Therefore, Christianity cannot escape the dark side of its history by converting to Jesus and his teaching, as is often said in Christian circles, since the seeds of the dissolution of Jewish life are already based in Jesus, in his person and message:

> Ex nihilo nihil fit [Nothing comes from nothing]: had not Jesus' teaching contained a kernel of opposition to Judaism, Paul could never *in the name of Jesus* have set aside the ceremonial laws, and broken through the barriers of national Judaism. There can be no doubt that in Jesus Paul found justifying support. (369)

According to Klausner, the unique element of Jesus' message consists in the fact that while basically everything that he taught can be found in the Jewish tradition, he presented it so pointedly and provocatively and bound to his person and in doing so entirely blended out other, fundamental aspects of the religious and societal life, so that the Jewish people had to reject his teaching if it did not want to be unfaithful to itself and its calling. Klausner elucidates this with reference to the moral law and the ceremonial law. Especially in the Sermon on the Mount, Jesus emphasizes the moral law over and against the ceremonial law so strongly that one could get the impression that he would almost abolish the ceremonial laws.

> But only "almost": Jesus never carried his teaching to its final conclusion. He himself observed the ceremonial laws (though not with the

---

See Joseph Klausner, *Jesus von Nazareth. Seine Zeit und seine Lehre* (Christian Wiese, ed.; Berlin: Suhrkamp Verlag / Jüdischer Verlag, 2021).

> scrupulousness and pedantry of the Pharisees) till the last night of his life. Such a conclusion—the abolition of the ceremonial laws and the consequent opening of the doors to the uncircumcised gentiles—it was left for another, a Pharisee also, to reach—namely, Saul of Tarsus after he was become Paul the Apostle. But had not Jesus lent some support towards this negative attitude to the ceremonial law and to the body of traditional belief transmitted, generation by generation, from Moses to the Pharisees, Paul would never have supported himself on Jesus in his efforts to overcome the "Christian-Judaism" founded by Simon Peter and James the brother of the Lord. (371)

Klausner continues:

> But Judaism could not agree with such an attitude. For the Jews their religion was more than simple belief and more than simple moral guidance: it was *a way of life*—all life was embraced in their religion. A people does not endure on a foundation of general human faith and morality; it needs a "practical religiousness," a ceremonial form of religion which shall embody religious ideas and also crown every-day life with a halo of sanctity. Jesus did not give any new ceremonial law to replace the old (except, perhaps, the brief form of prayer, "Our Father, which art in heaven . . ."), and so he taught no new national ways of life in spite of abolishing, or hinting at the abolition of the old ways. By this very fact he raised the nation out of its national confines: for is there not but one moral law for all nations alike? (371)

In other words, Jesus advocated a teaching that, in its conception, destroys Judaism as a way of life, and thereby leaves behind a void that nascent Christianity filled in with questionable borrowings from paganism as a stopgap. The fact that Judaism in its main streams resisted this process was correct and was the guarantee that it would not sink in the sea of the world of nations.

Klausner now adduces a series of examples from the Gospels to support this thesis. Jesus had relativized fundamental institutions of the Jewish people, such as Sabbath, family, civil justice, ownership, and much more in such a way that this was rightly perceived as a dangerous development by the leading representatives of Judaism. Curiously, Klausner views Jesus' exaggerated Jewishness as the reason for this:

> In all this, Jesus is the most Jewish of Jews, more Jewish than Simeon ben Shetah, more Jewish even than Hillel. Yet nothing is more dangerous to national Judaism than this exaggerated Judaism; it is the ruin of national culture, the national state, and national life. Where there is no call for the enactment of laws, for justice, for national statecraft, where belief in God and the practice of an extreme and one-sided ethic is in

> itself enough—there we have the negation of national life and of the national state. (374)

Basically, according to Klausner, Jesus was a religious enthusiast. The fascination of his personality consisted in the distinctive joining and juxtaposition of great meekness and mercy on the one side, and utmost strictness and sharpness in rebuke on the other side (410). Extremes of this kind in a personality in connection with an extraordinary self-consciousness and a deeply felt connection to God often arouse "astonishment, enthusiasm, and admiration" (408), especially among simple people. This is how it was with Jesus. According to Klausner,

> it is unquestionable that throughout his entire teaching there is nothing that can serve to the upkeep of the state or serve toward the maintenance of order in the existing world . . . Hence, the nation as a whole could only see in such public ideals as those of Jesus, an abnormal and even dangerous phantasy; the majority. . . . could *on no account* accept Jesus' teaching. This teaching Jesus had imbibed from the breast of Prophetic and, to a certain extent, Pharisaic Judaism; yet it became, on the one hand, the negation of everything that had vitalized Judaism; and, on the other hand, it brought Judaism to such an extreme that it became, in a sense, *non-Judaism*. (376)

In the final chapter of his book, Klausner asks, "What is Jesus for the Jews?" (413–14). For the Jewish people, Jesus is *"a great teacher of morality and an artist in parable.* He is *the* moralist for whom, in the religious life, morality counts as—everything" (414). But it is "no ethical code for the nations and the social order of today" (414). Thus "there was in him something out of which arose 'non-Judaism'" (413).

In conclusion, Klausner's major book about Jesus of Nazareth starts from the famous statement of Julius Wellhausen: "Jesus was not a Christian: he was a Jew" (413). Klausner modifies this sentence, by writing: "Jesus was not a Christian, but he *became* a Christian. His teaching and his history have been severed from Israel. To this day the Jews have never accepted him, while his disciples and followers of every generation have scoffed at and persecuted the Jews and Judaism" (413).

5. Joseph Ratzinger and Jacob Neusner: On the relevance of Klausner's critique of Jesus and his message

Klausner's criticism of Jesus' teaching has lost none of its relevance. It is justified if one separates Jesus' life and message from the writings of the

Old Testament. Only in connection with them and in an interpretation that knows itself to be obligated to the *hermeneutic of canonical discourse* does the message from and about Jesus of Nazareth make sense—to put it more precisely, that particular sense that the Church has recognized as the true and binding meaning for its teaching. The dialogue with Messianic Jews can remind Christian theology to revive these insights in order to avoid falling into the trap of a decontextualized Christology. That this danger continues to be present will be illustrated with reference to two recent examples.

If there is an image of Jesus that Joseph Ratzinger decisively rejects, then it is that of the religious and political revolutionary. Such an image is, however, widespread, even in theological circles. The radical message of the Nazarene has challenged established religious and political orders in the sharpest possible way. The Church—thus a common allegation—has tamed the Galilean and made him bourgeois. Joseph Klausner exposed this nerve when he charged that Jesus' message carries the seed for the destruction of Jewish life. Precisely this charge was taken up again about eighty years later by the rabbi Jacob Neusner. Had he been present two thousand years ago, he would not have followed Jesus. According to Neusner, the Sermon on the Mount is one-sided and neglects a crucial dimension of human life:

> And that counsel on prayer stands for much more in this torah for the inner life. In fact, the power of the Sermon on the Mount, so far as I can comprehend it, governs one dimension of my existence: the individual. Two other dimensions of human existence—community and family—are sadly omitted. In their natural order, first comes the family, then the village—and only then does the individual find his or her position in the scheme of things. But the first two dimensions of life I thought neglected by the torah I heard from the mountaintop.[30]

According to Neusner, Jesus' message dissolves the natural bonds of the family and destroys the proven social forms of life that are essential for the existence of the people of God:

> And yet, if I do what he says, I abandon my father and my mother, my brothers and sisters, my wife and my children. Then what is to be of Israel? For if all of us do what he wants, then the family disintegrates, the home collapses, and what holds the village and the land together,

30. Jacob Neusner, *A Rabbi Talks with Jesus* (Montreal and Kingston: McGill-Queen's University Press, rev. edn 2000 [1993]): 55.

> the body of the family, gives way. To follow him, do I have to violate one of the Ten Commandments?[31]

As radical movements in the history of Christianity up until the present-day show, this charge is not plucked out of the air. It is little wonder that Joseph Ratzinger / Benedict XVI sees it as necessary to deal with it in his Jesus trilogy. It is clear to him that the objections from the Jewish side cannot be disarmed with an emphatic rhetorical reference to the radicalism of Jesus' message. It is understandable therefore that he gives considerable room to the discussion with Rabbi Neusner in his Jesus book. He takes the objections of the Jewish rabbi very seriously:

> More than any other interpretations known to me, this respectful and frank dispute between a believing Jew and Jesus, the son of Abraham, has opened my eyes to the greatness of Jesus' words and to the choice that the gospel places before us. In the second section, then, I would like as a Christian to join in the rabbi's conversation with Jesus, so as to be guided toward a better understanding of the authentic Jewishness and the mystery of Jesus.[32]

The decisive reason why Neusner does not wish to follow Jesus but rather to remain "with eternal Israel" is the "I" that Jesus attaches to his message: "Because I really believe there is a difference between 'You shall be holy, for I the Lord your God am holy' and 'If you would be perfect, go, sell all you have and come, follow me.'"[33] According to Joseph Ratzinger / Benedict XVI, Jacob Neusner saw very clearly that the all-deciding difference lies here. Jesus was not the liberal rabbi who, according to a widespread view,

> broke open a narrow-minded, legalistic practice and replaced it with a more generous, more liberal view, and thereby opened the door for acting rationally in accord with the given situation. Jesus' statement that "the sabbath was made for man, not man for the sabbath" (Mark 2:27) is cited as evidence, the idea being that it represents an anthropocentric view of reality, from which a "liberal" interpretation of the commandments supposedly follows naturally. It was, in fact, the Sabbath disputes

31. *Ibid.*, 58.

32. Joseph Ratzinger / Benedict XVI, *Jesus of Nazareth: From the Baptism in the Jordan to the Transfiguration*, trans. A.J. Walker (New York: Doubleday, 2007): 69–70. For the German original, see Joseph Ratzinger / Benedict XVI, *Jesus von Nazareth. Erster Teil: Von der Taufe im Jordan bis zur Verklärung* (Freiburg i. Br.: Herder, 2007): 99.

33. Neusner, *A Rabbi Talks with Jesus* (see note 30), 114.

> that became the basis for the image of the liberal Jesus. His critique of the Judaism of his time, so it is said, was a freedom-loving and rational man's critique of an ossified legalism—hypocritical to the core and guilty of dragging religion down to the level of a slavish system of utterly unreasonable obligations that hold man back from developing his work and his freedom. It goes without saying that this interpretation did not favor a particularly friendly image of Judaism. Of course, the modern critique—beginning with the Reformation—saw in Catholicism the return of this supposedly "Jewish" element.[34]

Against the background of Neusner's criticism, Ratzinger poses the self-critical question: "Was it a good idea to jeopardize the great social function of the Sabbath, to break up Israel's sacred order for the sake of a community of disciples that is defined, as it were, solely in terms of the figure of Jesus?"[35] According to Ratzinger, the justification lies solely in the person of Jesus, who speaks not for himself but from God because he is the Christ, the Son of the living God (Matt 16:16). As far as the social function of the sabbath is concerned, Ratzinger shows that in the history of the Church, Jesus' critique of sabbath commandment has not served to destroy its social content. Rather, this has been placed in a new light through Jesus' death and resurrection and passed over to the first day of the week:

> The Church thus recuperated the social function of the Sabbath as well, always in relation to the "Son of Man." An unmistakable signal of this was the fact that Constantine's Christian-inspired reform of the legal system granted slaves certain freedoms on Sundays; the Lord's day was thus introduced as a day of freedom and rest into a legal system now shaped on Christian principles. I find it extremely worrying that modern liturgists want to dismiss this social function of Sunday as a Constantinian aberration, despite the fact that it stands in continuity with the Torah of Israel.[36]

As with the case of the sabbath commandment, Joseph Ratzinger / Benedict XVI extensively discusses the Decalogue's commandment to honor father and mother, its interpretation by Jesus, and Neusner's criticism. This will not be presented in further detail at this point. The

34. Ratzinger / Benedict XVI, *Jesus of Nazareth* (see note 32), 106–107 (German, 138).

35. *Ibid.*, 112 (German, 144).

36. *Ibid.*, 112 (German, 144–45).

leading hermeneutic here is "the proper interplay of Old and New Testaments."[37] Israel's faith and hope are not cast aside but rather universalized. In this move a dynamic is picked up that has a basis in the Scriptures of Israel. It is

> tied to Jesus' authority and his claim to Sonship. [This means that] It loses its historical weight and its whole foundation if Jesus is interpreted merely as a liberal reform rabbi. A liberal interpretation of the Torah would be nothing but the personal opinion of one teacher—it would have no power to shape history. It would also relativize both the Torah itself and its origin in God's will. For each statement there would be only human authority: the authority of one scholar. There can be no new faith community built upon that. The leap into universality, the new freedom that such a leap requires, is possible only on the basis of a greater obedience. Its power to shape history can come into play only if the authority of the new interpretation is no less than the authority of the original: It must be a divine authority.[38]

The biblical hermeneutic that is presupposed here is just as constitutive for the Church as it is for the self-understanding of Messianic Judaism. Jesus as God's Messiah did not discard the Torah but fulfilled it:

> Jesus stands before us neither as rebel nor as liberal, but as the prophetic interpreter of the Torah. He does not abolish it, but he fulfills it, and he does so precisely by assigning reason its sphere of responsibility for acting within history. Consequently, Christianity constantly has to reshape and reformulate social structures and "Christian social teaching." There will always be new developments to correct what has gone before. In the inner structure of the Torah, in its further development under the critique of the Prophets, and in Jesus' message, which takes up both elements, Christianity finds the wide scope for necessary historical evolution as well as the solid ground that guarantees the dignity of man by rooting it in the dignity of God.[39]

6. *Christologically mediated unity of Old and New Testament*

It is worth touching briefly on a recent relevant discussion where the principle of canonical discourse played a key role. If one separates the New Testament from the Old Testament, then the Catholic office

37. *Ibid.*, 121 (German, 154).
38. *Ibid.*, 119–20 (German, 152).
39. *Ibid.*, 126–27 (German, 160).

of priest would not have any biblical foundation. This is the position advanced by New Testament scholar Martin Ebner in his work *Does the Catholic Church Need Priests? A Reassurance from the New Testament,* in which he enters into a debate in current Church politics. He aims to provide "material for argumentation—namely, from the founding documents of our Christian faith, which were put together in the New Testament as canon"—for those who, in the current discussion of the Church in Germany, advocate the position that the office of priest is superfluous.[40] To this, Old Testament scholar Dieter Böhler offered the following succinct remark:

> The New Testament is not a canon, but at best a canon fragment. . . . Detached from Torah and the prophets, a New Testament possesses no canonical authority at all. "A reassurance from the New Testament alone" is not yet biblical, for the Bible is much more. Even into the 1980s, a dominant tendency in both Catholic and Protestant theology was to let the New Testament and the newness of Christianity shine out brightly by setting it against a background of the Old Testament and Judaism that was painted as black as possible.[41]

Böhler refutes Ebner's position in detail and reaches the conclusion:

> Jesus remains, in the conception of the Book of Hebrews, the sole priest of the Church. But the fact that the triple office of the bishops, presbyters, and deacons is formed as a presentation of Jesus' priesthood "according to the order of Melchizedek" in analogy to the biblical priesthood of Aaron is not surprising, let alone inappropriate, but rather simply biblical—that is, when "Bible" comprises the whole Bible.[42]

40. "Argumentationsstoff liefern, und zwar aus den Urdokumenten unseres christlichen Glaubens heraus, die im Neuen Testament als Kanon zusammengestellt wurden."—Martin Ebner, *Braucht die katholische Kirche Priester? Eine Vergewisserung aus dem Neuen Testament* (Würzburg: Echter, 2022): 12.

41. "Das Neue Testament ist kein Kanon, sondern allenfalls ein Kanonfragment. . . . Abgelöst von Tora und Propheten besitzt ein Neues Testament keinerlei kanonische Autorität. 'Eine Vergewisserung aus dem Neuen Testament' allein ist noch nicht biblisch, denn die Bibel ist weit mehr. Es herrschte bis in die Achtzigerjahre in der katholischen und evangelischen Theologie eine starke Tendenz, das Neue Testament und das Neue des Christentums dadurch hell erstrahlen zu lassen, dass man es vor einen möglichst schwarz gemalten Hintergrund des Alten Testaments und des Judentums stellte."—Dieter Böhler, "Das kirchliche Amt ist biblisch. Zu Martin Ebners '*Braucht die Kirche Priester?*,'" *Herder Korrespondenz* (12/2022): 20–23, at 20.

42. "Jesus bleibt in der Konzeption des Hebräerbriefes der einzige Priester der Kirche. Doch dass das dreistufige Amt der Bischöfe, Presbyter und Diakone als

In a short commentary on the decree on the ministry and life of priests, *Presbyterorum Ordinis*, Joseph Ratzinger had already anticipated this debate some time ago. In doing so, he also put the finger in the wound of a separation of the New Testament from the Old, which has gained a foothold in some currents of New Testament exegesis and the theology that has been influenced by them:

> The very exegesis of the New Testament seemed to establish a non-sacral view of all ecclesial tasks, removing all continuity between the sacral functions of the Old Testament and the new ministries of the infant Church. Still less could any connection be discerned with pagan conceptions of the priesthood. The very novelty of Christianity appeared to consist precisely in the de-sacralization of ministries. The servants of the Christian community were not called *hiereis* (the Greek equivalent of the Latin *sacerdotes*) but *presbyteroi*—or "elders." Now although the Protestant origins of modern exegesis were essentially operative in this manner of interpreting the New Testament, nothing could change the evidence that appeared to justify the conclusion: on the contrary, the burning question at the time was whether Luther was right after all, and not the Council of Trent.[43]

Here too, as with the arch-heretic Marcion, the error lies in the separation of the New Testament from the Old: "The whole question of the relationship between the Old and New Testaments is at stake. Does the New Testament constitute what is essentially a break with the past or, rather, a fulfillment in which the old continues, but is completely transformed and, really, restored in the new?"[44] Ratzinger titles his last section "The Unity of Old and New Testaments in Christ." Here he not only rejects the thesis of a radical break between Old and New Testaments, but also the concept of a radical break between the Christian faith and religious history generally:

Darstellung von Jesu Priestertum 'nach der Ordnung des Melchisedek' in Analogie zum biblischen Priestertum Aarons ausgeformt wird, ist nicht verwunderlich oder gar verfehlt, sondern eben einfach biblisch – wenn denn 'Bibel' die ganze Bibel umfasst."—*Ibid.*, 23.

43. Joseph Ratzinger, "The Ministry and Life of Priests," in *Homiletic and Pastoral Review* (August/September 1997): 7–18, at 7–8. For the German version, see Joseph Ratzinger, "Dienst und Leben der Priester" (first published in 1996), in *Joseph Ratzinger Gesammelte Schriften*, vol. 7/2 – *Zur Lehre des Zweiten Vatikanischen Konzils: Formulierung – Vermittlung – Deutung* (Freiburg i. Br.: Herder, 2012): 897–915, at 898.

44. *Ibid.*, 17 (German, 913).

> We must therefore reject the view that the Church's worship and priesthood entails a clean break with the history of pre-Christian salvation, a view that consequently denies any continuity from the priesthood of the Old Testament to the priesthood of the New. For in this view, the New Testament would not be a fulfillment of the Old Covenant but would stand in opposition to it. This would effectively destroy the internal unity of the history of salvation. By means of the sacrifice of Christ and its acceptance in the Resurrection, the entire heritage of worship and priesthood of the Old Covenant is handed over to the Church. . . . Yes, the priesthood of the Church continues and renews the priesthood of the Old Testament, which finds its true fulfillment precisely in this radical and transforming newness. This position is important even for relations between Christianity and other world religions. Although Christianity is a new beginning—the greatest and most radically new reality that has come from God—it does not negate the efforts of other religions, in their Advent-like gestures toward the meaning of man's existence . . .[45]

The discussions presented here show that Messianic Judaism's concern to heal the breach has great theological relevance and urgency. At the same time, one must expect that when this justified concern is voiced, familiar discourse constellations—whether in Christian–Jewish dialogue, in the specification of the relationship of Old and New Testaments, or in the understanding of the person and message of Jesus—will be broken open and productive irritations will be set in motion.

(Translated by John David Martin, James Earle Patrick, and Wayne Coppins from the German: "Das Messianische Judentum und die Hermeneutik der kanonischen Dialogizität")

45. *Ibid.*, 17–18 (German, 914). The same problematic emerged again in connection with the discussion of the article, "Le sacerdote catholique" from Pope emeritus Benedict XVI, which was published in the book edited by Cardinal Robert Sarah, *Des profondeurs de nos coeurs* (Paris: Fayard, 2020). On this, see Ludger Schwienhorst-Schönberger, "Der verleugnete Tempel," *Herder Korrespondenz* (3/2020): 46–49.

Jesus, Messiah from Israel and for Israel

New Testament Perspectives

Michael Theobald

For the New Testament, from the first to the last book, one thing is clear: The confession of Jesus of Nazareth as *Messiah from Israel*. The genealogy of Jesus in Matthew 1:1–17—the entry portal not just to the first Gospel,[1] but to the whole New Testament—proclaims his descent from both Abraham and David and with this the fulfillment of God's promises of salvation for Israel and the nations, who receive a share in the "blessing" of Abraham through the Messiah Jesus.[2] The Revelation of John—capstone of the New Testament—praises Jesus as "the lion of the tribe of Judah and sprout from the root of David,"[3] who "conquered" in death and is the only one who can open the scroll in the hand of God (Rev 5:4–5; cf. 3:7): Through him, God will extend his kingdom over Israel and the nations, indeed over the whole of creation, defeating all powers and forces of this earth and making a "new heaven and a new earth," the heavenly Jerusalem, the perfect city.

1. Matt 1:1—"Book of the origin of Jesus Christ, the son of David, the son of Abraham" is the heading to the genealogy in 1:2–16, and at the same time to the prologue 1:2–4:16, and to the whole Gospel. See Matthias Konradt, *Das Evangelium nach Matthäus* (Das Neue Testament Deutsch, 1; Göttingen: Vandenhoeck & Ruprecht, 2015): 26.

2. Cf. Gal 3:1–29.

3. Cf. Gen 49:39 as well as Isa 11:1–10; additionally, *TestJud* 24:5; 4 Ezra 12:31–32; etc.

If Jesus is Messiah *from Israel*, as the New Testament unanimously confesses,[4] then he is and remains also Messiah *for Israel*. To the same degree in which the second half of this statement was already soon forgotten in the faith consciousness of the Church, the first half of the statement also faded in the same move and lost its power. To be sure, the Church was fighting against the constant temptation to tear Jesus from his rootedness in Israel, in a gnostic-dualistic manner as the heavenly redeemer. But in the process of confessing the incarnation of the Son of God, they largely forgot his Jewishness and called the conviction into question under the impression that great parts of his people had said "no" to the gospel. Even under these conditions, Jesus is and remains *Messiah for Israel*. It darkened its confession of Jesus' resurrection and exaltation to "Lord" of all the nations with the claim that God had allegedly turned away from his people and only still granted it a future in the form of the conversion of *individuals* to the new people of God. Since the days of patristic theology, the doctrine of the Church as the new people of God, even if this is denied to this day,[5] has carried with it the rejection of Israel as God's people as a dark shadow or has degraded the old people of God to a preparatory stage of the Church, which is said to have been superseded by this, as the Old Covenant allegedly was by the New. In its declaration *Nostra Aetate* 4, the Second Vatican Council corrected this centuries-long attitude in crucial points and set the course for overcoming the so-called "doctrine of substitution," but this declaration from the year 1965—this has become exceedingly clear after more than fifty years—was only a beginning, nothing less, but also nothing more.[6]

4. For the Gospels, cf. also Mark 10:48; 11:9–10; 12:35–37; Luke 2:10–11; 4:16–30; John 4:22, 25. For the Epistles, cf. Rom 1:3; 15:12; and 2 Tim 2:8, as well as Heb 7:14.

5. Michael Theobald, "Von der Karfreitagsfürbitte zur Revision der Formel vom 'nie gekündigten Bund.' Joseph Ratzinger's 'Anmerkungen zum Traktat *De Iudaeis*,'" in *Grenzen überschreiten – Verbindendes entdecken – Neues wagen (FS Hubert Frankemölle zum 80. Geburtstag)*, ed. Angelika Strotmann and Monika Schrader-Bewermeier (Stuttgarter Biblische Beiträge, 77; Stuttgart: Katholisches Bibelwerk, 2019): 254–68.

6. As already stated by the French Bishops' Committee for Relations with Jews in a statement on April 16, 1973: "The position taken by the Second Vatican Council should be considered a beginning rather than a final achievement." But it "breaks with the mentality of the past. It calls all Christians to a new vision of the Jewish people, not only on the level of human relations but also on that

If the Church is the *new* people of God, as *Nostra Aetate* and other Conciliar texts say it is,[7] what then is the status of the *present* Jewish people? While *Nostra Aetate* does explain that the Jews are not to be depicted as either "rejected" or "cursed," it avoids speaking of them as a *populus = people*.[8] This omission is problematic so long as the recognition of the enduring "people of God" status of Israel is not, along the track of Romans 11, expressly recognized,[9] which the Council texts are nowhere prepared to do. The texts contain in unconnected juxtaposition elements of an unconquered "theory of substitution" and of a new Israel theology, a sure sign that most of the Conciliar fathers were not yet conscious of the problem with its dramatic consequences for ecclesiology. On the question of the Messianic identity of Jesus, it is noteworthy that while *Nostra Aetate* states in connection with Romans 9:4–5 that "from them (i.e. the kindred of Paul) is the Christ according to the flesh,"

of faith."—Cited according to the translation at https://ccjr.us/dialogika-resources/documents-and-statements/roman-catholic/other-conferences-of-catholic-bishops/cefr1973 (accessed April 11, 2025). ["La prise de position conciliaire doit être considérée davantage comme un commencement que comme un aboutissement." / "... elle rompt avec l'attitude de tout un passé. Elle appelle désormais un nouveau regard des Chrétiens sur le peuple juif, non seulement dans l'ordre des rapports humains mais aussi dans l'ordre de la foi."]—Conférence épiscopale française, "L'attitude des chrétiens à l'égard du judaïsme. Orientations pastorales du Comité épiscopal pour les relations avec le judaïsme" (Documents Épiscopat; Bulletin de la Conférence épiscopale française, n. 10, April 1973): section 2. https://eglise.catholique.fr/wp-content/uploads/sites/2/2017/02/1973_Eglise-de-France-%E2%80%93-Orientations-pastorales.pdf (accessed April 11, 2025).

7. *Nostra Aetate [NA]* 4.6; *Lumen Gentium [LG]* 9.1 and elsewhere; *LG* 9.3 contrasts the "new Israel" with the Israel of the wilderness period, which is called "secundum carnem," "Dei ecclesia." The document does not speak of the *present* Jewish people as people of God.

8. The draft of *Nostra Aetate* from November 1964 still spoke of "the people of the Jews." In the final version, Johannes Oesterreicher—"Die viel kritisierte letzte Textfassung," in *Die Autorität der Freiheit*, Vol. 3 (Johann C. Hampe, ed.; Munich: Kösel, 1967): 498–512, at 500—admittedly sees only a linguistic "replacement . . . without theological significance" ["Auswechslung . . . ohne theologische Bedeutung"]. But this omission remains concerning. In contrast to the first draft from 1961 (in *Herders Theologischer Kommentar zum Zweiten Vatikanischen Konzil*, III, ed. Bernd Jochen Hilberath and Peter Hünermann [Freiburg i. Br.: Herder, 2009]: 637–38), the *post Christum* Jews are *nowhere* referred to as a "people" in the final text!

9. Roman Siebenrock over this: "All statements that sound like replacement are avoided" ["Alle Aussagen, die nach Substitution klingen, werden vermieden"]—in *Herders Theologischer Kommentar* (see note 8), 662.

that is, that Jesus is *Messiah from Israel*, the necessary New Testament counterpart—Jesus, *Messiah for Israel*—is not mentioned at all. Romans 11:11–32 is referenced in a footnote to a sentence that expresses the eschatological hope of the Church in the form of a contourless universalism without reference to Christology as follows: "In company with the Prophets and the same Apostle (i.e. Paul), the Church awaits that day, known to God alone, on which all peoples will address the Lord in a single voice and 'serve him shoulder to shoulder' (Zeph 3:9)." Against Paul, this sentence says nothing about Israel, which is subsumed here under "the peoples," and also nothing about its Messiah. For the sake of giving a proper account of history, however, it should be added that the rediscovery of Romans 9–11 for the new formulation of a Messianic Christology and ecclesiology still lay in the future in the 1960s and was alongside other influences first initiated by *Nostra Aetate*. Among the Conciliar generation who made enduring contributions, the Old Testament scholar Norbert Lohfink and the New Testament scholar Franz Mußner may be mentioned here.[10]

In what follows, I will elucidate the specific eschatological aspect of the theme—Jesus, *Messiah for Israel*—with reference to two corresponding New Testament conceptions, with reference to Paul and Luke. At the end, the relevance of future eschatology for an Israel theology will be considered.

1. "From Zion will come the Deliverer" (Rom 11:26)

Paul gave expression to the enduring significance of Jesus as Messiah for Israel in his last writing, in the Epistle to the Romans.[11] He does so

10. Norbert Lohfink, "Methodenprobleme zu einem christlichen 'Traktat über die Juden,'" in Norbert Lohfink, *Bibelauslegung im Wandel* (Frankfurt a. Main: Knecht, 1967): 214–37; Norbert Lohfink, "Gottesvolk. Alttestamentliches zu einem Zentralbegriff im konziliaren Wortfeuerwerk," in Norbert Lohfink, *Unsere großen Wörter. Das Alte Testament zu Themen dieser Jahre* (Freiburg i. Br.: Herder, 1977): 111–26; Franz Mußner, *Traktat über die Juden* (Göttingen: Vandenhoeck & Ruprecht, 2009—new edn with preface by M. Theobald).

11. For extensive remarks on the passages of Romans that are discussed in what follows (Rom 1:3–4; 15:7–13) see Michael Theobald, "'Dem Juden zuerst und auch dem Heiden.' Die paulinische Auslegung der Glaubensformel Röm 1,3f.," in Michael Theobald, *Studien zum Römerbrief* (Wissenschaftliche Untersuchungen zum Neuen Testament, 136; Tübingen: Mohr Siebeck, 2001): 102–18; Michael Theobald,

already in the prescript, 1:1–7, where he introduces himself together with the gospel to his addressees. And he does this a final time in the *peroratio* (15:7–13), which, at the end of the detailed theological elucidation of the gospel, expresses its content in a nutshell.[12] Both texts, which frame the work as a kind of *inclusio*, demonstrate the centrality of the confession of Jesus as Messiah. The high point of the "gospel letter"[13] are the Israel chapters 9–11.

(1) The core of the prescript, 1:1–7, is the formula of faith in vv.3–4, which makes the gospel of the Son of God—which Paul sees himself called to proclaim—more precise in two ways. An initial statement affirms the origin of Jesus as the Davidic Messiah from Israel (= A), and a second, surpassing statement confesses his Easter enthronement as "Son of God in power" and "Lord" (κύριος) of all nations (= B). To these the Jew Paul, due to the universal exalted status of the Resurrected One, knows himself to be obligated as "apostle to the nations," as he states to his addressees in Rome right after this:

> [1] Paul, the servant of the Messiah Jesus,
> called apostle,
> set apart for the gospel of God . . .
> [3] about his *Son*,
>   who came from the seed of David *according to the flesh* [= A],
>   [4] who was enthroned as Son of God in power according to *the Spirit of holiness since* the resurrection of the dead [= B],
> *Jesus Messiah, our Lord* [Ἰησοῦ Χριστοῦ τοῦ κυρίου ἡμῶν],
> through whom we have received grace and our apostleship . . . among all the nations . . .

"'Geboren aus dem Samen Davids . . .' (Röm 1,3). Wandlungen im paulinischen Christus-Bild?," *Zeitschrift für die neutestamentliche Wissenschaft* 102 (2011): 235–60; on Romans 9–11, see: Michael Theobald, "Unterschiedliche Gottesbilder in Röm 9–11? Die Israel-Kapitel als Anfrage an die Einheit des theologischen Diskurses bei Paulus," in *The Letter to the Romans*, ed. Udo Schnelle (Bibliotheca Ephemeridum Theologicarum Lovaniensium, 226; Leuven: Peeters, 2009): 135–77; Michael Theobald, "Gottes Barmherzigkeit und Gottes Zorn. Turbulenzen um das Gottesbild in Röm 9–11," in *Mitleid und Mitleiden*, ed. Volker Leppin and Samuel Vollenweider et al. (Jahrbuch für Biblische Theologie 30 [2015]; Neukirchen-Vluyn: Neukirchener Theologie, 2018): 159–82.

12. Gerhard Sass, "Röm. 15, 7–13 – als Summe des Römerbriefs gelesen," *Evangelische Theologie* 53 (1993): 510–27.

13. Hans Schlier, *Der Römerbrief* (Herders Theologischer Kommentar, VI; Freiburg i. Br.: Herder, 1977): 9.

Romans 1:3–4, with its confession of the earthly-fleshly existence of Jesus and of his Spirit-determined mode of being, had already become in the second century a foundational text for the so-called "two natures" doctrine, which led to the abstraction from the historical-concrete figure of Jesus. After this dogmatic reading grid had broken down in the time of the Enlightenment, a "two-stage model"[14] gained the upper hand: The first level, Jesus' earthly descent "from the seed of David," is superseded and surpassed by a second level, that of his Easter-appointed position of rulership.[15] To the extent that research took seriously the fact that the confession should be read in light of Old Testament pre-texts, it also became clear how the expansion of the first line through the second is to be read in the sense of Pauline theology: Jesus, who "came from the seed of David," is Messiah of Israel from the beginning and remains so; on Easter he was enthroned as "the Son of God in power" in accordance with the words of Psalm 2: "You are my son! Today I have begotten you! Ask of me, and I will give (to you) nations

14. The term and model of interpretation go back to Eduard Schweizer, "Röm 1,3f. und der Gegensatz von Fleisch und Geist vor und bei Paulus," in *Neotestamentica. Deutsche und Englische Aufsätze 1951–1963* (Zürich / Stuttgart: Zwingli Verlag, 1963): 180–89.

15. This could go hand in hand with a devaluation of the earthly Jesus in favor of the one proclaimed after Easter, not least under the impression of a misguided interpretation of 2 Cor 5:16—"If we have known Christ *according to the flesh,* now we know (him) no longer." Cf. Rudolf Bultmann, *Theologie des Neuen Testaments* (Tübingen: Mohr Siebeck, 6th edn 1968): 293–94: "Jesus' death and resurrection is . . . what is decisive, indeed, it is basically the only thing that is important for Paul about the person and fate of Jesus—included here is the incarnation and the earthly life of Jesus as facts, i.e., in their *that*; in their *how* only insofar as Jesus was a concrete, specific human being, a Jew"; his Jewishness is admittedly scarcely developed on its own in its theological relevance. *Ibid.,* 52, on the "title 'Son of David' . . . which is synonymous in terms of substance with 'Messiah'": Paul must "have found it as in circulation before him. For while the title has no importance for Paul himself, he does refer to it in Rom 1:3, namely in a sentence that apparently relies on a formula that was handed down to him." ["Tod und Auferstehung Jesu ist . . . das Entscheidende, ja im Grunde das Einzige, was für Paulus an der Person und dem Schicksal Jesu wichtig ist, – einbegriffen ist dabei die Menschwerdung und das Erdenleben Jesu als Tatsache, d. h. in ihrem *Daß*; – in ihrem *Wie* nur insofern, als Jesus ein konkreter, bestimmter Mensch, ein Jude, war" // "sachlich mit 'Messias' gleichbedeutend (en) . . . Titel 'Davidsohn'" // "ihn als geläufigen vorgefunden haben. Denn für ihn selbst hat der Titel zwar keine Bedeutung, er nimmt aber auf ihn Bezug Rm 1,3 und zwar in einem Satz, der sich offenbar an eine ihm überlieferte Formel anlehnt."]

as your inheritance and the ends of the earth as your property . . ." (Ps 2:7–8). The Easter-appointed position of rulership of Jesus neither supersedes his earthly messianic function nor relativizes it; instead, it is, according to the testimony of Scripture, its necessary consequence.

(2) In the *peroratio*, 15:7–13, at the end of the writing, Paul confirms the enduring messianic significance of the earthly Jesus in that he underscores its role in God's plan of salvation. This *summarium* is embedded in Paul's admonition to the addressees, that the pagan majority and the Jewish-living minority of the Roman *ekklesia* should "receive" one another—accept and tolerate[16]—as they were both allowed to experience this from the Messiah Jesus:

> 7 Therefore receive one another,
> as also the Messiah [ὁ Χριστός] received you to the glory of God!
> 8 For I say:
> [The] Messiah [Χριστόν] became a servant of the circumcision
> *for the sake of the truth of God* [ὑπὲρ ἀληθείας θεοῦ],
> [that means:] in order to confirm the promises of the fathers [= A],
> 9 but the gentiles glorify God *for the sake of* [*his*] *mer*cy [ὑπὲρ ἐλέους] [= B],
> as it is written:
> Therefore, I will confess you among the gentiles and sing praises to your name [Ps 18:50].
> 10 And again, it (Scripture) says,
> Rejoice, gentiles, with his people [Deut 32:43^{LXX}]. . . .

According to this *summarium*, the earthly Jesus is God's authorized representative (= *diakonos*) for the Jews (= the circumcision)[17] in order to

16. Michael Wolter, *Der Brief an die Römer* (Part 2: Rom 9–16) (Evangelisch-Katholischer Kommentar, VI/2; Ostfildern / Göttingen: Vandenhoeck & Ruprecht, 2019), 404—Paul demands "that they, with one another and as different as they are, practice a fellowship that gives a social shape to their togetherness. Paul does not say what he is thinking of concretely, but one would not be mistaken in postulating that he had in mind the worship service gathering with the table fellowship that was practiced there." [". . . dass sie miteinander und unterschiedlich, wie sie sind, eine Gemeinschaft praktizieren, die ihrer Zusammengehörigkeit eine soziale Gestalt gibt. Paulus sagt nicht, woran er konkret denkt, doch wird man keinen Fehler machen, wenn man vermutet, dass er die gottesdienstliche Versammlung mit der dabei praktizierten Mahlgemeinschaft im Sinn hatte."]

17. On the terminology, see Anni Hentschel, *Diakonia im Neuen Testament. Studien zur Semantik unter besonderer Berücksichtigung der Rolle der Frauen* (Wissenschaftliche Untersuchungen zum Neuen Testament, II/226; Tübingen: Mohr Siebeck, 2007).

confirm "the truth" of God, which means his reliability[18] and his faithfulness to the promises that were given long ago to the fathers. Jesus is the guarantor of the reliability of God already through his existence as Messiah. This declaration pertaining to Israel (= A) is expanded in v. 9 (analogous to the prescript) through a second to the nations (= B): these may glorify God for the sake of his "mercy," which he turned to them—this is to be understood—through the one who was enthroned as "Lord of all" at Easter (10:12) in the justification of sinners out of pure grace. The unimaginable becomes true: "gentiles," who often enough are hostile to the people of God and oppress them, unite themselves with the Jews in the *ekklesia* in the praise of God (v. 10). The terms ἀλήθεια and ἔλεος, which respectively express the theological core of the two sentences of the *summarium* in a nutshell, strike, with their polarity of "faithfulness" and "mercy," the binding of God to his people Israel and his freedom to receive all humans in his love, the center of the Pauline image of God.[19]

What the "truth" of God, that is his reliability and faithfulness to the promises he once gave to the fathers, means is explicated by Paul in his Israel chapters, where he wrestles theologically to gain insight into the reason for the "no" of many in his people to the gospel. At the end of his winding paths of thought, he reaches an insight that was—as he signals—granted to him in prayer:[20] At the Parousia of the Lord "all of Israel"—in correspondence to the principle of the justification of sinners—will also itself experience "salvation" solely from grace (11:26a).

According to the argumentation of Paul, the reliable sign of God's faithfulness is the so-called "remnant" of the Jews (ὑπόλειμμα / λεῖμμα—9:27 / 11:5).[21] This has "according to the election of grace" (κατ' ἐκλογὴν χάριτος—11:5) attained to faith in the Messiah Jesus, among

18. ἀλήθεια is here to be understood from the biblical אמת, for which the LXX offer derivatives of ἀληθ- in 100 of 127 instances: Hans Wildberger, "אמן *'mn* fest, sicher [firm, sure]," in *Theologisches Handwörterbuch zum Alten Testament* vol. I, ed. Ernst Jenni (Munich: Chr. Kaiser, 1971): 177–209, at 201.

19. For development of this topic, cf. Theobald, "Gottes Barmherzigkeit" (see note 11).

20. Cf. Rom 11:25 (μυστήριον) with 10:1—If Paul in 10:1 engages in "intercession with God" for the "salvation" of Israel, then the revelation of the mystery of its salvation is the answer to this intercession.

21. With the "remnant" idea, Paul builds on Isa 10:22; for the use in the Old Testament and in early Judaism, cf. Hans Wildberger, "שאר *š'r* übrig sein [to be left over]," in *Theologisches Handwörterbuch zum Alten Testament*, vol. II, ed. Ernst Jenni (Munich: Chr. Kaiser, 1976): 844–55.

whom he is ranked, as he explains in 11:1–2: "Has God rejected his people? By no means! For I too am an Israelite, a descendant of Abraham, from the tribe of Benjamin. God has not rejected His people whom He chose beforehand" (cf. 11:28b). A Church that behaves exclusively in a Gentile Christian way and does not recognize Jews who believe in the Messiah Jesus as such, as was the rule from the second century onward, cannot appeal to Paul. On the contrary, for him the *communio* of Gentile-Christian communities with Jewish Christians in Jerusalem is fundamental for truly being the *ekklesia*,[22] and the dynamic of worldwide mission is no argument for denying the Jerusalem connection of the *ekklesia*.

A confirmation of this is provided by the way in which Paul underpins the "mystery" of the salvation of all Israel (11:26a) with the subsequent word of God from Scripture; characteristic for the mixed citation is its Zion-centeredness:

1 *From Zion* will come the Deliverer,
2 he will remove (the) godlessness from Jacob.
3 And this (is) [the fulfillment of] the from me (coming) covenant (διαθήκη),
4 when I take away their sins.

Paul refers his Gentile-Christian addressees in Rome to Jesus' descent as Messiah *from Israel* at the beginning of his argumentation in 9:4–5—"They are Israelites, . . . whose are the fathers, and from whom is *the Messiah according to the flesh* (ὁ Χριστὸς τὸ κατὰ σάρκα)." Now, at the end, he closes the circle with his confession of Jesus as Messiah *for Israel*. There are several important arguments that speak against a purely theocentric understanding of the first line, which echoes Isaiah 59:20—"From Zion will come the Deliverer (ἥξει ἐκ Σιὼν ὁ ῥυόμενος)"[23]—namely, the *inclusio*

22. Michael Theobald, "Kirche nach dem Neuen Testament. Ein ekklesiologischer Entwurf in vierundzwanzig Thesen," *Zeitschrift für Theologie und Kirche* 117 (2020): 377–408, at 394–95, 401.

23. Isa 59:20^{LXX}: καὶ ἥξει ἕνεκεν Σιὼν ὁ ῥυόμενος καὶ ἀποστρέψει ἀσεβείας ἀπὸ Ἰακώβ. καὶ αὕτη ἡ παρ' ἐμοῦ διαθήκη . . . ; which Paul combines with Isa 27:9^{LXX} (. . . ὅταν ἀφέλωμαι αὐτοῦ τὴν ἁμαρτίαν) to form a stylized quatrain (see above). For a reference of ῥυόμενος to God ultimately, see Wolter, *Römer* II (see note 16), 213–15; for a reference to Christ, see Martin Karrer, "Paulus, Jesaja und Israel – Beobachtungen zu Röm 11,26f.," in *Die Septuaginta – Themen, Manuskripte, Wirkungen. Septuaginta-Konferenz Wuppertal 2018*, ed. Eberhard Bons et al. (Wissenschaftliche Untersuchungen zum Neuen Testament, 444; Tübingen: Mohr Siebeck, 2020): 703–27; cf. also Tobias Nicklas, "Paulus und die Errettung Israels: Röm 11,25–32 in der exegetischen Diskussion und im jüdisch-christlichen Dialog," *Early Christianity* 2 (2011): 173–97.

with 9:5, the parallel to 1 Thes 1:10,[24] and above all the configuration of the four-line passage as an *utterance of God* (". . . this is for them the covenant from me") with the consequence that the "Deliverer" from Zion must be someone other than the "I" who proclaims his coming.[25]

The messianic contour of the Parousia expectation articulated in this saying is clear: "The Deliverer" will come not for the benefit of an individual but for the benefit of the *collective* Jacob. He will remove all godlessness from him, whereby God will fulfill his covenant with the fathers. And "the Deliverer" will come "from Zion" whence Israel has from of old awaited salvation,[26] be it from the earthly or from the heavenly Jerusalem; Paul probably sees both in one.[27]

What is decisive is that the saving initiative proceeds from God according to 11:25–27. "All Israel" will be saved when the measure of the time is fulfilled and the Messiah Jesus is revealed. Paul does not say that Israel must first accept the gospel and come to faith, *so that the Deliverer comes*. The prophecy of the salvation of "all Israel" goes forth *unconditioned*. When the Deliverer comes, God will "take away their sins" and turn the "righteousness" to Jacob, the fruit of the Messiah's giving of his life. The unconditional nature of this pronouncement is what

24. 1 Thes 1:10—"and to await his Son from heaven, whom he raised from the dead, Jesus, who saves us (τὸν ῥυόμενον ἡμᾶς) from the coming wrath"; oddly enough, Wolter, *Römer* II (see note 16), 213–15, does not discuss this parallel.

25. For details, cf. Theobald, "Unterschiedliche Gottesbilder in Röm 9–11?" (see note 11), 175–76; on the stylization of Scriptural quotes to utterances of God in Rom 9–11, cf. Hans Hübner, *Gottes Ich und Israel Zum Schriftgebrauch des Paulus in Römer 9–11* (Forschungen zur Religion und Literatur des Alten und Neuen Testaments, 136; Göttingen: Vandenhoeck & Ruprecht, 1984).

26. Ps 14(13):7; 50(49):2; 53(52):7; 4 Ezra 13:35; 4*Flor* I.11–13, etc.

27. In Rom 9:33 ("See, I lay in Zion, a stumbling block, a rock of offense . . ." [cf. Isa 28:16 with 8:14]) the saving death of Jesus is connected to the (earthly) Zion, to which the coming of the Savior "from Zion" is probably contextually connected; on the "above (= heavenly) Jerusalem" cf. Gal 4:26. Otfried Hofius, "Das Evangelium und Israel Erwägungen zu Römer 9–11," in Otfried Hofius, *Paulusstudien* (Wissenschaftliche Untersuchungen zum Neuen Testament, 51; Tübingen: Mohr Siebeck, 2nd edn 1994): 175–202, at 196: "The specification that the ῥυόμενος will come 'from Zion' does not necessarily have to be interpreted with reference to the appearing of Christ from the heavenly Jerusalem. Paul could very well be thinking of the earthly Zion, on which Christ will reveal himself at the Parousia and from which he will complete his saving work on Israel." ["Die Angabe, dass der ῥυόμενος 'aus Zion' kommen wird, muss nicht notwendig auf das Erscheinen Christi vom himmlischen Jerusalem her gedeutet werden. Paulus kann sehr wohl an den irdischen Zion denken, auf dem sich Christus bei der Parusie offenbaren und von dem aus er sein Rettungswerk an Israel vollführen wird."]

differentiates the future vision of Paul from that of Luke, as I will show in what follows. But this too is grounded in Scripture; only it follows a different biblical model of thought.

2. Repent, so that "he may send the promised Messiah"! (Acts 3:20)

The question of the future of Israel as the chosen people of God plays a decisive role not only for Paul but also for Luke. In the words of Christoph Schaefer (in his Israel study), in biblical tradition both hold

> fast to an eschatological hope for Israel, but take up thereby elements of (Old Testament–) biblical theology in respectively specific ways. In this regard, a salvation-historical view that above all stands in the tradition of Deuteronomistic narrations of history plays a key role for Luke, insofar as it always reckons with the disobedience of Israel as well as the wrath and punishment of God, and yet also contains the call to repentance, which makes possible the saving turning of God. With regard to the future of Israel, Paul, by contrast, exhibits in Rom 11 a view that is oriented to the so-called "grace theology" of the Priestly (writing) tradition, insofar as it emphasizes the unconditionally given promises of God, who in his omnipotence takes responsibility for the present hardening as well as the eschatological acceptance of Israel.[28]

From the very beginning of the Lukan "double work,"[29] it is clear that Israel possesses enduring future prospects in the Messiah Jesus.

28. "an einer eschatologischen Hoffnung für Israel fest, rezipieren dabei jedoch Elemente (alttestamentlich-) biblischer Theologie in je spezifischer Weise. Dabei spielt für Lukas eine heilsgeschichtliche Sicht, die vor allem in der Tradition deuteronomistischer Geschichtserzählungen steht, eine wesentliche Rolle, insofern diese immer schon mit dem Ungehorsam Israels sowie mit Zorn und Strafe Gottes rechnen, stets aber auch den Ruf zur Umkehr enthält, welcher die heilvolle Zuwendung Gottes wieder ermöglicht. Paulus hingegen zeigt in Röm 11 bezüglich der Zukunft Israels eine Sicht, die sich an der sog. 'Gnadentheologie' priester(schrift)licher Tradition orientiert, insofern sie die bedingungslos gegebenen Verheißungen Gottes hervorhebt, der in seiner Allmacht die gegenwärtige Verstockung wie auch die eschatologische Annahme Israels verantwortet"—Christian Schaefer, *Die Zukunft Israels bei Lukas. Biblisch-frühjüdische Zukunftsvorstellungen im lukanischen Doppelwerk im Vergleich zu Röm 9–11* (Beihefte zur Zeitschrift für die neutestamentliche Wissenschaft, 190; Berlin: De Gruyter, 2012): 6–7; cf. his analysis of the relevant texts of the double work on pages 105–384 ("Israels Zukunft im lukanischen Doppelwerk" ["Israel's Future in the Lukan Double Work"]).

29. Knut Backhaus, *Das lukanische Doppelwerk. Zur literarischen Basis frühchristlicher Geschichtsdeutung* (Beihefte zur Zeitschrift für die neutestamentliche Wissenschaft, 240; Berlin: De Gruyter, 2022).

(1) In the so-called prehistory of Luke 1–2, the overture of that Gospel, Luke allows the theme to be heard programmatically, at first from Gabriel, the heavenly messenger, in the announcement of the birth of Jesus (Luke 1:30b-33):

> [30b] Do not be afraid Mary; for you have found favor with God.
> [31] And behold, you will become pregnant
> and bear a son
> and you shall name him Jesus.
> [32] This one will be great and will be called Son of the Most High.
> *And God, the Lord, will give him the throne of his father David,*
> [33] *and he will reign over the house of Jacob forever,*
> *and of his reign there will be no end.*

This birth announcement with its punchline—"he shall reign over the house of Jacob forever"—should not be forgotten when the double work recounts how the gospel of Jesus Christ, starting from Galilee and Judea, spread in the world of the *Imperium Romanum*. Nor is it revoked by the fact that Jesus' messengers, in the continuation of the narrated story, experience rejection time and again from the synagogues, up to and including in Rome. What is true for Paul (cf. Rom 9:6), holds true in the same way for Luke: The word of God does not fail, it endures.[30]

Correspondingly, the *Benedictus* of Zechariah (Luke 1:68–79), which is likewise largely woven from Scripture, begins with the praise:

> [68] Blessed be the Lord God of Israel!
> For he has visited us and accomplished redemption for his people;
> [69] *he has raised up a horn of salvation for us in the house of his servant David.*
> [70] So did he promise from of old through the mouth of his holy prophets. . . .[31]

30. Luke 1:32–33 echoes a number of biblical promises, in addition to Isa 9:6; Mic 4:7; and Dan 7:14; above all that of the prophet Nathan, which God sends to David through him (2 Sam 7:8–16): ". . . [12] When your days are fulfilled and you lie down with your fathers, I will raise up your offspring after you, who will come forth from your body, and I will establish his kingdom. [13] He shall build a house for my name, and I will establish the throne of his kingdom forever. . . . [15] But I will not take my steadfast love from him, as I took it from Saul, whom I put away from before you. [16] Your house and your kingdom shall be made sure forever before you; your throne shall be established forever." Luke then legitimizes the promise of eternal rule, now related to the Messiah Jesus, in two ways: through Scripture, and in such a way that a heavenly messenger, Gabriel, expressly confirms it for Jesus, from above, so to speak.

31. Walter Radl, *Das Evangelium nach Lukas. Kommentar. Erster Teil: 1,1–9,50* (Freiburg i. Br.: Herder, 2003): 95: "Luke repeats this appeal to the word of the

Finally, the birth of Jesus in Luke 2:11 is proclaimed to the shepherds by the heavenly messengers with these words:

> Today has been born to you in the city of David the Deliverer,
> who is [the] Messiah, [the] Lord.

(2) Does Jesus remain the Messiah for Israel even if he is rejected by his people? In the middle of the so-called "travel narrative," the narrative of Jesus' trek from Galilee to Jerusalem (Luke 9:51–19:27), we find a saying of Jesus that looks ahead to the meeting of the returning Son of Man with those who will reject him in his earthly life, lastly in Jerusalem (Luke 13:34–35):[32]

> 34 Jerusalem, Jerusalem,
> the one who kills the prophets
> and stones those sent to her:
> How often I wanted to gather your children,
> as a hen gathers her chicks under the wings,
> and you would not have it.
> 35a Behold, your house is left to you [by God].
>
> 35b But [δέ] I say to you:
> You will not see me,
> until it[33] [or: he[34]] comes [ἕως ἥξει],
> that you say [ὅτε εἴπητε]:
> Blessed is the one who comes [ὁ ἐρχόμενος] in the name of the Lord!
> [Ps 118:26]

Verses 34–35a have to do with a self-contained judgment word of Jesus against city and temple. With the afterword in v.35b, it takes a

---

prophets almost word for word in Acts 3:21. It retains its validity for the future as well, until the consummation of salvation history" ["Diese Berufung auf das Wort der Propheten wiederholt Lukas fast deckungsgleich Apg 3,21. Sie hat ihre Gültigkeit auch für die Zukunft, bis zur Vollendung der Heilsgeschichte"]. On Acts 3:21, see below under (4). Cf. *ibid.* 93–94 on the rich Scriptural cross-references in the cited opening of the *Benedictus*.

32. On this word, which originates in the Sayings Source Q, cf. Michael Theobald, "Von der Henne und ihren Küken (Lk. 13,34f. par. Mt. 23,37–39). Ein Gerichtswort Jesu?," in *Altes und Neues hervorholen (Mt 13,52). Debatten zur Bibel in Theologie und Kirche – Festschrift für Lorenz Oberlinner zum 80. Geburtstag*, ed. Gerd Häfner, Ferdinand R. Prostmeier, and Thomas Schumacher (Stuttgarter Bibelstudien, 254; Stuttgart: Katholisches Bibelwerk, 2022): 124–59.

33. To be supplemented in the Greek: "the hour" or "the day."

34. If ἥξει is 3rd pers. masc., much speaks for the view that "the Son of Man" is meant: H.T. Fleddermann, *Q. A Reconstruction and Commentary* (Biblical Tools and Studies, 1; Leuven / Paris / Dudley: Peeters, 2005): 706.

turn, in which it is not clear at first glance whether, in continuation of the pronouncement of doom, a "horrifying seeing again" is prophesied to those who rejected Jesus during his lifetime,[35] or whether a salvific perspective is not, after all, opened up for them. Later, when Jesus approaches Jerusalem from the Mount of Olives, his own following greet him with the very welcome greeting from Psalm 118 that in Luke 13:35 is put into the mouths of the "children" of Jerusalem at their encounter with the Parousia Christ,[36] which is likewise to be thought of in Jerusalem (19:37–38). This could indicate that, in the jubilation of Jesus' following over his appearance on the Mount of Olives, Luke sees an anticipation of what he has said in 13:35 about Jesus' eschatological "coming": Even those who still oppose him now will one day open themselves to him. They will "greet Jesus as their Messiah . . .—when he returns at the end of days."[37] At very least,

35. Cf. Dieter Zeller, "Entrückung zur Ankunft als Menschensohn (Lk 13,34f.; 11,29f.)," in Dieter Zeller, *Jesus – Logienquelle – Evangelien* (Stuttgarter biblische Aufsatzbände [Neues Testament], 53); Stuttgart: Katholisches Bibelwerk, 2012): 151–65, at 154; Michael Wolter, *Das Lukasevangelium* (Handbuchs zum Neuen Testament, 5; Tübingen: Mohr Siebeck, 2008): 499; this is also the conventional interpretation of the parallel passage in Matt 23:37–39—Ulrich Luz, *Das Evangelium nach Matthäus (Mt. 18–25)* (Evangelisch-Katholischer Kommentar, 1/3; Zürich / Neukirchen-Vluyn: Benziger / Neukirchener, 1997): 384.

36. The priests customarily called out the word of blessing from Ps 118:26 at the Feast of Booths (*mSuk* 3.9) to those who were going up into the temple; later the word was also interpreted as messianic: *Midrash Ps 118* §22 (244a), cf. Andrew C. Brunson, *Psalm 118 in the Gospel of John. An Intertextual Study on the New Exodus Pattern in the Theology of John* (Wissenschaftliche Untersuchungen zum Neuen Testament, 2/158; Tübingen: Mohr Siebeck, 2003): 22–101 ("Psalm 118 in Its Jewish Setting"). On the localization of the Parousia of the Messiah from the Mount of Olives, cf. Schaefer, *Die Zukunft Israels bei Lukas* (see note 28), 198–204.

37. "Jesus als ihren Messias begrüßen . . . – bei seiner Wiederkunft am Ende der Tage"—Franz Mußner, "Die Stellung zum Judentum in der 'Redenquelle' und in ihrer Verarbeitung bei Matthäus," in Franz Mußner, *Dieses Geschlecht wird nicht vergehen* (Freiburg i. Br.: Herder, 1991): 87–100, at 96 with note 34: "This agrees with the prophetic statement by Paul in Rom 11:26" ["Das trifft sich mit der prophetischen Ansage des Paulus in Röm 11,26"]; Helmut Merkel, "Israel im lukanischen Werk," *New Testament Studies* 40 (1994): 371–98, at 382: Luke 13:34–45 gives "hope that the Jerusalem inhabitants who refuse to be gathered by Jesus will pay homage to him at the Parousia with the praise, 'Benedictus qui venit in nomine Domini'" ["[lässt] hoffen, dass die Jerusalemer, die sich der Sammlung durch Jesus verweigern, bei der Parusie ihm mit dem Lobpreis huldigen 'Benedictus qui venit in nomine Domini'"]. In favor of this interpretation is not only the aforementioned particle δέ, with which the prophecy v.35b is contrasted with the preceding word of judgment ("*But* I tell you"), but also the Lukan context as a whole: Schaefer, *Die Zukunft Israels bei Lukas* (see note 28), 149; François

the saying holds up the "hope" that "enemies" will become "friends" when they see him again.[38]

(3) With the last word of the Resurrected One to his own, the opening scene of Acts programmatically shows the direction of the book. Despite the directive to worldwide mission, it continues to uphold the Israel-centered perspective of the Gospel:

> [6] When they had come together,
> they were asking him:
> *Lord,*
> *are you at this time restoring the kingdom for Israel*
> [εἰ ἐν τῷ χρόνῳ τούτῳ ἀποκαθιστάνεις τὴν βασιλείαν τῷ Ἰσραήλ;]*?*
> [7] He said to them:
> It is not for you
> to know times or periods
> which the Father has fixed by his own authority.
> [8] But you will receive power
> when the Holy Spirit has come upon you;
> and you will be my witnesses in Jerusalem and in all Judea and Samaria and
> to the ends of the earth.

The Lukan Jesus does not correct the disciples' question about whether he "is restoring (ἀποκαθιστάνεις) the kingdom for Israel in this time" in terms of content. Rather, he points to the sole sovereignty of the Father over the course of time and explains to the disciples what is incumbent upon them until the end of time: They are to be Jesus' "witnesses . . . to the ends of the earth." The centrifugal force of the mission beyond Judea and Samaria, which is determined by the Spirit of God, does not abolish the connection back to the center, the holy city of Jerusalem.

Bovon, *Das Evangelium nach Lukas, vol. 2 (Lk. 9,51–14,35)* (Evangelisch-Katholischer Kommentar, 3/2; Zürich / Neukirchen-Vluyn: Benziger / Neukirchener, 1996): 460. "In Acts, the apostles offer Israel and its leaders, who are responsible 'out of ignorance' for the demise of Jesus, a final opportunity for conversion. Despite the hardening that persists, Luke leaves a final offer of forgiveness open until the end of his work." ["In der Apostelgeschichte bieten die Apostel Israel und seinen Führern, die 'aus Unwissenheit' verantwortlich sind für das Verschwinden Jesu, eine letzte Gelegenheit zur Bekehrung an. Trotz der Verhärtung, die weiterbesteht, lässt Lukas ein letztes Angebot der Vergebung bis zum Ende seines Werkes offen."]

38. Bovon, *Lukas* II (see note 37), 460; *ibid.* 445: The saying in v.35b opens up "an enigmatic future, of which we do not learn whether it will be dark or light." [". . . eine rätselhafte Zukunft, von der wir nicht erfahren, ob sie dunkel oder hell sein wird."]

(4) According to the content summary of the book of Acts, the *propositio* in Acts 1:7, the book initially narrates how Jerusalem, with the proclamation of the gospel by the messengers of Jesus, gets a new chance to convert to its Messiah. Alongside the Pentecost scene in Acts 2:1–41, Peter's speech at the temple courtyard—which is appended to the healing of the man lame from birth at the gate called Beautiful—is of primary significance (see Acts 3:12–26) because it portrays the encounter of Israel with its Messiah at the Parousia—in contrast to the first encounter with the earthly Jesus—as salvific. The retrospective view on those calamitous days flows into their salvation-historical evaluation (vv. 17–18) and a renewed call to repentance (vv. 19–21):

> 17 And now, brothers,
> I know that
> you acted in ignorance,
> just as your rulers did also.
> 18 But God has thus fulfilled
> what he proclaimed beforehand through the mouth of all the prophets:
> that his Christ would suffer.
>
> 19 Therefore repent and return,
> so that your sins may be wiped away,
> 20 in order that times [καιροί] of refreshing may come from the presence of the Lord
> and that he may send *the preordained-for-you Messiah Jesus*
> [τὸν προκεχειρισμένον ὑμῖν χριστὸν Ἰησοῦν],
> 21 whom heaven must receive until the *times of the restoration of all things*
> [ἄχρι χρόνων ἀποκαταστάσεως πάντων],
> about which God spoke through the mouth of his holy prophets from of old.[39]

With the theme of "restoration," the *apokatastasis*, 3:21 takes up 1:6 and characterizes this in connection with v. 20 as a time of "refreshing" for Israel, which would be grounded in the sending of the hitherto hidden Messiah for Israel's salvation. The notion—known from Luke 13:35b—of the absence of the Messiah until the point in time of his sending again at the Parousia is lightly varied but clearly recognizable.[40] What

39. For this phrase see above, note 31; it may be a conscious reference back to the *Benedictus*.

40. While Luke 13:35b gets by without the Christ title (the Son of Man conception is probably in the background), Acts 3:20 speaks of the "Messiah"; while Luke 13:35 concerns Jesus' withdrawal, this is filled out in Acts 3:21 from the "ascension narrative" ("whom heaven must receive"). The reference to the Parousia

is crucial is that Jerusalem, and with it all Israel, seize the chance to repent, so that God sends the "Messiah preordained" for the people also really unto their salvation. If they seize the chance, then at the end of times Israel will enter into the consummation together with the converts from the nations.

3. *The future of Israel—a look ahead*

An astonishing number of things unite Paul and Luke in their view of Israel:[41] Both view the people of God, because of their history since Abraham, as the natural first addressees of the gospel (πρῶτον—Rom 1:16, par. Acts 3:26). Both connect the "no" of the majority of Jews to Jesus with the subsequent mission among the Gentiles (Rom 11:25–26; see also Luke 21:24[42] with 13:35). Both see in all of this the will of God, indeed his preordination at work, and hope—after the completion of the mission to the nations—for Israel's encounter again with its Messiah, then in the bright light of the Parousia. Both are rooted in Scripture, only they follow different biblical thought patterns: While Paul, with the Priestly writing, starts from the unshakeability of the promises of God and thus definitively announces the salvation of Israel, Luke conditions this in accord with his Deuteronomistic understanding of history, but never gives up the hope in the Messiah for Israel.[43]

---

in Acts 3:21 is disputed by Gerhard Lohfink, "Christologie und Geschichtsbild in Apg. 3,19–21," *Biblische Zeitschrift* 13 (1969): 223–41, without providing convincing reasons.

41. Cf. the insightful overview in Schaefer, *Die Zukunft Israels bei Lukas* (see note 28), 11–16, from which only the most important motifs and themes are mentioned in what follows; Daniel A. Gleich, *Die Lukanischen Paulusreden. Ein sprachlicher und inhaltlicher Vergleich zwischen dem paulinischen Redestoff in Apg. 9–28 und dem Corpus Paulinum* (Arbeiten zur Bibel und ihrer Geschichte, 70; Leipzig: Evangelische Verlagsanstalt, 2021), who is interested in the "authentic statements of Paul" ["authentische Aussagen des Paulus"] in Acts (323), leaves aside the parallels in the remaining parts of the book.

42. The motif of the "*full number* of the [Gentile] nations (τὸ *πλήρωμα* τῶν ἐθνῶν)" determined by God as the goal of the worldwide mission (Rom 11:25) and as the point in time for the "salvation" of Israel (Rom 11:25) and/or Jerusalem that then takes place is attested also in Luke 21:24—"and they will fall by the edge of the sword and be led captive among all the nations, and Jerusalem will be trampled by the nations until the times of the *nations* are *fulfilled* (ἄχρι οὗ *πληρωθῶσιν* καιροὶ *ἐθνῶν*)"; immediately afterwards comes the prophecy of the return of the Son of Man (Luke 21:25–28)—corresponding to Rom 11:26.

43. Schaefer, *Die Zukunft Israels bei Lukas* (see note 28), 6–7.

The significance of the two conceptions becomes clear from a comparison with Ephesians and the Gospel of John, which, unlike Paul and Luke, have given up the specifically messianic-eschatological perspective in favor of a presentist or individual eschatology oriented to the death of each individual. Ephesians deserves the highest esteem because it warns the Gentile Christians of Asia Minor against the increasing forgetfulness of Israel and makes clear to them that the *ekklesia*'s dignity is grounded in its sharing in the prerogatives of Israel: "Remember that at one time you, the nations (τὰ ἔθνη) . . . were without the Messiah, excluded from the commonwealth of Israel and strangers to the covenants of promise, without hope and godless in the world. But now in Messiah Jesus you who were once far off have come near through the blood of Messiah" (Eph 2:11–13).[44] The purpose of the writing did not incline the author to speak of the future of Israel. But his presentist eschatology would also hardly have allowed him to do so. The one who assumes that those who believe in Jesus have already been raised with him in baptism and seated in the heavenly places (Eph 2:5–7) expects only this one thing from the future—the status that has already been achieved will only be confirmed in bodily death. The Gospel of John shows clearly what a burden a presentist eschatology places on the Israel question. Like Paul, the author of the book does not end by assigning guilt to the Jews on account of their "no" to Jesus but rather places all the responsibility on God himself. At the end of the first half of the book it says with unsurpassable clarity (John 12:37–40):

> Though he [i.e., Jesus] had performed such great signs before them,
> they were not believing in him,
> [38] in order that the word of Isaiah, the prophet, might be fulfilled,
> which he had spoken:
>
> > Lord,
> > who has believed our report,
> > and the arm of the Lord,
> > to whom has been revealed? [Isa 53:1]
>
> [39] *For this reason they could not believe,*
> *for Isaiah again said:*
>
> > He has blinded their eyes
> > and he hardened their heart,
> > in order that they would not see with the eyes

44. For details, cf. the commentary on 2:11–22 in Michael Theobald, *Mit den Augen des Herzens sehen. Der Epheserbrief als Leitfaden für Spiritualität und Kirche* (Würzburg: Echter, 2000): 81–98.

and understand with their heart
and turn
and I will [then] heal them [Isa 6:10].[45]

According to Paul, too, it was God who provoked the "no" of the Jews through the hardening of their hearts (Rom 11:8–10, 25c). But the apostle moves this insight into a broader horizon and thus takes away its final sharpness: God hardened the hearts of the Jewish people in order that as a consequence of this the gospel might reach the Gentile world; and when he has reached his goal and "the full number of the gentiles has come in," "the hardening" of the Jews who are saying "no" to the gospel will be taken away again and "all Israel will be saved" (Rom 11:25–26). In contrast to this grandiose vision of the future, the divine enigma of the "blinding" of the Jews in the face of Jesus' message is frighteningly isolated in John. It experiences no resolution because the Gospel's presentist understanding of salvation permits only an individual eschatology and the subsequently added references to an end-times judgment according to works[46] focus only on the individuals and do not open up a collective perspective along the line of a salvation history with Israel.[47] When the Jerusalem authorities obtain the handing over of Jesus from Pilate with their admission, "We have no king but Caesar!" (John 19:15), then, according to the Johannine presentation, with their submission to the rulers of the *imperium*, they abandon

45. On the quotation, cf. Walter Gross, "Kann Gottes Prophet scheitern? Gott verstockt Israel (Jes. 6,1–11)," in Walter Gross & Karl-Josef Kuschel, *"Ich schaffe Finsternis und Unheil!" Ist Gott verantwortlich für das Übel?* (Mainz: Matthias-Grünewald-Verlag, 1992): 15–33. No other New Testament writer, with his version of the Isaiah quotation (cf. otherwise Matt 13:14; Mark 3:5; 4:12; Luke 8:10; 19:42; Acts 28:26; Rom 11:8) assigns responsibility for the hardening of hearts and minds of the Jews in the face of the gospel so clearly to *God* as the fourth Evangelist. While Luke at the end of Acts interprets the "No" of a part of Israel to the message of Christ (cf. esp. Acts 28:24) along the lines of the Septuagint as "*self*-hardening" (cf. above all Acts 28:27), John 12:40 says, "*He* blinded their eyes." After other conceivable answers to the question of the "why" for Israel's "no," this was perhaps the last and actual "answer" that the Johannine circle was able to give: the recourse to the will of God.

46. Cf. John 5:28b, 29; also 12:48. On the subsequently added character of these passages, cf. Michael Theobald, *Das Evangelium nach Johannes. Kapitel 1–12* (Regensburger Neues Testament; Regensburg: Verlag Friedrich Pustet, 2009): 49–59, 72–74.

47. On the individual eschatology of the fourth Evangelist in the context of this theology of death, cf. Michael Theobald, "Futurische versus präsentische Eschatologie? Ein neuer Versuch zur Standortbestimmung der johanneischen Redaktion," in Michael Theobald, *Studien zum Corpus Iohanneum* (Wissenschaftliche Untersuchungen zum Neuen Testament, 267; Tübingen: Mohr Siebeck, 2010): 534–73.

the messianic hope of their people and with it its future. They obtain about the handing over of Jesus to death and paradoxically promote thereby the public proclamation of Jesus before the whole world as king on the cross, to the acknowledgment of which, according to the fourth Evangelist, there is no longer any alternative:[48] As Son of God and Son of Man, Jesus puts an end to all messianic dreams.

48. However, the evangelist handles the title with reserve: (a) the inchoate confession that Nathaniel makes to Jesus as "King of Israel" is surpassed by Jesus at the end through his reference to the "Son of Man" (cf. John 1:50–51; 9:35–38); (b) Jesus withdraws himself from the demands of the Galilean crowd to make him king (John 6:15); (c) the crowd's hailing of Jesus in Jerusalem with the cry of "King of Israel" is counteracted by the episode of Jesus' entry seated on a donkey foal in accord with Zec 9:9 (John 12:14–15); the evangelist adds to this that Jesus' disciples only understood this after Jesus' death (John 12:16); (d) in the dialogue with Pilate, Jesus distances himself from the title of king when he accepts its validity only in the sense of a royal testimony to the truth (John 18:37)—corresponding to the Platonic idea that if the philosopher as the lover of wisdom is the true king, all the more then the one who is the Wisdom of God, the Truth in person (14:6); see Michael Theobald, "Gattungswandel in der Johanneischen Passionserzählung. Die Verhöre Jesu durch Pilatus (Johannes 18:33–38; 19:8–12) im Licht der *Acta Isidori* und anderer Prozessdialoge," in *Studies in the Gospel of John and its Christology: Festschrift Gilbert Van Belle*, ed. Joseph Verheyden et al. (Bibliotheca Ephemeridum Theologicarum Lovaniensium, 265; Leuven: Peeters, 2014): 447–83, at 479–81.—The corridor in which the title for Jesus occurs in the New Testament is as a whole very narrow. Starting from the probably historical *titulus crucis* (Mark 15:26 par. Matt 27:37; Luke 23:38; John 19:19) [Michael Theobald, *Der Prozess Jesu. Geschichte und Theologie der Passionserzählungen* (Wissenschaftliche Untersuchungen zum Neuen Testament, 486; Tübingen: Mohr Siebeck, 2022]: 603–609)], the title is encountered on the one hand in the collocation "King of the Jews" in the mouths of non-Jews—thus with Pilate (Mark 15:2 par. Matt 27:11; Luke 23:3; John 18:33; Mark 15:9 par. John 18:39; Mark 15:12), the Roman soldiers (Mark 15:18 par. Matt 27:29; John 19:3) and the Magi (Matt 2:2)—and on the other hand in the collocation "King of Israel" in the mouths of Jews—thus with Nathaniel (John 1:49), the crowd who greets Jesus in Jerusalem (John 12:13; cf. already 6:15), and the chief priests who mock the crucified one (Mark 15:32 par. Matt 27:42). The growing reserve of the New Testament with regard to the title of king (it is completely absent from Acts and the *Corpus Paulinum*) is probably related to the risk of its political misunderstanding in the context of the Roman Empire, which its Christological use in Revelation (1:5; 17:14; 19:16) with its explicitly critical discourse on rulership confirms in its own way. Mark S. Kinzer ("Is Jesus of Nazareth Still King of the Jews? New Testament Christology and the Jewish People," in *Jesus, King of the Jews? Messianic Judaism, Jewish Christians, and Theology Beyond Supersessionism*, ed. James E. Patrick (Vienna: Toward Jerusalem Council II, 2021]: 43–55), who, based on the New Testament, favors a "king-of-the-Jews-Christology," will refer, against the thesis of a New Testament marginality of the title of king advocated here, to its implication in the confession of Jesus as Messiah, which is accurate for the concept of Davidic messiahship in itself. But in the New Testament there is a clear disentanglement of the

For the confession that Jesus is not only *Messiah from Israel* but also *for Israel* one needs—this is shown by the above comparison of the divergent New Testament conceptions—a messianically contoured theology of the future. What this could look like is, due to the towering difficulties associated with it, not easy to say. Developing it is an interdisciplinary theological task that is urgently needed. Conceptions of the Parousia, and not just the apocalyptic variety of the Pauline near expectation, are subject to a fundamental suspicion of mythology. This entails a dramatic loss of plausibility which has not yet found its way into the general consciousness of faith. Such conceptions (also judgment scenarios and judgment statements of the New Testament) must be interpreted and translated in the context of a messianic theology of the future. To this may be added the serious finding that the Apostle's vision of a Church consisting of Jews and Gentiles was soon abandoned by Christianity. Conversions of Jews, which were often enough forced, were understood as a rejection of their Judaism, to which the Church no longer wanted to grant a right of residence. Viewed in this way, Paul's argumentation in Romans 11 only still has historical value, because its decisive pillar—the so-called Jewish-Christian "remnant" as a sign of God's faithfulness to Israel—was soon broken away. The horrifying rupture in civilization of the Shoah in the twentieth century, for which the anti-Judaism of Christendom in its various forms prepared the ground, gradually made the Churches aware of the need for an Israel theology. Now, Paul and Luke—admittedly under completely changed conditions and with the renunciation of any biblicism—can once again become the leaven for a theological renewal. John may tell us what mission can only still be today: bearing witness to God's love in his Messiah Jesus in word and in deed, or, as the Sermon on the Mount

---

messianic confession from the king conception, as the following examples already show: (a) Rom 1:3–4 does not adopt the βασιλεύς title for Jesus' enthronement at Easter but rather the title of κύριος (with significant consequences for Christology); (b) Luke, who understands the Messiah title of Jesus from the anointing of the baptized Jesus with the "Holy Spirit," brings it closer to the title of prophet (cf. Luke 1:35; 3:21–22; 4:1, 18 [Isa 61:1]; 10:21; Acts 4:27; 10:38); (c) the old passion narrative fills the Messiah title with new content when it interprets Jesus' path into death from the psalms of the suffering Righteous One or of the suffering and persecuted David (cf. Theobald, *Der Prozess Jesu* (see above): 76–79; see further note 50). When Kinzer pleads for a "King-of-the-Jews Christology" with the rationale that only this truly guarantees Christology's connection to Israel, the answer must be: for all of the aforementioned transformations, this connection is fundamental.

puts it, "Let your light shine before men, so that they may see your good deeds and praise your Father in heaven" (Matt 5:16).[49]

If, after everything that has happened, Jews today come to faith in the Messiah Jesus, then this is an unexpected gift that simultaneously shames and enriches the Church, and one that demands her reverence. It could be, and would be desirable, that this small seed would lead to a change in the consciousness of the Church, as a result of which the talk of Israel as the root of the Church, as taken up by the Second Vatican Council, would become a living experience in her own midst. The confession of Jesus as Messiah from Israel and for Israel, which Christians must still discover in its enduring polarity, includes many things: the recognition without reservation of the ways of Judaism under the sign of the never-revoked and eternal covenant of God with his people; not coopting Jesus as Israel's Messiah for their own faith; showing respect when Jews not only acknowledge Jesus as their "brother," but also honor him even as a prophet and perceive him as the servant of God who suffered and was maltreated like so unendingly many of his sisters and brothers;[50] not dismissing the uncertain future of the state of Israel from the messianic hope in spite of all of the human abysses of hatred and violence in the Palestinian conflict; internalizing the fact that salvation and rescue also occur apart from the Church and without her: "O, the depth of the riches and wisdom and knowledge of God! How unfathomable are his decisions, how inscrutable his ways! . . . ," Paul declares at the end of his Israel chapters, and thereby invites us, in his inimitable fashion, to praise the *Deus absconditus*, whose mystery infinitely transcends all human thinking (Rom 11:33–36; cf. Eph 3:20).

(Translated by John David Martin, James Earle Patrick, and Wayne Coppins from the German: "Jesus, Messias aus Israel und für Israel. Neutestamentliche Perspektiven")

49. Michael Theobald, "'Wie mich der Vater gesandt hat, so sende ich euch' (Jn. 20:21). Missionarische Gestalten im Johannesevangelium" (2008), in Michael Theobald, *Studien zum Corpus Iohanneum* (Wissenschaftliche Untersuchungen zum Neuen Testament, 267; Tübingen: Mohr Siebeck, 2010): 472–89.

50. Bound up with Jesus' cross is a change in the concept of the "messianic"; suffering and being persecuted receive their own quality as "messianic birth pangs." Here, too, we may recall the collective interpretation of the Servant Songs, especially Isa 52:13–53:12; cf. Mußner, *Traktat über die Juden* (see note 10), 74–78 ("Israel als Gottesknecht" ["Israel as Servant of God"]).

On Lukan and Pauline Preservation of Identity

Response to Michael Theobald

Henk Bakker

FIRST, I WISH TO EXPRESS MY APPRECIATION for Michael Theobald's fine and scholarly address regarding major Christological aspects within Pauline and Lukan thinking, in particular as related to the issue how, if at all, and why, Jesus was for Paul, and for Luke, the Messiah for the Jewish people for their time.

Let me briefly respond to some of Theobald's argumentation, and then conclude with pointing in a direction to which our discussion may be heading, I hope. Theobald sets out with the observation that the mainstream of the early Church's multifaceted communities, indeed, stood the test of persistent temptation ("ständige Versuchung") to make it succumb to gnostic-dualistic ways of interpreting Jesus and earliest Christian traditions.[1] However, and the conjunction is his "certainly . . . but" ("gewiss . . . aber"), overall, the mainstream of the early orthodox Church neglected to take Jesus' Jewishness seriously into account. Yes, they respected the incarnation ("Menschwerdung"), but at the high cost of Jesus' Jewish identity ("Jude-Sein"). And, for that matter, I think, the Church has ever since suffered from a new form

1. Loofs classifies this temptation as "the most perilous crisis" ["die gefährlichste Krisis"] in early Christian times; see Friedrich Loofs, *Leitfaden zum Studium der Dogmengeschichte* (Tübingen: Max Niemeyer Verlag, 7th edn 1968): 98.

of docetism, which does not renounce Jesus' humanity, not even his humanity within his deity, but a docetism which takes pride in embracing Jesus' incarnation by declaring his Jewishness void. He became man (and therefore ethical model, even *norma normans* [a normalizing norm], for what humanity and the humane is all about), and the Jewishness he took upon himself was something extra, just to let his people know that Jewish religion can do without its rituals and identity markers. By consequence, these two sides of Jesus (man + Jew) were played out against each other, for as the "perfect man" he could be critical of his own, and stand at a moral distance from Israel, for he was not really one of them.[2] I will return to this presumption later, and first formulate my hypothesis, which is that according to Scripture Jesus did not become man *and* Jew, but, since he became a Jew, he evidently became man.

Theobald, then, accurately notices that the Jewish people have dogmatically been degraded to become merely the forerunner of the Church ("Vorstufe der Kirche"). As a consequence, the Church forgot about its Jewish roots and built its history in the air,[3] an aberration which I classify as a form of ecclesiological docetism that disabled the mainline worldwide Churches from looking critically at their own history and genuinely evaluating the devastation of this loss.[4]

Furthermore, Theobald observes traces of Israel's protracted bond with God as a Jewish people in Paul's letter to the Romans, and in Luke's book on the earliest whereabouts of the Church, the Book of Acts. In Romans 11:25–36 he underscores the eschatological Zion-centeredness of Paul's perspective, and the lasting role of the remnant (*š*^{e}*'ērîṯ*) in Israel's moments of crisis, which validates the promise, unconditionally, that "all Israel" will be saved. In utter adoration, Paul

2. This was one of the turns the German liberal school took in the nineteenth century, and to which Karl Barth objected in the second decade of the twentieth century. Jesus showed quintessential morals, from man to man, and even though he held a high standard, decent Christians do quite well in following him.

3. Cf. Karl R. Hagenbach, *Lehrbuch der Dogmengeschichte* (Leipzig: Verlag von S. Hirzel, 3rd edn 1853): 36, with regard to Marcion, who renounced anything Jewish in the gospel, and who, by consequence, built "Christianity in the air" ["das Christentum in die Luft"].

4. Cf. Karl Barth, *Kirchliche Dogmatik* IV.1 par. 62 (Zürich: Theologischer Verlag Zürich, 1986): 729: "There is an ecclesiological docetism . . ." ["Es gibt einen ekklesiologischen Doketismus . . ."]

could only express the sheer wonder of this grace by affirming it by doxology (*autōi hē doxa*), and by mystery (*mustērion*), and in climactic wording ("Höhepunkt"). Moreover, in Acts 3:20, Luke seems to reckon with the possibility that this promised end could occur if, and only if, Jerusalem's leaders would repent and convert. Then the *apokatastasis pantōn* for Israel would commence ("Zeit des Aufatmens für Israel"), and Jesus would be sent to Israel again, Peter affirmed. Accordingly, I take Luke's underlying premise to be that the predicted fate of the temple Jesus spoke about did not have to happen after all.[5] Indeed, I think this was the reason why James, Jesus' brother, was portrayed in early Christian texts as a Jew who was allowed permanent entrance to the temple, who prayed unremittingly for his people, and who was truly respected by many.[6] My strong opinion is that Christian Jews lived with the expectation that the temple, "this place,"[7] could be saved, rededicated, and re-inaugurated to the Eternal One.[8]

Theobald concludes with suggesting that the words "from Israel" ("aus Israel") certainly imply "for Israel" ("für Israel"). Israel's vocation remains, well preserved in God's providence, although all too often he conceals himself (*Deus absconditus*). Yet, he was, still is, and remains entirely present. Hence Theobald's summon to expect the unexpected, to deem conversions of Jews to Jesus as humbling reminders of their

5. The author, Luke (who supposedly used several sources, and developed some of his own), composed his Gospel and the Book of Acts in retrospect of his dealings with some of the apostles, and probably with Paul as well. Of course, he incorporated narratives and sayings which merely served his cause, as to make his point. I take it that Luke wants to illustrate by delineating early Christian history and development, as he envisages how the gospel spreads in his days, how churches multiply and traverse national and adjacent borders, illustrating that the kingdom of God is near, and the Jewish country and its temple eventually will be purified and transformed. This expectation will certainly have been pinpointed and adjusted to match with all kinds of situations, incidents, occurrences, and speculations. The presumption that the downfall of the temple "did not have to happen" is part and parcel of early Christian eschatological thinking.

6. Many priests were converted to the Christian faith in the early years of the young Christian Church, see Acts 6:7, "a large number of priests [*polus te ochlos tōn hierōn*] became obedient to the faith."

7. See for example Acts 6:13, 14; 7:7; 21:28 (Hebr. *hammāqôm hazzeh*).

8. Cf. forthcoming, Henk Bakker, "Αὕτη ἡ ἀνάστασις ἡ πρώτη (Rev 20:5b): Making Sense of the Apocalypse's Prefinal Phase" (Festschrift Riemer Roukema, 2023).

grace and our (Gentile Christian) arrogance, and to be open to welcome Jewish people as a people of God, regardless of their position toward the Christian faith.

I do concur with Theobald's balanced conclusions, but I suggest they be supplemented or augmented by vital notions of a well-considered Spirit-Christology, hinted at by Paul, and indicated by Luke as well.[9] According to Luke and Paul, the Spirit signifies (and carries) the designated fullness of God who establishes and preserves the identity of the Jewish people,[10] and for that matter also its collective embodiment in the *māšîaḥ*.

As of consequence, Jesus the ideal man, model for humanity and the humane, set at a distance from his own people (merely appearing to be Jewish, but not really so in his very personhood), did not exist. This is obvious in the Gospel of John, because the eternal *logos* of God (Word, Wisdom), cannot be identified as a *logos asarkos*,[11] for at the closing of the prologue the *logos* is indicated as God's "only one" (*monogenēs*), the predicate used in the LXX for Isaac, and for Jephthah's daughter.[12] Eternal Word-ness and Jewish identity seem to go together quite well in the

9. See Luke 1:35; 3:22; 10:21; Acts 10:38; 16:7 (cf. Matt 1:18, 20), and in Paul: Gal 4:4; Rom 1:4; 8:9, 15; 15:16; 1 Cor 12:3 (*kurios Iēsous*), and 2 Cor 3:17 (*ho de kurios to pneuma estin*). Cf. Cornelis van der Kooi, *This Incredibly Benevolent Force: The Holy Spirit in Reformed Theology and Spirituality* (Grand Rapids, MI: Eerdmans, 2018), and Henk Bakker, *Jezus. Reconstructie en revisie* (Utrecht: Kok Boekencentrum, 3rd print 2021): 139–49. See also publications on Spirit-Christology by Piet Schoonenberg, Harold Hunter, Robert Jenson, Myk Habets and David Coffey.

10. On the Spirit and the emergence, preservation, and conservation of identity, see particularly (in Torah:) Gen 1:2 (cf. Job 33:4; Ps 33:6); Num 11:17, 24, 25, 29; 27:18; Deut 34:9; (in the Prophets:) Jdg 6:34 (and other judges); 1 Sam 16:13; Isa 11:2; 42:1; 44:3; 59:21; 61:1; 63:10–11; Ezek 36:27; 37:14; 39:29; Joel 2:28–29; Hag 2:6; Zec 12:10; (in the Gospels:) Matt 3:11, 16; 12:18; Luke 4:18; John 1:33; 14:17, 26; (in the Letters:) Rom 1:4; 8:14–16; 1 Cor 12:13; 2 Cor 3:3, 6, 17–18; Gal 4:6; and (in the other books:) Acts 2:4, 17–18; 15:28.

11. Instead of *logos asarkos*—so in Hippolytus, *Contra Noëtum* 4.7, 10, 11, 12—it is better to use *logos presarkos*; see David Griffin, *The Word Became Flesh: A Rapprochement of Christian Natural Law and Radical Christological Ethics* (Australian College of Theology Monograph Series; Eugene, OR: Wipf & Stock, 2016): 152—"*asarkos* is better substituted by *presarkos*, as '*presarkos*' provides the temporal aspect essential to a Christian theory of reality, and also implies the later *ensarkos*."

12. Gen 22:2, 12, 16 (3x *monogenēs* [LXX]), and Jdg 11:34 (*monogenēs* [LXX]).

prologue of the fourth Gospel.[13] However, John's view is certainly not adoptionistic in scope, since Spirit and Son share the same qualities and profession. Both are addressed as "Counsellor" (*paraklētos*).[14] In concurrent Christian literature, too, features of a pre-critical Spirit-Christology seem equally traceable (e.g., *Odes of Solomon, 2 Clement, The Shepherd of Hermas*).[15]

Since the downgrading of identity from the onset of the new millennium until now—indeed, the distortion and loss of identity—seems to be a strategy of all sorts of extremisms, such as antisemitism, I would certainly not wish to keep the identity of *logos* too vague. *Logos* and *pneuma*, from eternity, go together in bringing about salvation history, which starts with creation and follows the vocation of the Jewish people of Israel, in particular its "remnant," embodied in its Messiah Jesus Christ, for "salvation is from the Jews" (John 4:22).

13. Cf. John 1:14, 18. The enduring presence of the Logos/Wisdom at the "bosom" of the Father (*ho ōn eis ton kolpon tou patros*) confirms, and affirms, the identity of the *monogenēs* as (both!) Israel's *and* God's son.

14. John 14:16 (cf. 1 John 2:1). Paul, too, conceives of the Spirit and the Christ as unremittingly interceding for the Church (Rom 8:26, 34).

15. *Odes of Solomon* 19.1–5; 24.1–2; 36.1–7 (cf. 12.12; 41.9, 14–15), *2 Clement* 9.5; 14.4, *Shepherd of Hermas* 58.1–2; 59.5; 78.1; 89.1–2; 91.5. See also Theophilus of Antioch, *Ad Autolycum* 2.10 (*Logos = pneuma*), and Tertullian, *Adversus Marcionem* III.16.5 ("*Spiritus Creatoris qui est Christus*"). Cf. Henk Bakker, "Pneuma-Christology as Applied Christology: Intimacy and Immediacy in the *Odes of Solomon*," in *The Spirit is Moving: New Pathways in Pneumatology*, ed. Gijsbert van den Brink, Eveline van Staalduine-Sulman, and Maarten Wisse (Studies in Reformed Theology, 38; Leiden: Brill, 2019): 93–108; and Henk Bakker, "Kissing Hermas: Convertive Mystagogy in the *Shepherd*," in *Early Christian Mystagogy and the Body*, ed. Nienke Vos and Paul van Geest (Annua Nuntia Lovaniensia, 83; Leuven: Peeters, 2022): 21–47.

The Jewishness of Jesus and Its Significance for Christology

Helmut Hoping

JESUS OF NAZARETH was born of a Jewish woman (Gal 4:4) and circumcised on the eighth day (Luke 2:21), as the law for Jewish boys prescribes (Gen 17:9–14). Jesus was a Jew; he lived as a Jew and died as a Jew. To be sure, Jesus' Jewishness was usually not contested in theology or the Church, but its theological meaning was not fully recognized until the twentieth century in the wake of the rediscovery of the Jewish element in Christianity.

The first impetus toward engagement with the Jewish Jesus came from Jewish scholars. Alongside Abraham Geiger (1810–1874),[1] one should mention above all Joseph Klausner (1874–1958) whose book *Jesus of Nazareth: His Time, His Life and His Teaching* (1930) was published in German shortly before the National Socialists seized power.[2] Among the Jesus books that Jewish scholars published after the Shoah, the

1. Cf. Susannah Heschel, *Der jüdische Jesus und das Christentum. Abraham Geigers Herausforderung an die christliche Theologie* (Berlin: Jüdische Verlagsanstalt, 2001).

2. Cf. Joseph Klausner, *Jesus von Nazareth. Seine Zeit, sein Leben und seine Lehre*, ed. Christian Wiese (Berlin: Suhrkamp / Jüdischer Verlag, 2021), reissuing the German translation of Klausner's third, revised edition from 1952. His Hebrew original was published in 1921, and appeared in English soon after: Joseph Klausner, *Jesus of Nazareth: His Life, Times, and Teaching*, trans. Herbert Danby (New York: Macmillan, 1925).

Jesus book by David Flusser (1917–2000) probably experienced the widest distribution in the German language.[3]

According to the Christian confession, Jesus is not just a Galilean prophet or teacher of wisdom, but the incarnate Son of God. The themes of this article are the identity of the incarnate Son of God as a circumcised Jew, the Messiahship of Jesus, the relationship of the people of Israel to the body of the crucified, resurrected, and exalted Messiah Jesus, and the question of the validity of the land promise.

1. The Son—God's Word becomes Jewish flesh

Denial of the true Jewishness of Jesus was part of National Socialist ideology. Alfred Rosenberg (1893–1946), the chief ideologue of German National Socialism, spread the myth of the Aryan Jesus.[4] Shortly after the end of the National Socialist reign of terror and the Shoah, Karl Barth (1886–1968) declared that Jesus Christ and Israel are "two inseparable realities, not only at that time but also for all of history, indeed for all eternity." The opinion cannot be that "we believe in Jesus Christ who just happened *by chance* to be an Israelite, but who could just as well have come from another people. No, here one must think very strictly. For Jesus Christ . . . was *necessarily a Jew.* There is no overlooking this fact; rather, it belongs to the concrete reality of God and his revelation."[5] Barth spelled out the Jewishness of Jesus starting from the theology of the Johannine prologue: "The Word became—not 'flesh,' man, humiliated and suffering man in some sort of generality, but *Jewish* flesh."[6] God's Word became "messianic man."[7]

3. Cf. David Flusser, *Jesus* (Reinbeck bei Hamburg: Rowohlt, 22nd edn 2000 [1968]).

4. Susannah Heschel, *The Aryan Jesus: Christian Theologians and the Bible in Nazi Germany* (Princeton: Princeton University Press, 2008).

5. "zwei nicht zu trennende Wirklichkeiten, nicht nur damals, sondern für die ganze Geschichte, ja für alle Ewigkeit" // "dass wir an Jesus Christus glauben, der nun eben zufällig ein Israelit war, der aber ebenso gut auch einem anderen Volk hätte entstammen können. Nein, hier muss man ganz streng denken. Denn Jesus Christus . . . war notwendig Jude. An dieser Tatsache ist nicht vorbeizusehen, sondern sie gehört zu der konkreten Wirklichkeit Gottes und seiner Offenbarung"—Karl Barth, *Dogmatik im Grundriß. Vorlesungen gehalten im Sommersemester 1946 an der Universität* (Bonn / Zollikon / Zürich: Evangelischer Verlag, 1947): 84.

6. "das Wort wurde–nicht 'Fleisch,' Mensch, erniedrigter und leidender Mensch in irgendeiner Allgemeinheit, sondern jüdisches Fleisch"—Karl Barth, *Die Kirchliche Dogmatik* IV/1 (Studienausgabe; Zürich: Theologischer Verlag, 1986): 181.

7. Jochen Denker, *Das Wort wurde messianischer Mensch. Die Theologie Karl Barths und die Theologie des Johannesprologs* (Neukirchen-Vluyn: Neukirchener-Verlag, 2002).

Jesus was a circumcised Jew from Nazareth in Galilee. The Feast of the Circumcision of the Lord (*Circumcisio Domini*) existed in the Roman Rite until the Vatican liturgical reform. Why the feast was done away with after the Shoah is difficult to comprehend.[8] In very recent times, individual theologians have spoken out in favor of reintroducing the Feast of the Circumcision of the Lord into the Catholic liturgy.[9]

For the Jewish people, circumcision is a sign of the covenant: "So shall my covenant, whose sign you bear in your flesh, be an everlasting covenant" (Gen 17:13). The Apostle Paul views the circumcision of Jesus as the confirmation of the promises to the patriarchs, Abraham, Isaac, and Jacob/Israel: "Christ has become a servant to the circumcision on behalf of the truth of God to confirm the promises to the fathers" (Rom 15:8). Theologians from antiquity and the medieval period understood the circumcision of Jesus later primarily as a sign of the cultural difference between Judaism and Christianity.[10] The demand for a federal ban on circumcision, as it was raised in Germany a few years ago, was perceived by Jews as an attack on their identity.[11]

If God's Word became Jewish flesh, then the Jewishness of Jesus cannot be of incidental relevance to Christology. It is not a human nature that is born but rather a concrete human being, to whom also his or her gendered identity belongs.[12] Therefore, God's incarnation cannot be adequately expressed in language if one says that God's Word took on human nature, became man, but not a circumcised Jew. This is said

8. Alex Stock, *Poetische Dogmatik. Christologie: 1. Namen* (Paderborn / Munich / Vienna / Zürich: Schöningh, 1995).

9. Christian Rutishauser, "Das Fest der Beschneidung des Herrn – ein Plädoyer für dessen Rückgewinnung," in Christian Rutishauser, *Christlichen Glauben denken. Im Dialog mit der jüdischen Tradition* (Forum Christen und Juden, 15; Münster: LIT, 2016): 233–48; Jan-Heiner Tück, "Beschneidung des Herrn. Warum Papst Franziskus eine Lücke in der katholischen Gedenkkultur schließen sollte," *Communio: Internationale Katholische Zeitschrift* 48 (2019), 216–30; Jan-Heiner Tück (ed.), *Die Beschneidung Jesu. Was sie Juden und Christen heute bedeutet* (Freiburg i. Br. / Basel / Vienna: Herder, 2020).

10. Andrew S. Jacobs, *Christ Circumcised: A Study in Early Christian History and Difference* (Philadelphia, PA: Penn Press, 2012).

11. Alfred Bodenheimer, *Haut ab! Die Juden in der Beschneidungsdebatte* (Göttingen: Wallstein, 2012).

12. Helmut Hoping, "Ein Gottessohn, der nicht Mann sein soll. Der Knabe in der Krippe gerät in die Mühlen der Genderdebatte: Wie lässt sich Weihnachten geschlechtergerecht feiern?," *Frankfurter Allgemeine Zeitung* (Feuilleton) 28 Nov 2020: 9.

to be important historically but not theologically.[13] But whoever considers the Jewishness of Jesus as theologically unimportant commits—thus already Pinchas Lapide (1922–1997) with respect to Karl Rahner (1904–1984)—"*disincarnation*: the reduction of a living human form to an abstract, bodyless idea."[14]

The Jewishness of the incarnate Son of God must become a central interpretive tool of incarnation theology. The Jewish identity of Jesus requires an *interpretatio iudaica* of the Christology of the *vere Deus—vere homo* (Nicea 325).[15] In this context, Hans Hermann Henrix has spoken of the incarnation of God as his "inJewation" or "Jew becoming" (*Judewerdung*).[16] What this means concretely can be shown, for example, using the idiolect of the prophetic proclamation and prayer language of Jesus. However, the incarnation of the Word of God must not be understood in the sense of an absorption of the divine in the human. Even in his utmost condescension in the Jew Jesus, God remains the exalted and eternal God.[17] The "unmixed" (ασυγγύτως) of the formulation of the Council of Chalcedon (451) is the "Jewish thorn in Christology."[18]

In conversation with Jacob Neusner, Joseph Ratzinger / Benedict XVI says in his much-discussed Jesus book that Jesus understood "himself as the Torah—as the word of God in person."[19] Here, Ratzinger presupposes the understanding of Torah as *instruction, teaching, word of God*

13. Cf. Ingolf U. Dalferth, "Gott für uns. Die Bedeutung des christologischen Dogmas für die christliche Theologie," in *Denkwürdiges Geheimnis. Beiträge zur Gotteslehre. Festschrift für Eberhard Jüngel*, ed. Ingolf U. Dalferth et al. (Tübingen: Mohr Siebeck, 2004): 51–75, at 74.

14. "*Desinkarnation* – die Reduktion einer lebendigen Menschengestalt zu einer abstrakten, leiblosen Idee," Pinchas Lapide and Karl Rahner, *Heil von den Juden? Ein Gespräch* (Mainz: Grünewald, 1983): 62.

15. Cf. Helmut Hoping, "Gottes Wort in jüdischem Fleisch. Jesus von Nazareth und der Gedanke der Inkarnation," in *Christologie zwischen Judentum und Christentum. Jesus der Jude aus Galiäa, und der christliche Erlöser*, ed. Christian Danz, Kathy Ehrensperger and Walter Homolka (Tübingen: Mohr Siebeck, 2020): 229–46, at 239–45.

16. Cf. Hans Hermann Henrix, "Menschwerdung Gottes konkret: Judewerdung," in *Wendung nach Jerusalem. Friedrich-Wilhem Marquardts Theologie im Gespräch*, ed. Hanna Leming (Gütersloh: Kaiser, 1999): 256–69.

17. Helmut Hoping, *Jesus aus Galiläa. Messias und Gottes Sohn* (Freiburg i. Br. / Basel / Vienna: Herder, 2019): 345–46.

18. Joseph Wohlmuth, *Die Tora spricht die Sprache der Menschen. Theologische Aufsätze und Meditationen zur Beziehung von Judentum und Christentum* (Paderborn / Munich / Vienna / Zürich: Schöningh, 2019): 182.

19. Joseph Ratzinger / Benedict XVI, *Jesus of Nazareth: From the Baptism in the Jordan to the Transfiguration*, trans. Adrian J. Walker (New York: Doubleday, 2007): 110.

and *revelation* and not the narrow concentration on the law with its individual stipulations.[20] The Pontifical Commission for Religious Relations with Judaism calls Jesus the "living Torah of God" in its document for the fifty-year anniversary of *Nostra Aetate* (1965).[21] This designation is justified by saying that for the Jews it is in the Torah that God's word is present.

The talk of Jesus as "Torah in person," which has appeared in theology now for about twenty years,[22] has not gone unchallenged; after all, it can easily be understood as a new form of substitution—the law of Christ supplants the Torah of Moses.[23] But Jesus does not take the place of God's instruction for Israel. Klaus Berger has objected that the Torah is "not a human being" and can "not be replaced."[24] According to the Christian confession, Jesus is also more than the authentic interpretation of the Torah—thus the objection raised by Karl-Heinz Menke.[25]

A more suitable approach to the notion of incarnation may be the indwelling of God (*Shekinah*) in his people and in the Holy of Holies of the Temple, even if an incarnation of God may also go beyond that.[26]

20. Cf. Jan-Heiner Tück, "Der Jude Jesus – 'die Tora in Person'?," in *Christologie zwischen Judentum und Christentum. Jesus der Jude aus Galiläa, und der christliche Erlöser*, ed. Christian Danz, Kathy Ehrensperger and Walter Homolka (Tübingen: Mohr Siebeck, 2020): 183–207.

21. Papal Commission for Religious Relations with the Jews, *"The Gifts and the Calling of God Are Irrevocable" (Rom 11:29): A Reflection on Theological Questions Pertaining to Catholic–Jewish Relations on the Occasion of the 50th Anniversary of "Nostra ætate" (No. 4)* (Dec 10, 2015): no. 26.

22. Cf. Jacobus Schoneveld, "Die Tora in Person. Eine Lektüre des Prologs des Johannesevangeliums als Beitrag zu einer Christologie ohne Antijudaismus," *Kirche und Bibel* 5 (1990): 40–52.

23. Cf. Eberhard Jüngel, "Der hypothetische Jesus, Anmerkungen zum Jesus-Buch des Papstes," in *Annäherungen an Jesus von Nazareth. Das Buch des Papstes in der Diskussion*, ed. Jan-Heiner Tück (Ostfildern: Grünewald, 2008): 94–103; Paul Petzel, "'Ich sage nur ein höfliches Nein und gehe meine Wege.' Zu Joseph Ratzingers / Benedikts XVI. Lektüre von Jacob Neusners Jesusbuch," *Orientierung* 72 (2008): 167–74.

24. "kein Mensch," "nicht ersetzt warden"—Klaus Berger, "Kant sowie ältere protestantische Systematik. Anfragen des Exegeten an Benedikt XVI.," in *Jesus von Nazareth kontrovers. Rückfragen an Joseph Ratzinger*, ed. Karl Lehmann (Berlin: LIT, 2007): 27–40, at 33.

25. Karl-Heinz Menke, *Jesus ist Gott der Sohn. Denkformen und Brennpunkte der Christologie* (Regensburg: Pustet, 2008).

26. Cf. Hoping, *Jesus aus Galiläa* (see note 17), 203–207; Tück, "Der Jude Jesus" (see note 20), 203–207.

In the prologue of the fourth Gospel, the Word, who was in the beginning with God and "became flesh and camped among us" (ὁ λογός σαρξ ἐγένετο καί ἐσκήνωμεν ἐν ὑμὶν—John 1:14) is identified with the Messiah Jesus, of whom it is said that he is the "only begotten (μονογενής), who is God and rests on the heart of the Father" (John 1:18).

2. *Yeshua haMashiach—Jesus Christ*

If Jesus himself professed his messiahship, then it was probably only toward the end of his life. The "messianic secret" thesis (Mark 8:27–32), according to which Jesus initially kept his messiahship secret because of possible political misunderstandings, was called into question by William Wrede (1859–1906), cofounder of the history of religions school.[27] Shortly before his death, he corrected his position in a letter of January 2, 1905 to Adolf von Harnack (1851–1930): "I am more inclined than earlier to believe that Jesus regarded himself as designated to be the Messiah."[28]

There is also no reason to doubt that Jesus declared, at the latest before the Sanhedrin and Pilate, his messiahship (Mark 14:61–62) or royal dignity (Mark 15:2; John 18:33–38).[29] Otherwise, the *titulus crucis* "Jesus of Nazareth King of the Jews" (Mark 15:26; John 19:19–22), on which the Roman governor Pilate insisted against the Sanhedrin, would also not be able to be explained. For after the end of the political kingship in Israel, "King of the Jews" could only mean the Messiah of Israel (Ps Sol 17.3–4, 32).

Moses ben Maimon (1135–1204) counts the expectation of the Messiah among the fundamental doctrines of the Jewish faith. In his Mishnah commentary on *Sanhedrin,* Maimonides writes: The twelfth of the thirteen fundamental doctrines "refers to the Messianic era. We are to believe as fact that the Messiah will come and not consider him late. If

27. Cf. William Wrede, *Das Messiasgeheimnis in den Evangelien. Zugleich ein Beitrag zum Verständnis des Markusevangeliums* (Göttingen: Vandenhoeck & Ruprecht, 1969 [1901]).

28. "Ich bin geneigter als früher zu glauben, daß Jesus selbst sich als zum Messias ausersehen betrachtet hat."—cited according to Hans Rollmann and Werner Zager, "Unveröffentlichte Briefe William Wredes zur Problematisierung des messianischen Selbstverständnisses Jesu," *Zeitschrift für Neuere Theologiegeschichte* 8/2 (2001): 274–322, at 317.

29. Hoping, *Jesus aus Galiläa* (see note 17), 106–108.

he delays, wait for him (Hab. 2:3); set no time limit for his coming. . . . A corollary of this principle is the assertion that the king of Israel must come only from the house of David. . . ."[30] In the Jewish morning prayer of Orthodox Jews, the expectation of the Messiah is formulated as follows in the *Yigdal,* the opening hymn of the prayer service: "He will send our anointed at the end of days, to redeem them that wait for the end—his salvation. In the abundance of his lovingkindness God will quicken the dead. Blessed for evermore be his glorious name."[31]

Even though in Judaism over the centuries the expectation of the Messiah has remained alive,[32] it has nevertheless faded since the nineteenth century, especially in liberal or progressive Judaism. *The Messiah Isn't Coming. Farewell to the Jewish Redeemer*—so reads the title of a book by Walter Homolka, Juni Hoppe, and Daniel Krochmalnik, which was published by Herder at the beginning of 2022.[33] The idea of Messiah—so Homolka in his introduction—cannot be a bridge for the dialogue between Jews and Christians.

Homolka cites the Jewish scientist and philosopher of religion Yeshayahu Leibowitz (1903–1994), who, in his Conversations About God and the World, said: "Every Messiah who comes in the present is a false Messiah."[34] Leibowitz was an orthodox Jew who defined his Judaism in terms of observing the *mitzvot* of the *Torah.* He criticized Christianity as a religion without *mitzvot.* But Leibowitz did not advocate a messianism without a Messiah: "Of course, I also believe that the Messiah will come," thus Leibowitz, but the coming of Messiah remains "a future coming."[35]

30. Maimonides on Mishnah Sanhedrin 10:1:29—Isadore Twersky (ed.), *A Maimonides Reader* (Springfield, NJ: Behrman House, Inc., 1972): 422. Twersky credits the translation to Arnold J. Wolf, "Maimonides on Immortality and the Principles of Judaism," *Helek: Sanhedrin, Chapter Ten* (American Jewish Congress, 1966).

31. Israel Abrahams (ed.), *Annotated Edition of the Authorised Daily Prayer Book,* trans. Simeon Singer (London: Eyre and Spottiswoode, 5674—1914): 3.

32. Nathan Peter Levinson, *Der Messias* (Stuttgart: Kreuz, 2007).

33. Cf. Walter Homolka, Juni Hoppe, and Daniel Krochmalnik, *Der Messias kommt nicht. Abschied vom jüdischen Erlöser* (Afterword: Magnus Striet; Freiburg i. Br. / Basel / Vienna: Herder, 2022).

34. "Jeder Messias, der in der Gegenwart kommt, ist ein falscher Messias," Jeshajahu Leibowitz and Jeshajahu Shashar, *Gespräche über Gott und die Welt,* ed. Michael Shashar; trans. Matthias Schmidt (Frankfurt a. Main: Dvorah, 1990): 148.

35. "Natürlich, auch ich glaube daran, dass der Messias kommen wird" . . . "ein zukünftiges Kommen"—*Ibid.,* 148.

The origin of the Messiah from the lineage of David forms a central part of the New Testament proclamation. The birth narratives in the Gospels of Matthew and Luke give Bethlehem, the city of David, as the place of Jesus' birth (Matt 2:1; Luke 2:11). However, as what was decisive for Jesus' messiahship—as the interpretation of Psalm 110:1 in Mark 12:35–37 shows—is not the sonship of David, since David himself—thus the teaching of Jesus about the Messiah—calls him Lord (κύριον). Therefore, the Messiah must be more than "David's Son"; he is the Son of Man, the Son of God. The Revelation of John also makes clear that the Messiah Jesus is more than the "Son of David." At the end of Revelation, the resurrected and exalted Lord says of himself: "I am the root and the stem of David, the bright morning-star" (Rev 22:16).

3. The People Israel and the Body of Christ

According to the genealogy of the Gospel of Matthew, Jesus is not only the "son of David" but also the "son of Abraham" (Matt 1:1), and yet as the Messiah of Israel he is greater than Abraham as well as Isaac and Jacob, to whom the name Israel was given because he had struggled with God (Gen 32:29), and also than Moses (Heb 3:1–5). This is why Mark S. Kinzer calls Jesus, the son of Mary, "the representative and individual embodiment of the entire people of Israel."[36]

In the Jew Jesus of Nazareth, the God of Israel confirmed his faithfulness to his people, whom he had acquired as his special possession. Jesus is the "Yes" of God to the promises to Israel, God's "Amen": "For he is the 'yes' (ναί) to everything that God has promised. Therefore, also through him comes the Amen (ἀμὴν) to the praise of God, mediated through us" (2 Cor 1:20). "On behalf of the truth of God, Christ has become a servant to the circumcision to confirm the promises to the fathers" (Rom 15:8). The Christological significance of Jesus' Jewishness, which was demonstrated in the first section, excludes any form of *replacement theology* and/or *supersessionism*, respectively. If Jesus of Nazareth as *Torah* of God in person is the Messiah of Israel, who gave his life for the many, then God cannot have rejected the Jewish people whom

36. Mark S. Kinzer, *Postmissionary Messianic Judaism. Redefining Christian Engagement with the Jewish People* (Grand Rapids, MI: Brazos, 2005): 219.

he chose as his special possession, and this means that his promises to his people remain in force.

The election of Israel as God's special possession is thus not a *perfectum*, a completed action, but also continues *post Christum natum*. For Israel—so the Apostle Paul—is not rejected; it has the sonship, the covenants, the instruction, the sacred service, and the promises (Rom 9:4). Through their election, the Jews are loved by God for the sake of the fathers (cf. Rom 11:28b). "For the grace and calling that God bestows are irrevocable" (Rom 11:29). Christians and Jews have in common the belief in the one God, the God of Abraham, Isaac, and Jacob, who was also the God of Jesus. Jesus summarized the *Torah*, which for him was God's instruction, in the two commandments of love for God and love for neighbor (cf. Deut 6:4–5; Lev 19:18). Jesus does not mean the end of the law, its abolition; Jesus is the goal (τέλος) of the law (Rom 10:4).

Nowhere in the New Testament is the Church of Christ called the "new Israel." The Church should give up this self-designation since it is associated with the idea of a substitution of Israel by the Church. By contrast, the Church as the "messianic people" should be held onto, since the Church is the body of Christ, of the Messiah Jesus. In the constitution on the Church, *Lumen Gentium* (1964), those who believe in Jesus, the Christ from Israel, are said to be the "messianic people" who have "Christ for its head," "'who was delivered up [*passivum divinum; author's note*] for our sins, and rose again for our justification' (Rom 4:25), and now, having won a name which is above all names (Phil 2:6), reigns in glory in heaven." The messianic people of the Church of Christ is the "people of the acquirement" (λαὸς εἰς περιποίησιν—1 Pet 2:9). The messianic time is the time of the Church, which will be completed at the end of time, "when Christ, our life (cf. Col 3:4), shall appear, and 'creation itself will be delivered from its slavery to corruption into the freedom of the glory of the sons of God' (Rom 8:21)."[37]

The Jewish people is the messianic people of God by descent. The Jews remain the first owners of the Holy Scriptures vis-à-vis the Christians, so as to bear witness to the one and only God. The distinction between the Jews, to whom God has given the *Torah*, and the *goyim*—so

37. *LG* 9.

Bruce Marshall—is constitutive.[38] But one can speak rightly of a people of God from Jews and Gentiles, independently of the existence of converted or Messianic Jews, who acknowledge Jesus as Messiah. The Noachide covenant of God with all creatures is to be distinguished from the Sinai covenant and the new covenant in Christ Jesus. It is the presupposition for the special election of Israel and the acquirement of the Church as people of God.

If—as Christians and Messianic Jews believe—at the right hand of the Father is none other than Jesus of Nazareth, who as a Jew lived, died, and was resurrected from the dead, then the Body of the risen Jewish Messiah cannot be halved; in that case, there belong to him, alongside those who are united in his Church with the Risen One through baptism and faith, also those who, according to the flesh, are united with him as children of Abraham and Sarah. This has been rightly emphasized by Robert William Jenson (1930–2017), one of the most significant Lutheran theologians of the twentieth century.[39] Jews, for whom the Messiah is yet to come or will never come, because he is not a real person but a personification of messianic hopes, will object to the existence of a two-part Body of the Messiah of Israel, which as people of God consists of Synagogue and Church. By contrast, Messianic Jews—so Mark Kinzer—can understand themselves as members of the Body of the crucified and risen *Yeshua haMashiach*.[40]

In Romans 11:25–27, Paul speaks of a mystery (μυστήριον) of the end-time salvation of "all Israel" (πᾶς Ἰσραὴλ). Based on the Zion tradition of the *Tanakh*, the Savior from Zion would be thought of as the God of Israel and not as his Messiah, but Paul evidently identifies the Savior from Zion with the Messiah Jesus. It was on this basis that Franz Mussner (1916–2016) developed his theory of a special way (*Sonderweg*) to salvation for Israel.[41]

38. Cf. Bruce D. Marshall, "Christ and the Cultures: The Jewish People and Christian Theology," in *The Cambridge Companion of Christian Doctrine*, ed. Colin E. Gunton (Cambridge: Cambridge University Press, 1997): 91–92.

39. Cf. Robert W. Jenson, "Toward a Christian Theology of Judaism," in *Jews and Christians*, ed. Carl E. Braaten and Robert W. Jenson (Grand Rapids, MI: Eerdmans, 1997): 12–13.

40. Cf. Kinzer, *Postmissionary Messianic Judaism* (see note 36), 263–302.

41. Franz Mußner, *Die Kraft der Wurzel. Judentum – Jesus – Kirche* (Freiburg i. Br. / Basel / Vienna: Herder, 1987): 39–54.

In contrast, Klaus Wengst called for the abandonment of the claim that Jesus is the Messiah for Israel.[42] Jesus may be the "Messiah from Israel for the nations," but not the "Messiah of Israel."[43] According to Wengst, what "for the Church is there mediated through the Messiah Jesus" applied "for Israel already beforehand and also continues to apply without such mediation."[44] But what does it mean if the Messiah of Israel and the Messiah from Israel for the nations (*goyim*) are not identical?

Like Christianity, Judaism also knows the hope that in the end all the righteous will be saved. In his book, *Wesen des Judentums* [*Essence of Judaism*], Leo Baeck (1873–1956) cites the following sentence, which is a classic statement for Jewish universal salvation: "Even the pious who are not Israelites have a share in the eternal blessedness."[45] According to Joseph Ratzinger, it is the joint responsibility of Jews and Christians "to represent the truth of the one will of God before the world and to place man before his inner truth, which is at the same time his way."[46] According to the conviction of Christians and Messianic Jews, the common path leads to eternal fellowship with God and his Messiah Jesus.

4. Christian Zionism? Eretz *and* Medinat Israel

The promises to Abraham, Isaac, and Jacob (Israel) also include the land of the promise (Gen 12:7; 26:3; 28:13), *Eretz Israel*.[47] It seems to me quite unlikely that among the promises that Paul says belong to the Jews, such as sonship, covenants, Law and sacred service and the

42. Klaus Wengst, *Jesus zwischen Juden und Christen* (Stuttgart: Kohlhammer, 1999): 14–15.

43. "Messias aus Israel für die Völker" . . . "Messias Israels"—*Ibid.*, 76.

44. "für die Kirche durch den Messias Jesus vermittelt da ist" . . . "für Israel schon vorher und gilt auch weiterhin ohne solche Vermittlung"—*Ibid.*, 81.

45. "Auch die Frommen, die nicht Israeliten sind, haben an der ewigen Seligkeit teil."—Leo Baeck, *Das Wesen des Judentums* (Wiesbaden: Fourier, 1998): 98.

46. "die Wahrheit des einen Gotteswillens vor der Welt zu vertreten und den Menschen vor seine innere Wahrheit zu stellen, die zugleich sein Weg ist"—Joseph Ratzinger, *Die Vielfalt der Religionen und der Eine Bund* (Hagen: Urfeld, 1998): 32.

47. Cf. Erich Zenger, "'Deinen Nachkommen gebe ich dieses Land' (Gen 12,7). Überlegungen zum christlichen Umgang mit den Landverheißungen des Ersten Testaments," in *Zion – Ort der Begegnung. FS Laurentius Klein*, ed. Ferdinand Hahn et al. (Bodenheim: Athenäum-Hain-Hanstein, 1993): 141–61.

fathers (Rom 9:4), he does not also reckon the land of the promise, with Jerusalem as the dwelling place of Israel's God. Although Paul does not specifically discuss the land promise in Romans 9–11, he nowhere calls into question the connection of people and land, even though he does not comment on the future of the people whom God has chosen as his special possession—except for its eschatological future. How the future of the people of Israel will look in detail remains entrusted to God. But I see no basis in the New Testament for N.T. Wright's thesis that Jesus, as the "climax of Israel's story,"[48] has made the land promise obsolete.[49]

In terms of Israel theology, it is not sufficient in my view to ground the foundation of the modern State of Israel after the *Shoah* exclusively in terms of natural law. In his article on the theology of Judaism, "Grace and Calling Without Remorse" (2018), the emeritus Pope Benedict XVI explained "that the Jewish people, like every people, possesses a claim to their own land based on natural law" but that a Jewish state "cannot be derived directly from Holy Scripture," even though "in a broader sense . . . God's faithfulness to the people of Israel"[50] finds expression in it.[51] In the weekly newspaper *Jüdische Allgemeine*, Rabbi Arie Folger demanded: "Yes, it is time that the Church recognized that the return to Zion is religiously significant."[52]

Already one year earlier, the declaration "Between Jerusalem and Rome" (February 1, 2017), published by the Conference of European

48. Nicholas Thomas Wright, *The New Testament and the People of God* (Minneapolis, MN: Fortress, 1992): 401–402.

49. Cf. *ibid.*, 246–57.

50. Joseph Ratzinger / Benedict XVI, "Gnade und Berufung ohne Reue. Anmerkungen zum Traktat 'De Iudaeis,'" *Communio: Internationale Katholische Zeitschrift* 47 (2018): 387–406, at 401; the translation into English is imprecise here: Joseph Ratzinger / Benedict XVI, "Grace and Vocation Without Remorse. Comments on the Treatise *De Iudaeis*," *Communio: International Catholic Review* 45 (2018): 163–84, at 178–79.

51. Cf. Helmut Hoping, "Joseph Ratzinger / Benedikt XVI. über das Judentum. Bemerkungen aus aktuellem Anlass," *Communio: Internationale Katholische Zeitschrift* 47 (2018): 618–31.

52. "Ja, es ist Zeit, dass die Kirche einsieht, dass die Rückkehr nach Zion religiös bedeutend ist."—Arie Folger, "Gefahr für den Dialog? Das jüngste Traktat von Benedikt XVI. zum katholischen Verständnis des Judentums wird heftig kritisiert. Eine Einordnung aus rabbinischer Sicht," *Jüdische Allgemeine*, July 19, 2018; cf. also Folger's letter to Benedict XVI—Arie Folger, "Brief an Papa Benedikt XVI / Joseph Ratzinger," *Communio: Internationale Katholische Zeitschrift* 47 (2018): 614–17.

Rabbis together with the Rabbinical Council of America, stated that "God's eternal covenant" with Israel showed itself not only through the fact that after the *Shoah* Jewish life in the Diaspora was revived but also through the fact that many Jews answered the call "to return to *Eretz Yisrael*, where a sovereign Jewish state arose." If the promise of the land was not abrogated by the appearance of the Messiah Jesus, then from the Christian side one will not be permitted to call into question the inseparable connection between people and land of Israel.[53]

However, a "Greater-Israel theology" by no means follows from this form of Christian Zionism, especially since the borders of *Eretz Israel* are not defined precisely in the biblical writings—1 Kings 5:5 speaks of the kingdoms of Israel and Judah as stretching "from Dan to Beersheba." Nor does a Christian-Zionist end-times doctrine (Armageddon / messianic millenarianism), as this has developed above all in the evangelical sphere from the traditional chiliasm and the dispensationalism of the nineteenth century, follow from the validity of the land promise.

5. Closing remarks

The conversation between Jews, Messianic Jews, and Christians is particularly sensitive. It demands, from all those involved, respect for the faith of the others as well as the readiness to mutually recognize one another as children of Abraham, be it the children of Abraham according to the flesh, children of Abraham according to the flesh and in faith in the Messiah Jesus, or the children of Abraham acquired additionally from the nations (*goyim*) through Christ. Insofar as Messianic Jews clearly distance themselves from the mission of Jews, the dialogue between Christians and Messianic Jews need not lead to alienation of Christians and Jews who do not profess *Yeshua haMashiach*.

(Translated by John David Martin, James Earle Patrick, and Wayne Coppins from the German: "Das Judesein Jesu und seine Bedeutung für die Christologie")

53. Willehad Paul Eckert, Nathan Peter Levinson, and Martin Stöhr, eds., *Jüdisches Volk, gelobtes Land. Die biblischen Landverheißungen als Problem des jüdischen Selbstverständnisses und der christlichen Theologie* (Abhandlungen zum christlich-jüdischen Dialog, 3; Munich: Kaiser, 1970); Martin Stöhr (ed.), *Zionismus. Beiträge zur Diskussion* (Abhandlungen zum christlich-jüdischen Dialog, 9; Munich: Kaiser, 1980).

The Jewish Christ, His People, and the Torah

In Dialogue with Helmut Hoping

Markus Bockmuehl

At the heart of this colloquium's concern lies a tragic nexus of Christian history, indeed a kind of tragic double helix. This is not primarily the phenomenon that Gentile Christianity's triumph entailed the gradual loss and suppression of Jewish ways of believing in Jesus, although that is sad enough. Nor do I mean the inevitable consequence that Jews and Christians soon *diverged* more and more—about Torah and about the practical life of faith, about the promise of the world to come, or about the election, identity, and future of the people of God.

No, the tragic double helix is this: Jews and Christians may have disagreed about most of their core convictions, but they *agreed* on this one point: It is impossible to be both a Jew and a Christian. More sharply put for our purposes: A follower of Jesus cannot be a Jew and a Jew cannot be a follower of Jesus. Already by the early second century, Ignatius of Antioch insisted "it is perverse to talk of Jesus Christ and to practice Judaism."[1] Meanwhile Rabbi Eliezer Ben Hyrcanus was excommunicated by his colleagues for discussing a halakhic opinion of Jesus with Jacob of Kfar Sakhnin, a messianic Jew.[2]

1. *Magn* 10.3 (ἄτοπόν ἐστιν, Ἰησοῦν Χριστὸν λαλεῖν καὶ ἰουδαΐζειν); cf. 8.1–2; *Phld* 6.1.

2. *B. Abod. Zar.* 16b–17a (פעם אחת הייתי מהלך בשוק העליון של ציפורי ומצאתי אחד ומתלמידי ישו הנוצרי ויעקב איש כפר סכניא שמו); cf. *t. ḥul.* 2.7; *Qoh. R.* 1.8.3.

Although never totally without its dissenters, this bipolar position certainly attained the status of orthodoxy in both communities. Indeed it seems important to acknowledge that *on both sides* this conviction typically grounded what became a position of explicit supersession and replacement of Jewish faith in Jesus. Expressed in terms of a Venn diagram, what became jointly superseded and replaced by both Judaism and Christianity was any intersection between them. One might go so far as to say that the result was to asphyxiate Messianic Judaisms of this or perhaps any kind.

All this clearly places Christology at the heart of any Jewish ways of believing in Jesus. And this is where Professor Hoping's contribution to this volume strikes such an important note. I am in substantial agreement with his development of core theses about (1) the Son of God becoming Jewish flesh not incidentally but at the heart of his incarnation, (2) Jesus the Messiah being both Son of David and more than Son of David, and (3) the Church as Body of Christ is the messianic people of God of Gentile and Jewish Jesus-believers.

Certainly among the key insights is the acknowledgement that we need an *interpretatio Judaica* of Christology (see pp. 178–79 of this volume). Professor Hoping rightly notes that Israel's historical and Christological absence is a notorious lacuna in the Christian Creed.[3] Precisely this lacuna must be addressed if we are to understand the essential dogmatic implication that the Word became Jewish flesh, died, and rose in his Jewish body (see pp. 179, 184 of this volume). From the perspective of a "systematic Christology" there is perhaps room here to elaborate further on what this may or must mean for the Messiah of Israel ascended and "seated at the right hand of the Father": Jesus Christ is of Israel not merely incarnate and risen, but does not cease to be so as the Son coming in glory.

Professor Hoping is quite right, too, to insist that we must not settle for pious but ultimately supersessionist accounts that allow the essential Jewishness of Christology to be subsumed under vague and ill-conceived notions of "Jesus as the Torah in person." Well before Joseph Ratzinger, twentieth-century scholars in Germany and elsewhere had

3. Note, at the same time, the possibility that the diversity of second- and third-century views on the place of Israel may potentially render its absence from the creed the lesser of two evils: cf. also Nathan MacDonald, "Israel and the Old Testament Story in Irenaeus's Presentation of the Rule of Faith," *Journal of Theological Interpretation* 3 (2009): 281–98, at 295–98.

advocated for clichés of this sort. Leaving aside what exactly might be meant by Jesus as the Torah, it is undoubtedly problematic if it encourages a Christology for which the coming of Jesus means that God's word and promise to Israel are now revoked and replaced.

Theology of the land

The previous theme relates closely to the promise entailed in a theology of the Land, which Professor Hoping subtly balances in the tension between Land and State, *Eretz Israel* vs *Medinat Israel*. At the same time, I would agree with his critique of my colleague and friend N.T. Wright. On this as on several related questions, Wright's position seems difficult to distinguish from certain kinds of replacement theology, however much he insists on a rhetoric of continuity.

At the same time, I suggest that two aspects of Professor Hoping's remarks on this topic could usefully do with teasing out a little more, not least in relation to a systematic Christology.

First, and while acknowledging the return to the Land as religiously significant, it seems important to ask if on his reading a Christian theology of the Land must in practice simply cede its substance to a non-Christian Jewish perspective, whether ancient or contemporary, politically Zionist or otherwise. Contrary to much twentieth-century scholarship, contemporary interpreters of Jesus, Matthew, or even Paul "within Judaism" tend more commonly to recognize New Testament hints at a Christian theology of the Land. The fact that the Land sustains a wealth of metaphorical and symbolic significance in both Christian and even in Jewish texts in no way invalidates a literal meaning; indeed, in important ways it presupposes it. Matthew, and Matthew's Jesus, give expression to a poignant theology of the Land, whether in relation to the northern tribes or the witness of persecution through all the towns of Israel (e.g., 4:13–15; 10:6, 23; 15:24). Periodic scholarly denials notwithstanding, the earthly Jerusalem present and future similarly matters to Luke and Acts, to Paul and James, as well as to John of Patmos.

There is a second and more difficult aspect to which contributors to this volume have given conflicting answers. Professor Hoping is right to resist a Christian Zionism that makes common cause with a "Greater Israel" theology and politics. And yet, does a systematic Christology, informed by messianic faith, require explicit theological and perhaps eschatological convictions about the twentieth-century return to the Land? It very well may—but further discussion is needed. Elsewhere in this volume, David Neuhaus alludes to the problem of whether Messianic Judaism requires a religious allegiance to Zionism—and more specifically to the political state of Israel as in principle a monocultural, mono-ethnic "Jewish State"—rather than, for example, shared with Messianic Arabs as equal partners and stakeholders. That question goes to the heart of the problem, and a Christian theology of the Land cannot finally side-step this challenge.

Three questions

Three concluding specific questions must here suffice by way of further response and discussion of Prof. Hoping's essay.

1. It is true and important to acknowledge (see p. 183 of this volume) that Christian preoccupation with a Jewish Messiah actually leaves the majority of Jews uninterested. Despite the emphasis on Messiah and eschatology in the last three of Maimonides' Thirteen Principles (*ikkarim*), most Jews today—as perhaps throughout most of Jewish history—are not particularly invested in messianism. What does the problem of such Jewish skepticism entail for the possibility of contemporary inner-Jewish dialogue about the Messiah—whether Jesus or for that matter any other messiah, like Chabad's Rebbe Schneerson? Is Messianic Judaism *of any stripe* now inevitably marginal and irrelevant?
2. A second question relates to the evocative passing reference to Yeshayahu Leibowitz (1903–1994), a fierce critic of religious interpretations of the State of Israel. Professor Hoping cites his charge that Christianity is a faith without *mitzvot* (see p. 183 of this volume). Messianic Jews will mostly disagree with this view, but it is hard to deny that Western liberal theology and *Kulturprotestantismus* have left unnumbered hostages on this front, whether with or without Kant. Scholars of Matthew's Gospel might note here the importance of repeated talk of the *mitzvot* or *entolai* of Jesus in that text. Paul has long been widely (many now think wrongly!) assumed to take a different view. Rightly or wrongly, that charge against antinomian Christianity is far from trivial, and not without considerable support in the history

of theology. A version of it is also frequently heard from Muslims. A "systematic" messianic Christology cannot bypass the question: What is the place of Torah in the churches of the Messiah?

3. Professor Hoping's conclusion, finally, calls for Messianic Jews to abandon a mission to Jews, even though elsewhere (see p. 186 of this volume) he rightly insists that it is nonsense to consider Jesus the Messiah only for the Gentiles. Galatians 2:7–8 clearly distinguishes between an apostolic mission to Gentiles (carried out by the Jewish Paul with Gentile assistance) and an apostolic mission to the Jewish people that is (solely, it seems) the domain of Jewish apostles. On this latter point Galatians appears at one with the Gospel of Matthew: Passages like 10:23 encapsulate that messianic invitation to Israel and arguably hint at its long delay. In practice, today *both* the Messianic Jewish witness to Israel and the call to refrain from such a witness are profoundly problematic. Regardless of how one hopes to resolve the horns of that dilemma, what sense does it make for *Gentiles* to demand that *Jewish* believers in Jesus abandon their Jewish testimony, purely for the sake of a Gentile–Jewish dialogue?

Post-Supersessionist Messianology

The Present and Future Jewish King

Mark S. Kinzer

1. Jesus' enduring Jewish identity

THE JEWISHNESS of the *historical* Jesus is now taken for granted. But the reality and significance of Jesus' *enduring* Jewish identity is only gradually becoming a subject of theological reflection. At the beginning of this century, Robert Jenson pointed to its significance:

> The risen Jesus is also flesh, in that he is risen bodily, for to be an embodied creature is to be flesh. Now, flesh is never an individual possession; that we are flesh means among other things that we have parents and ancestors, who—at least until we get to Adam—are not everyone's parents and ancestors. The Word who has come in the flesh belongs to the lineage of Abraham and Sarah, and this fact belongs to his identity, to what traditional Christology calls the "one hypostasis" of the Word who is Jesus . . .[1]

Jenson describes the resurrected Jesus as the bearer of Jewish flesh, and suggests that this is an essential feature of his glorified identity.

1. Robert W. Jenson, "Toward a Christian Theology of Judaism," in *Jews and Christians, People of God*, ed. Carl E. Braaten and Robert W. Jenson (Grand Rapids, MI: Eerdmans, 2003): 1–13, at 12–13. This volume consists of papers delivered at a conference in 2001. Jenson's text had been published earlier in *Pro Ecclesia* 9.1 (2000): 43–56.

Moreover, he proposes that this identity implies an enduring association with those of the same lineage, namely, the Jewish people.

In the same year, Bruce Marshall offered a similar proposal, in even more explicit language:

> [I]n the person of the Logos God makes his own the flesh of this particular Jew, Jesus of Nazareth. *God's ownership of this Jewish flesh is permanent.* In the end, when all flesh shall see the glory of the Lord, the vision of God will, so the traditional Christian teaching goes, be bound up ineluctably with the vision of this Jew seated at God's right hand. So in willing his own incarnation, it seems that God wills the permanence, indeed the eschatological permanence, of the distinction between Jews and Gentiles. *But Jesus cannot be a Jew, or be identified as such (as he will be even in the eschaton), all by himself, in isolation from his people.* He is a Jew, like any other, only in virtue of his descent from Abraham, and thus in virtue of his relationship to the Jewish people as a whole. And this suggests that in owning with unsurpassable intimacy the particular Jewish flesh of Jesus, God also owns the Jewish people as a whole, precisely in their distinction from us Gentiles; he cannot own the one without also owning the other.[2]

Marshall's formulation could not be clearer: "God's ownership of this Jewish flesh is permanent." And, since Jewish identity is inherently corporate, the resurrected Jesus retains a distinctive relationship with the Jewish people as a whole. Marshall infers from this the striking claim that Jewish identity itself carries over into the eschaton.

Neither Jenson nor Marshall explored the wide-ranging ramifications of these bold assertions, and few other prominent theologians of this century have ventured further along the same path. But two recent publications—one by Kayko Driedger Hesslein and the other by Barbara Meyer—have begun to explore this new terrain.[3] Each reflects deeply on the Jewish identity of the resurrected Jesus. Barbara Meyer's *Jesus the Jew in Christian Memory* is of particular interest for the purposes of the present volume, since it devotes concentrated attention to the implications of Jesus' ongoing Jewish identity for the Church's relationship to the Jewish people.

2. Bruce D. Marshall, *Trinity and Truth* (Cambridge: Cambridge University Press, 2000): 178 (emphasis added).

3. Kayko D. Hesslein, *Dual Citizenship: Two Natures Christologies and the Jewish Jesus* (London: Bloomsbury T&T Clark, 2015); Barbara U. Meyer, *Jesus the Jew in Christian Memory: Theological and Philosophical Explorations* (Cambridge: Cambridge University Press, 2020).

Like Jenson and Marshall, Meyer assumes the resurrection of Jesus and the Christology of the ecumenical councils, and reflects on the Jewishness of Jesus in that context. In doing so, she acknowledges the novelty of such a project: "Jesus *was* a Jew, and it is correct for Christians to say that Jesus Christ *is* Jewish and *will always remain* Jewish. Yet historical Jesus research and [Chalcedonian] Christology remain at odds."[4] "Hundreds of books have been written about the '*Historical* Jesus' and quite a few about Jesus the Jew *in history*. Christologies focusing on Jesus the Jew that use the *present* tense are fewer."[5] Like Jenson and Marshall, Meyer also perceives that the Jewishness of the resurrected Jesus implies his ongoing relationship with the Jewish people, and thus also with the shape-shifting historical reality of Jewish identity. "Speaking about Jesus in the *present* tense seems to belong to an exclusively Christian confessional language. But here we see that Christology is not just concerned with *historical* Judaism but also has a stake in *contemporary* Jewish self-understanding as well as everything that happened in between—from post-Second Temple Jewish history to the present."[6] Moreover, since the resurrected Jesus is also the Jesus of the world to come, one must add Christological assertions in the *future* tense, and reckon with the necessary implications concerning Jewish identity: "What does it mean that Jesus Christ *will be* Jewish? . . . We do not know how Jewishness will be expressed at the end of times. Jewishness was differently expressed in the first and twenty-first centuries . . . What we do know, however, is that this Jewish self-expression will not be disconnected from other Jewish lives."[7]

Meyer concludes the paragraph just cited by enunciating the central thesis of her entire volume: "This means that Jesus' otherness for Christian non-Jews will not be dissolved either."[8] As she states in her introduction, "my key argument is that the Jewishness of Jesus Christ engenders an otherness that opens up new intellectual, spiritual, and ethical horizons for the non-Jewish Christian."[9] She builds here on the philosophical exploration of otherness in the work of Levinas and those

4. Meyer, *Jesus the Jew* (see note 3), 5 (emphasis added).
5. *Ibid.*, 11 (emphasis added).
6. *Ibid.*, 66 (emphasis added).
7. *Ibid.*, 103 (emphasis added).
8. *Ibid.*, 103.
9. *Ibid.*, 11.

influenced by him. Since the overwhelming majority of "Christians" are non-Jews, the Jewish identity of Jesus creates a potentially fruitful distance between the master and those who in other respects are united to him by faith and baptism. And since his Jewish identity has content only in relation to the life of the Jewish people throughout history, it also establishes a potentially fruitful dependence of his disciples on the life and tradition of a community external to their own immediate socio-cultural identity. Meyer employs the term "vulnerability" to describe this fruitful dependence:

> Jesus' Jewishness is the most apparent signifier of Christianity's vulnerability. With Jesus the Jew at its heart, the Christian faith cannot succeed in isolation but holds an inbuilt connection to Judaism and Jews. After overcoming the aggression of rejecting this bond, Christians have the chance to experience the blessings of connectedness. Vulnerability is increased by attachment, but so is the vitality of the Christian community. I would go so far as to connect the vitality of Christ himself to the Christian attachment to the people of Israel.[10]

But what about *Jewish* disciples of Jesus? Meyer acknowledges our existence, and the fact that our relation to the Jewish Jesus differs from that of Gentile Christians. After asserting that "the Jewish Jesus can never be in the Christian's domestic domain," she includes a qualifying footnote: "Except for people of Jewish family background and Christian belief, whether they understand themselves as Christian Jews or Jewish Christians."[11] But she never explicitly affirms the theological significance of that difference, or details its meaning.

Meyer has taken the discussion further than those who preceded her. But there is still further to go.

2. *Bearing witness to Jesus as* King *of the Jews*

Meyer teaches at the University of Tel Aviv. The Jewish / Christian conversation occupies a central place in her life, as well as in her theology. In the first words of her acknowledgments, the author identifies herself as "an anti-missionary Christian theologian." While she discusses Jewish views of Jesus, her explicitly identified audience consists of

10. *Ibid.*, 178–79.
11. *Ibid.*, 73 n.24.

"non-Jewish Christians," and her primary purpose consists in persuading that audience of its Christological dependence upon the Jewish people. Jesus is himself dependent upon the Jewish people for an essential aspect of his own identity, and as a result the followers of Jesus—who do not share his Jewish identity—need the Jews to be themselves so that their resurrected master can continue to be himself.

Meyer's anti-missionary stance, anti-supersessionist purpose, and Gentile-Christian audience cohere with her reluctance to consider a proposition that goes beyond Jesus' Jewish identity—namely, that he is and forever will be the *King* of the Jews, and thus also the *Lord* of Jewish identity. A Messianology such as this also takes us beyond the preliminary Christological soundings of Jenson and Marshall. If Jesus is the *King* of the Jews, he is indeed dependent upon them, for the word "king" (like the word "father") is intrinsically relational in meaning: A king without subjects is no king. But the subjects of this peculiar king (who uniquely is both human and divine) depend upon *him* even more than he depends upon *them*. The precise character of this dependence remains hidden, for the presence of the resurrected Jesus has gone largely unrecognized by the family over whom he reigns. But if in fact this particular Jew who was crucified as the King of the Jews has also been raised from the dead, and if in his resurrection he *remains* the King of the Jews, and if he is both human and divine, then over them he truly does reign.

Explicit (though fragmentary) witness to the resurrected Messiah has been maintained historically only in the life of the Church, a community largely composed of those who are not his natural subjects. This establishes a hidden mutuality between the Jewish people and the Church, a mutuality denied by Meyer, for whom Jesus is a Jew but not clearly the *King* of the Jews, and for whom Christians are dependent upon Jews but Jews are not marked by the same relational vulnerability. Whenever Jesus is acknowledged by members of either community to be the King of the Jews, this hidden mutuality becomes manifest. Such people realise that they must look to and receive from members of another community and tradition in order fully to be themselves. Few on either side now confess Jesus to be the resurrected King of the Jews, or discern the communal mutuality this confession entails. Historical blinders (providentially permitted) still limit the epistemological capacities of these two intertwined communities, but their mutual dependence remains an ontological fact.

Speaking as one of those Jews referred to in Meyer's footnote, and as also one who confesses Jesus to be the King of the Jews, I would propose that Jewish disciples of Jesus are called to embody, and bear witness to, this mutual dependence. As Meyer realizes, Jesus the Jew creates no distance for us in our relationship to him. His Jewish identity sustains our own Jewish identity. But the historical alienation of the two communities with which we identify opens up a different kind of *otherness* in our lives. Both our Jewish and Christian environments continually call into question the Jewish identity that Jesus has renewed, and now sustains. Our uncanny controverted presence within these two worlds parallels that of the King of the Jews. This is because we represent the troubling communal mutuality his resurrected Jewishness entails. If we did not sense his intimate presence as our resurrected royal brother, we would quickly retreat into a less ambiguous Jewish or Christian pattern of life.

3. Jesus as "King of the Jews" in the Passion narrative

Those who first bore witness to Jesus' identity as King of the Jews were themselves Jews and not Gentiles. Their witness comes to us through the passion narrative of all four canonical Gospels, in which this title plays a prominent role. Nevertheless, as Wongi Park has shown, exegetes and theologians over the centuries have given little attention to the title's distinctive significance. They have generally treated the phrase as equivalent in meaning to "King of Israel." The effect, as Park shows, is that Jesus' kingship (i.e., his authority as *ho Basileus*, "the king") "obscures and overshadows his identity as *tōn Ioudaiōn*" ("of the Jews"). In other words, his "ethnoracial identity as an ethnic Judean is diminished and downplayed" by these interpreters.[12] Given the post-supersessionist recovery of Jesus' Jewish identity, however, this matter deserves new scrutiny.[13] Does this title, which all of the Gospels depict

12. Wongi Park, *The Politics of Race and Ethnicity in Matthew's Passion Narrative* (Cham: Springer Nature Switzerland, 2019): 18.

13. This section summarizes Mark S. Kinzer, "Is Jesus of Nazareth Still King of the Jews? New Testament Christology and the Jewish People," in *Jesus, King of the Jews? Messianic Judaism, Jewish Christians, and Theology Beyond Supersessionism*, ed. James E. Patrick (Vienna: TJCII, 2021): 43–55; first published in *Kesher* 39 (Summer / Fall 2021), article 1. For reflection on the term "post-supersessionist," see later in

as inscribed upon the Roman instrument of Jesus' execution, tell us anything about Jesus' past and present relationship to those sharing his Jewish lineage?

In the four passion narratives, the phrase is employed only by non-Jews, or by Jews in conversation with non-Jews (as in John 19:21). In contrast, when Jews in the Gospels refer to the royal identity of Jesus, they call him the "the King of *Israel*" (Mark 15:32; John 1:49; 12:13). This distinction in usage makes sense in first-century terms, for Jews at that time—and in the pre-modern period in general—preferred the self-designation "Israel" when speaking or writing in-house.[14] On the other hand, when speaking to or writing for Gentiles, or when speaking or writing about situations in which Jews and Gentiles interact, the name "Israel" tends to give way to the name "the Jews." Therefore, when the Gospels depict people referring to Israel's Messiah as "the King of the Jews," they are highlighting the Gentile identity of those using the title.

The distinction between the titles "King of Israel" and "King of the Jews" has great theological import. In the post–New Testament Christian world, the term "Israel" has been used in a way that detaches it from its exclusive reference to the nation which traces its genealogical origins to Abraham, Isaac, and Jacob, Sarah, Rebecca, Rachel, and Leah. When Christians acclaim Jesus as "the King of Israel," they may readily equate Israel with the Church, and imply nothing more than the fact that Jesus rules over those who have been baptized in his name. While Gentile Christians have claimed to be Israel, they have not claimed to be "Jews." That name in the New Testament is unambiguous in meaning and reference, and it remained unambiguous in the centuries that followed.

So, when Jesus is mocked by Pilate and the Roman soldiers as "King of the Jews," we have no doubt what the title means. He is honored and mocked as the rightful ruler of the Jewish people—a people to which the Gentile speakers in the narrative do not belong, a people identified in relation to common ancestors, a common history, a common way of life, a common geographical center. Jesus is honored and mocked with a title that has indisputable national, political, and

---

this volume—Mark S. Kinzer, "Post-Supersessionist Eschatology: Welcoming Jesus at the Mount of Olives."

14. Cynthia M. Baker, *Jew* (New Brunswick, NJ: Rutgers University Press, 2017).

territorial connotations—a title that obstinately resists universalization and spiritualization.[15]

Moreover, from the perspective of Pilate and the Roman soldiers, the true object of mockery is not Jesus but the contemptible people he represents. As Park notes, "Jesus is made inferior as a Judean subject through a parody of what has been called 'the mocking of a king.' This ancient practice of miming conquered kings occurred in Alexandria. . . . Jesus is made to represent a conquered Judean king and the conquered territory of Judea and its inhabitants. In this way, *the message of Roman superiority and Judean inferiority* is dramatically enacted by the entire Roman garrison."[16] Park's analysis focuses on the Gospel of Matthew, but the theme is even more pronounced in the Gospel of John (19:19–22), which recounts the following tense interchange between Pilate and the Jewish chief priests:

> Pilate also had an inscription written and put on the cross. It read, "Jesus of Nazareth, the King of the Jews." Many of the Jews read this inscription, because the place where Jesus was crucified was near the city; and it was written in Hebrew, in Latin, and in Greek. Then the chief priests of the Jews said to Pilate, "Do not write, 'The King of the Jews,' but, 'This man said, I am King of the Jews.'" Pilate answered, "What I have written I have written."

The chief priests do not object to the publication of the Roman charge that Jesus *claimed to be* the king of the Jews. On the other hand, they object vigorously to the wording of the charge which Pilate actually

15. In his dialogue with Pilate in the Gospel of John, Jesus states that his kingship is "not of this cosmos" (18:36). This has often been understood as a rejection of a "Jewish" conception of messiahship, in which the king has a special relation to a particular nation or territory, and rules over an earthly (rather than a purely heavenly) domain. But this is not what John means by the phrase "this cosmos." For John, the phrase resembles the rabbinic term *olam hazeh*, and refers to the current age and order of the world, which (for John) is subject to the power of dark forces. Jesus comes to save and give life to the world (John 3:16–17; 4:42; 12:47), but to do so he must deliver it from the power of the one who currently dominates its affairs (12:31). Jesus' kingship is not exercised according to the pattern on public display in the royal courts of the ancient world; nevertheless, he was crucified as the king of the Jews, and this title connects Jesus to a particular nation, territory, and political institution. There is no contradiction between these two assertions. In fact, as we will see, the first assertion explains the significance of the second. See George R. Beasley-Murray, *John* (Word Biblical Commentary, 36; Waco, TX: Word, 1987): 331.

16. Park, *The Politics of Race and Ethnicity in Matthew's Passion Narrative* (see note 12), 124–25 (emphasis added).

posted—for that wording implies that Jesus not only *claimed* this title, but rightfully owned it. And that is why he was crucified. Pilate implies that when the Jews look at him, hanging naked on a cross, they are looking at their king, they are looking at themselves. And in forty years, this metaphor would become a literal reality: The land will be littered with Jewish corpses amid the smoke rising from a smoldering Jerusalem.

This was Pilate's malicious intent according to the Gospels, whose readers all knew that Jerusalem herself had indeed been crucified in the likeness of her king. But the Jewish authors saw a deeper meaning in the title inscribed upon Jesus' cross. Pilate sought to contrast the glory and overwhelming force of Roman imperial rule with the lowly subservience of Judea and of Judea's king. The early followers of Jesus welcomed this contrast and made it central to their message, just as they eventually turned the brutal Roman mode of execution into a shocking symbol of their movement.

4. Jewish kingship as servant-kingship

If the resurrected Jesus is the same man who was nailed to the cross, albeit in an eschatologically transformed condition, then he remains today the King of the Jews. This establishes a relationship of interdependence between him and the Jewish people.

To assert such a mutual dependence would likely raise concerns for Meyer and other Christian theologians engaged in Jewish–Christian dialogue. And rightly so. There is a danger here of spiritualizing and christianizing the gritty particularity of Jewish history, identity, and discourse. Under a philosemitic cloak could lurk a Christian imperialism asserting hegemony over the "partial truths" of a subordinate Jewish religious tradition.

I have already noted one source of protection against this danger, namely, the dependence of this sovereign on his subjects. While they are more dependent on him than he is on them—he is, after all, their ruler, and divine as well as human—he truly needs them in order to be himself, a Jewish king of the Jews. As Meyer stresses, this intimacy between Jesus and the Jewish people creates a salutary distance between Jesus and the Church of the nations, and even establishes Christian dependence upon a religious community socially external to itself. The Church's historical failure to acknowledge this dependence should chasten and humble her, and help to guard against the imperialist temptation.

Recovery of the title "King of the Jews" in its narrative context provides an additional source of protection against this temptation. As argued above, this title functions in the passion narrative as Roman imperial ridicule—not primarily directed at Jesus himself, but at the Jewish people. The Roman authorities treat Jesus as a stand-in, a living effigy, for this people whom they despise. They thereby signal their own power and superiority. But the Gospel tradition turns this ridicule upside down, transforming it into a judgment of Roman imperial authority and of the Jewish rulers whom the Romans have co-opted. Pilate sees Jesus as a non-entity, and sets him up as a fitting representative for the national non-entity to whom he belongs. The Evangelists, on the other hand, see Jesus as the resurrected Lord and Messiah, who dies and rises to redeem and glorify his people. Through this crucifixion, the Roman governor intends to humiliate the Jews. The Evangelists imply that the event does the opposite.

The synoptic story of the request of James and John anticipates and interprets the passion narrative in just this way:

> James and John, the sons of Zebedee, came forward to him and said to him, "Teacher, we want you to do for us whatever we ask of you." And he said to them, "What is it you want me to do for you?" And they said to him, "Appoint us to sit, one at your right hand and one at your left, in your glory." But Jesus said to them, "You do not know what you are asking. Are you able to drink the cup that I drink or be baptized with the baptism that I am baptized with?" They replied, "We are able." Then Jesus said to them, "The cup that I drink you will drink, and with the baptism with which I am baptized you will be baptized, but to sit at my right hand or at my left is not mine to appoint, but it is for those for whom it has been prepared." When the ten heard this, they began to be angry with James and John. So Jesus called them and said to them, "You know that among the gentiles those whom they recognize as their rulers lord it over them, and their great ones are tyrants over them. But it is not so among you; instead, whoever wishes to become great among you must be your servant, and whoever wishes to be first among you must be slave of all. For the Son of Man came not to be served but to serve and to give his life a ransom for many." (Mark 10:35–45; see Matt 20:20–28)

The story contrasts the character of true leadership in Israel with the manner in which the Gentiles—and paradigmatically the Romans—exercise authority. James and John, thirsting for honor, wealth, and power, unwittingly imitate the imperial despots who lord it over the Jews, rather than the master on his way to Golgotha. Jesus is the rightful King of Israel, and that means governing not for his own benefit, but for the benefit of his subjects. It also means governing in a way that equips those governed to become responsible agents rather than disempowered slaves.

This interpretation of the passion narrative warns us against conceiving of the Jewish kingship of Jesus along the lines of those Roman authorities whose ways, according to that narrative, he condemned. The hidden rule of the resurrected Messiah over Israel can only be viewed as that of the servant-lord who washes the feet of his disciples. He is the king who empowers his subjects to share in his rule. Such a vision fits well with the audacious rabbinic conception of authority which asserts the independence of the sages, even from God (or at least from a *bat kol,* i.e., a heavenly voice), while at the same time including all of their ostensibly "independent" rulings within the divine revelation to Moses at Sinai (e.g., *b.* Bava Metzia 59b; *Exod. Rab.* 28.6; 47.1)! Like the government of the God depicted in rabbinic literature, the royal rule of the resurrected Messiah unleashes Jewish agency. If Jesus is the living King of the Jews who has ruled the Jewish people since his death and resurrection, his hidden messianic government has generated, or at least blessed, the emergence of that very tradition which has so boldly re-envisioned the relationship between divine sovereignty and responsible human action. The fact that his messianic government is veiled from those he governs only reinforces the servant-character of his rule.

Once we grasp the meaning of the title "King of the Jews" in the context of the passion narrative, we will reject any triumphalist reading of Jewish history which assumes an established Christian image of Jesus, and then superimposes it upon a simplified or spiritualized picture of the Jewish experience. Israel receives its name as the result of a wrestling match with God, and the Jewish people have never stopped wrestling. Israel's struggle with God is not a zero-sum competition, for the victory of each depends upon that of the other. This is how the God of Israel governs, and it is likewise the mode of authority exercised by his Anointed One.

5. Jesus as the future King of the Jews

To confess Jesus as the past and present King of the Jews is to affirm a mysterious truth, a reality now veiled from sight. To confess Jesus as the future (i.e., eschatological) King of the Jews is to hope in the mystery unveiled.

The expectation that the Jews will "convert to Christianity" at the end of the age has long been a staple of Christian eschatological menus. It has also posed a stumbling block for post-supersessionist Christian theologians such as Barbara Meyer. Their resistance to this traditional motif is well justified. Triumphalist Christian thinking has pictured the revelation of Jesus to the Jews at the end of the age as a negation of the Jewish historical experience. In such a scheme, the Jesus revealed to the Jews is the King of the Gentiles, and the Jewish "conversion to Christianity" means the de-Judaization of the Jews.[17]

If Jesus is the past, present, and future King of the Jews, then the eschatological unveiling of this mystery will challenge, chasten, refine, and consummate the historical experience of *both* the Jewish people and the Church. It will reveal the mutual dependence which each has persistently contested. It will do so by manifesting to the Church of the Gentiles that their Lord is preeminently the King of the *Jews*, and by making known to the Jewish people that the name of their king has been, is, and forever shall be, Yeshua haNotzri, Jesus of Nazareth.[18]

In the context of such a King-of-the-Jews Messianology, Jewish disciples of Jesus do more than witness to the mutual dependence of Israel and the Church. Like John the Baptist, we bear witness to the Coming One, who as King of the Jews scandalizes both communities. Yet, as that very King, he also is the One who fulfills the truths guarded and treasured by each tradition, and satisfies the longing of every heart. May he come soon, speedily, and in our days.

17. For further discussion of the eschatological "conversion of the Jews," see later in this volume—Kinzer, "Post-Supersessionist Eschatology" (see note 13).

18. For a fuller exposition of an eschatology that takes into account Jesus' eternal identity as King of the Jews, see later in this volume—Kinzer, "Post-Supersessionist Eschatology" (see note 13).

The Eschatological King and His People of Jews and Gentiles

Response to Mark S. Kinzer, "The Present and Future Jewish King"

Bernard Mallmann

THE "JEWISH FLESH," which for Karl Barth is the historically decisive category for Jesus,[1] is for Mark Kinzer equally decisive for the glorified Christ. Jewish flesh has enduring significance in the state of glory. Mark Kinzer supplies the inquiry into the historical Jesus with an eschatological orientation. To maintain this thesis, he must assume a strong continuity between the order of creation and the order of redemption. An important pointer already lies therein: With the thought of Kinzer, Christian theology, and especially Christology, has the painful thorn in its own flesh, not to succumb to the Marcionite temptation to decouple protology from eschatology, but to think through both from the actual center of Christology,[2] and to affirm the canonical unity of

1. Cf. Karl Barth, *Kirchliche Dogmatik IV/1: Die Lehre von der Versöhnung* (Zürich: Theologischer Verlag, 1953): 181—"The Word became—not 'flesh,' man, humiliated and suffering man in some sort of general sense, but Jewish flesh" ["Das Wort wurde – nicht 'Fleisch,' Mensch, erniedrigter und leidender Mensch in irgendeiner Allgemeinheit, sondern jüdisches Fleisch."]. In addition, Helmut Hoping, *Jesus aus Galiläa. Messias und Gottes Sohn* (Freiburg i. Br.: Herder, 2019); Jan-Heiner Tück, "Beschneidung Jesu. Ein Zeichen gegen die latente Israelvergessenheit der Kirche," in *Beschneidung Jesu. Was sie Juden und Christen heute bedeutet.* Mit einem Geleitwort von Walter Kardinal Kasper, ed. Jan-Heiner Tück (Freiburg i. Br.: Herder, 2020): 27–61.

2. Even the Gospel of John underscores an anti-Marcionite and gnostic reading when it says: "My kingdom is not *from* this world [ἐκ τοῦ κόσμου]" (John 18:36).

the Old and New Testaments.[3] Only if the two-in-oneness of the Christian Bible is taken seriously in its theological sense does the thesis gain plausibility that Jesus not only was the King of the Jews but also remains so as the Exalted One.

What the title on the cross of Jesus says historically[4] refers in historical retrospect to Jesus' sending. Just as the title of king is a term expressing mutual relationship between king and people, so the term "sending" can only be understood as relationship. As a "real symbol" of the Heavenly Father, Jesus understands his sending first to the "lost sheep of the house of Israel" (Matt 10:6); his sending is a manifestation of the pro-existence of Jesus which has its outworking in the sending "for the people of Israel" and in which he displays his authority as Messiah.[5] Because in him true deity and true humanity come together, he

---

Gnostic texts such as the Acts of Pilate write "My kingdom is not *in* this world," implying a separation of the world and the kingdom of Christ. On this, cf. Ignace de la Potterie S.J., *Die Passion nach Johannes. Der Text und sein Geist*, trans. Hans Urs von Balthasar (Einsiedeln: Johannesverlag, 1987): 71.

3. On the canonical unity of the Old and New Testaments, see Bernard Mallmann, *Dekanonisierung des Alten Testaments? Rückfragen an Notger Slenczka aus Sicht katholischer Theologie* (Studien zur systematischen und spirituellen Theologie, 57; Würzburg: Echter, 2021): esp. 304–507.

4. On the historicity of the cross title, see Martin Hengel, "Jesus der Messias Israels," in *Der messianische Anspruch Jesu und die Anfänge der Christologie. Vier Studien*, ed. Martin Hengel and Anna Maria Schwemer (Wissenschaftliche Untersuchungen zum Neuen Testament, 138; Tübingen: Mohr Siebeck, 2001): 1–80, at 48–60. See further de la Potterie, *Die Passion nach Johannes* (see note 2), 61–89; Klaus Berger, *Wozu ist Jesus am Kreuz gestorben?* (Gütersloh: Gütersloher Verlagshaus, 1998): 14–17.

5. Cf. Thomas Söding, "'Für das Volk.' Die Sendung Jesu und die Hoffnung Israels," in *Streitfall Christologie. Vergewisserungen nach der Shoah*, ed. Helmut Hoping and Jan-Heiner Tück (Quaestiones Disputatae, 214; Freiburg i. Br.: Herder, 2005): 73–124. Gerhard Lohfink shows that the Lucan double work is about nothing else than the gathering of the people of Israel. The individual audience groups, the temple, and individual persons serve as representatives of the whole people, to which the message and teaching of Jesus applies. In this connection, there is a continuity between the pre-Easter hearers of Jesus and the post-Easter community. Cf. Gerhard Lohfink, *Die Sammlung Israels. Eine Untersuchung zur lukanischen Ekklesiologie* (Studien zum Alten und Neuen Testament, 39; Munich: Kösel, 1975). The Church thus arises from the people of God. Luke does not introduce the Church until Acts 5. Cf. Lohfink, *Sammlung* (see above), 56: "For Luke, the Church is not an entity that is simply there on the day of Pentecost but a reality that must first come into being, and that has really come into being for the first time at the moment when a large part of Israel has gathered around the apostles and disciples of Jesus." ["Die Kirche ist für Lukas nicht eine Größe, die am Pfingsttag einfachhin da ist, sondern eine Wirklichkeit, die erst noch entstehen muß und die erst in dem Augenblick

can reveal the Father in order to gather his flock. What comes to expression in the sending of Jesus is therefore nothing else than the absolute theocentricity of his being, which legitimizes him as the Messiah of God. A sending-Christology has theocentricity as its core, inasmuch as his pro-existence can be again interpreted doubly: The "for the people" dimension is to be thought together with Jesus' orientation "for God."

The *homoousios* of divinity must, however, also apply to the *homoousios* of humanity if his historical life is to be understood as a revelatory "real symbol." Only in this doubled sameness of being can his sending be understood as kingship for the Jews. Here, it has significance for Judaism as well as for Christianity as *signum rememorativum, demonstrativum,* and *prognosticum.*[6] With Jean-Marie Lustiger, Mark Kinzer repeatedly refers to the fact that Jesus as a Jew embodies the whole people of Israel.[7] In his life as the hidden and revealed King of the Jews, he realizes the calling that is given and promised to Israel. He embodies the life and the promissory history without falling away from the will of God, which finds its expression in the Torah, in the process. His kingship can further be interpreted as a kind of *recapitulatio* of the history of Israel, which corresponds to the kingship of YHWH, which he wants to establish for his people (*rememorativum*). As a present sign (*demonstrativum*), the kingly rule of Jesus realizes itself in the fact that the particular election of Israel always carries with it a universal mandate. When Jesus confesses in the Gospel of John that his kingdom is not of this

---

wirklich entstanden ist, als sich ein großer Teil Israels um die Apostel und Jünger Jesu gesammelt hat."] With the Stephen pericope, the separation between believing Israel as Church and unbelieving Israel as Judaism emerges. Only after this does Luke transfer the term λαός to the Church. Just as God himself created his people in the Old Testament, so in parallel, the Church is created anew by God out of the Gentile Christians (cf. Acts 18). But: "In the sense of Luke, one must probably even formulate it like this: *the true Israel is only arrived at when the gentiles have been brought into the fellowship of God's people.* But that means: There is only one λαός; this is at the same time the λαὸς ἐξ Ἰουδαίων gathered after Pentecost *and* the λαὸς ἐξ ἐθνῶν that comes in addition in the time that follows" ["Im Sinne des Lukas muß man wohl sogar so formulieren: *das wahre Israel ist erst dann erreicht, wenn die Heiden in die Gemeinschaft des Gottesvolkes eingebracht worden sind.* Das heißt aber: Es gibt nur einen λαός, dieser ist zugleich der nach Pfingsten gesammelte λαὸς ἐξ Ἰουδαίων *und* der in der Folgezeit hinzukommende λαὸς ἐξ ἐθνῶν"]—*ibid.*, 60.

6. For the terminology, cf. Thomas Aquinas, *Summa Theologica* III[a], Q.60, Art.3, on the conception of the sacraments that encompasses the past, present, and future.

7. Cf. Mark S. Kinzer, *Searching Her Own Mystery:* Nostra Aetate, *the Jewish People, and the Identity of the Church* (Eugene, OR: Cascade Books, 2015): 12–16.

world (cf. John 18:36), it is implied that the Old *and* New Testaments carry a surplus of promises in themselves, which still await the ultimate fulfillment in the kingdom of God (*prognosticum*).

The revelation of the Father in the sending of the Son is, however, not an action that lies outside of the election and promise of Israel, but can, if the Son truly reveals the Father, only be conceived of in the covenant history of Israel. The Son does not reveal a second covenant of God that would stand alongside the covenant with the chosen people. Jesus as King of the Jews is the one who is deeply rooted in the covenant history of Israel and who identifies with the promise of God in his sending: Jesus, the King of the Jews is in his life the concretization of the covenant history of God with humanity and the eschatological revelation that God is faithful to his promise and will fulfill it.[8] With this, the theological basis is withdrawn for every mission to the Jews. The only mission to Judaism is the sending of the Son to the people of God, whom he chose in order to enter into his covenant with them—a covenant, however, into which Israel and the nations are gathered.[9] Judaism believes in the God for whom the King of the Jews wants to bear witness in truth. That is why there can only be dialogue with Judaism about the Word of God (τὸν λόγον τοῦ θεοῦ), who has, as the content of his sending, the confirmation of the covenant for Israel.

Jean-Marie Lustiger illustrates this with the kingship of Jesus. In doing so he recalls that Jesus' kingly dignity is not first ascribed to him

8. Mark Kinzer emphasizes that Jesus does not replace the covenant history of Israel but truly realizes it, which he shows at the baptism of Jesus in the Jordan. Cf. Kinzer, *Searching Her Own Mystery* (see note 7), 95–99.

9. For this, cf. Christian Rutishauser, "Christian Mission to the Jews Revisited: Exploring the Logic of the Vatican Document 'The Gifts and Calling of God Are Irrevocable,'" *Studies in Christian–Jewish Relations* 14.1 (2019): 1–16. See also Christian Rutishauser, "'Ungekündigter Alter Bund' und 'Heil für alle Völker in Christus' – Katholische Glaubenssätze im Widerspruch?," in *Christlichen Glauben denken. Im Dialog mit der jüdischen Tradition*, ed. Christian Rutishauser (Forum Christen und Juden, 15; Vienna: LIT Verlag, 2016): 93–109, at 99: "The one God from Mount Sinai lets his Jewish Messiah become the light and salvation of the world and, through the outpouring of the Holy Spirit, makes it possible for God-fearing gentiles to enter into the covenant with God as well. There should arise one covenant in Christ, one people from Jews and gentiles." ["Der eine Gott vom Berg Sinai lässt seinen jüdischen Messias zum Licht und Heil der Welt werden und ermöglicht es durch die Ausgießung des Heiligen Geistes den gottesfürchtigen Heiden, ebenfalls in den Bund mit Gott einzutreten. Es soll ein Bund in Christus, ein Volk aus Juden und Heiden entstehen."]

at the cross but already in the account of the adoration of the Magi (Matt 2:1–12), who ask about the "newborn king of the Jews." The former Parisian cardinal, Jew and Catholic, reads the pericope in the logic of the contrast between Jesus as king and Herod as king. Jesus is the actual king of Israel, not Herod, who presents himself as the supposed king of Israel and does not recognize Jesus' sending. The sin of Herod is, according to Lustiger, that he "refuses Israel's Election in order to claim it for himself, to set himself up in place of Israel. The king given by God is his enemy since Herod has made himself king and usurped God's place with his people."[10] The sin of the Gentiles, into which Christian confession can also fall back, is the denial of the election of Israel, in which Jesus not only lives but is at the same time the "real symbol" of this election. Faith in Jesus as the Christ must therefore include respect for the enduring and given election of Israel. Jesus is the God-appointed and God-confirmed king, who lives out, opens, and confirms this election. For Christianity, this can mean not just self-critically working through replacement theology, but also revising "structural supersessionism"[11] in all theological treatises and clearly naming the enduring significance of the Jewish flesh of Jesus.

Moreover, the confession of Jesus as the "King of the Jews" has *ecclesiological* consequences. If one takes the title "King of the Jews" seriously in a theological sense, then the Church has the task of testifying kenotically to the kingly rule of God. An ecclesiology is thus to be spelled out kenotically, in that the Church lets herself be integrated into the sending of Jesus' own kingship in which the kingly rule of God breaks through.[12] In the constitution on the Church, *Lumen Gentium* 8,

10. Jean-Marie Lustiger, *The Promise* (Grand Rapids, MI: Eerdmans, 2007): 34. For the interpretation of Matt 2:1–12, see *ibid.*, 49–57.

11. R. Kendall Soulen, *The God of Israel and Christian Theology* (Minneapolis, MN: Fortress, 1996): 31–32.

12. Cf. Hengel, "Jesus der Messias Israels" (see note 4), 58: "Yet Jesus is for him [John the Evangelist; *author's note*]—much more than with Mark—not only Son of Man and Messiah, but at the same time as such the true 'king of God's people Israel' (John 1:49; 12:13; cf. also 11:52), i.e., the Son who is one with the Father and is sent by him into the world. Therefore in him, the kingly rule of God and that of Christ merge—they are identical (John 3:35; 18:36–37)" ["Jesus ist für ihn [den Evangelisten Johannes; *Anm. d. Verf.*] dabei – viel mehr als bei Markus – nicht nur Menschensohn und Messias, sondern zugleich als solcher der wahre 'König des Gottesvolkes Israel' (Joh 1,49; 12,13; vgl. auch 11,52), d.h., der vom Vater in die Welt gesandte gottgleiche Sohn. Die Königsherrschaft Gottes und die Christi fallen bei ihm daher zusammen: Sie sind identisch (Joh 3,35; 18,36f.)."]

the Second Vatican Council describes the relationship of the Church of Jesus Christ to the Catholic Church with the term *subsistit in*—"is actualized in." This rules out a rigid, absolute identification, as it was still firmly written with *est* ("is") in Pius XII's encyclical *Mystici Corporis*, and the concept of the Church is expanded. The privative term *subsistit in* expands the Church of Jesus Christ and deprives her of a usurpative appropriation.[13] Analogously, the kingship of Jesus will also have to be interpreted in the analogy of this "one complex reality" (cf. *LG* 8). The kingship of Jesus will not consist in a visible people of Judaism or of Christianity but in the togetherness of both entities. However, the kingship of Jesus as "one complex reality" itself has to be put into perspective again in such a way that it does not limit itself solely to Judaism or Christianity or to both entities.

Lumen Gentium 8 introduces the Christological "no weak analogy." Just as divine and human nature come together in Jesus Christ, so the togetherness of "the earthly Church and the Church enriched with heavenly things" can be understood as Church. The kingdom of Jesus "which is not of this world" (John 18:36), is also historically "one complex reality" in which Judaism and Christianity come together. However, this can only be interpreted as standing together in the sense of "undivided and unmixed." It is the reality of the King of the Jews, "who united the two parts and tore down the dividing wall of hostility in his flesh" (Eph 2:14). Yet it remains an open question what exactly the *ecclesia ex circumcisione* means in her connection to the *ecclesia ex gentibus*, and which ecclesiological place she can occupy without ecclesiologically usurping Judaism.[14] The kingdom of Jesus, which is not identical with the Church, is, in the person of Jesus as King of the Jews, the spiritual bond between Judaism and Christianity.[15]

13. Cf. Jan-Heiner Tück, *Römisches Monopol? Der Streit um die Einheit der Kirche* (Theologie kontrovers; Freiburg i.Br.: Herder, 2008).

14. Cf. Mark S. Kinzer, *Postmissionary Messianic Judaism: Redefining Christian Engagement with the Jewish People* (Grand Rapids, MI: Brazos Press, 2005): 151–79.

15. "Jesus himself—the Messiah of Israel and the individual embodiment of the Jewish people—is the fundamental spiritual bond linking the Church to the Jewish people"—Kinzer, *Searching Her Own Mystery* (see note 7), 18. See also Rutishauser, "Katholische Glaubenssätze" (see note 9), 99–100—"The Jewish Messiah has become the bridge between Jews and gentiles, and so the New Testament Scriptures recognize Jesus in a dual role: On the one hand, he is the King of the Jews who brings the way of salvation of the Jews to fullness and to its goal (Matt 5:18–19; Passion narratives). . . . On the other hand, Jewish messianism, an end-time phenomenon

The decisive thing here will be in what way the kingship of Jesus stands in relation to the Old Testament kingship of YHWH. Are two different reigns spoken of here? Or is the kingship of Jesus integrated into the kingship of YHWH? Or is the latter even represented by the former and historically concretized by it? For Rabbinic Judaism, the kingdom of God is present in the praying of *Shema Yisrael.*[16] The person praying opens himself to the kingdom of God and concretizes it in the doing of the Torah, through which YHWH becomes present in his people. But the expectation nevertheless remains that this kingdom will become universal and extend to the whole of creation. The kingdom of Jesus will need to be read in such a way that it clarifies and at the same time eschatologically universalizes the kingdom of YHWH in a singular way. On the cross, Jesus concretely realizes the obedience with respect to the Torah, in that here the love of God and neighbor is revealed as the content of his sending. Through his pro-existence on the cross for all human beings, he opens the kingdom of God for all human beings. The "βασιλεία *Christi*" ["kingdom of Christ"] in John 18:36 may not, however, be equated with the "βασιλεία τοῦ θεοῦ" ["kingdom of God"] of

---

in dialectic transition in the New Testament, becomes both the Christology of the original Church from the Gentiles and the starting point of a new covenant for the nations. Thus, Jesus Christ as the incarnation of the Jewish way of salvation, becomes universal salvation for all nations, through the mysterious transition from Jews to Gentiles, from death to resurrection. Jewish messianism mutates into the Christology of the Church. What appears from a Jewish perspective to be the end of time and the fulfillment of the Law, becomes from a Christian perspective the beginning and wellspring of a new covenant history for the nations in the Church." ["Der jüdische Messias ist zur Brücke zwischen Juden und Heiden geworden, und so erkennen die neutestamentlichen Schriften Jesus in einer doppelten Funktion: Einerseits ist er der König der Juden, der den Heilsweg der Juden zur Fülle und zum Ziel bringt (Mt 5,18f.; Passionsgeschichten). . . . Anderseits wird der jüdische Messianismus, ein Endzeitphänomen, im Neuen Testament in einem dialektischen Umschwung zur Christologie der Urkirche aus dem Heidentum und zum Ausgangspunkt des neuen Bundes für die Völker. So wird Jesus Christus als Inkarnation des jüdischen Heilswegs durch den geheimnisvollen Übergang von Juden zu Heiden, von Tod zu Auferstehung zum universalen Heil für alle Völker. Der jüdische Messianismus mutiert zur Christologie der Kirche. Was aus jüdischer Perspektive als Ende der Zeit und Erfüllung des Gesetzes erscheint, wird aus christlicher Perspektive zum Anfang und Ursprung einer neuen Bundesgeschichte für die Völker in der Kirche."] Also, Rudolf Pesch, *Gott ist gegenwärtig. Die Versammlung des Volkes Gottes in Synagoge und Kirche* (Augsburg: Sankt-Ulrich-Verlag, 2006), 96.

16. Cf. also Hanspeter Ernst, "Reich Gottes im rabbinischen Judentum. Gegenwärtig in Israel und zukünftig in der Welt," *Bibel und Kirche* 62 (2007): 109–112.

the Synoptic tradition,[17] but rather displays an eschatological-sacramental orientation. His reign will be for those whom he gathers in "spirit and truth" (cf. John 4:23–24). The Johannine concept of incarnation culminates on the cross and is the moment of history universalized "in Christ."

Faith in Jesus as the King of the Jews is an eschatological faith, and as such is messianic in character. However, the decisive and enduring question is whether, from an eschatological point of view, all of Judaism will confess Jesus as their king. In this regard, Mark Kinzer cites a passage from Robert W. Jenson:

> Can there be a present body of the risen Jew, Jesus of Nazareth, in which the lineage of Abraham and Sarah so vanishes into a congregation of gentiles as it does in the church? My final—and perhaps most radical—suggestion to Christian theology . . . is that . . . the embodiment of the risen Christ is whole only in the form of the church *and* an identifiable community of Abraham and Sarah's descendants. The church and the synagogue are together and only together the present availability to the world of the risen Jesus Christ.[18]

Judaism and Christianity together await the messianic kingdom that the coming Messiah ushers in. Jesus as the king of the Jews, who not only represents the kingship of YHWH but incarnates it, opens the kingdom for his people as the servant king. The confession that Jesus' reign does not mean a messianic earthly theocracy is an expression of the strict monotheistic faith of Jesus, which must be the foundation of any Christology.[19] Faith in Jesus, the King of the Jews, is faith in the God of the promise: "Faith in Christ is consistent faith in God."[20] In the kingly rule for which the Son of God takes responsibility, there is no

17. Cf. Volker Gäckle, "Das Reich Gottes im Johannesevangelium," in *Das Reich Gottes im Neuen Testament. Auslegungen – Anfragen – Alternativen*, ed. Volker Gäckle (Biblisch-Theologische Studien, 176; Göttingen: Vandenhoeck & Ruprecht, 2018): 179–92.

18. Robert W. Jenson, "Towards a Christian Theology of Judaism," in *Jews and Christians: People of God*, ed. Carl E. Braaten and Robert W. Jenson (Grand Rapids, MI: Eerdmans, 2003): 1–13, at 13 (emphasis original). Cf. also Jürgen Moltmann, *The Coming of God: Christian Eschatology*, trans. Margaret Kohl (Minneapolis, MN: Fortress, 1996): 198—"The common focus of Jewish and Christian hopes is the coming of the Messiah to his messianic kingdom. Only *the Christ of the Parousia* will save 'all Israel' (Rom 11.26). The acceptance of all Israel will be 'life from the dead' (Rom. 11.15f.). Consequently, Israel's Messiah must be the risen One" (emphasis original).

19. Cf. Rutishauser, "Katholische Glaubenssätze" (see note 9), 100.

20. "Christusglaube ist konsequenter Gottesglaube."—Söding, "'Für das Volk'" (see note 5), 102.

connection between throne and altar, neither does it culminate in the deification of the political ruler. For the Johannine testimony of Jesus as the King of the Jews, he is not only a forerunner and herald of this kingdom of God, but he is bound up with this kingly rule, as he and the Father are one (cf. John 10:30), so that it is the one reign that binds Father and Son together.

The reign of God is indeed not *from* this world, but it is in the world, in that it becomes present there. "To the extent that people hear the voice of the shepherd ([John] 10:3), or as the Book of Revelation says, 'follow the Lamb wherever he goes' ([Rev] 14:4), the kingship of Christ realizes itself in the hearts of his own and they are 'in the truth.'"[21] Christianity is thus placed in solidarity with Judaism, and the Church is "bound together in a messianic community-of-the-way with the Jews"[22] or, as Jean-Marie Lustiger expresses this, with "freely given reciprocity."[23] This dimension of the "messianic community-of-the-way" of the Jewish people and Christians will have to take into view more strongly the Feast of Christ the King, which liturgically recalls the eschatological kingship of Jesus.[24] When the liturgical texts say that Christ is the

21. "In dem Maß, als die Menschen die Stimme des Hirten hören (10,3) oder, wie die Apokalypse sagt, 'dem Lamme folgen, wohin immer es geht' (14,4), verwirklicht sich Christi Königtum in den Herzen der Seinen und sind sie 'in der Wahrheit.'"—De la Potterie, *Die Passion nach Johannes* (see note 2), 74–75. However, de la Potterie understands the gathering of the sheep by the shepherd Jesus as the withdrawal of the Church from the Synagogue. Here the consequence of a "structural supersessionism" becomes apparent (cf. R. Kendall Soulen, *The God of Israel and Christian Theology* (see note 11), 31–32), in the fact that Israel's heritage is not adequately appreciated in the theological structure of the reflections.

22. "zusammengebunden in einer messianischen Weggemeinschaft mit den Juden"—Erich Zenger, "Das Erste Testament als Herausforderung christlicher Liturgie," in *Leseordnung. Altes and Neues Testament in der Liturgie*, ed. Georg Steins (Stuttgart: Katholisches Bibelwerk, 1997): 11–28, at 28. Christian Rutishauser describes the relationship between Judaism and Christianity as "a dual people of God with a dialogical existence" ["ein doppeltes Gottesvolk von einer dialogischen Existenz"]—"Katholische Glaubenssätze" (see note 9), 109.

23. Cf. Lustiger, *The Promise* (see note 10), 99–102, here 101—"the pagans must recognize in Jesus the grace given to Israel, because they share in that grace; and Israel must welcome the hope manifested by the wonders that God accomplishes among the pagans. Thus, each group bears witness to the other that it is an unearned gift that it has received. It is this mutual recognition, this freely given reciprocity that is the object of our hope."

24. Cf. also Regina Wildgruber, "Sackgasse oder Spur messianischer Weggemeinschaft? Der Christkönigssonntag im Lesejahr B," *Bibel und Liturgie* 82 (2009):

King of all creation, and at the same time also Head of the new creation, this underscores the relative character of Jesus' kingship in relation to the eschatological consummation.[25] The Christology of King Jesus only does justice to its explosive nature as King of the Jews when this kingship is read in relation to the theocentricity of the consummation. The kingly rule of God is the kingly rule of Jesus, which the Jewish Messiah Jesus has definitively established,[26] and toward which the "messianic community-on-the-way" is traveling.

(Translated by John David Martin, James Earle Patrick, and Wayne Coppins from the German: "Der eschatologische König für das eine Volk aus Juden und Heiden. Antwort auf Mark S. Kinzer")

45–55. For the Feast of Christ the King, see: Christoph Joosten, *Das Christkönigsfest. Liturgie im Spannungsfeld zwischen Frömmigkeit und Politik* (Pietas Liturgica, 12; Tübingen / Basel: Francke, 2002).

25. Cf. Maria Neubrand, "'Ein Volk aus Nichtjuden' (Apg 15,14). Die bleibende Erwählung Israels und die Erwählung aus den Völkern im lukanischen Doppelwerk," in *Das Heil der Anderen. Problemfeld: "Judenmission,"* ed. Hubert Frankemölle and Josef Wohlmuth (Quaestiones Disputatae, 238; Freiburg i. Br.: Herder, 2010): 289–310, at 308–310, here 308: "The definitive establishment of the Davidic-messianic kingly rule belongs to the Jewish–Christian future hope. For although, according to the testimony of the New Testament, Jesus is validly confirmed as Davidic Messiah through his resurrection and exaltation and installed in his rulership (cf. Acts 2:29–36; Rom 1:3–4), until his return the ultimate establishment of the hoped-for messianic rule and with it the kingdom of God 'to the ends of the earth' is, nevertheless, still pending (cf. Acts 1:6; 3:21)" ["Die endgültige Errichtung der davidisch-messianischen Königsherrschaft gehört zur jüdisch-christlichen Zukunftshoffnung. Denn zwar ist nach dem neutestamentlichen Zeugnis Jesus durch seine Auferweckung und Erhöhung als davidischer Messias gültig bestätigt und in seine Herrschaft eingesetzt (vgl. Apg 2,29–36; Röm 1,3f.), doch steht bis zu seiner Wiederkehr die endgültige Errichtung der erhofften messianischen Herrschaft und mit ihr das Reich Gottes 'bis an die Grenze der Erde' noch aus (vgl. Apg 1,6; 3,21)"].

26. Cf. Hengel, "Jesus der Messias Israels" (see note 4), 60: "The one who denies every messianic claim of Jesus can just as little provide a historically satisfying explanation for the execution of Jesus as s/he can for the emergence of early Christology and the massive transfer of the Messiah title to the Risen One, a title that was so closely connected to his person that it quickly became a proper name and circa ten years later gave to Christians their name which is still valid today." ["Wer jeden messianischen Anspruch Jesu leugnet, kann die Hinrichtung Jesu so wenig historisch befriedigend klären wie die Entstehung der frühen Christologie und die massive Übertragung des Messiastitels auf den Auferstandenen, ein Titel, der so sehr mit seiner Person verbunden wurde, daß er rasch zum Eigennamen wurde und den Christen ca. zehn Jahre später ihren bis heute gültigen Namen gab."]

United in Diversity

Plurality as a Characteristic of Early Christian Ecclesiology

Thomas Schumacher

1. Introduction and outline of the problem

The insight that the roots of Christianity are to be found in Judaism, and that consequently the origins of Christianity can only be adequately interpreted and classified against their Jewish background, can now be considered as self-evident in theological reflection. Nevertheless, tracing the historical development of the disengagement of Christianity from Judaism proves itself to be a highly complex task. The issues associated with this question are subsumed and discussed under the catchphrase, "Parting of the ways"; but it can hardly be claimed that a clear consensus has been established in this area with regard to a description and categorization of the processes in question so far.

Whatever these processes may have looked like, however, one consequence of the disengagement of Christianity from Judaism is, in retrospect, impossible to overlook: If one asks about the perception of the relationship between these two religions in Western Church history and theological history, a binary juxtaposition is the predominant paradigm for interpretation. Judaism and Christianity are customarily seen as two unambiguously mutually demarcated monotheistic religious systems, which, despite a certain common ground in traditions and faith convictions, differ fundamentally from one another, and most particularly in one essential respect: Whereas the confession of Jesus of Nazareth as

Messiah counts as one of the core convictions relevant for the Christian tradition, in the Jewish context Jesus mostly plays the role of a prophetic figure.[1] According to this classical interpretation, the confession of Jesus as the Messiah functions as a sharply defined *identity marker* so that the concept of conversion—of a conscious change of religion—becomes applicable to the transition between Judaism and Christianity.

This binary scheme of thought determined theological reflections over the centuries and was also applied to the interpretation of early Church developments. This can be illustrated paradigmatically using the biography of Paul, in which the binary model is brought in with the widespread interpretation of his breakthrough experience near Damascus as a *conversion*. The christophany to Paul and his turning toward a relationship with Christ is seen ultimately as a rejection of the Jewish tradition and a turning to Christianity—an interpretation which in the Catholic tradition has found expression and resonance in the Feast of the Conversion of Saint Paul and which is linked with a reception of Paul, which also imports a binary model of the juxtaposition of Christianity and Judaism into the interpretation of his writings.

But when it comes to doing conceptual justice to the phenomenon of Messianic Judaism, which is currently gaining strength and moving stronger into theological consciousness, then the binary paradigm proves itself entirely unsuitable. For in the self-understanding of the Jewish-Messianic stream, Jewish identity is combined with the confession of the Messiahship of Jesus Christ—a constellation that breaks open the binary scheme. Thus, this movement represents a theological provocation, which implies the necessity to put classic patterns of interpretation to the test.

Certainly, fundamental inquiries into the construction of Christian identity by demarcation from Judaism are historically already linked with the early days of the Quest for the Historical Jesus. From its outset, it has claimed the hermeneutical consideration of the Jewish context and the Jewish identity of Jesus,[2] and its postulates in this regard are

1. For a Jewish perspective on Jesus, cf., e.g., Walter Homolka, *Der Jude Jesus – Eine Heimholung. Mit einem Geleitwort von Jan-Heiner Tück* (Freiburg i. Br.: Herder, 2020).

2. Cf. on this already Hermann Samuel Reimarus: "By the way, he was a Jew by birth and wanted to remain so; he testifies that he has not come to abolish the law, but to fulfill it; he only points out that the most important thing in the law

now generally received affirmatively. Thus, despite the Christological differences that separate Christianity and non-Messianic Judaism from each other, the historical Jesus himself becomes the link with the Jewish tradition. An analogous position can now also be identified within the research on Paul: Here the breakthrough essentially goes back to the so-called "New Perspective on Paul,"[3] which still understands Paul as a Jew even after the Damascus experience, fundamentally calling into question a conversion interpretation. In light of the relevant considerations and findings, it has now become clear, not least in the "Paul within Judaism" debate,[4] that the older binary model of understanding was not only insufficient to adequately explain the textual phenomena, but also quite often yielded a distorting interpretation of New Testament writings and a false perspective on Judaism.

To avoid corresponding hermeneutical short-circuits in exegesis, it is therefore of central importance when interpreting New Testament writings to keep in mind that early Christian constructions of identity should be understood as highly plural entities—and this observation

---

does not depend on the external things" ["Uebrigens war er ein gebohrner Jude und wollte es auch bleiben: er bezeuget er sey nicht kommen das Gesetz abzuschaffen, sondern zu erfüllen: er weiset nur, daß das hauptsächlichste im Gesetze nicht auf die äusserlichen Dinge ankäme"]—Anonymous, *Von dem Zwecke Jesu und seiner Jünger. Noch ein Fragment des Wolfenbüttelschen Ungenannten*, ed. Gotthold E. Lessing (Braunschweig, 1778): 19–20.

3. For a survey of the history of research, cf., e.g., Christian Strecker, "Paulus aus einer 'neuen Perspektive.' Der Paradigmenwechsel in der jüngeren Paulusforschung," *Kirche und Israel* 11 (1996): 3–18; Michael Wolter, "Eine neue paulinische Perspektive," *Zeitschrift für Neues Testament* 14 (2004): 2–9; Michael Bachmann, ed., *Lutherische und Neue Paulusperspektive. Beiträge zu einem Schlüsselproblem der gegenwärtigen exegetischen Diskussion* (Wissenschaftliche Untersuchungen zum Neuen Testament, 182; Tübingen: Mohr Siebeck, 2005); Stefan Schreiber, "Paulus und die Tradition. Zur Hermeneutik der 'Rechtfertigung' in neuer Perspektive," *Theologische Revue* 105 (2009): 91–102; Christine Gerber, "Blicke auf Paulus. Die New Perspective on Paul in der jüngeren Diskussion," *Verkündigung und Forschung* 55 (2010): 4–60.

4. Cf., e.g., Mark D. Nanos and Magnus Zetterholm, eds., *Paul within Judaism: Restoring the First-Century Context to the Apostle* (Minneapolis, MN: Fortress, 2015); John M.G. Barclay, "Paul, Judaism, and the Jewish People," in *The Blackwell Companion to Paul*, ed. Stephen Westerholm (Chichester: Wiley-Blackwell, 2011): 188–201; Kathy Ehrensperger, "Die 'Paul within Judaism'-Perspektive. Eine Übersicht," *Evangelische Theologie* 80 (2020): 455–64; Kathy Ehrensperger, "Paulus und die Völker – Aspekte der 'Paul within Judaism'-Perspektive," *Kirche und Israel* 35 (2020): 118–31.

should also be of theological and exegetical interest in view of Messianic Judaism. A look in the Pauline writings, that is, in the oldest texts of a religious tradition shaped by the confession of Christ, quickly reveals that the above-mentioned plurality is a basic feature of the early Christ-movement. For even after Damascus, Paul quite naturally claims a Jewish identity for himself, and in that respect, he is representative of other Christ-believing Jews, whereas according to the Pauline tradition non-Jewish believers in Christ for their part do not perform a conversion to Judaism, even if they disengage themselves in a conversion-like manner from their original pagan religiosity.

Thus, the stereotypical talk of "Jewish Christians" and "Gentile Christians" established in exegetical discourse is to be assessed as problematic, since it insinuates a parallelism of their respective entry into the relationship with Christ and the resulting consequences for the religion of origin, and at the same time implies an ecclesiological homogeneity. It would be conceptually much more appropriate to speak of "Christ-believing Jews" and "Christ-believers from the nations," and thus to express terminologically the outlines of the difference and the plurality within early Christianity.[5] And unquestionably it is very important to keep in mind when interpreting the Pauline writings that Paul is primarily addressing a non-Jewish audience and formulates his positions in an audience-specific way. Thus, his text may not be interpreted in such a way that the standards he formulates with regard to non-Jewish believers in Christ are simply and uncritically also applied to a Jewish audience. When looking at the New Testament, one will

5. This differentiation should also be relevant for the interpretation of the famous mosaic from the entrance wall of Santa Sabina in Rome, which is repeatedly referred to in the context of Messianic Judaism, on which the personifications of the *ecclesia ex circumcisione* and the *ecclesia ex gentibus* are placed in relation to one another; cf.on this for example the book cover by Mark S. Kinzer, *Searching Her Own Mystery:* Nostra Aetate, *the Jewish People, and the Identity of the Church. With a Foreword by Christoph Cardinal Schönborn* (Eugene, OR: Cascade Books, 2015), as well as the comments on this iconographic conception by Antoine Lévy, "Restoration of the *Ecclesia ex Circumcisione*?" in the present volume. For if a parallel formulation is chosen in this inscription by means of the preposition *ex*, then this speaks for a break both *ecclesiae* make with their respective original dimensions, i.e., Jews (*ex circumcisione*) and nations (*ex gentibus*). But this already reflects a marked shift compared to the New Testament finding, for which such a parallel interpretation of the respective religious backgrounds does not yet apply; cf. on this also note 9 in this article.

consequently have to take much more account of early Christian plurality than it is customarily done.

2. Intra-Christian plurality in Paul

With regard to the Pauline writings, the aforementioned plurality can be recognized in many respects. This may be illustrated for instance with regard to Romans—that piece of writing which is generally esteemed as the overall presentation of Paul's theology. Already in the so-called theme verse of this writing, in Romans 1:16–17, the explicit mention of Jews and non-Jews as addressees of the gospel catches the eye, when the first named group, the Jews, is given priority (Ἰουδαίῳ τε πρῶτον καὶ Ἕλληνι). And this differentiation seems to continue even after a pagan's acceptance of the gospel and after his turning to Jesus Christ. In this respect, consider the differentiation between διὰ πίστεως and ἐκ πίστεως in Romans 3:30 (εἴπερ εἷς ὁ θεὸς ὃς δικαιώσει περιτομὴν ἐκ πίστεως καὶ ἀκροβυστίαν διὰ τῆς πίστεως) which probably represents not so much a mere linguistic variation as a relevant group-specific distinction.

The parable of the olive tree in Romans 11:16b–24 also points in this direction since in this passage Paul interestingly utilizes the noun "branches" (κλάδοι) as a kind of honorific title and only with regard to Jews, whereas for Christians of the nations he uses the somewhat awkward-sounding formulation "you, being a wild olive tree" (σὺ δὲ ἀγριέλαιος ὢν).[6] Despite the Christ relationship which binds Christ-believing Jews and Christians of the nations together, conceptually both groups are clearly distinguished from each other. This gives the impression that the Jewish identity continues to exist even after turning to Christ, whereas for non-Jews the entry into a relationship with Christ seems to be thought of much more in the category of conversion.

Also speaking in favor of this is the striking fact that Paul qualifies the turning of Jews to Jesus Christ as ἐπίγνωσις (and so not as γνῶσις), that is, as a supplementing and deepening of knowledge, such

6. Cf. Thomas Schumacher, "'Gott hat sein Volk nicht verstoßen!' (Röm 11,2). Anmerkungen zu den Substitutionsmotiven in Röm 9–11," in *Antijudaismen in der Exegese? Eine Diskussion 50 Jahre nach* Nostra Aetate, and Stefan Schreiber and Thomas Schumacher (Freiburg i. Br.: Herder, 2015): 232–77, at 255–57, 261.

that the Christ relationship is quite obviously not interpreted as a break with previous Jewish identity.[7] On the other hand, Paul understands the process of non-Jews turning to Christ much more as a caesura and break with the respective past religious beliefs.

Even the formulation in Romans 10:4 according to which Christ is τέλος νόμου does not speak against this position. In the history of exegesis, this phrase was repeatedly interpreted in such a way that the law as the *identity marker* of Judaism came to an end with Christ, but as the semantic spectrum of τέλος and also the newer readings of this passage attest, this interpretation is in no way compelling. In any case, it would be difficult to reconcile it with the positive statements about the law in Romans 7 and the thought from Romans 3:21, according to which the πίστις relationship to Christ "establishes the law" (νόμον ἱστάνομεν). Hence it would be much more appropriate to translate τέλος in Romans 10:4 not as "end" but as "goal" or "highest form" of the law.[8]

So, it should be noted that in Romans Paul clearly distinguishes between the salvation-historical status of Jews and non-Jews or of Christ-believing Jews and Christians of the nations, respectively, and thus assumes an intra-Christian plurality. For this, we could also refer to a detail from the list of greetings where Romans 16:4 mentions the gratitude of the "assemblies from the nations" (αἱ ἐκκλησίαι τῶν ἐθνῶν) toward Prisca and Aquila—a formulation which by way of a conclusive analogy directly suggests the acceptance of the existence of assemblies (ἐκκλησίαι) of *Jewish* believers in Christ, and thereby makes the aforementioned intra-Christian plurality discernible once again.[9]

7. Cf. Norbert Baumert, "'Επίγνωσις bei Paulus. 'Eifer der Juden' – ohne 'Erkenntnis?,'" in *NOMOS und andere Vorarbeiten zur Reihe 'Paulus neu gelesen,'* ed. Norbert Baumert (Forschung zur Bibel, 122; Würzburg: Echter, 2010): 408–20; Maria-Irma Seewann, "Über die Zu-Erkenntnis (ἐπίγνωσις) der Juden. Bibeltheologische Überlegungen," in Baumert, ed., *NOMOS und andere Vorarbeiten*, 421–26; Schumacher, "Gott hat sein Volk nicht verstoßen!," (see note 6), 271–72.

8. Cf. Hans-Peter Riermeier, "'Höchste Stufe' von Gesetz ist Christus. Beobachtungen zur Semantik von τέλος (Röm 10,4)," in Baumert, ed., *NOMOS und andere Vorarbeiten*, (see note 7), 385–98.

9. In this context, the conspicuous fact certainly is worth mentioning that in New Testament parlance there is no parallel formulation such as ἐκκλησία ἐκ περιτομῆς ("Church from the circumcision") yet; with regard to Christ-believing Jews, rather expressions such as οἱ ἐκ περιτομῆς πιστοί ("the believers from the circumcision," Acts 10:45) or ἐκκλησιῶν τοῦ θεοῦ τῶν οὐσῶν ἐν τῇ Ἰουδαίᾳ ἐν Χριστῷ Ἰησοῦ ("churches of God that are in Judaea in Messiah Jesus," 1 Thes 2:14) were

3. *On problems of Galatians*

In Galatians, however, there appear to be some marked deviations from this finding, which are particularly concentrated in the reference to the incident at Antioch (Gal 2:11–21). They are first noticeable in Galatians 2:14, where Paul, according to the majority interpretation, formulates against Peter that the basis for a friction-free coexistence for Christians of the nations and Christ-believing Jews in the church of Antioch is that Peter in his function as representative of the Jewish wing lives in a "gentile" or "pagan" and no longer in a "Jewish way" (ἐθνικῶς καὶ οὐχὶ Ἰουδαϊκῶς ζῇς). Accordingly, the unity among Christians would require that Christ-believing Jews break with their own Jewish identity and this step would imply, as Hans-Dieter Betz phrased it, a "total emancipation from Judaism."[10]

The statements from Galatians 2:15–16 also seem to fit into this interpretation. For if in verse 15 it is formulated from a Jewish perspective that "We are Jews from birth and not sinners like the Gentiles," and this statement is read in opposition to verse 16—"But because we have recognized that man is not justified through works of the law, but through faith in Jesus Christ, we too have come to believe in Christ Jesus . . ."[11]—then Jewish identity and faith in Christ appear to be diametrically opposed to one another. The statement from Galatians 2:15–16 sounds as if Paul wanted to contrast two opposite ways of salvation, namely the Jewish, which is distinguished by Torah observance, and the Christian, whose key characteristic is faith in Christ. The adversative δὲ at the beginning of verse 16 (εἰδότες δὲ ὅτι) would thus mark

---

formed. The parallel phrase *ekklesia ex circumcisione* in Santa Sabina should therefore probably be evaluated as a secondary assimilation to αἱ ἐκκλησίαι τῶν ἐθνῶν and already presupposes the autonomy of a Christ-believing Jewish ἐκκλησία alongside non-Christ-believing Judaism. The *ekklesia ex circumcisione* represents, so to speak, the counterpart to the *ekklesia ex gentibus*. Moreover, it is quite striking that in Santa Sabina in both personifications the singular has already taken the place of the plural constructions of New Testament parlance.

10. Hans-Dieter Betz, *Galatians. A Commentary on Paul's Letter to the Churches in Galatia* (Hermeneia; Philadelphia, PA: Fortress, 1979), 112—in the original German: "völligen Emanzipation . . . vom Judentum."

11. This translation is based on the German "Einheitsübersetzung" from 1980; in the original it reads: "15 Wir sind zwar von Geburt Juden und nicht Sünder wie die Heiden. 16 Weil wir aber erkannt haben, dass der Mensch nicht durch Werke des Gesetzes gerecht wird, sondern durch den Glauben an Jesus Christus, sind auch wir dazu gekommen, an Christus Jesus zu glauben . . ."

the caesura between Judaism and Christianity, or accentuate a conversional interpretation. Correspondingly, with a view to the argumentative structure of Galatians 2:15–16, Heinrich Schlier formulates: "What Paul and the other Jewish Christians now know is therefore the fact that the righteousness of God does not prevail in performance at all, not even in the performance demanded by God. That is a knowledge that presupposes a complete break with Judaism."[12]

These interpretations give the impression that the emergence of a unified Christianity becomes tangible in Galatians, a form of Christianity which now also expects Christ-believing Jews to break with their religion of origin. This hermeneutical approach is also applied to evaluating the question of the opponents in Galatians, for if one imagines that with this letter Paul is reacting to early Christian preachers who have penetrated the churches he founded himself and who demand from the Galatian Christians of the nations an orientation toward Jewish law, then according to the majority opinion this applies best to *Jewish* opponents.[13] With regard to Christians of the nations, these Jewish opponents thus would not have esteemed justification—opened up through the relationship with Christ—as a community-enabling foundation; rather, they would have viewed compliance with the Jewish law, or ultimately membership in Judaism, as a prerequisite for an ecclesiological community. With this situational background in mind, Paul would bring forward his own break with Jewish identity in order to advance his argument.

4. Galatians under the magnifying glass

But this interpretation can be questioned in different ways. First, it should be pointed out that Paul's position outlined with recourse to Galatians 2:14 and Galatians 2:15–16 would ascribe a sin-forgiving

12. "Was Paulus und die anderen Judenchristen jetzt wissen, ist demnach die Tatsache, daß sich die Gerechtigkeit Gottes überhaupt nicht in Leistungen, auch nicht in den von Gott geforderten Leistungen durchsetzt. Das ist ein Wissen, das den völligen Bruch mit dem Judentum voraussetzt."—Heinrich Schlier, *Der Brief an die Galater* (Kritisch-exegetischer Kommentar – NT, 7; Göttingen: Vandenhoeck & Ruprecht, 5th edn 1971): 92.

13. For discussion, cf. Michael Bachmann, "Die 'Opponenten' des Paulus im (heilsgeschichtlich profilierten) Galaterbrief. Alte und neue Zugänge," *Zeitschrift für die Neutestamentliche Wissenschaft* 112 (2021): 145–79.

dimension to Torah or to Torah observance—as did the foreign missionaries' demand of a Torah-compliant life for Christians of the nations. This creates the impression that faith in Christ and Torah observance stand in relation to one another as two contrary, mutually exclusive ways of salvation: the Jewish way based on the law, and the Christian way that distanced itself from it. However, in the New Perspective on Paul inspired above all by the work of Ed Parish Sanders, it is strongly emphasized that such an evaluation of the Torah in no way is in accordance with the beliefs of ancient Judaism.[14] The law does not have the function of justifying the sinner and awarding him forgiveness of sins, but rather is oriented toward or subordinate to the covenant in a positive, protective manner; a narrative of "works righteousness" is therefore completely out of place in this regard.

Further peculiarities could be added to this, especially in the area of textual tradition. This first concerns the question of the textual reconstruction of Galatians 2:14, because in contrast to the aforementioned textual variant, Papyrus 46 and a few other textual witnesses only talk of Peter living in a "non-Jewish/pagan way" (ἐθνικῶς ζῇς). According to this shorter variant—εἰ σὺ Ἰουδαῖος ὑπάρχων ἐθνικῶς ζῇς, πῶς τὰ ἔθνη ἀναγκάζεις ἰουδαΐζειν—Paul would formulate the question in Galatians 2:14, "If you, as a Jew, live in a non-Jewish/pagan way, why then are you urging the Christians of the nations to adopt Jewish ways of behavior?" And the phrase ἐθνικῶς ζῇς should by no means be read in the sense of a conversion, but rather as an expression of an adaptation to customs of Christians of the nations, since the counter-term, that is, ἰουδαΐζειν, in turn denotes an imitative alignment to a Jewish lifestyle, as Dieter Sänger has convincingly worked out.[15] Thus, Galatians 2:14 is unlikely to be addressing a broadly "gentile" way of life of Peter, but

14. Cf. on this esp. Ed Parish Sanders, *Paul and Palestinian Judaism: A Comparison of Patterns of Religion* (Philadelphia, PA: Fortress / London: SCM, 1977): 107–25, 183–205, 409–18, as well as also Ed Parish Sanders, *Paul, the Law and the Jewish People* (Philadelphia, PA: Fortress, 1983). For the current assessment of Sanders' approach, cf. the concise presentation in Barclay, "Paul, Judaism, and the Jewish People" (see note 4), 191–92. For discussion, cf. also Ehrensperger, "Die 'Paul within Judaism'-Perspektive" (see note 4); Nanos and Zetterholm, eds., *Paul Within Judaism* (see note 4).

15. Cf. Dieter Sänger, "Ἰουδαϊσμός – ἰουδαΐζειν – ἰουδαϊκῶς. Sprachliche und semantische Überlegungen im Blick auf Gal 1,13f und 2,14," *Zeitschrift für die Neutestamentliche Wissenschaft* 108 (2017): 150–85.

rather ἐθνικῶς ζῇς would express a behavior oriented toward Christians of the nations. And against the background of the situation in Antioch, that most likely brings to mind the fellowship existing between Jewish and non-Jewish believers in Christ, which should not be confused with a "total emancipation from Judaism."[16]

But the syntactical structure of Galatians 2:15–16 is also worth discussing from a text-critical point of view. The particle δέ, which expresses the previously mentioned adversative contrast between verses 15 and 16, is text-critically so uncertain, that although it found its way into the main text in the Greek text edition by Nestle-Aland, it is placed in square brackets there. It is missing in the text handed down by Papyrus 46 and Codex Alexandrinus, among others, and even the Majority Text does not transmit this particle. This text-critical uncertainty, however, raises the question of whether Galatians 2:15–16 could not be read as one single complex sentence, albeit a long one. This variant is often excluded in the commentary literature, because a corresponding *participium coniunctum*, for example ὄντες or something similar, is missing in verse 15, which might stand in parallel to the participle εἰδότες in verse 16.[17] However, since Papyrus 46 *does* transmit the form ὄντες—regrettably there is no corresponding reference in the text-critical apparatus of Nestle-Aland—one should not be too quick to exclude this possibility. These two text-critical observations would even allow the conclusion that for Paul—and Peter would explicitly have to be included here—Jewish identity and faith in Christ are not mutually exclusive. But then the statement would be made here that the "knowledge" (εἰδότες) spoken of in Galatians 2:16—that is, the knowledge that the justification of the sinner cannot arise from observance of the Torah—is ultimately familiar to every Jew: "We, Jews by birth, . . . know that man is not justified by works of the law. . . ." And according to Papyrus 46, Paul would also emphasize that he still considers himself and also Peter to be Jews (Ἰουδαῖοι ὄντες). Consequently, a "total emancipation from Judaism"[18] or a conversion to Christianity is definitely not what this is about.

16. Betz, *Galatians*, (see note 10), 112.

17. Cf., e.g., Albrecht Oepke, *Der Brief des Paulus an die Galater* (Theologischer Handkommentar zum Neuen Testament, 9; Berlin: Evangelische Verlagsanstalt, 4th edn 1979): 90; Hans-Joachim Eckstein, *Verheißung und Gesetz. Eine exegetische Untersuchung zu Galater 2,15–4,7* (Wissenschaftliche Untersuchungen zum Neuen Testament, 86; Tübingen: Mohr Siebeck, 1996): 6.

18. Betz, *Galatians* (see note 10), 112.

But what do these considerations mean for the question of the opponents in Galatians? In the light of the above, the assumption of a "conversion" of Jews to a homogeneous Christianity seems more than questionable. On the contrary, the difference between Christ-believing Jews and Christians of the nations, which is also clearly recognizable elsewhere in the Pauline tradition, would remain present as the basic concept in Galatians. At the same time, however, this has implications for the answer to the opponents' question: If one considers that in Galatians 2:15–16 the Jewish conviction is formulated that the Torah has no sin-forgiving function, then the Galatian opponents, who apparently assumed just such a function, hardly seem to have been Jewish missionaries.

And this impression again leads to a text-critical question in the context of that passage in which Paul refers directly to the opponents (Gal 6:11–16). In Galatians 6:13, they are described, according to the *Novum Testamentum Graece*, as οἱ περιτεμνόμενοι, as "circumcised," which unquestionably makes one think of Jews or Christ-believing Jews. In the context of the identification of opponents, particular weight is attached to this statement. However, here too the manuscript findings are by no means unambiguous,[19] for (once again!) in Papyrus 46, in the Codex Vaticanus, and in some other majuscule and minuscule manuscripts, instead of a present participle the perfect participial construction περιτετμημένοι is transmitted, which can be understood either as middle or as passive. Going with the latter, a translation of "those who have been circumcised" would suggest itself, which likewise makes us think of Jews or Christ-believing Jews. But speaking very clearly against this interpretation is the fact that the use of οἱ περιτετμημένοι as a designation for Jews or Judaism would be extremely unusual; indeed, it would even be the only passage in the entire New Testament in which a construction of the verb περιτέμνω would be used as a designation for Jews. If this thought were to have been expressed, the widely attested nominal construction περιτομή or the coined phrase οἱ ἐκ περιτομῆς would have been more likely. Consequently, the middle interpretation might be considered more suitable for this reading. But then οἱ περιτετμημένοι would mean those "who have let themselves be circumcised," which insinuates the thought of people who themselves have made a conscious

19. On what follows also cf. Thomas Schumacher, "Juden oder Nichtjuden, das ist hier die Frage. Zur Identifizierung der Gegner im Galaterbrief," *Zeitschrift für die Neutestamentliche Wissenschaft* 113 (2022): 69–98.

decision for circumcision. But this generally makes one think less of Jewish boys who were circumcised as a rule in infancy, and much more of non-Jewish Christ-believers, who evidently felt compelled to take such a step as a result of their orientation toward Judaism. One could best designate this group as "Judaizing Christians of the nations."

Such an identification of the Galatian opponents would now relate conclusively to the previous reflections on Galatians 2:14 and Galatians 2:15–16, because the aforementioned passages now appear as a correction of a misguided and highly "un-Jewish" reception of Torah. When the Galatian opponents demanded circumcision along with other Jewish practices, they seem to have attributed to this step—contrary to Jewish tradition—a sin-forgiving dimension. And it is precisely this category error that Paul would pick up at the end of the biographical section, the so-called *narratio*, when he formulates from the perspective of Christ-believing Jews: "We, as native-born Jews, know that one does not acquire forgiveness of sins through the Torah."

In view of the presented manuscript findings, it is now highly conspicuous that all the highlighted textual variants are transmitted by Papyrus 46 and that this manuscript yields a consistent overall picture—incidentally also beyond the passages discussed here. This manuscript is the oldest and unquestionably the most valuable textual witness to Galatians. And in addition to this external criterion, there is an internal one, because with regard to the origin of manuscript variants or their interdependence, the textual variants of Papyrus 46 can hardly be explained as secondary. Since, if an intra-Christian plurality of Christ-believing Jews and Christians of the nations is still recognizable in this manuscript or in the associated manuscript tradition, then the corresponding variants can be made understandable as secondary through the early Christian developments reflected in the context of the "Parting of the Ways" debate—that is, an increasing marginalization of the Jewish stream within early Christianity, in the wake of which the idea of a homogeneous Christianity more and more became the background of understanding the text. On the contrary, attempts to identify the text variants of P 46 as secondary prove rather difficult, as the oft-repeated reference to possible scribal errors illustrates.[20]

20. Incidentally, a very similar finding can also be identified in this manuscript in the area of historical semantics, as becomes clear, e.g., in the textual variant of Eph 1:15 transmitted by Papyrus 46. For the influence of historical-semantic

With this it should have become clear, how much weight Paul places on the idea of an intra-Christian plurality in his view of early Christianity. He differentiates clearly between Jews and non-Jews, and between Christ-believing Jews and Christians of the nations, and reacts in a defensive way, regardless of all existing contacts and ties, against tendencies toward convergence in the area of religious identity. In any case, in the epistle to the Galatians, he affirms that the non-Jewish believers in Christ should value their own socio-religious status instead of imitating the Jewish lifestyle.

5. A side glance at the epistle of James

In the light of these textual observations and reflections, a side glance at the epistle of James may open up deeper insights. This epistle has often been set in opposition content-wise to the Pauline literature, an opposition that found its clearest expression in the hermeneutical and canonical queries of Martin Luther. They are reflected in the verdict of an "epistle of straw" expressed about James (WA, DB 6.10) as well as in the plan to "heat the oven" with this letter (WA, TR 5.382). As is well known, in the background of this negative assessment stands the statement expressed in James that faith without works is useless and that even Abraham was not regarded as a righteous person by God on account of his faith, his πίστις, but because of his works—a statement which in Luther's view was diametrically opposed to the affirmation of justification through faith alone, that is, to the Reformation *articulus stantis et cadentis Ecclesiae*, that is, the article by which the Church stands and falls.

In light of this issue, one must keep in view the different audiences of Pauline writings and of the epistle of James. Whereas Paul addresses himself primarily to a pagan audience and discusses topics like the acceptance of non-Jews by God, forgiveness of sins, and the constitution of a relationship with God through Christ, the situation is quite different in the epistle of James. Admittedly, for a long time this text was considered to be a writing addressed to a comprehensive Christian audience,

---

developments on the text transmission, cf. Thomas Schumacher, "Historische Semantik und Textüberlieferung. Anmerkungen zu einem vernachlässigten Wechselverhältnis in der neutestamentlichen Exegese," *Filología Neotestamentaria* 33 (2020): 133–59.

but now there are more and more voices that consider James to be an intra-Jewish text.[21] Conspicuous is the addressing of the "twelve tribes in the diaspora," who at the same time are qualified as Christ-believing. If one does not wish to interpret this in the sense of supersessionism, then the consequences for the question of audience are plain to see. Accordingly, Karl-Wilhelm Niebuhr also stated that, in James, "any sort of indication of non-Jews . . . is completely lacking."[22] Against this background, he speaks in a research survey of a "New Perspective on James"[23] and thus marks the classic assessment that James is an anti-Pauline document as radically questionable.

But what does this mean for the considerations presented here? If one reads the epistle of James as a letter written by the brother of the Lord (the other four Jameses hardly come into question as author, as recent scholarship on James holds almost unanimously) or as standing

21. Cf. Karl-Wilhelm Niebuhr, "Der Jakobusbrief im Licht frühjüdischer Diasporabriefe," *New Testament Studies* 44 (1998): 420–43, at 423—". . . the use of the metaphor 'twelve tribes' without being tied to belonging to the twelve-tribe people [is] in New Testament times, as far as I know, nowhere documented!" [". . . die Verwendung der Metapher 'zwölf Stämme' ohne Bindung an die Zugehörigkeit zum Zwölf-Stamme-Volk [ist] in neutestamentlicher Zeit m.W. nirgends belegt!"] Cf. on this also Manabu Tsuji, *Glaube zwischen Vollkommenheit und Verweltlichung. Eine Untersuchung zur literarischen Gestalt und zur inhaltlichen Kohärenz des Jakobusbriefes* (Wissenschaftliche Untersuchungen zum Neuen Testament, II/93; Tübingen: Mohr Siebeck, 1997): 47–49; Richard Bauckham, *James: Wisdom of James, Disciple of Jesus the Sage* (London / New York: Routledge, 1999): 11–25; Peter H. Davids, "Palestinian Traditions in the Epistle of James," in *James the Just and Christian Origins*, ed. Bruce D. Chilton and Craig A. Evans (Supplements to Novum Testamentum, 98; Leiden: Brill, 1999): 33–57; Scot McKnight, "A Parting Within the Way: Jesus and James on Israel and Purity," in Chilton and Evans, eds., *James the Just*: 83–129; Karl-Wilhelm Niebuhr, "Tora ohne Tempel. Paulus und der Jakobusbrief im Zusammenhang frühjüdischer Torarezeption für die Diaspora," in *Tora und Weisheit. Studien zur frühjüdischen Literatur*, ed. Karl-Wilhelm Niebuhr (Wissenschaftliche Untersuchungen zum Neuen Testament, 466; Tübingen: Mohr Siebeck, 2021) 175–207, at 204–206.

22. "überhaupt jeglicher Hinweis auf Nichtjuden . . . völlig fehlt"—Karl-Wilhelm Niebuhr, "Glaube im Stresstest. Πίστις im Jakobusbrief," in *Glaube. Das Verständnis des Glaubens im frühen Christentum und in seiner jüdischen und hellenistisch-römischen Umwelt*, ed. Jörg Frey, Benjamin Schliesser and Nadine Ueberschaer (Wissenschaftliche Untersuchungen zum Neuen Testament, 373; Tübingen: Mohr Siebeck, 2017): 473–501, at 498.

23. Karl-Wilhelm Niebuhr, "A New Perspective on James? Neuere Forschungen zum Jakobusbrief," *Theologische Literaturzeitung* 129 (2004): 1019–44.

in his tradition, then the thrust of this writing changes fundamentally. It is striking that James self-evidently presupposes Jewish traditions and at the same time places a clear focus on the reception of the Jesus tradition. This document is not about the question of justification or the prerequisites for entering into a relationship with God, as Paul discusses with regard to the nations, but much more about how the ethic of Jesus is to be lived out in the framework of Jewish identity.

If one bears in mind this basic argumentational orientation in the epistle of James, it is all the more striking how intensely and emphatically this letter insists on the statement that the faith relationship with God and with Christ is dead and futile without active and practical concretizing in works. From a Jewish perspective, for whom a life according to the Torah self-evidently implies a certain religiously motivated lifestyle and the expression of the relationship with God in actions, however, this is perfectly obvious—thus here a thought is highlighted which in the context of the audience can almost be described as a banality. In addition, this basic idea seems to be formulated in a certain way following Pauline concepts and motifs.

But how is it that such a basic trait of Jewish religiosity is highlighted so intensively in a letter addressed to a Jewish audience? One possible explanation for this could be that the respective basic idea had become questionable for the audience. If one now calls to mind the diaspora situation of the Jewish audience and considers that there were emerging churches made up of Christians of the nations in their immediate vicinity, as well as the fact that, according to the Pauline understanding, no Torah observance should be demanded of Christians of the nations, then the following suspicion arises: The law-free faith praxis of Christians of the nations may have exerted a certain fascination on Christ-believing Jews which might have induced them to fundamentally question the devotion to the Torah enshrined in their own Jewish religiosity. Against such a background, the insistence of the epistle's author on a practically realized performance of faith, grounded in the law, would be understandable, and from that perspective quite a few passages and formulations of this letter would also appear in a different light, for example the emphasis on the Torah as the perfect law of liberty. Considered in this way, the epistle of James would try to steer against certain tendencies among Christ-believing Jews to adapt to the religious practice characteristic of Christians of the nations.

6. Conclusion

If one follows these considerations, the situations in the Galatian churches (or in the sphere of influence of the Judaizing Christians of the nations missionizing there, respectively) on the one hand and among the addressees of the epistle of James on the other hand present themselves as being to a certain extent mirror-images of one another: The Galatian missionaries succumb to the category error that assigns a sin-forgiving impact to the Torah and accordingly represent a postulate of adaptation to a Jewish lifestyle, aimed at Christians of the nations. In Galatians, Paul reacts against these tendencies by reassuring his audience about their soteriological status, placing them on an equal footing with Christ-believing Jews with regard to their relationship to God, and on this basis repudiating as a misorientation a lifestyle that imitates Judaism on the part of Christians of the nations. The epistle of James, on the other hand, problematizes an opposite tendency when it recommends to a Jewish audience that Torah observance and a faith concretized in works is a permanently relevant religious orientation for them. The target group of James is also indirectly warned against imitating a lifestyle that does not correspond to their socio-religious status. And here too, a misunderstanding appears to exist, such that the Pauline πίστις-theology is falsely understood as liberating from an active and practical concretization of faith in human performance.

If one brings these two lines together, they not only bear eloquent witness to the fact that, in view of the existing fellowship between Christ-believing Jews and Christians of the nations, there were evidently tendencies toward convergence between both groups. At the same time, they also formulate a clear statement in favor of maintaining an intra-Christian plurality of the two basic streams of early Christianity. Thus, the autonomy of Messianic Judaism is to a certain extent founded already in the New Testament. Early Christianity was no homogeneous stream and obviously did not intend to be. It is in light of this benchmark that Christian churches and denominations should also view the present phenomenon of Messianic Judaism.

(Translated by John David Martin and James Earle Patrick from the German: "Verbunden in Verschiedenheit. Pluralität als Wesensmerkmal frühchristlicher Ekklesiologie")

Response to Thomas Schumacher, "United in Diversity"

Markus Tiwald

THANK YOU, THOMAS, for your very convincing and fascinating paper! I really enjoyed how you insisted on pluriformity in early Judaism but also in the beginning of Christianity.[1] You are perfectly right that the binary paradigm of a juxtaposition of "Judaism" and "Christianity" (both terms put under quotation marks!) indeed is anachronistic at least for the first century CE. I am also fully convinced by your exegesis of Romans 10:4 regarding the phrase τέλος γὰρ νόμου Χριστὸς εἰς δικαιοσύνην παντὶ τῷ πιστεύοντι. The New Revised Standard Version still translates: "For Christ is the *end* of the law so that there may be righteousness for everyone who believes," but it certainly should be the "fulfillment" of the law, not the "end," as you Thomas have convincingly shown. Thankfully, the revised German 'Einheitsübersetzung' from 2016 has corrected the translation "end of the law" (cf. the earlier version of the Einheitsübersetzung) with "fulfillment of the law."

1. On pluriformity in early Judaism, cf. Markus Tiwald, *Das Frühjudentum und die Anfänge des Christentums* (Beiträge zur Wissenschaft vom Alten und Neuen Testament, 208; Stuttgart: Kohlhammer, 2016): 28–30. There existed no "normative Judaism" in these days; cf. Günter Stemberger, *Einleitung in Talmud und Midrasch* (Munich: C.H. Beck, 8th edn 1992): 15; and Jacob Neusner, "The Formation of Rabbinic Judaism: Yavneh (Jamnia) from A.D. 70 to 100," in *Aufstieg und Niedergang der Römischen Welt II 19/2*, ed. Wolfgang Haase (Berlin: De Gruyter, 1979): 3–42, at 42.

There are only a few points where I might place some comments. I have noticed that you repeatedly refer to the Torah no longer having soteriological relevance. For example: ". . . that in Gal 2:15–16 the Jewish conviction is formulated that the Torah has no soteriological relevance . . ."[2] As you have shown in your paper, you are here indebted to Ed Parish Sanders. Sanders' publications were indeed groundbreaking and necessary for the seventies and eighties of the last century, especially in developing the "New Perspective on Paul."[3] Sanders is perfectly right that Judaism was never a legalistic and narrow-minded religion of "works of the law." Depicting the Pharisees as a merely legalistic movement is certainly some sort of caricature that Christian exegetes have anachronistically imposed on this group. Sanders has rightly demonstrated that this is an entirely wrong assessment of Judaism—merely based on a negative Christian bias against Jews. Nevertheless, Sanders' works were written nearly half a century ago and thus are out of date in some other points. For example, Sanders considers "Torah" in a very static way. One could say: Even if Sanders' merits were huge, he did not go far enough. Today we know that "Torah" in early Judaism was not mainly considered as a compendium of commandments—what Paul calls the "works of the law," ἔργα νόμου (Gal 2:16; Rom 3:20–21, 28; 4:6)—but was seen as the life-inspiring law of nature.[4]

Already starting in the Book of Proverbs, in Jesus Sirach, and in the Book of Wisdom, Torah is depicted as the personification of God's wisdom. Proverbs 8:22–31 and Sirach 24 depict the Torah already pre-existent "before the ages, in the beginning" (Sir 24:9), being present in the process of creation of this world. Later, this pre-existent wisdom of God found its dwelling in the holy tent in Zion and became the βίβλος διαθήκης θεοῦ ὑψίστου νόμον ὃν ἐνετείλατο ἡμῖν Μωυσῆς, "the book of the covenant of the Most High God, the law that Moses commanded us" (Sir 24:23).[5] Considering the fact that the Torah was present in

2. This was the formulation in the paper held at the conference. It is laudable that Thomas Schumacher—after our discussions at the conference—has softened this expression in the version printed in this volume to: "that the Torah has no sin-forgiving function" instead of "that the Torah has no soteriological relevance."

3. Ed Parish Sanders, *Paul and Palestinian Judaism: A Comparison of Patterns of Religion* (Philadelphia, PA: Fortress / London: SCM, 1977): *passim*.

4. For the following, cf. Tiwald, *Frühjudentum* (see note 1), 296–304.

5. Cf. Hindy Najman, "Torah and Tradition," in *The Eerdmans Dictionary of Early Judaism*, ed. John J. Collins and Daniel C. Harlow (Grand Rapids, MI / Cambridge: Eerdmans, 2010): 1316–1317, at 1317.

the moment of creation, Torah later could be interpreted as the law of nature, the general order pervading the whole cosmos. This line of interpretation was already present in Qumran. The Qumran expert Heinz-Josef Fabry thus concludes that Torah in Qumran had a broad range of meaning,

> which quietly moves away from a lawbook with statute law to an entity that bursts all contours, which transcends away from the book into the divine, maybe even into the cosmic realm. In Qumran, one saw the Torah everywhere, or rather, in everything and behind everything. This totality is perhaps best understood if one accepts the Torah as the cosmic order instituted by God in the world . . .[6]

Especially in *Musar leMevin* ("Instruction to a Student")[7] this concept—interpreting the Torah as cosmological order of nature—can be found explicitly. The document was found in six copies in Qumran,[8] so that we can conclude the high significance that this document had for the Qumranites. *Musar leMevin* mentions the רז נהיה (*raz nihyeh*), the "mystery of being." This formulaic expression[9] depicts the whole order of nature from which we can deduce correct ethical behavior. This clearly corresponds to the "Torah" in its entirety, spanning from the order of nature to the ethical instructions for humankind.[10] According to the

6. "der sich unter der Hand wegbewegt von einem Gesetzbuch mit gesatztem Recht zu einer Größe, die alle Konturen sprengt, die sich vom Buch weg transzendiert in den göttlichen, vielleicht sogar in den kosmischen Bereich hinein. In Qumran sah man überall, besser: in allem und hinter allem die Tora. Diese Totalität ist wohl am besten zu verstehen, wenn man die Tora als die von Gott der Welt eingestiftete kosmische Ordnung akzeptiert . . ."—Heinz-Josef Fabry, "Der Umgang mit der kanonisierten Tora in Qumran," in *Die Tora als Kanon für Juden und Christen*, ed. Erich Zenger (Herders Biblische Studien, 10; Freiburg i. Br.: Herder, 1996): 293–327, at 322.

7. Concerning *Musar LeMevin*, cf. John Kampen, *Wisdom Literature* (Eerdmans Commentaries on the Dead Sea Scrolls; Grand Rapids, MI / Cambridge: Eerdmans, 2011): 43. Earlier the manuscript was called *4QInstruction*, but the text also comprehends fragments of Cave 1 and can be found in: 1Q26, 4Q415–418, 4Q423.

8. Cf. Matthew J. Goff, *The Worldly and Heavenly Wisdom of 4 QInstruction* (Studies on the Texts of the Desert of Judah, 50; Leiden: Brill, 2003): 1–2.

9. Armin Lange, *Weisheit und Prädestination. Weisheitliche Urordnung und Prädestination in den Textfunden von Qumran* (Studies on the Texts of the Desert of Judah, 18; Leiden: Brill, 1995): 58—"downright solidified formulaically" ["geradezu formelhaft verfestigt"].

10. Lange, *Weisheit und Prädestination* (see note 9), 60—". . . a world order and creation order that contains ethical and historical components and will one day be fulfilled in the eschaton. Thus, in the term רז נהיה, the ethical and moral elements of the primordial order of wisdom begin to merge with the idea of a predestinational

Qumranites, the right interpretation of this "mystery" (רז נהיה—*raz nihyeh*), is only given to the Teacher of Righteousness. According to 1QH[a] XII.27–28, the Teacher of Righteousness thanks God with the words: "For you have given me understanding of the mysteries of your wonder, and in your wondrous council you have confirmed me."

But also in Diaspora-Judaism, the perception of Torah as order of nature was widespread. Thus, the letter of Aristeas, written in the second century BCE in Egypt, talks about the λόγος φυσικός (§143), the "law of nature." Later, Philo Alexandrinus in *De Vita Mosis* 2:37 explains:[11] κοσμοποιία γὰρ ἡ τῶν νόμων ἐστὶν ἀρχή ("the creation of the world is the beginning of the law"). Consequently, he talks about the ἄγραφος νομοθεσία ("unwritten law of nature") in *De Abrahamo* 5–6, and thus interprets the Sinaitic Torah as a subsequently formulated wording of the unwritten law of nature. Other than the Qumranites, for Philo the order of nature is no mystery, but can be understood with human reason. God's laws are λογικοὶ νόμοι (*Abr* 5), "rational laws." Even if the patriarchs lived long before the Torah was proclaimed on Mount Sinai, they nevertheless were able to live according to the "Torah" in the sense of the order of nature, which could be perceived by human reason. Thus, the Sinaitic Torah according to *Abr* 5 is only a "reminder" to the law of nature: τοὺς τεθέντας νόμους μηδὲν ἄλλ' ἢ ὑπομνήματα εἶναι ("the written laws are nothing more than a memorial"). This corresponds to Romans 1:20—"Ever since the creation of the world [ἀπὸ κτίσεως κόσμου] his eternal power and divine nature, invisible though they are, have been understood and seen through the things he has made [τοῖς ποιήμασιν—the works of God's creation]."

According to these reflections, I cannot agree with the argument made that the Torah, according to early Jewish thought, had no soteriological relevance. I certainly agree with Sanders and with you Thomas (and also with the Apostle Paul) that the Jewish Law does not *mechanically* redeem any persons by working off a catalogue of "works of the law" (cf. Gal 2:16; Rom 3:20–21, 28; 4:6). But according to early Jewish

---

order of history leading to the eschaton." [". . . eine Welt- und Schöpfungsordnung, die ethische und historische Komponenten enthält und sich dereinst im Eschaton erfüllt. Es beginnen sich also im Begriff רז נהיה die ethisch-sittlichen Elemente der weisheitlichen Urordnung mit der Vorstellung einer prädestinatianischen, auf das Eschaton zulaufenden Geschichtsordnung zu vereinigen."]

11. Concerning Philo's perception of the law, cf. Tiwald, *Frühjudentum* (see note 1), 167–69.

thought, Torah certainly contains the vivid will of God—and this always has a soteriological function.

Following these considerations, I would also advise caution with the opinion that the Pauline mission to the nations was "law-free"[12] (quote from page 231: "that, according to the Pauline understanding, no Torah observance should be demanded of Christians of the nations" and on the same page "law-free faith praxis of Christians of the nations"). I have argued elsewhere that we should better distinguish Torah as the law of nature and Torah as a compendium of ritual commandments.[13] An ethical interpretation of the ritual aspects of the Torah can already be found in the *Letter of Aristeas*, in the books of Philo, and also in the letters of the Apostle Paul. The *Letter of Aristeas* § 143 underscores that πρὸς τὸν φυσικὸν λόγον ("according to the law of nature") nothing is impure.[14] Only because the ritually impure animals lead an immoral life they are forbidden to be eaten, as § 147 concludes:

> by naming them unclean, he [God] gave a sign by means of them that those, for whom the legislation was ordained, must practise righteousness in their hearts and not tyrannise over any one in reliance upon their own strength nor rob them of anything, but steer their course of life in accordance with justice, just as the tame birds, already mentioned [i.e. the ritually pure birds], consume the different kinds of pulse that grow upon the earth and do not tyrannise to the destruction of their own kindred.[15]

Following the same pattern, also Philo in *De Migratione Abrahami* 89–93 talks about the so called "radical allegorists,"[16] liberal Jews, who only accept an ethical interpretation of the Torah. For example, the

12. Such expressions are frequent in scholarly literature. For further examples see Markus Tiwald, "'Wir richten das Gesetz auf' νόμον ἱστάνομεν (Röm 3,31): Die bleibende Gültigkeit der Tora im Christentum," in *"Dein Wort ist meinem Fuß eine Leuchte." Festschrift für Ludger Schwienhorst-Schönberger*, ed. Georg Braulik, Agnethe Siquans, and Jan-Heiner Tück (Freiburg i. Br.: Herder, 2022): 334–47.

13. Cf. Tiwald, *Frühjudentum* (see note 1), 296–304.

14. Cf. Folker Siegert, "Early Jewish Interpretation in a Hellenistic Style," in *Hebrew Bible / Old Testament: The History of Its Interpretation*, ed. Magne Sæbø (Göttingen: Vandenhoeck & Ruprecht, 1996): 130–98, at 151—"Nothing is impure by nature, sect. 143 concedes."

15. Edition: Robert H. Charles, *The Apocrypha and Pseudepigrapha of the Old Testament in English* (Oxford: Clarendon Press, 1913).

16. Concerning the "radical allegorists," cf. Lutz Doering, *Schabbat. Sabbathalacha und -praxis im antiken Judentum und Urchristentum* (Texts and Studies in Ancient Judaism, 78; Tübingen: Mohr Siebeck, 1999): 347–48.

circumcision is interpreted allegorically as "an emblem of the excision of pleasures and of all the passions" (*Migr* 92) and the Sabbath as a day of philosophical contemplation. On the one hand, Philo criticizes that these liberal Jews neglect the ritual aspects of the Torah—for example, the bodily circumcision or the observation of sabbatical rest. On the other hand, he himself underscores that the true meaning of Torah consists in morally correct behavior. Following the same trajectory, Philo concludes in *De Specialibus Legibus* 2.63 that the whole Torah consists of two κεφάλαια ("head-commandments") which he identifies as "one's conduct towards God by the rules of piety and holiness, and of one's conduct towards men by the rules of humanity and justice." The Apostle Paul uses the same word stem, when he underscores in Romans 13:9 that all the commandments are "briefly comprehended [ἀνακεφαλαιοῦται—summed up as a head-commandment] in this saying, namely, Thou shalt love thy neighbor as thyself. . . . Love therefore is the fulfillment of the law."

We therefore can conclude: In some circles of early Judaism, Torah was seen as the vivid will of God pervading the whole of nature and leading to a morally correct way of life. Paul, after his conversion, adopted the liberal view that the Torah can be fulfilled by the commandment of love. When Paul rejects the "works of the law," this only focuses on ritual purity norms, but not on the Torah as commandment of love.[17] He herewith followed a pattern of interpretation that can already be seen in the argumentation of the "radical allegorists." Even if the complete neglecting of ritual commandments was too liberal for some other Jews, it nevertheless was a possibility in the wide range of Torah-interpretations in the variegated theologies of early Judaism. Following the idea that the double commandment of love is the fulfillment of Torah, Paul did certainly *not* abrogate the Torah, and his mission was not "law-free."

17. See, for detailed argumentation: Markus Tiwald, "Gesetz," in *Neues Testament. Zentrale Themen*, ed. Lukas Bormann (Neukirchen-Vluyn: Neukirchener Theologie, 2014): 295–314, at 304–308; and Tiwald, *Frühjudentum* (see note 1), 296–304.

Assessing Jewish Christianity

The Lessons of the "Parting of the Ways"

Étienne Vetö, ICN

1. Introduction

An assessment of contemporary Messianic Judaism and Jewish Christianity can greatly benefit from analyzing the reality of Jewish disciples of Yeshua/Jesus and their disappearance in the first centuries CE. Three aspects will be addressed. The first two concern the chronology and the causes of their disappearance. What is at stake is to know if they are a viable reality: The longer they have existed and thrived, the more reason there is to believe they can exist and play a role in the future. Likewise, analyzing the obstacles to Jewish-Christian existence in the first centuries CE can help gauge if today's situation is more favorable and/or if some of these hindrances can be worked on and removed. The third aspect will be to consider the wider framework of the demise of Jewish Christ-confessors. I will argue that it is deeply intertwined with the "parting of the ways," the process that brought about Judaism and Christianity as two distinct and antagonistic religious traditions. Their disappearance is the result and the symptom of the difficulty for both the people of Israel and the nascent Christian *ekklesia* to live out their identity and mission as "people of God" that bring together Jews and Gentiles. This is what is truly at stake, and the historical and theological meaning of Jewish Christianity cannot be fully grasped outside of this context.

One of the difficulties of this approach is that it is at the boundary between history and theology. The last question, for instance, cannot be answered only through historical considerations. This paper will thus have no claim to offer a complete study or solution of the matter at hand. Moreover, I am not a historian, so the historical aspects will never come from first-hand research. However, as I have been doing this research, I have come to realize that synthesizing large quantities of historical research with the eye of an "outsider" and guided by theological questions allows one to come to new insights. I hope that the historical aspects retain their solidity and that I have avoided undue collusion of history and theology.

Much of the terminology that will be used is debatable and debated. Although many criticize the expression "parting of the way(s)"[1]—I will sometimes refer to other possible wordings—it still is the most used terminology for the process that led to the existence of the related but distinct religions of Rabbinic Judaism and Christianity. Likewise, with some flexibility, because of the fluidity of the religious and chronological "borders" we will consider, I will use "Jewish disciples of Yeshua/Jesus" mainly for the first generations, while preferring "Judeo-Christians" for the later generations. As we will see, the latter are more distinct from other strands of Judaism, and some are not ethnically Jewish. Sometimes, when the historical period or the distinction between Jew and Gentile are not relevant, I will simply use the expression: "Christ-confessor." I will use both names and designations: Jesus/Christ and Yeshua/Messiah, since we are considering Jews who speak Aramaic and/or Greek.

Although we will see that the process is "messier" than what was imagined until a few decades ago, it still is a process, so I have divided the study in four historical periods or situations: the Jewish *ekklesia* (2), the mixed Jewish-Gentile *ekklesia* (3), the "parting of the ways" (4–5), and Judaism and Christianity (6). I will dwell at length on the third aspect to analyze the causes of the parting. The final section (7) will draw some conclusions of the present study for a possible (re)union of the ways that would include Jewish believers in Yeshua/Jesus.

1. See Adele Reinhartz, "Slip-Slidin' Away: Rethinking the 'Parting of the Ways,'" in *Negotiating Identities: Conflict, Conversion, and Consolidation in Early Judaism and Christianity (200 BCE–600 CE)*, ed. Karin Hedner-Zetterholm et al. (Coniectanea Biblica; Lanham, MD: Lexington / Fortress Academic, 2022): 103–28, at 113.

2. *The Jewish* ekklesia

This section will be especially synthetic. The first stage of what would eventually become "Christianity" was a messianic movement inside the Jewish world. Following quite an extensive review of scholars, especially from the field of "Jewish Jesus Research,"[2] it is quite plausible to state that Jesus lived and died as a Torah-observant Jew. This means he wore tassels, he observed *kashrut* and *shabbat*.[3] In that period of great religious dynamism and creativity, where Sadducees, Pharisees, Essenes, Galileans coexisted, interacted, and competed, Jesus' teaching and practice fit into the debates of the time. For instance, siding with the Pharisees against the Sadducees, he believed in angels and demons and in the resurrection of the dead; however, with the Sadducees, he refused to follow the Pharisees' additional purity rules on handwashing or on food.

Moreover, his disciples were all Jewish. Living with Jesus and following his teaching, they too were Law-observant, participated in the life of the synagogue and in the Temple-worship, even though after his passion and resurrection they also celebrated the "Lord's supper" in their homes, probably after *shabbat*. They were one religious current inside the multifaceted traditions of the Jewish people and received names such as "Nazarenes" (Acts 24:5) in Aramaic-speaking milieus, or "Christians" (Acts 11:26) in Greek-speaking ones; they themselves probably used more often the name "the Way" (Acts 19:9).

This means that Jesus had no plans of initiating a new religion or of forming another people than the Jewish people. However, he did appoint leaders, the Twelve. They were Jewish, and their number indicates that they were designed both to represent the twelve tribes of Israel and to symbolize their full gathering once again. They are thus anchored in the history and the hope of the people of Israel. But it is possible that Jesus meant to replace the leaders of the people, that is, the elders, priests, scribes, and Pharisees. This is the most convincing interpretation of the parable of the vineyard (the people of Israel) entrusted

2. Many scholars can be cited, such as D. Flusser, J. Neusner, D. Boyarin, A. Reinhartz, A.-J. Levine, G. Boccaccini.

3. On *kashrut* see, e.g., Daniel Boyarin, *The Jewish Gospels: The Story of the Jewish Christ* (New York: The New Press, 2012): 106–28; on *shabbat*, see David Flusser, *Jesus* (New York: Herder & Herder, 1969): 48–52, and Boyarin, *The Jewish Gospels* (see above), 52–69.

to new tenants (the apostles?) (Matt 21:33–46 //). Perhaps the seeds for subsequent tensions and divisions were sown here.

3. *The mixed Jewish–Gentile* ekklesia

A second "stage" of the evolution of the *ekklesia* of believers in Jesus came into being with the entrance of the first Gentiles. If we follow the Acts of the Apostles, this happened quite late: The first Gentile to come to faith in Jesus was probably Cornelius (Acts 10:1–11:18). Indeed, those who joined after Pentecost were Jews from many countries and proselytes who had fully joined the Jewish people (Acts 2:5, 9–11, 14, 19–22). The early *ekklesia* was composed of Hellenists and Hebrews (Acts 6:1), all of them Jewish. The first step outside the Jewish people was with the Samaritans (Acts 8:5–25), who were not Gentiles. The Ethiopian eunuch was probably a proselyte, since he was reading the Prophets and had been to Jerusalem to worship God (Acts 8:27–28).[4]

However, the opening to the Gentiles was not an error or even an accident. It corresponds both to the mission given by the Risen Lord to the Eleven to "make disciples of all nations" (Matt 28:19) and to how providence used the persecution of the *ekklesia* in Jerusalem. However, questions and tensions appear: Should the Gentiles be circumcised? Should they observe *kashrut*? How can there be common prayer and meals with Jewish and Gentile Christ-confessors? We are in a moment in which many Gentiles become proselytes or God-fearers, and the "Nazarenes" have the same question as the rest of the Jewish people.[5] The watershed moment, also in the structure of Acts, is the assembly of Jerusalem which decides that the Gentiles do not need to observe the Torah, that is, they do not need to become Jews. The rules for the Gentile believers are to "abstain from what has been sacrificed to idols and from blood and from what is strangled and from sexual immorality" (Acts 15:29). These rules can be understood as expressions of either the Noachide Laws (*Sanhedrin* 56b), or the rules for *gerim*, the resident

4. See Jean-Pierre Lémonon, *Les débuts du Christianisme: de 30 à 135* (Paris: Les Éditions de l'Atelier, 2003): 127 n.14.

5. Paula Fredriksen, *Paul, the Pagans' Apostle* (New Haven, CT: Yale University Press, 2017): 96–98.

aliens living in the community of Israel (Lev 17–18), or again, specific rules for Gentiles grafted into Israel through the Messiah.[6]

Nothing specific is asked of the Jewish members of the *ekklesia*. That indicates quite clearly that they are to continue to observe the Torah.[7] If they did not practice *kashrut* or observe ritual purity, for instance, the debate between Paul and Peter narrated in Galatians 2 or Peter's vision in Acts 10 would not make sense. Even this last text should not be understood as a divine injunction to bring an end to *kashrut*. It concerns people, not food, if we follow the conclusion Peter draws: "God has shown me that I should not call anyone profane or unclean" (Acts 10:28). It is a divine intervention that "makes" so to speak the Gentiles pure, perhaps through their faith in Jesus, which frees them from idolatry. The concrete implication is the possibility to share meals together—which is in fact a return to what is allowed by the Torah over and against the Pharisaic practices.[8]

6. Some manuscripts of Acts 15 add to the rules "and do not do to others what you would not want them to do to you" (Western MSS), a negatively phrased version of the Golden Rule that echoes a famous saying through which Hillel the Elder synthesizes the whole Torah (*b. Shabbat* 31a). This would mean that the Gentiles who enter the New Covenant are obligated by the Torah, with special provisions according to their status as "messianically renewed Gentiles." They are not only bound by Noachide rules or rules for the *gerim*, but rather they have entered a new dimension, as members of a Covenant that also obligates "messianically renewed Jews"—in a specific way as well.

7. I do not agree with Antoine Lévy when he says that there is no sign that the early Jewish disciples of Jesus were Torah-observant because "there is no material record of an official attempt at imposing the observance of *mitzvot* on Jewish disciples"—*Jewish Church: A Catholic Approach to Messianic Judaism* (Washington, DC: Lexington Books, 2021): 184). That Jews should observe the Torah was so obvious that we would rather need an "explicitly promulgated" rule stating that Jewish members of the *ekklesia* were not bound by the *mitzvot* (as understood in the first century CE, before the written rabbinic codifications) to conclude that they did not do so. That would be so momentous a change that it would need an explicit debate and decision at least as significant as what is narrated in Acts 15.

8. See Damien Artiges, *La singularité d'Israël, Un défi pour l'unité des chrétiens* (unpublished doctoral dissertation; Brussels: Institut d'Études Théologiques, 2018): 200–204. The same general interpretation of Gal 2:11–14, as touching the people one can share a meal with rather than *kashrut*, can be found in Mark S. Kinzer, *Postmissionary Messianic Judaism: Redefining Christian Engagement with the Jewish People* (Grand Rapids, MI: Brazos, 2005): 82–85.

Therefore, this second stage of the movement of Yeshua/Christ-confessors is that of a "mixed" community, composed of Torah-observant Jewish Yeshua/Christ-confessors and non-Torah-observant Gentile Yeshua/Christ-confessors who follow minimal practices which allow them to share the table with the Jewish members. It is still a Jewish movement, although it welcomes Gentiles, and the Yeshua-confessing Jews anchor it into the Jewish world and provide a bridge between the Gentiles and the whole people of Israel. Historically speaking, many biblical scholars believe that the Book of Acts presents an "idealized" view of the early *ekklesia*, where everyone puts everything in common and lives in perfect harmony (Acts 2:42–47)—and thus where Jews and Gentile believers in Jesus live in harmony. Shared meals and the celebration of the Lord's supper were probably still complex. The "Jerusalem synod" creatively opened a way fraught with perils and instability. However, theologically speaking, the way proposed by Acts 15 is that of a "composite" or "dual" *ekklesia*, bringing into unity Jews and Gentiles who maintain their respective identity.

4. The chronological, social, and geographical complexity of the "parting of the ways"

This true but unstable situation unravels in a third stage of existence of the early Yeshua/Christ-confessing community, in a process of "parting of the ways," during which Judaism and Christianity crystallize into two different traditions. Indeed, more than a clear cut "moment," it is a long and messy development, and there is no real consensus on what date to give. There seem to be conflicting data: One can find communities of Judeo-Christians in Syria in the fourth century and perhaps even until the sixth century, but in Roman cemeteries already at the end of the first century, tombs bear different symbols, pointing to either belief in Christ or belonging to the Jewish people. I will argue that there are in fact a plurality of dates to consider, because the "parting" happens at different rhythms according to who is involved and in what regions.[9]

9. "Our sources suggest that the parting of the ways was an uneven and messy process, occurring in different times in different places and for different reasons"—Reinhartz, "Slip-Slidin' Away" (see note 1), 115.

For instance, much will depend on the social level, education, and responsibility of the people in society and religious institutions. The more educated and those who are more involved in the institutions, the bishop-theologians and the rabbis, will be the first to underline the differences and consider them incompatible. We already have texts from the early second century by Ignatius of Antioch exhorting his flocks not to "judaize"; he is also one of the first authors to speak extensively of "Christianity."[10] Daniel Boyarin considers that, in what will become the Christian world, the notion of heresy as criterion of exclusion based on faith-content, is coined at the middle of the second century, in great part by Justin Martyr (c.100–c.165 CE). Justin asserts that those who do not believe that God has a *Logos* are heretics. However, this is not a description of a distinction of beliefs between the "Synagogue" and the "Church" of the second century, because many Jews who did not follow Jesus believed that there was a divine *Memra*, while some Christ-confessors did not (not all had access to the Fourth Gospel, for instance). This was a non-separating difference of theological opinion inside of the Jewish world, which Justin turns into a crystallizing factor of mutual exclusion between traditions that are thus being constructed. We see a parallel phenomenon happen with the idea of *minim* in rabbinic literature.[11] While it truly develops only in later texts, the notion appears in rabbinic literature in third-century documents.[12] It probably concerns Christ-confessors and their faith less than what was once believed, since in general people left the synagogal practice for many reasons,[13] but it works in the same excluding way as the notion of heresy. The heads of the communities and the scholars promote themselves as border guards and set up the borders at the same time.

Conversely, the common people take much more time to part clearly. If Ignatius rants against judaizers, it means that they exist. Justin himself insists on keeping Gentiles from observing Jewish practices. He admits that members of the Jewish people who believe in Jesus can

10. Judith Lieu, "'The Parting of the Ways': Theological Construct or Historical Reality?," *Journal for the Study of the New Testament* 17 (1995): 101–119, at 114.

11. Daniel Boyarin, *Border Lines: The Partition of Judaeo-Christianity* (Philadelphia, PA: University of Pennsylvania Press, 2004): 41.

12. *Tosefta Bereshit* 3.25; see Boyarin, *Border Lines* (see note 11), 43.

13. See Adiel Schremer, *Brothers Estranged: Heresy, Christianity and Jewish Identity in Late Antiquity* (Oxford: Oxford University Press, 2010).

continue to observe the Mosaic Law as long as they understand that it is not salvific. However, "Gentiles who believe in Christ" should not observe the Law, even though Justin says that those who do will still be saved.[14] Clearly, Justin is addressing concrete situations of the mid-second century, probably in Rome. The borders that are being set up are still quite porous for the common people.

Another factor to be considered is culture and geography. Sources show that the "parting" happened more quickly in the Western part of the Roman Empire—as the examples of the Roman cemeteries and of Justin Martyr attest. Conversely, in the zones of Semitic culture, as in the Aramaic-speaking Syrian Province of the Empire, or outside of the Empire in Mesopotamia, the process was much slower. Situations that Justin confronts in the second century are still being addressed in the mid-fourth century by John Chrysostom in Antioch, who dedicates a series of sermons on the occasion of Jewish festivals to oppose judaizing.[15] Although he is more worried about Gentile Christians going to the synagogue than about the practice of the Law by Judeo-Christians, it shows that the crisscrossing between communities and traditions is still alive. Indeed, in Syria there are possible traces of Judeo-Christian practices until the sixth century.[16]

These different factors show that the "parting of the ways" is a complex process. It is drawn-out and messy, with fluid borders between religious observances and communities. One can add a further complexity, namely that of the different ways of being Judeo-Christians. There are at least three main recognizable strands, the Nazarenes, the Ebionites and the Elcesaites, with different understandings of the person of

14. Justin Martyr, *Dialogue with Trypho*, 47:2. See Artiges, *La singularité d'Israël* (see note 8), 251–55.

15. John Chrysostom, "Against the Jews"; see Pieter van der Horst, "Jews and Christians in Antioch at the End of the IVth Century," in *Christian–Jewish Relations Through the Centuries*, ed. Stanley E. Porter and Brook W.R. Pearson (Sheffield: Sheffield Academic Press, 2000): 228–38. Interestingly, van der Horst shows that a contemporary document from fourth-century Antioch, the *Apostolic Constitution*, suggests another solution to the same situation: to integrate synagogal prayers into church liturgies.

16. Shlomo Pines, *The Jewish Christians of the Early Centuries of Christianity According to a New Source* (Jerusalem: Israel Academy of Sciences and Humanities, 1996): 211–310.

Jesus, of Scripture, and of the relationship to Gentiles or to the rabbis.[17] The latter point is significant since some admitted Gentiles: not all were ethnically Jewish, although in different ways they related to the Mosaic Law and their religious-cultural paradigms were Semitic.[18] For this reason, instead of a parting of the ways or even "partings" of the ways,[19] the most accurate metaphor is that of a crisscrossing of muddy tracks.[20]

If one insists on establishing a chronology—a perilous endeavor indeed!—I would argue that the tipping point that brought about "Judaism" and "Christianity" as identifiable traditions and communities was reached in Rome in the first half of the second century for the elite and religious leaders, while it probably was closer to the end of the second century for the common people. In the Greek part of the Empire this happened at the end of the second century for the leaders and in the early third century for the people. And in Antioch and outside the Roman Empire in Mesopotamia, the process stretched on to the third and fourth century respectively for leaders and people, with some pockets where it happened even later.

5. The causes of the partings of the ways

In the same way as the process itself was complex, the reasons that underlaid it were multiple: They touch on faith-content, practice and worship, competition between leaders, tensions between Jews and Gentiles, and the impact of the laws and wars of the Roman Empire.

The classical renderings of the partition between Judaism and Christianity, especially on the Christian side, insist on the doctrinal differences which slowly coalesced into irreconcilable oppositions. J. Dunn, for instance, underlines how the doctrinal tensions were probably

17. Some scholars believe that the Ebionites were considered by the rabbis as *posche Israel*, dissidents of Israel, and not only as Christian heretics, for much longer than the other strands—cf. Marcel Simon, *Verus Israel: Étude sur les relations entre Chrétiens et Juifs dans l'empire Romain (135–425)* (Paris: Éditions E. De Boccard, 1964): 299–300.

18. See Artiges, *La singularité d'Israël* (see note 8), 258–77; Simon, *Verus Israel* (see note 17), 280; Marcel Simon and André Benoît, *Le judaïsme et le christianisme antique* (Paris: Presses Universitaires de France, 1968): 266–77; Simon C. Mimouni, *Les chrétiens d'origine juive dans l'antiquité* (Paris: Albin Michel, 2004).

19. James D.G. Dunn, *The Partings of the Ways Between Judaism and Christianity and Their Significance for the Character of Christianity* (London: SCM Press, 2006).

20. Lieu, "'The Parting of the Ways'" (see note 10), 119.

concentrated along the lines of the four main pillars of what he calls "Jewish faith" in the first century, and led to a series of antagonisms, which developed in the following chronological order: the importance and validity of the Temple and the Temple sacrifices, observance of the Torah, the election of Israel and the relationship between Jews and Gentiles, and the faith in the divinity of Jesus and its (in)compatibility with faith in the One God.[21] Certainly, doctrinal questions were a significant element. However, one would need to nuance the way Dunn presents these points and his chronology. Is the Temple questioned already in Stephen's speech (Acts 7),[22] or after and because of its destruction? Is the problem with the Law Torah-observance *tout court*, or more precisely its purpose, that is, whether it is necessary for salvation or rather a question of faithfulness to God's command?[23] Also: rather than the theological meaning of the Law, was it not the way it was observed—the way *shabbat* was observed for instance[24]—that could lead to conflict? Or again, was there a resistance to the charismatic-ecstatic dimension of the worship of Jewish disciples?[25] In the Jewish world, concrete observance and forms of worship are often more of a dividing factor than the faith-content. Finally, is the idea of a divine Messiah and of a certain plurality in God, or of a suffering Messiah, so foreign to Jewish thought in that period?[26] Faith-based distinctions, especially

21. Dunn, *Partings of the Ways* (see note 19), 318–38.

22. *Ibid.*, 126.

23. Jean-Pierre Lémenon, *Les judeo-chrétiens: des témoins oubliés?* (Paris: Cerf, 2006): 8.

24. The present consensus on the reasons for which the members of the Johannine community feared to be excluded from the synagogues (*aposynagōgos*) is that it was not because of their faith in Jesus but rather because of the way they observed *shabbat*—cf. John S. Kloppenborg, "Disaffiliation in Associations and the ἀποσυναγωγός of John," *HTS Teologiese Studies / Theological Studies* 67.1 (2011): Art. #962, 16 pages; https://doi.org/10.4102/hts.v67i1.962; Myrte C. de Boer, "Expulsion from the Synagogue: J.L. Martyn's *History and Theology in the Fourth Gospel* Revisited," *New Testament Studies* 66 (2020): 367–91.

25. See Amy-Jill Levine, *The Misunderstood Jew: The Church and the Scandal of the Jewish Jesus* (San Francisco, CA: HarperOne, 2006): 109.

26. See, among many others, Boyarin, *Jewish Gospels* (see note 3), 25–51; Fredriksen, *Paul, the Pagans' Apostle* (see note 5), 111–117. The main difficulty with the affirmation of the Messiahship of Jesus was probably not the question of his divinity and of the One God, but the discrepancy between the fruit of the Passion and Resurrection and the Messianic promises of the prophets—see Levine, *Misunderstood Jew* (see note 25), 56–61.

according to a "Jewish" and "Christian" line, are partly a retro-projection. The same synagogue could easily be attended by Christ-confessors and non-Christ-confessors, while coalescing along the lines of culture, such as Hebrew or Hellenistic.[27]

Indeed, another aspect, and perhaps a more significant one especially in the first period, was conflicts of leadership. We saw that the Jewish disciples of Jesus had their own leaders, the apostles, and those who were instituted by them: the elders, the supervisors or *episkopoi* (who gradually become the leading figures), and the deacons. In parallel to this was established the class of the rabbis. Recent scholarship thinks that these took quite some time to impose themselves,[28] but as their authority grew, it meant that there were two types of religious leaders competing for their flock: Christ-confessing elders and rabbis. The establishment of institutions certainly came before that of doctrine. Indeed, if the notion of heresy came into being in the middle of the second century, doctrinal or dogmatic decisions had to wait until the fourth century. This is clear in Christianity with the Council of Nicaea (325 CE). Likewise, there is a fierce debate in the scholarly world about when the "synod of Yavneh" took place or whether it was a reconstruction by later rabbis, but many think it reflects a situation that is also from the fourth century.[29] Indeed, the leaders and institutions are the ones who, by pushing for the unity of their flock and their own control over them, felt the need to articulate distinctions and contributed in a decisive way to the establishment of two clearly distinct faiths, of two "religions." As in many divisions in society and religious institutions, conflicts of leadership had a great weight.

A third major cause of tensions and divisions is the difficult coexistence between Jews and Gentiles. S. Cohen suggests that this was the main issue.[30] The first two aspects we have considered, faith-content

27. See Boyarin, *Jewish Gospels* (see note 3), 1–24.

28. See Natalie B. Dohrmann, "Jews in the West: From Herod to Constantine the Great," in *Judaism*, vol. I: *History*, ed. Michael Tilly and Burton Visotzky (Stuttgart: Kohlhammer, 2021): 100–104.

29. Daniel Boyarin, "A Tale of Two Synods, Nicaea, Yavneh and Rabbinic Ecclesiology," *Exemplaria* 12.1 (2000): 21–62.

30. Shaye Cohen, "The Ways That Parted: Jews, Christians and Jewish-Christians, ca 100–150CE," in *Jews and Christians in the First and Second Centuries: The Interbellum 70–132 CE*, ed. Joshua Schwartz (Leiden: Brill, 2017): 310.

and competition of leadership, are tensions which developed partly inside the Jewish world, between Judeo-Christians and Jews that were not Yeshua/Christ-confessors, although both were certainly exasperated by the evolutions brought on by the influx of Gentiles. However, this influx needs to be taken into consideration in its own right. As we have seen, the solution established by Acts 15 seems to have been an unstable one. Already in Justin's account of the different positions he meets with, we find antagonisms: There are Jewish disciples of Jesus who still want to impose the observance of the Mosaic Law on Gentiles; there are Gentile believers in Christ who want nothing to do with Jewish Christ-confessors, and "refuse to share table or converse with people of that kind."[31] A.-J. Levine underlines that it was possible to live and share the eucharistic table together when one believed that the Messiah would be back soon, but as the early *ekklesia* understood that the Parousia was for a more distant future, daily differences concerning food or the observance of *shabbat*, or the prospect of intermarriage between Jews and Gentiles, became much thornier.[32] The two-track solution offered by Acts 15 broke down. The first community seemed to have been confronted with the choice of reverting to being a movement for Jews and proselytes or else of becoming a Gentile movement. Two factors contributed to the traction given to the latter option: the growing numerical imbalance between Jews and Gentiles among the Christ-confessors[33] and the spiritual and cultural weakening of the Judeo-Christians once they lost their center of gravity and point of reference with the destruction of the Temple and the banning of Jews from Jerusalem. This led to a marginalization of the Judeo-Christians with respect to the Gentiles and an inversion of the question that had been addressed in Acts 15: not how should Gentile Christ-confessors live, but

31. Justin Martyr, *Dialogue with Trypho*, 47:2.

32. "To circumcise or not to circumcise; to keep kosher or to eat pork and shrimp; to have one church for both Jews and Gentiles or to have separate tables, beliefs, and practices. . . . The church was fighting for its life"—Levine, *Misunderstood Jew* (see note 25), 74; see 70–84.

33. For example, with the expulsion of Jews from Rome under Claudius (c. 49 CE?) the Gentiles became a majority in the Christ-confession communities (see Dunn, *Partings of the Ways* [see note 19], 33–34). This prepared the way for Rome to be one of the earliest places where Judaism and Christianity were distinguished, as we have seen above.

rather how should Judeo-Christians live? The Christ-confessing Jews, who in the stage of the mixed Jewish–Gentile *ekklesia* were bridges between Jews and Gentiles, became a tiny, imperiled no-man's land between two realities which increasingly defined themselves against the other. The cultural environment had its importance: we have seen above that the regions where a Judeo-Christian presence lasted the longest were the Aramaic-speaking ones. Those were the regions where they could also be more easily accepted in a majority-Gentile Church, because of cultural similarities.

The last cause for the parting of the ways that we will consider is the pressure from the Roman Empire, which gained from a division it greatly contributed to creating. After the Great Fire of Rome (64 CE), Nero did not want to antagonize the rather well-integrated Jewish community, but the charismatic and ecstatic disciples of Jesus amid that community and the Gentile members were an easy scapegoat and were thus accused. And those who were not blamed tended to keep their distance from those who were. Another wedge between the different strands of Jews was the *fiscus iudaicus,* a tax levied on the Jews from 73 CE after the destruction of the Temple and the first Jewish–Roman war. Though it concerned all Jews, it was collected from observant Jews: This certainly pushed the Gentile members of the *ekklesia* to distance themselves from the Jews, and the Jewish disciples of Jesus to refrain from Torah-observance. The same phenomena happened again, to avoid persecution, when Jews, including Judeo-Christians, were evicted from Jerusalem in 135 CE. The destruction of the Temple and the banishment of the Jews from Jerusalem had a huge impact on the parting of the ways. These momentous events shook the Jewish world to its foundation and paved the way for new ways of interpreting the age-old traditions found in the Torah and the Prophets and for the new leaderships of the elders and bishops and of the rabbis. Moreover, when in the second to third centuries the empire started a more systematic persecution of Christians, Jews—who at that period were well accepted and protected—had a clear interest in distancing themselves as much as possible from the latter. Also, Jews were keen on maintaining the exceptional right they had received not to worship the emperor as divine: they were worried that, if a great number of Christ-confessing Gentiles claimed the same right as heirs of the revelation of the One God of Israel, the right may be brought into question. An easy solution was to stress their religious differences. In the end, Christianity was recognized as a specific religion in 313 by an empire that had a significative hand in establishing it as such.

6. Judaism and Christianity: Antagonism between two religions or the "ways that never parted"?

With the fourth century, one can truly speak of two distinct religions. However, they can be seen both as increasingly antagonistic and also, paradoxically, as maintaining a deep bond. The antagonism started quite early, with the idea found in some authors already during the second century that the Christian *ekklesia* replaced the Jewish people,[34] and that the Jews were guilty of the unheard of crime of killing the Messiah,[35] which would lead to the infamous accusations of deicide.[36] These tropes never became Catholic magisterium, but they were the majority opinion for centuries. Rabbinic literature is quite sober on Christianity and on Jesus but there are scathing texts presenting the latter in Sheol under the latrine of the High Priest's palace.[37] The practices of each tradition established themselves so to speak against the other. This is quite explicit on the Christian side, with the decision at the Council of Nicaea I (325) not to follow the Jewish custom in establishing the date of Easter, and at Nicaea II (787) to prohibit the converts from Judaism to Christianity from observing the Law, confirmed centuries later at the Council of Florence (1442) by the canons prohibiting "judaizing." Judaism chose to ignore Christianity as much as it could in its texts, but it is interesting to see how the practice of circumcision, which *de facto* was not always observed by all, especially while it was banned by Roman law in the second century, became one of the main markers of Judaism once it was not practiced any more by most Christians.[38] The origin of the *kippa* is difficult to pinpoint, but it is quite probable that it is more recent than the similar skullcap of Christian abbots and bishops.

Paradoxically, this way of setting up each tradition as "what is not the other" witnesses to a permanent and profound relationship between

34. See *Epistle of Barnabas* 4:6–7; Justin Martyr, *Dialogue with Trypho*, 11.

35. See Melito of Sardis, *Easter Homily*, 92.

36. See John Chrysostom, *Against the Jews*, 7.

37. See *b. Gittin* 56b–57a.

38. See Shaye Cohen, *The Beginnings of Jewishness: Boundaries, Varieties, Uncertainties* (Berkeley, CA: University of California Press, 2001): 39–49.

them. Rabbinic literature picks up on patristic tropes—for example, in representing Isaac carrying a cross.[39] Israel Yuval has shown quite convincingly how Jewish liturgy has been deeply influenced by Christian worship, by rejecting it but also by receiving some themes that "rub off" on it—for instance, in the *Haggadah* of *Pesach*.[40] Although the two traditions developed under their own inner impetus and under the influence of many factors, they always kept in contact, and some authors and periods show very explicit mutual influences.[41] This has led some scholars to propose other metaphors than the "parting of the ways," such as that of two siblings who come from the same "mother."[42] At the very least, one needs to complexify the notion of the "parting of the ways," as does Daniel Boyarin when he insists that they constituted and in a way still constitute continuous roadways with imperceptible boundaries,[43] or as do thinkers who speak of "the ways that have never parted."[44]

7. Conclusions: From the "parting of the ways" to a "(re)union of the ways"?

In an echo of the three aspects underlined in the introduction of this paper, I will draw three conclusions.

Let us start with the third, because it is the most decisive. I believe our study has confirmed that we are confronted with two different but

39. See *Genesis Rabbah* 56:3, (ed. Theodor – Albeck, 598), quoted by Maren Niehoff, "Origen as a Key in Genesis Rabbah," in *Genesis Rabbah in Text and Context*, ed. Sarit K. Gribetz et al. (Texts and Studies in Ancient Judaism, 166; Tübingen: Mohr Siebeck, 2016): 139.

40. Israel Yuval, *Two Nations in Your Womb* (Berkeley, CA: University of California Press, 2008): see esp. 62–67.

41. E.g., on Kabbalah (Jewish and Christian) and Hasidism, see Moshe Idel, *Hasidism: Between Ecstasy and Magic* (Albany, NY: State University of New York Press, 1995); or Shaul Magid, *Hasidism Incarnate: Hasidism, Christianity, and the Construction of Modern Judaism* (Redwood City, CA: Stanford University Press, 2014); see also my recent entry "Spirit," in *Encyclopedia of Jewish–Christian Relations* (2022). https://www.degruyter.com/database/EJCRO/entry/ejcro.13901391/html (accessed April 11, 2025).

42. See Alan L. Segal, *Rebecca's Children: Judaism and Christianity in the Roman World* (Cambridge, MA: Harvard University Press, 1986); see also the different metaphors studied in Reinhartz, "Slip-Slidin' Away," (see note 1), 103–20.

43. See Daniel Boyarin, *Dying for God, Martyrdom and the Making of Christianity and Judaism* (Stanford, CA: Stanford University Press, 1999): 9.

44. See Adam H. Becker and Annette Yoshiko Reed, eds., *The Ways That Never Parted: Jews and Christians in Late Antiquity and the Early Middle Ages* (Texts and Studies in Ancient Judaism, 95; Tübingen: Mohr Siebeck, 2003).

related questions: that of the disappearance of Yeshua/Christ-confessing Jews who maintain a Jewish identity, and that of the wider process of partition inside the "people of God." These are inseparable and cannot be understood one without the other. Christ-confessing Jews were the first victims of the "parting of the ways" and they were the indicator that the ways were parting, because they were gradually torn between the two emerging traditions. This also means in the present and for the future that one cannot concentrate only on the theme of Jewish disciples of Yeshua: If it is right for these to have their space in the world of disciples of Jesus and if the time is ripe, they can only exist in a stable way as part of a process that brings together Jews and Gentiles, the whole of the people of Israel and the whole of Christianity. What is at stake is wider and deeper than the question of Jewish disciples of Jesus because the parting of the ways concerns the whole of the "people of God"—the whole of Israel, and the whole of the Gentiles who, according to the NT, have been grafted onto the chosen people. The whole people of God are wounded, in both of their lungs or branches. What is at stake is recovering or, better said, finally attaining, the unity and "catholicity" which are the vocation of the people of God, made of Jews and Gentiles.

However, we are facing a form of virtuous circle: Jewish "Christianity" cannot exist without the wider process, but this process itself cannot happen without Jewish disciples of Jesus. They are the bridge that can connect the ways that parted; they will be and are already the first fruits and sign that the ways may unite. They are indispensable for the wholeness of the Church and of the people of God—which will happen in God's time and according to the ways God knows.

This said, we can now turn to the first two themes evoked in the introduction, concerning the chronology and then the reasons for the disappearance of Jewish Christ-confessors, knowing that it took place in a wider process.

The chronology we have defined shows that the phenomenon that became the two distinct religions of Judaism and Christianity was once one, and for a period that spanned one, two, and in some places and parts of society, three centuries. Jews who have believed in Jesus have been able, in many different ways, to maintain their identity and to consider themselves part of the Jewish people. This means that this composite unity is possible. Moreover, even since they have crystallized into distinct traditions, they have maintained through the ages a deep relationship. To a certain extent, one can understand this to be the sign of a profound, structural, although deeply hidden and very complex tendency toward the unity of the whole "people of God," composed of Jews and Gentiles. It is also comparable to embers of the composite Jewish-Christian identity buried under the ashes and ready to be revived if the right wind blows.

Of course, the simple fact that a reality has existed and can exist does not mean it will or even should exist again, even in a new form. One can wonder if there was not a certain degree of necessity, or at the very least, inevitability, in the parting of the ways and the disappearance of Judeo-Christianity.[45] Paul insists that the "hardening of Israel" allows the Gentiles to enter into the (new) covenant (Rom 11:25); this may well be because Paul perceives the difficulty for Jews to accept that Gentiles can join without becoming Jews. One could also say that this hardening was a protection of the people of Israel facing a Church that was always more intent on "swallowing up" the Jewish people and integrating them into an indistinct form of universality.[46] A.-J. Levine believes that the parting of the ways was the only realistic solution for both the gospel to spread to all humanity and the chosen people to maintain their identity: "Had the church remained a Jewish sect, it would not have achieved its universal mission. Had Judaism given up its particularistic practices, it would have vanished from history. That the two movements eventually separated made possible the preservation of each."[47] The disappearance of Jewish Christians who maintain

45. Antoine Lévy is right to underline that reflecting on a role for Jewish Christians now and in the future has no meaning if their past demise corresponded to the nature of the Church and was thus so to speak necessary—*Jewish Church*, (see note 7), 183.

46. See Mark D. Nanos, *Reading Romans Within Judaism* (Eugene, OR: Cascade, 2018): 221; Étienne Vetö, "Jewish–Christian Dialogue and the Identity of the Church," in *Dialog Chrześcijańsko—Żydowski – Dialog Międzyreligijny czy Ekumeniczny? Christian—Jewish Dialogue – Interreligious or Ecumenical Dialogue?*, ed. Sławomir J. Żurek (Lublin: Towarzystwo Naukowe Katolickiego Uniwersytetu Lubelskiego Jana Pawła II, 2021): 13–34, at 33–34.

47. Levine, *Misunderstood Jew* (see note 25), 84. The orthodox rabbinic document *To Do the Will of Our Father in Heaven* (2015) also insists on the necessity of the development of Christianity to allow for the spreading of the knowledge of the God of Israel to all peoples (§3).

their identity was not a pure accident of history. However, what Paul evokes is an economic necessity, related to a period of salvation history. Likewise, the parting of the ways was inevitable only if the balance proposed by Acts 15 of a dual situation inside of the *ekklesia* / *am haElohim* did not hold. Conversely, although this would deserve an in-depth study of its own, Acts 15 seems like the fundamental ecclesiological proposal of the NT, the one that best corresponds to the promises of the *Tanakh*, and that has its own necessity. We are perhaps in the right moment of salvation history to finally enact it.

That does not mean it will be simple. It never has been. But whenever and wherever it may happen and it already happens, it truly will be a fruit and a sure sign of the messianic age. If the parting was a long, messy, and varied process, the same is and will be true of the unification of the ways. It will entail "grey zones" where borders are fluid, as well as provisional solutions, experimentation in different ways of being Judeo-Christians, and envisioning different ways of bringing closer together Jews and Christians, as well as Jews and Gentiles. In a way, the twenty-first century being a time of fluid identities and affiliations makes it a favorable period for this process.

Moreover, we cannot "go back" after eighteen hundred years of parting. We cannot simply wish away the long history of antagonism and of construction of specific identities. The wounds of history call for penance and *tikkun olam*. To take just one example, the Church should not only address the whole Jewish people when she confesses her past errors, but more precisely the Jewish believers in Jesus who have been obliged to forgo the observance of the Torah and to separate themselves from their people. Likewise, one can understand the great difficulty that mainstream rabbinic Judaism has with Messianic Judaism and Jewish Christianity—even in a period in which other traditional boundaries, between Judaism and Buddhism for example, are becoming more porous. The name of Jesus has been associated for centuries with persecution, and for centuries the Jewish people have been confronted with a seemingly irrepressible urge by the Church to swallow them up. Building trust is a long process and will entail forgoing missionary activity in a clear and decisive manner. It also means being very clear about respecting and upholding Jewish identity and way of life. Jewish disciples of Jesus who have not been proselytized, but who undertake their own faith journey and, moreover, who maintain their Jewish identity and observance, are in the paradoxical situation of being the main sticking point but also the possible witnesses that the Churches are taking these questions earnestly.

However, taking seriously the depth and reality of history also means welcoming the richness that has been developed over the centuries by each tradition. For Christians (and Messianic Jews), this means recognizing that, if God has always continued to accompany God's people, many aspects of rabbinic tradition are inspired by the Holy Spirit. For Rabbinic Judaism (and Messianic Jews), the same can be said of Christian tradition, even when it has gradually left the Semitic world and become Greco-Latin and then opened to the immense variety of civilizations of the nations. All of these are part of the gifts of the Spirit and should be welcomed as such.

In this long, messy, but hope-filled and hope-inspiring process, we may be helped by taking into account, as the third aspect of this conclusion, the causes of the partings of the ways and of the disappearance of Jewish disciples in Jesus that have been brought to the light in this paper. If the parting has a plurality of factors, so will the path toward unity.

Doctrine counts but is not the only aspect. Conceptions about God, identity of Jesus, understanding of election and of the role of the Law, of the land of Israel and of the Temple—these questions are part of the dialogue and debate to be held between Jews and Christians, between the Church and Jewish believers in Jesus, between Jewish believers and the wider Jewish world. However, many other questions are to be confronted and, even if they make for a more complicated picture, they may also offer avenues for unexpected breakthroughs where doctrinal questions are sticking points. Practice and observance are a significant aspect to consider. There may be possible points of convergence to explore in observance and mystical life, that do not follow doctrinal differences or antagonism, for instance between Messianic Jews and Rabbinic Judaism or between Hasidism and Charismatic Christianity.

Likewise, it is time to implore and prophetically cry out against petty competition and power struggles between leaders and the faithful of all Churches and Jewish institutions. The words God asked Ezekiel to proclaim are still topical: "Prophesy against the shepherds of Israel; prophesy and say to them: To the shepherds—thus says the Lord God: Woe, you shepherds of Israel who have been feeding yourselves! Should not shepherds feed the sheep?" (Ezek 34:1–2). What truly will feed the sheep if not to recover unity?

Furthermore, now as in late antiquity, social and political forces are to be considered. The geopolitical situation of the present age is quite different, and there is no reality comparable to the Roman Empire that would directly benefit from an antagonism between Jews and Christians. Many Church institutions and a greater part of Rabbinic Judaism are related to the "Western World"—even in Israel—and would in fact value as much unity as possible between Jews and Christians, who share the same conception of the dignity of the human being in the image of God, and many of the same ethical principles. However, there is a risk that the growth of Christianity in the Southern Hemisphere and in the East, which have little historical contact with Jews, will lead to less interest in and less affinity with the Jews. Moreover, the Israeli–Palestinian conflict pushes many Christians, especially in the Middle East, to reject the Jewish people. Yet these forces are still in the making and are not set in stone—they can and should be addressed.

Finally, we have seen that tension between Jews and Gentiles was a decisive factor in the parting of the ways. It is an obvious difficulty: Why would Jews want to "share" the covenant with others? Why would Gentiles want to become adopted or grafted members of a covenant that is made with the Jews? I believe that it is the will of God as expressed in the Scripture, but distortions need to be rectified so that the prospect may truly be "good news" for both Jews and Gentiles. Once again, let me insist on the need for Christianity to develop a theology and a practice that upholds a strong conception of the permanence of the election of Israel *qua* Israel. Judaism also needs to address seriously what it means for the people of Israel to be a "blessing for all the families of the earth" (Gen 12:3) and a "light for the nations" (Isa 42:6; 49:6). Both traditions will also need to develop a theology of election that holds together a true distinction for Israel with a full equality of Jews and Gentiles.

All this put together will not bring about the messianic healing and fullness of all the branches of God's people: Only God and the Messiah can do that. But we can hope that it will pave the way.

Response to Étienne Vetö, "Assessing Jewish Christianity"

Mariusz Rosik

FOR SEVERAL DECADES, the problem of the parting of the ways has received increasing interest from researchers. Dozens of books and hundreds of articles have been written on the subject. Almost all of them show that the separation of Church from Synagogue (Christianity from Judaism) was not a one-time act, but a long-lasting, multilayered, and diversified process.[1] Judeo-Christians played a significant—I would even say, a decisive—role in this process. They were the ones who argued in favor of Jesus of Nazareth as the Messiah expected by the Jews, and at the same time they opened the door of the new faith for the Hellenistic and Roman cultures, not linked to Judaism. In this short presentation, I would like to clarify more precisely the meaning of the term "parting of the ways," point out the role of Judeo-Christians in this process, and highlight the value of Professor Étienne Vetö's important comments on the issue of interest to us.

1. Wayne A. Meeks, after analyzing the texts of the New Testament and in view of the relationship of the Church with representatives of Judaism, comes to a simple conclusion: "The path of separation, then, was not single or uniform"—Wayne A. Meeks, *In Search of the Early Christians: Selected Essays* (New Haven, CT: Yale University Press, 2001): 132.

1. What is "parting of the ways"?

There is a need to define more precisely the technical term "parting of the ways." This term refers us back to the model of description of the process according to which two religions emerged from biblical Judaism: Christianity and rabbinic Judaism (in this chronological order). In other words, from one "way" two different "ways" emerged. Although the validity of the above view cannot be denied, one should be aware of the fact that Judaism of the first century did not represent one way. Apart from the groups within Judaism as they are traditionally enumerated in handbooks (pharisaism, sadduceism, essenism, zealotry with its radical wing of *sicarii*, Herodians, scribes, supporters of John the Baptist sometimes described as the Baptists, and possibly also the Samaritans as the heirs to the Mosaic religion), there were also currents associated with apocalyptic literature and with the mystical trend, as well as the ordinary *am-ha'aretz*, that is shepherds not knowing the Law, and the poorest people of Eretz Israel.[2] Different faces of Judaism in the Diaspora should also be added to the list, for example, the Egyptian *Therapeutae*.[3]

Therefore, many authors prefer to speak about "Judaisms" in the first century.[4] The ways of practicing Judaism were very different and sometimes distant from each other. And from them two separate religions, Christianity and rabbinic Judaism, emerged. What is more, both emphasized the "way," which means the manner of cultivating the bond with God, and both saw themselves as the "way." Rabbis developed *halakha*, in other words, "the way" of interpreting and applying

2. Andrzej Mrozek, "Chrześcijaństwo jako herezja judaizmu," *The Polish Journal of the Arts and Culture* 5 (2013): 9–25, at 10. The author uses the term "heresy" in the same sense in which it was used in the writings of Jewish historians of the first century and in the New Testament: Josephus and Philo used the term *hairesis* "to determine not only philosophical schools but also religious groups within Judaism such as the Essenes, the Sadducees, and the Pharisees. The meaning of the term *hairesis* in the New Testament is close to that which we find in Hellenistic texts and in Judaism"—*Ibid.*, 12.

3. Torrey Seland, "Once More—The Hellenists, Hebrews, and Stephen: Conflicts and Conflict-Management in Acts 6–7," in *Recruitment, Conquest, and Conflict: Strategies in Judaism, Early Christianity, and the Greco-Roman World*, ed. Peder Borgen, Vernon K. Robbins, and David B. Gowler (Emory Studies in Early Christianity; Atlanta, GA: Scholars Press, 1998): 179–200.

4. Bruce Chilton and Jacob Neusner, *Judaism in the New Testament: Practices and Beliefs* (London / New York: Routledge, 1995): xviii.

the Law in everyday life.[5] Similarly, Christianity was seen as "a way" (Acts 9:2) and Christ himself declared that he was "the way" leading toward God (John 14:6). What is more, because the process of disunion between the two religious communities took place in different places and at different times, and was motivated by various factors, many authors prefer to speak of *partings* (plural) of Judaism and Christianity.

The issue that still calls for in-depth consideration is the complexity of the image of Christianity which was not homogeneous throughout the Roman Empire in the three first centuries. Apart from Judeo-Christians and ethno-Christians, there appeared communities like the Ebionites, the Elcesaites, or the Nazarenes.[6] The followers of Marcion or of Montanus also aspired to the name of Christians; they were excluded from the Church community, but that did not mean that the Jews did not see them as Christians. Hence, among the opinions about the different faces of the Church in the first centuries, one can come across the view represented for example by R. Kraft who prefers to speak of "Christianities" rather than a single Christianity of that time. In any case, it is clear that the simple image of the tearing of one canvas of Judaism into two parts (like the tearing of the Temple's curtain at the moment of Jesus' death) is not adequate to express the very complex process of the emergence of the two religions.[7]

5. In a similar way, the residents of Qumran saw their community as "the way" (1QS 4.22; 8.10, 18, 21; 9.5).

6. For more about these groups, see: Karl Baus, *Von der Urgemeinde zur frühchristlichen Grosskirche* (Handbuch der Kirchengeschichte, 1; Freiburg i. Br.: Herder, 1963); Matt Jackson-McCabe, "Ebionites and Nazoraeans: Christians or Jews?," in *Partings: How Judaism and Christianity Became Two*, ed. Hershel Shanks (Washington, DC: Biblical Archaeology Society, 2013): 187–205; Petri Luomanen, "Ebionites and Nazarenes," in *Jewish Christianity Reconsidered: Rethinking of Ancient Groups and Texts*, ed. Matt Jackson-McCabe (Minneapolis, MN: Augsburg Fortress, 2007): 81–118; Simon C. Mimouni, "Réflexions sur le judéo-christianisme," in *Christianity, Judaism and Other Greco-Roman Cults: Studies for Morton Smith at Sixty*, vol. II – *Early Christianity*, ed. Jacob Neusner (Leiden: Brill, 1975): 53–76; Richard Bauckham, "The Origin of the Ebionites," in *The Image of Judaeo-Christians in Ancient Jewish and Christian Literature*, ed. Peter J. Tomson and Doris Lambers-Petry (Wissenschaftliche Untersuchungen zum Neuen Testament, 158; Tübingen: Mohr Siebeck, 2003): 162–81; Joseph Verheyden, "Epiphanius on the Ebionites," in Tomson and Lambers-Petry (see above), 182–208.

7. Mariusz Rosik, *Church and Synagogue (30–313 AD): Parting of the Ways* (European Studies in Theology, Philosophy and History of Religions; Bern: Haupt, 2019): 466.

2. The role of Judeo-Christians in the "parting of the ways" process

The parting of the ways between Church and Synagogue is based on two unquestionable facts: its evolutionary character[8] and the role of Christians descended from Judaism.[9] These two issues are the backbone of first the tension, then the conflict, and finally even the mutual disfavor and hostility which to a great extent was characteristic of the history of Church and Synagogue in the first three centuries. Tension, conflict, and disfavor arose around the person of Christ and interpretation of his role in the history of salvation and around consequences (theological, liturgical, and social) resulting from this interpretation.[10]

Generally speaking, the process of the creation of rabbinic Judaism and Christianity as separate religions concerns mainly Judeo-Christians. It is hard to speak about the "parting of the ways" of ethno-Christians and the Jews who were not Christian since their ways were never common. Even the most Hellenized Jews in the Diaspora (such as Philo of Alexandria) belonged to Jewish communities which gathered on the Sabbath in synagogues and carefully protected their identity as those who were different from "the Greeks." Pagans known as "God-fearers" could not fully participate in the life of Jewish communities unless they became proselytes. On the other hand, there is no evidence of any Jewish community not believing in Christ that would welcome ethno-Christians with open arms, especially if the latter refused to circumcise. Hence, there was no need for "the parting of ways" of Christians descending from pagan religions and the Jews not recognizing Christ.[11]

8. Martin Goodman, "Modelling the 'Parting of the Ways,'" in *The Ways That Never Parted: Jews and Christians in Late Antiquity and the Early Middle Ages*, ed. Adam H. Becker and Annette Yoshiko Reed (Texts and Studies in Ancient Judaism, 95; Tübingen: Mohr Siebeck, 2003): 119–29, at 122; Waldemar Chrostowski, "*Żydzi i religia żydowska a Maryja Matka Jezusa*," *Salvatoris Mater* 2.1 (2000): 215–33, at 219; Andrew S. Jacobs, "The Lion and the Lamb. Reconsidering Jewish–Christian Relations in Antiquity," in Becker and Yoshiko Reed, eds., *The Ways That Never Parted* (see above), 95–118, at 98.

9. James D.G. Dunn, *Christianity in Making*, 2, *Beginning from Jerusalem* (Grand Rapids, MI / Cambridge: Eerdmans, 2009): 133–38.

10. Mary C. Boys, "Doing Justice to Judaism: The Challenge to Christianity," *Journal of Ecumenical Studies* 49.1 (2014): 107–110, at 107–108; Peter Landesmann, *Anti-Judaism on the Way from Judaism to Christianity* (Wiener Vorlesungen: Forschungen, 5; Bern: Haupt, 2012): 51–54.

11. Rosik, *Church and Synagogue* (see note 7), 465–66.

There is no doubt that rabbinic Judaism and Christianity started to exist as separate religions in different places and at different times. It seems that, at the earliest, the division became reality in Rome when Nero accused the followers of Christ of starting the fire in the year 64, not identifying them with the Jews.[12] The Roman authorities distinguished the two religious groups already at the beginning of the second century. This is evidenced by the issue of *Fiscus Iudaicus* which, at that time, was not imposed on Christians, and also the issue of persecution. The tax imposed on the Jews by Vespasian after the destruction of the Temple in Jerusalem was maintained by his son Domitian (81–96) and it encompassed those who "lived the Jewish way" and those who had rejected their Jewish roots.[13] Not only the followers of Christ descended from Judaism (even though they were considered to be those who had actually rejected their Jewish identity) but also probably Christians of pagan descent were included in the first group. Since the time of the successor of Domitian, Nerva (96), Christians were exempt from the payment of the *Fiscus Iudaicus*. The persecution against Christians did not encompass the Jews, and vice versa. After the Bar Kokhba revolt (132–135), the sharp edge of imperial policy was directed against the Jews (Rabbi Akiba became a famous Jewish martyr) and this time the followers of Christ were not bothered. On the other hand, Bar Kokhba himself persecuted Judeo-Christians for the reason that they recognized the Messiah in Jesus, and not in him.[14] In Palestine, Jews and

12. "Separation of Christians from Jews, then, must have started extremely early in the imperial capital, if within a generation of the death of Jesus of Nazareth neither the common people nor the authorities had any difficulty in distinguishing between the adherents of those two closely related 'superstitions,' as elite Roman writers disparagingly referred to them"—Margaret H. Williams, "Jews and Christians at Rome: An Early Parting of the Ways," in *Partings. How Judaism and Christianity Became Two*, ed. Hershel Shanks (Washington, DC: Biblical Archaeology Society, 2013): 151–78, at 152.

13. Marius Heemstra, *How Rome's Administration of* Fiscus Judaicus *Accelerated the Parting of the Ways between Judaism and Christianity: Rereading 1 Peter, Revelation, the Letter to the Hebrews, and the Gospel of John in their Roman and Jewish Context* (PhD thesis; Groningen, 2009): 14. According to some authors, the tax applied to every Jew aged between three and sixty; Martin Goodman, "Diaspora Reactions to the Destruction of the Temple," in *Jews and Christians: The Parting of the Ways AD 70 to 135*, ed. James D.G. Dunn (Grand Rapids, MI / Cambridge: Eerdmans, 1999): 27–38, 30.

14. Richard Bauckham, "Jews and Christians in the Land of Israel at the Time of the Bar Kochba War, with Special Reference to the Apocalypse of Peter," in

Christians saw each other as two completely separate religious communities after the creation of the Academy in Yavneh around the year 90.[15] Both the Jerusalem Talmud and the Babylonian Talmud confirm that the 'blessing' of *minim* from the "Eighteen Blessings" prayer was created at that time.[16]

3. Three possibilities

The question of internal tensions in Christian communities in the first century undoubtedly affected most powerfully the Jewish followers of Christ. They had to decide if they should:

(1) join the communities in which an increasingly large group consisted of ethno-Christians,
(2) try to stay within the Jewish communities which did not accept Christ, or maybe
(3) make an effort to develop their own religious structures comprising only Judeo-Christians.

The first possibility, most often confirmed by the New Testament writings, resulted over time in the loss of Jewish identity by the Jews believing in Christ. The second possibility did not stand the test of time: the Jews believing in Christ were recognized as apostates and excluded from synagogue by official (rabbinic) Judaism.[17] The supporters of the

---

Tolerance and Intolerance in Early Judaism and Christianity, ed. Graham N. Stanton and Guy G. Stroumsa (Cambridge: Cambridge University Press, 1998): 228–38, at 228–31.

15. Daniel Boyarin of the University of California, Berkeley, believes that researchers interpret the "Yavneh effect" incorrectly: "All of the institutions of rabbinic Judaism are projected in rabbinic narrative to an origin called Yavneh. Yavneh, seen in this way, is the effect, not the cause"—Daniel Boyarin, *Border Lines: The Partition of Judaeo-Christianity* (Philadelphia, PA: University of Pennsylvania Press, 2004): 48.

16. William Horbury, "The Benediction of the Minim and Early Jewish–Christian Controversy," *Journal of Theological Studies* 33 (1982): 19–61, at 19–20; Jacob Mann, "Genizah Fragments of the Palestinian Order of Service," *Hebrew Union College Annual* 2 (1925): 269–338, at 306.

17. Mirosław Wróbel, "*Birkat ha-Minim* and the Process of Separation Between Judaism and Christianity," *The Polish Journal of Biblical Research* 5.2 (2006): 99–120; Frédéric Manns, *John and Jamnia: How the Break Occurred Between Jews and Christians*

third possibility, forming communities of Judeo-Christians (related to the Ebionites, the Nazarenes, and the Elcesaites) had to find an intermediate status between Christians of pagan descent and Jews rejecting the faith in Jesus as the Messiah.[18] Communities of that type, even if they managed to form coherent religious structures, did not survive long.

The theological and historical analyses have brought to light many nuances linked to this issue. It turns out that there were Judeo-Christians who had departed from practicing the Law of Moses (like circumcision, celebration of the Sabbath, observance of religious dietary rules of *kashrut*) almost completely, and those who, believing in Christ, still observed the Jewish customs. In this perspective, the Judaizers coming from paganism also played a major role. Although they entered the Christian community from a pagan community, along with the discovery of the new faith they discovered Judaism and leaned toward it, sometimes even more than Judeo-Christians. In addition, various communities whose members were Judeo-Christians and/or Judaizers were characterized by stronger or less strong attachment to the Jewish tradition, customs, and rules.

What is more, they did not disappear from the religious scene of the ancient world as quickly as has been widely assumed in scholarship until recently. Researchers dealing with the issue of the parting of the ways essentially concentrated on relations between Christian and Jewish communities around the Mediterranean and thus on the territories where Greco-Hellenistic and Roman cultures dominated. However, the development of Christianity was directed not only to the west of Palestine. The followers of Christ equally quickly brought the good news to the east, to regions where Semitic mentality dominated. There, especially in Syria, Judeo-Christian communities were developing their activities over a much longer period of time than in Europe; some of them survived even until the beginnings of the fourth century (as Vetö has noted).[19]

---

c. 80–100 A.D., trans. Mildred Duel and Marina Riadi (Jerusalem: Franciscan Printing Press, 1988).

18. Stanley Jones, *Pseudoclementina Elchasaiticaque inter Judaeochristiana: Collected Studies* (Orientalia Lovaniensia Analecta, 203; Leuven: Peeters, 2012).

19. Annette Yoshiko Reed, "'Jewish Christianity' After the 'Parting of the Ways': Approaches to Historiography and Self-Definition in the Pseudo-Clementines," in Becker and Yoshiko Reed, eds., *The Ways That Never Parted,* (see note 8), 189–231.

4. *Étienne Vetö about the "parting of the ways"*

Among many of the qualities of Vetö's paper, I would like to highlight three:

(1) The first seems to be the most fundamental: showing that research on the parting of the ways can make a significant contribution to the grounding and more precise definition of the identity of contemporary Messianic Jewish communities. In the long run, it may turn out that contemporary Messianic Jewish communities can become important environments for Christian–Jewish dialogue.

(2) The second concerns the question of the choice of terminology. From a methodological point of view, the latest research on the emergence of two separate religions from biblical Judaism encounters some terminological difficulties. Researchers in both academic and popular works use in an ambiguous way the terms "Judeo-Christianity," "Judeo-Christian," "Judaizers," "Jewish Christianity," or "Christian Judaism." The meaning of these terms used by individual authors differs significantly. In some works, the term "Judeo-Christians" is used to refer to the baptized Jews who joined the Church, others use it to describe Christians descending from pagan religions (ethno-Christians) who tended to observe Jewish practices. In the latter case, there is no clear border between "Judeo-Christians" and "Judaizers."

Vetö uses the expression "Jewish disciples of Yeshua/Jesus" mainly for designating the first generations, while he prefers "Judeo-Christians" for the later generations. He adds that "the latter are more distinct from other strands of Judaism, and some are not ethnically Jewish." I think that the acceptance of such terminology would greatly facilitate the whole debate on the parting of the ways.

(3) A third and equally important value of Vetö's paper is that he looks at the question of the parting of the ways through the eyes of a Judeo-Christian. Today's research presents the process of parting of the ways of Church and Synagogue either from the perspective of Christianity,[20]

20. John G. Gager, "The Parting of the Ways; A View from the Perspective of Early Christianity: 'A Christian Perspective,'" in *Interwoven Destinies: Jews and Christians Through the Ages*, ed. Eugene Fisher (New York: Paulist Print, 1993): 62–73, at 70–73.

or of rabbinic Judaism.[21] It seems that modern scholars have somewhat lost this most important perspective: that of the Jewish disciples of Christ (the first generation) and that of the Judeo-Christians (the later generations). This observation seems to be an important clue for contemporary Christian–Jewish dialogue: In order for this dialogue to become truly fruitful, it is necessary, above all, to listen to the voice of contemporary Messianic Jewish communities.[22]

21. Martha Himmelfarb, "The Parting of the Ways Reconsidered: Diversity in Judaism and Jewish–Christian Relations in the Roman Empire. 'A Jewish Perspective,'" in *Interwoven Destinies*, ed. Fisher (see note 20), 47–61.

22. Rosik, *Church and Synagogue* (see note 7), 550–51.

Turning Away from Replacement Theology and Rediscovering the Ecclesia ex Circumcisione

Ecclesiological Reflections in Light of Messianic Judaism

Ursula Schumacher

1. Introduction

THE Messianic Jewish movement presents a challenge for Catholic theology—not only because prominent positions in Messianic Jewish theology demand a dialogical engagement with Catholic theology, but also because they see this dialogue as implicated in Catholic theological *self-understanding*. The issue arising from such positions which in the following shall be taken up theologically both as stimulus and challenge can be summarized as follows: According to *Nostra Aetate* 4 and its later magisterial explication, especially by Pope John Paul II, there is a "bond that spiritually ties the people of the New Covenant to Abraham's stock" (*NA* 4); "all who believe in Christ—Abraham's sons according to faith—are included in the same Patriarch's call" (*NA* 4); and the Church "draws sustenance from the root of that well-cultivated olive tree" (*NA* 4). Ecclesiologically formulated: The Church's relationship to Judaism has an enduring, foundational, and intrinsically important significance for ecclesiology, not merely an external or superseded one.

When we take the soteriological implications of this relationship seriously, Israel and the Church cannot be viewed as two separate entities in salvation history, a consequence which already has been formulated by both the magisterium and theology. The movement of Christ followers with its openness for non-Jews—resulting from the non-recognition of Jesus' Messiahship by the majority of Judaism of his time—is therefore not to be seen as a separate way of salvation independent of Israel,[1] but rather as an opening of the relationship to Israel's God for the nations and as a beginning fulfillment of the promise of the nations' pilgrimage, which in a personalized interpretation can be understood as a turning to Jesus Christ.[2] Certainly, the Christian anti-Jewish history of guilt has perverted and obscured this foundational relationship between Judaism and Christianity; it is therefore all the more important to formulate and to affirm this relationship ecclesiologically in all clarity. Let us thus state it explicitly once again: The Church has to be seen as a community whose election by God not only does not replace Israel and whose dependence on Israel also is not merely in terms of its chronological succession or the continuation of an external preparation. Rather, the Church is to be understood as standing in an enduring inner connection to Israel.

A foundational relationship of this kind between the Church and Israel has massive implications for ecclesiological reflection—in the words of Mark Kinzer: "If the Body of Christ is an eschatologically renewed and expanded form of genealogical-Israel, rather than a separate entity created by God *ex nihilo* and only prefigured by the Israel of the old covenant, then one would expect that the presence of Jews in her midst would be an essential component of her identity."[3] And the ecclesiological consequences of a renewed Israel theology can therefore not be exhausted in piecemeal adaptations, but are to be seen as a foundational perspective whose echo must resonate throughout all

1. Clearly stated in the document "'The Gifts and the Calling of God Are Irrevocable' (Rom 11:29): A Reflection on Theological Questions Pertaining to Catholic–Jewish Relations on the Occasion of the 50th Anniversary of '*Nostra aetate*' (No. 4)," *Papal Commission for Religious Relations with the Jews*, December 10, 2015, Nos. 25, 35.

2. Cf. as an example Thomas Schumacher, "Jüdischer König und Weltenherrscher. Christologische und heilsgeschichtliche Perspektiven in der großen Inklusion des Matthäusevangeliums. Zugleich ein Beitrag zur Rezeption des Motivs der Völkerwallfahrt," in *Sprachbilder und Bildsprache. Studien zur Kontextualisierung biblischer Texte. FS Max Küchler*, ed. Thomas Schumacher, Markus Lau, and Karl Matthias Schmidt (Novum Testamentum et Orbis Antiquus / Studien zur Umwelt des Neuen Testaments, 121; Göttingen: Vandenhoeck & Ruprecht, 2019): 201–25.

3. Mark S. Kinzer, *Searching Her Own Mystery:* Nostra Aetate, *the Jewish People, and the Identity of the Church* (Eugene, OR: Cascade, 2015): 57–58.

of ecclesiology (and not only here[4]): The existence and the promise of Judaism, its life, and its relationship to God have formative, essential, and identity-shaping relevance for the Church; the Church stands "in a permanent theological reference to Israel."[5] She thus can think and express "her own reality only in the mode of a referential identity."[6] Or again in other words: "The entire Church, beyond any specific Church tradition, is ontologically related to Israel. Everything that the Catholic Church has, including the rich variety of her ecclesial traditions, she originally received from the Jewish nation and its spiritual legacy."[7]

Of course, the existence of Messianic Judaism is no *necessary* prerequisite for the affirmation of this fundamental theological insight. The phenomenon of Messianic Judaism does, however, imply a certain intensification of the ecclesiological challenge outlined above and thus without a doubt requires theological reflection—which has, up to now, hardly been done by Catholic theology; this reflection is necessary already because every form of an explicit confession of Christ has ecclesiological relevance. In the case of Messianic Judaism, however, two additional aspects are of special importance for the link between Israel theology and ecclesiology. First, the connection between Judaism and Christianity manifests and concretizes itself here in a particularly solid way. This applies naturally also for those with Jewish ancestry who become members of Christian Churches. Second, Messianic Judaism confronts a Christian ecclesiology particularly intensely with the question of the foundational relationship between Judaism and Christianity, since a Messianic Jewish perspective does not regard external institutional conversion as a necessary consequence of confessing Jesus as the Messiah, but rather lives its relationship to Christ as a variety of *Jewish* identity. Precisely that is why it poses a challenge for the theological self-reflection of the Church.

4. Mark Kinzer formulates this with great clarity and quite rightly: "The affirmations of *Nostra Aetate* 4 reverberate throughout the entire system of Catholic theology—Christology, ecclesiology, sacramental teaching, and all that remains," Kinzer, *Searching Her Own Mystery* (see note 3), 9.

5. "in einem theologischen Dauerbezug zu Israel"—Gregor M. Hoff, *Ekklesiologie* (Gegenwärtig Glauben denken, 6; Paderborn: Schöningh, 2011): 51.

6. "ihre eigene Wirklichkeit nicht anders als im Modus einer verwiesenen Identität"—*Ibid.*, 51.

7. Antoine Lévy, *Jewish Church: A Catholic Approach to Messianic Judaism* (Lanham, MD: Lexington Books, 2021): 241. Cf. also "The Gifts and the Calling of God Are Irrevocable" (see note 1), Nos. 28, 33–34.

Certainly, such attribution of relevance can be questioned. For example, Messianic Judaism that is presently heterogeneous and, in terms of numbers, a marginal phenomenon can be relativized as an isolated and contingent occurrence, to which the Church should not attribute a fundamental and intrinsic significance. Against such a relativizing stance however, one must duly consider that an ecclesiological relevance of Jews who believe in Christ cannot be casually dismissed—at least not if one takes seriously the biblical finding that Jesus was first sent to Israel, and if one does not want to assume that the fact that Jesus' first followers were Jews lost every salvation-historical relevance after they established the mission to the nations and opened up the Jesus movement for non-Jews. Naturally the question of how to interpret the figure of Jesus Christ is of foundational importance here—more concretely, the question of whether Jesus Christ is to be seen as relevant for Israel. If one does not wish to simply exclude the latter (which would be problematic considering Jesus' own self-understanding and the New Testament finding[8]) then every form of Jewish Christianity including Messianic Judaism must be taken as a realization of the will of Jesus and as relevant to salvation history. Such a position, however, must by no means be permitted to fall back into the old pattern of replacement theology: The assumption of Jesus' relevance for Israel may not be interpreted as if Jesus first had to lead Israel into a relationship with God as is the case with gentile Christians. Theology must firmly object to any relativization of Israel's lasting significance in salvation history and of the soteriological worth of her relationship to God—as well as to every legitimization of missional activity toward the Jewish people. With his concept of a post-missionary Messianic Judaism,[9] Mark Kinzer has marked out standards, which must also apply for a Christian Israel theology in encounter and dialogue with Messianic Judaism. If one takes this grounding in Israel theology seriously and combines a theological appreciation of Messianic Judaism with a clear rejection of every form of supersessionist theology and mission to the Jews, then it should also be possible to disarm concerns that see in the dialogue with Messianic Jews the danger of blurring the Church's firm rejection of missionary activity among Jews.

8. Cf., e.g., the article by Michael Theobald in the present volume.

9. Mark S. Kinzer, *Post-Missionary Messianic Judaism: Redefining Christian Engagement with the Jewish People* (Grand Rapids, MI: Brazos, 2005).

A relativization of the significance of Messianic Judaism, however, could also begin with the questioning of the *Jewishness* of Messianic Jews.[10] Is Messianic Judaism, because of its confession of Christ, to be denied the honorary title of belonging to "Israel," as Jewish voices repeatedly state? This is a question which a non-Jewish perspective must not presume to decide. It does, however, raise quite a few issues, insofar as here—if one considers the self-assessment of at least a part of Messianic Judaism—we are evidently confronted with an inner-Jewish difference of opinion in the assessment of an identity problem. In any case, Jews who believe in Christ could only be denied *Judaism*, not *Jewishness*—only belonging to a religious community, not being Jewish as such. Perhaps, however, the question may be asked whether here, under other auspices, the basic assumption returns that Judaism and Christianity can only be defined in a relationship of reciprocal exclusion—an assumption which shaped Christian theology for a long time. And is it not due rather to the history of Christian offences against Jews than to the matter itself that from a Jewish perspective, a confession of Jesus as the Messiah cannot (or only in rare exceptions) be viewed as part of a legitimate intra-Jewish diversity of opinion?

Thus, it remains the case that the existence of Messianic Judaism must concern Christian theology and specifically ecclesiology. The questions that arise from this shall be approached in the following from the perspective of a Catholic dogmatic theologian without Jewish roots. The subsequent reflections owe their intellectual stimuli strongly to the Israel-theologically sensitive voices in ecclesiological discourse and even more to the ecclesiological reflections of Jewish-Christian authors. Based on these valuable approaches, we can state that ecclesiologically, indirect and direct consequences arise from the challenge posed by Messianic Judaism:

(1) Indirect consequences result from the fact that Messianic Judaism—that is, the biographies and religious convictions of Jewish

10. Such a relativization occurs allusively for example in the formulation of Hans H. Henrix: "The root of the Church is the biblical Israel, whose ongoing continuity can be seen most of all in the Judaism of today" ["Die Wurzel der Kirche ist das biblische Israel, dessen fortlaufende Kontinuität vor allem im heutigen Judentum zu sehen ist"]—Hans H. Henrix, "Messianisches Judentum heute. Eine überraschende Wirklichkeit und Irritation im christlich–jüdischen Verhältnis," *Stimmen der Zeit* 229 (2011): 519–30, at 527.

persons who recognize Jesus as Messiah without, however, deriving from this the consequence of an external institutional conversion to Christianity—once again and with particular urgency places the questions of an Israel theology on the agenda of Christian or, concretely, Catholic ecclesiology. The existence of Jews who believe in Christ (both *in* an institutional Church affiliation, but probably even more so *outside* of it) functions as an effective driving factor for a further, even stronger awareness of the Church's foundational relationship to Israel and of the need for a deepening of corresponding ecclesiological reflections. This is not trivial, and it is an important service which Jews who believe in Christ—and, concretely, Messianic Judaism—render to the Church, and arguably to Judaism. Richard Harvey clearly articulates this as a mission given to Messianic Jews: "They are to bear witness to the enduring election of Israel (the Jewish people), to be partners with the nations in the '*one* new humanity' that is the Church, and, finally, to be visible as an eschatological sign of the enduring purposes which God has for his people."[11]

(2) One must, however, also consider direct ecclesiological consequences, insofar as the existence of Messianic Judaism itself requires ecclesiological reflection, but also insofar as Messianic Judaism accentuates anew the question of the ecclesiological significance of Jews who believe in Christ and who stand in an institutional connection with the Church. Both aspects by their nature touch each other, but, on the other hand, are not simply identical and do not have the same ecclesiological implications.

The following reflections will remain selective and partial. Neither the Christological foundations nor the sacramental concretizations of the ecclesiological questions can be addressed; and the following is not about problems of concrete organizational integration of Messianic Judaism into Church structures, either. It is about a question that precedes institutional ecclesiological structures: the question of a theological

11. "Sie sollen die bleibende Erwählung Israels (des jüdischen Volks) bezeugen, sie sollen Partner sein mit den Völkern in dem '*einen* neuen Menschen,' der die Kirche ist, und schließlich als ein eschatologisches Zeichen für die bleibenden Absichten sichtbar sein, die Gott mit seinem Volk hat"—Richard Harvey, "Messianisches Judentum im deutschen Kontext. Gedanken eines Beobachters," in *Messianische Juden – eine Provokation*, ed. Ulrich Laepple (Göttingen: Vandenhoeck & Ruprecht, 2016): 127–39, at 133.

interpretation of the Church of Jesus Christ, and, concretely, of the ecclesiological implications of Messianic Judaism. To that end, three theses will be discussed in the following sections.

Thesis 1: The phenomenon of Messianic Judaism has fundamental implications for the field of ecclesiology, requiring further development or revision (section 2).

Thesis 2: This raises the ecclesiological question of how an overarching meaning of the particular can be theologically conceived (section 3).

Thesis 3: The relationship of the Church to Christ-believing Jews is so fundamental that it cannot be adequately described in the category of an *ecumenical* relation—or if so, only at the risk of fundamental misunderstandings (section 4).

2. Ecclesiological impulses and advancements

2.1. Overcoming residues of replacement theology in ecclesiology

Thinking in terms of replacement theology is regrettably tenacious—decades of a now unequivocal theological rejection of this figure of thought in the wake of *Nostra Aetate* notwithstanding. There are undoubtedly subcutaneous remnants of the old Israel theology, even if an Israel-sensitive wording becomes increasingly prevalent in more recent texts. Thus, references to the Church as the "new Israel" have largely disappeared from newer ecclesiological literature (though presumably not completely). There are, however, other ecclesiological positions which are likewise to be regarded as residues and ongoing after-effects of replacement thinking and must as a result be questioned. This can be illustrated, for example, by a look at the people-of-God ecclesiology, which should not be formulated without also including the statement that *Israel* is first, primarily, and continuously the people of God, and that the Church only participates in this election. The talk of the "new, eschatological people of God, that is . . . the Church"[12] is therefore to be regarded as problematic, if the immediate context lacks a corresponding clarification with regard to Israel. Examples of an implicitly

12. "neuen eschatologischen Volk Gottes, eben . . . der Kirche"—Georg Kraus, *Die Kirche. Gemeinschaft des Heils. Ekklesiologie im Geist des Zweiten Vatikanischen Konzils* (Regensburg: Pustet, 2012): 51, cf. also 148–50.

supersessionist reception of Bible passages can also still be found, for example when the Church is regarded, with reference to Isaiah 11:10, 12, as a "sign to the nations," *"signum levatum in nationes"*—without taking into consideration that in the Old Testament context, an individual savior figure with divine authority is meant here, the shoot from the stump of Jesse.

In a certain way it is itself a consequence of replacement thinking that, despite a strongly increased sensitivity to the theology of Israel, the awareness of a merely participatory and not absolute election of the Church is not yet consistently taken into account. Presumably, the model of concentric circles often used in the interpretation of *Lumen Gentium* (*LG* 14–16) has a counterproductive effect here—all the more so because it has, like the hypothesis of being taken into the relationship with the God of Israel, a spatial-metaphorical connotation: Applied to the relationship with Christ, the model of concentric circles, in which Judaism is regarded as the circle closest to the center in the realm of non-Christian religions, certainly has its justification—but the effect is completely misleading when the proximity to the center is not interpreted as a metaphor for the Christ relationship, but for the relevance in salvation history or for the quality of a relationship with God. The existence of Jews who believe in Christ, and specifically of Messianic Judaism, unquestionably constitutes a call for Catholic ecclesiology to eliminate such after-effects of supersessionist theology.

2.2. Critical scrutiny of a certain type of ecclesial self-centeredness

The previously sketched relationship between the Church and Israel implies a fundamental relativity of the Church: Already from her origin, the Church is relative to Israel, to the original chosen people, and in this respect the Church is de-centered. With the marginalization and breaking away of a perceivable group of Jewish Christians in the Church, however, the constant reminder of God's grace in having opened his offer of relationship to the nations got lost.[13] This development toward

13. Cf., e.g., Johannes Cornides, "The Cost to the Church of Losing the Jews. Christian Doctrine as a History of Forgetting," in *Jesus, King of the Jews? Messianic Judaism, Jewish Christians, and Theology Beyond Supersessionism*, ed. James Earle Patrick (Vienna: Toward Jerusalem Council II, 2021): 33–42, at 36.

a purely gentile Church thus at least contributed to the formation of an ecclesiological triumphalism, which allowed a humble awareness of the graciousness and relativity of the Church's election to recede very much into the background.

Here the ecclesiological perception of Christ-believing Jews (and especially of Messianic Judaism, which lives its Christ relationship beyond an institutional, ecclesiastical integration) can function as an impulse to make theology more aware again of the graciousness of the Church's calling and genesis[14]—or, to put it another way: to recognize the salvation-historical fact that the members of the *ecclesia ex gentibus* up to this day are nothing other than the branches from the wild olive tree which receive their fecundity from the cultivated olive tree (Rom 11:17–24), or the dogs that eat from their master's table what the children drop (Matt 15:27). In systematic theology, often the "relativity" of the Church is mentioned; this mainly refers to foundational aspects in ecclesiology such as the Church's being ordered toward Jesus Christ and toward the kingdom of God.[15] Here it would be necessary to put greater emphasis on the fact that the *ecclesia ex gentibus* is only called in and through the election of Israel. And this relativity has not been abolished with the historical separation of Judaism and Christianity, even if the numerical relations suggest this misconception.

2.3. Developing ecclesiology in the light of Israel theology: The example of notae ecclesiae

With regard to an exemplary issue, I now want to give a rough sketch of how ecclesiological thinking could and should be developed further in light of the challenge stated at the beginning of this article: It is about the *notae ecclesiae*, the essential characteristics of the Church. Israel-sensitive ecclesiological reflections have demanded to include the Church's relationship to Israel among the *notae ecclesiae*.[16] If, in-

14. Cf. Peter Hirschberg, "Messianische Juden: Gefahr oder Chance für den christlich-jüdischen Dialog?," in *Messianische Juden*, ed. Laepple (see note 11), 71–108, at 99.

15. Cf. as an example Jürgen Werbick, *Den Glauben verantworten. Eine Fundamentaltheologie* (Freiburg i. Br.: Herder, 4th edn 2010): 831–34; Siegfried Wiedenhofer, "Ekklesiologie," in *Handbuch der Dogmatik*, Vol. 2, ed. Theodor Schneider (Düsseldorf: Grünewald, 2000): 47–154, at 101.

16. Cf., e.g., Franz Mussner, *Traktat über die Juden* (Munich: Kösel, 2nd edn 1988): 175; Lévy, *Jewish Church* (see note 7), 241.

stead, one wishes to adhere to the four *notae ecclesiae* mentioned in the Nicene-Constantinopolitan creed, then one option would be to reinterpret the four essential characteristics of the Church in terms of Israel theology—an option which can also be seen as ecclesiologically fertile insofar as it opens up more differentiated possibilities for reflecting on Jews who believe in Christ or, specifically, on Messianic Judaism as a part of the Church of Jesus Christ. In the following, I will outline a few thoughts in this direction.

(1) Unity as an essential characteristic of the Church refers to the bond of the members united in the body of Christ—irrespective of all the differences that exist between them. This unity is grounded in the relationship with Christ. And it should be interpreted as a unity of those from Israel and those from among the nations who believe in Christ, which as such also goes back to the fact that only in Jesus are the nations called into the unifying relationship with the God of Israel. The unity in diversity that is characteristic of the Church and unites, among others, Jews and non-Jews who believe in Christ, thus has a deep and inextinguishable connection to Israel, insofar as the Christ relationship grants a share in Israel's promises to the nations.

(2) God is the one who is actually and intrinsically holy. The holiness of the Church, the second *nota ecclesiae*, owes itself to the presence of God in her and to the mission of the Church to make God recognizable and perceptible in the world. This sacramental function of the Church, however, implies a permanent reconnection with the first-chosen people, since the Church is only holy because and insofar as she has received a share in *Israel*'s relationship with God. Christ-believing Jews and the current of Messianic Judaism can therefore quite concretely be regarded as a special form of expression of this God relationship that constitutes the Church's holiness. It is not just any god whom the Church is supposed to make perceptible in the world, but the God of Abraham, Isaac, and Jacob. And the fact that the Church did not just forget this relatedness to Israel that is fundamental to her holiness but has even become guilty of anti-Judaistic attitudes and actions, must be seen as a fundamental dimension of the sinfulness of a Church which is called to holiness.

(3) When one speaks of catholicity as the third essential characteristic of the Church, the term refers to "fullness" and "perfection,"[17]

17. "Fülle," "Vollkommenheit"—Wiedenhofer, "Ekklesiologie" (see note 15), 125.

to the idea "that the Church realizes herself in a comprehensiveness and wholeness, a universality and totality,"[18] and ultimately to an all-encompassing claim to validity, which is grounded in the conviction that all human beings, without exception, are called to salvation and into communion with God. This third *nota ecclesiae* is also related to Israel and concretely to Jews who believe in Christ or to Messianic Judaism, because the Church's mission to all the world is, by its nature, unthinkable and incomprehensible without her foundational origin in the election of Israel. But even more: Precisely when one also means by "catholicity" the dimension of "temporal continuity in abiding faithfulness to the origins,"[19] the relationship with Jews who believe in Christ constitutes an aspect of ecclesial catholicity. From a biblical perspective, the *ecclesia ex gentibus* is not to be seen as something absolute (the specification of the name already implies this), but rather as fundamentally being related to the *ecclesia ex circumcisione*—and so fundamentally in fact, that the gentile Church cannot regard herself as truly catholic without the Church of Christ-believing Jews.

(4) The apostolicity of the Church, the fourth *nota ecclesiae*, finally expresses that the Church is linked in a special way to her origin and that "the validity of this original testimony [becomes] a standard and legitimation of the continuing history of the Church."[20] Now, the Church's "original testimony" is unquestionably Jewish, and Christ-believing Jews and Messianic Judaism can consequently be considered as a specific vivification and representation of the apostolic dimension of the Church. Against this view, the question could be raised whether this position does not imply a theological exaggeration of one contingent datum—the Jewishness of the first disciples of Jesus. However, a quick glance at the meaning of the calling of the twelve disciples, the "primordial Apostles,"[21] already speaks against this: According to

18. "dass sich die Kirche in einer Allumfassendheit und Ganzheit, in einer Universalität und Totalität verwirklicht"—Kraus, *Die Kirche* (see note 12), 411.

19. "zeitlicher Kontinuität in bleibender Ursprungstreue"—*Ibid.*, 419.

20. "die Geltung dieses Ursprungszeugnisses wird zum Maßstab und zur Legitimation der weiteren Kirchengeschichte"—Wiedenhofer, "Ekklesiologie" (see note 15), 131; cf. Kraus, *Die Kirche* (see note 12), 68, 429; Wolfgang Beinert, "Apostolizität der Kirche," in *Lexikon für Theologie und Kirche*, vol. 1 (Freiburg i. Br.: Herder, 3rd edn, 2017): 881–82, at 881.

21. "Urapostel"—Kraus, *Die Kirche* (see note 12), 432.

a basic exegetical assumption, Jesus in fact calls the twelve Apostles as representatives of the twelve tribes of Israel and as a sign that his gathering movement aims at *all of Israel*.[22] And so, the apostolicity of the Church is very specifically linked with a Jewish dimension from its very origin—a theological insight whose anamnetic focus is completely obscured if one sees the ecclesiological relevance of the Apostles only in their function as witnesses to the faith and as leadership figures. Again, one may object here that in its journey through time and under the influence of the Holy Spirit, the Church of the nations has developed her own forms of keeping her apostolic origin alive. This indeed is a justified objection, but it does not oblige one to understand this process as a *suppression* of the specifically Jewish dimension of the Church's apostolicity—an interpretation which actually would imply a supersessionist position. In fact, if every trace of replacement theology is supposed to be eliminated from such a consideration, the apostolic ministry in the gentile Church would have to be interpreted in its foundational reconnection to the original Jewish dimension of apostolicity, which in Paul's mission is transferred into the realm of the gentile Church, and whose particular representation can be seen in Jews who believe in Christ or Messianic Jews, respectively.[23]

3. Sacramentality and representation as ecclesiological categories

From the beginning, it was a nuisance that according to both Jewish and Christian understanding God brought about the redemption of the world by means of the concrete—via the concreteness of a single people chosen out of the peoples to be set apart, and through the concreteness of a single man in whom God communicates himself. It is thus a fundamental characteristic of the divine entering into relationship with the human that this takes shape through individual relationships and that God brings his salvation into the world via the particular. One may

22. Cf. for example Matthias Konradt, *Israel, Church, and the Gentiles in the Gospel of Matthew*, trans. Kathleen Ess (Baylor-Mohr Siebeck Studies in Early Christianity; Waco, TX: Baylor University Press, 2014): 76; Matthias Konradt, *Das Evangelium nach Matthäus* (Göttingen: Vandenhoeck & Ruprecht, 2015): 160.

23. Cf. also Jean-Miguel Garrigues, "The Jewishness of the Apostles and Its Implications for the Apostolic Church," in Kinzer, *Searching Her Own Mystery* (see note 3), 198–215, esp. 202–204.

even see in this a characteristic of a historically rather than cosmically conceived form of religiosity, insofar as particularity and individuality are fundamental dimensions of historicity. And this *universale concretissimum*, as Hans Urs von Balthasar formulated it with a Christological intention, now bears Jewish features—as does God's election of the people of Israel. This may be perceived as an irritation or even as a barrier to reception—but from the Judaeo-Christian perspective on the history of revelation it is a fact inescapably assigned to theology for reflection.

For the analysis of this apparent "aporia of the concrete," theological categories such as sacramentality—that is, symbolism combined with impact potential of a concrete corporal entity—and representation[24] were used. Ecclesiology in this context often refers to the Second Vatican Council's dogmatic constitution *Lumen Gentium* (no. 9) which says:

> So it is that that messianic people, although it does not actually include all men, and at times may look like a small flock, is nonetheless a lasting and sure seed of unity, hope and salvation for the whole human race. Established by Christ as a communion of life, charity and truth, it is also used by Him as an instrument for the redemption of all, and is sent forth into the whole world as the light of the world and the salt of the earth. (Cf. Mt. 5:13–16.)

In what follows, however, it is not primarily the sacramental or representational mission of the Church for the world that is to be considered, but its fundament, that is, the Church's relationship to Israel, and the question of how sacramentality or even representation realizes itself therein.

In the Old Testament, the category of representation refers primarily to individuals,[25] but against the background of increasingly evident "universalistic features in the religion of Israel,"[26] one can also apply this category to all of Israel. At least the election of Israel can be thought

24. "direct proportionality of unity and diversity between a representing and represented reality" ["direkte Proportionalität von Einheit und Verschiedenheit zwischen einer vertretenden und einer vertretenen Wirklichkeit"]—Karl-Heinz Menke, *Stellvertretung. Schlüsselbegriff christlichen Lebens und theologische Grundkategorie* (Sammlung Horizonte, N.F. 29; Einsiedeln: Johannesverlag, 1991): 20.

25. *Ibid.*, 30–33.

26. "universalistischen Zug in der Religion Israels"—Joseph Ratzinger, *Glaube – Wahrheit – Toleranz. Das Christentum und die Weltreligionen* (Freiburg i. Br.: Herder, 2003): 123.

of as comprising a fruitful symbolism or a sacramental openness: "The gentile nations are . . . inscribed in Israel's election even before Israel exists as such."[27] Israel is a blessing for the nations (Gen 12:3), an "instrument . . . by which other human beings may come to know Him,"[28] and Israel's calling is a "beginning . . . to be completed in that the chosen people will also invite the nations to worship the true God."[29] Israel can thus be seen in a symbolic or even representational role among the nations, until they themselves turn toward the God of Israel; Israel should be an effective, that is, a credible sign for the relationship to God, and Israel holds a place open for others to join in the worship of God. This, however, does not imply that the salvation-historical mission of Israel comes to an end with the creation of the Church: The Old Testament idea of the pilgrimage of the nations to Zion can resonate with the hope that one day all nations as a representation of the whole of humanity will pray to the God of Israel—a promise whose *telos* has obviously not yet become reality, with the effect that the symbolism or the representativity of the election of Israel remains. An analogous interpretation of the Church's sacramentality would therefore have to be seen as a prolongation of the sacramentality of Israel under the specific conditions of the universal mission and world-encompassing openness of the Church.

Conversely, it may be argued that the Church as the Body of Christ—or, originally and principally the Jewish-Christian current within it—should, according to the divine will, stand in a salvation-historical service to Judaism. That God, "out of his free choice gave to some, who look like a remnant, an additional knowledge [*Zu-Erkenntnis*] and that

27. "Die ausländischen Nationen sind . . . , schon bevor Israel als solches existiert, in dessen Erwählung eingeschrieben."—Michael P. Maier, *Völkerwallfahrt im Jesajabuch* (Beihefte zur Zeitschrift für die alttestamentliche Wissenschaft, 474; Berlin: De Gruyter, 2016): 4.

28. "Werkzeug . . . , damit die anderen Menschen Ihn kennenlernen können"—*Ibid.*, 6.

29. "Anfang . . . , der sich darin vollenden soll, daß das erwählte Volk auch die Völker zur Verehrung des wahren Gottes einladen wird"—Richard Schaeffler, *Philosophische Einübung in die Theologie*, vol. 3: *Philosophische Einübung in die Ekklesiologie und Christologie* (Scientia & Religio 1/3; Freiburg i. Br.: Alber, 2004): 137. Cf., e.g., also Hans W. Wolff, "Zur Hermeneutik des Alten Testaments," in *Probleme alttestamentlicher Hermeneutik. Aufsätze zum Verstehen des Alten Testaments*, ed. Claus Westermann (Theologische Bücherei, 11,3; Munich: Kaiser, 1968): 140–80, at 153.

these have accepted Christ, is for 'the whole of Israel' a sign that God has not rejected the rest either";[30] the salvation that God wants to bring about through the community of those who are in a relationship with Christ, is not a salvation *against* Israel or *bypassing* Israel, but *for* Israel. In a special way, Jews who believe in Christ are called to be a sign for Jews who do not believe in Christ or even to represent them in an explicit relation to Christ—through a lifestyle that makes it recognizable that there is a relationship to the *God of Israel*. This genuinely Jewish-Christian task may in the course of time have been conferred also upon the non-Jewish Christian community—which, however, deeply failed in this regard and instead of being a sign "stood there as an obstacle . . . , as a shadow between God and his people and the land of Israel."[31]

Thus, we can identify a certain functional reciprocity here: Just as Israel has a symbolic (or a representative) function for the nations and the nations can in a sense only find God *in* Israel, Christians (Jewish and non-Jewish believers in Christ) can be a sign for Israel or can assume a representative role for Israel in an explicit Christ relationship. Mark Kinzer, too, conceives of a reciprocal representative relationship when he assumes that, on the one hand, the sacramental life of Judaism is effective in the Church in a vicarious way after the marginalization of Jewish Christendom,[32] while, on the other hand, God accepts the worship of Jesus Christ, Israel's Messiah, through the Church as vicarious for a corresponding practice in Israel.[33] Expressed more simply: Israel representatively leads a sacramental life for the Church, and the Church worships the Jewish Messiah of Israel, Jesus Christ, in representation of Israel. Thus, it can be theologically assumed both for Israel's relationship with God and for the Church's relationship with Christ that each can unfold a hidden effective power which, according to the

30. "aus seiner freien Wahl einigen, die wie ein Rest aussehen, eine Zu-Erkenntnis schenkte, und diese Christus angenommen haben, ist für 'Ganz-Israel' ein Zeichen, daß Gott auch die übrigen nicht verstoßen hat"—Maria-Irma Seewann, "Über die Zu-Erkenntnis (ἐπίγνωσις) der Juden. Bibeltheologische Überlegungen," in *NOMOS und andere Vorarbeiten zur Reihe "Paulus neu gelesen,"* ed. Norbert Baumert (Forschung zur Bibel, 122; Würzburg: Echter, 2010): 421–26, at 424.

31. "als Hindernis . . . , als Schatten da[stand] zwischen Gott und seinem Volk und Land Israel"—*Ibid.*, 425.

32. Cf. Kinzer, *Searching Her Own Mystery* (see note 3), 168.

33. *Ibid.*, 170.

saving will of God, functions as sign and as instrument for a salvific reality that transcends their own individual realm—in a hidden way that is ordered toward the still-pending full realization and that, until the time of its occurrence, represents a weakened form of its fulfillment. With this, a hidden mutual reference is expressed as well as the hope that both forms of religious life can exercise for the other a healing and correcting power.[34]

Admittedly, further reflection would be required on the question of whether it is the category of effective symbolism (sacramentality) or that of representation that enables a more appropriate theological interpretation of the respective forms of being-for one another. This question is complex and cannot be decided in a general way. Biblically and in terms of magisterial teaching, sacramentality appears to be the better-founded category, and with regard to an ecclesiological use of the category of representation, admittedly there remains need for further clarification. For both figures of thought, however, the connection of a basic theocentric dimension with an anthropological component is fundamental: It is God who gives a sacramental significance and effectiveness to a relation constituted by him, and it is also God who bestows on a contingent and temporal entity a representative power beyond its own capabilities. Both figures of thought thus denote the participation of finite entities in God's work of salvation which can only be explained from the divine power itself.

But however one interprets this reciprocal sacramentality or representation, one thing is certainly implied: Christ-believing Jews or members of the Messianic Jewish current compose the nucleus of this in a unique way. This can be said because in them the two services overlap: On the one hand, they stand in a symbolic or representative way for the nations in a relationship to the God of Israel, and on the other hand, they stand in a symbolic or representative way for Israel in a relationship to the Messiah, Jesus Christ. At least partially this entails the possibility of a proleptic, symbolic approximation of the full form of a bond between Judaism and Christianity which, however, cannot be achieved in the individual existence of Jewish Christ-believers, but

34. Cf. Mark S. Kinzer, "Finding Our Way Through Nicaea. The Deity of Yeshua, Bilateral Ecclesiology, and Redemptive Encounter with the Living God," *Kesher* 24 (2019): 29–52, at 34.

only in a broadly communal, Spirit-led way that brings outer and inner ecclesial realities into congruence with each other.

4. A question of ecumenism?

All these considerations, however, lead to one fundamental follow-up question: How is the present relationship between the Messianic Jewish current, which sees itself as part of Judaism, and the institutionally constituted Catholic Church to be evaluated? If the previous considerations were primarily aimed at the Church of Jesus Christ as a spiritually hidden (and historically again and again also obscured) entity, then the question unavoidably arises—not least in light of the self-understanding of the Catholic Church (*LG* 8)—whether or how the foundational relationship between the *ecclesia ex gentibus* and the *ecclesia ex circumcisione* can become visible in an institutional way. This problem will be discussed here in the form of a very concrete question: Is the relation of the *ecclesia ex gentibus* to the *ecclesia ex circumcisione* a question of ecumenical theology, as it is often referred to in discussions?

In a certain way this seems not only comprehensible, but even highly convincing, insofar as differences between varying external forms of lived Christ relationship are usually treated as a question of ecumenism and insofar as the concern to make the *ecclesia ex circumcisione* in the form of Christ-believing Jews recognizable and present inside the Church is ecclesiologically justified. Of course, the institutional realization of the Church is to be measured by the extent to which it corresponds to or represents the inner reality of grace which is hiddenly present in it. If it is true that the Church in her innermost essence refers to Israel and is constituted in a foundational and irreducible inner plurality[35] of Jewish believers and a gentile Christian branch—as Mark Kinzer says, in a "bilateral ecclesiology"[36]—then it should even be postulated that there is also an external, palpable, and institutional echo

35. This is formulated clearly in the document "The Gifts and the Calling of God Are Irrevocable" (see note 1), No. 43—"It is and remains a qualitative definition of the Church of the New Covenant that it consists of Jews and Gentiles, even if the quantitative proportions of Jewish and Gentile Christians may initially give a different impression." On the biblical basis of this view, cf. the article by Thomas Schumacher in the present volume.

36. Developed in detail in Kinzer, *Post-Missionary Messianic Judaism* (see note 9).

of this inner dimension of her being. And this would also justify the concern to seek this form by means of ecumenical efforts.

On the other hand, there remain some fundamental questions with regard to the classification of the relationship between the *ecclesia ex circumcisione* and the *ecclesia ex gentibus* as an ecumenical relationship: Firstly, from an ecclesiological point of view the relation of the *ecclesia ex gentibus* and the *ecclesia ex circumcisione* is about something even more important and deeper than is generally the case in ecumenical relations. And secondly, the ecumenical approach, at least for the time being, is associated with a danger that must be taken seriously. I shall explain both aspects in more detail in the following.

(1) In the first instance, it must be asked: Is not the relationship to Christ-believing or Messianic Judaism so foundational for the Church that it constitutes a basic dimension of every ecclesiology rather than a question of ecumenism? This formulation in no way intends to diminish the ecclesiological importance of ecumenical efforts. But ecclesiologically it is at least not impossible to regard ecumenical efforts as a subordinate problem, whose approach comes onto the theological agenda only as a follow-up question to an independently constituted full ecclesiality of one's own denomination—and that would, according to the previous considerations, unquestionably be too little when it is about the relationship to the Jewish-Christian branch of the Church: What is at stake here is rather the very essence of the Church herself. In addition, the category of an "ecumenical" relationship does not completely clarify the objectives connected with it; concretely, what degree of internal differentiation the community to be achieved by ecumenical efforts should have. Certainly, it has become increasingly clear throughout the history of the ecumenical movement that a uniform Church in which the multiplicity of distinct Christian traditions and styles of faith would be blurred is not particularly desirable. With regard to the relationship between the *ecclesia ex circumcisione* and the *ecclesia ex gentibus,* however, a specific clarification of the goal of any possible approximation should be stated: Under no circumstances may it ever happen (again) that a Jewish-Christian current is simply absorbed by the Church of the nations in such a way that it merges with it and vanishes in it forever. The *ecclesia ex circumcisione* must be recognizable in the Church and must remain distinguishable; a unity worthy to be striven for would therefore definitely have to be a unity with clear markers of

a fundamental intra-ecclesial distinction on the institutional level—a formulation which probably cannot be held in the same clarity with regard to the aims usually associated with ecumenical efforts and which accordingly marks a fundamental divergence between the non-Jewish Christian ecumenism on the one hand and the relationship between the *ecclesia ex circumcisione* and the *ecclesia ex gentibus* on the other. To classify the latter relationship as a question of ecumenism would always be in danger of conceptually blurring and thus leveling the aforementioned fundamental differences, since the concept of ecumenism is incapable of representing those differences terminologically. A use of the category of ecumenism in view of the relationship between the *ecclesia ex circumcisione* and the *ecclesia ex gentibus*, although it is not altogether wrong, thus causes more unclarity and misunderstanding than it avoids. Such an outcome should be reason enough to challenge and find alternatives for any terminology—in this case the language of ecumenism.

(2) Admittedly, this problem of terminological ambiguity could be addressed by demanding greater terminological precision; thus, it would be conceivable and sensible, for example, to speak of "proto-ecumenism" or of a "proto-ecumenical" connection with regard to the relationship between *ecclesia ex circumcisione* and *ecclesia ex gentibus* and in this way avoid or at least reduce the potential for misunderstanding that accompanies the use of this term. Nevertheless, there would remain a danger that does not lie in terminology, but in the matter itself—that is, in the institutional integration of Messianic Judaism into the Church: the danger of appropriating something unavailable, which should remain in consciousness *as such*. The questions that arise in this context are the following: Would not an institutional incorporation of Messianic Judaism into the Church strengthen an intra-Jewish split? And above all: May not the striving for an institutional integration in a certain way again become the expression of a desire to settle, to classify, to conform, and to domesticate—even up to the danger of finding oneself again on the slippery slope toward forced conversion, and the danger of institutionally obscuring the unearned grace of being invited into a relationship with the God of Israel? Or, to put it differently: Can it be reasonably ruled out at the present time and in light of the factual spread, depth, and rootedness of an Israel-theological sensitivity in the Church (and that means of course: in all her levels, concretizations, players, and currents) that an institutional integration could lead again

to the absorption of Jewish Christianity and thus to a repetition of an earlier, fatal aberration? This question could only be affirmed with clear conscience if Christ-believing Judaism were understood unequivocally and unanimously as a sacramental sign for the constitutive connection of the Church to the first-chosen people and as an essential feature of intra-Christian diversity. As long as this is not the case, the threat of renewed concealment, suppression, and eradication of Jewish identity in the Church remains—and this means that with regard to the relationship between the *ecclesia ex circumcisione* and the *ecclesia ex gentibus,* the classical objective of ecumenical efforts, the rapprochement or unification of separated Churches encompassing inner and outer dimensions of ecclesiality, must currently be assessed as problematic.

Of course, this reservation does not imply that no connection with Messianic Judaism should be sought on an institutional level, nor that the problem outlined here should be viewed as a constitutive problem (rather than a contingent one, that is, a problem due to a certain non-necessary circumstance)—and certainly not that the Messianic Jewish community should remain an amorphous, institutionally invisible entity. As long, however, as no fundamental changes with regard to the self-understanding of the Church and her relationship to Israel have been made, concerns can be expressed about any institutional *integration* of Messianic Judaism into the Church. As a consequence of the guilty self-absolutization of the *ecclesia ex gentibus,* there is still a way to go here before the ecclesiologically important approximation of the Church's external constitution and her inner reality can take place. An ecclesiological renunciation in this regard, or a temporary suspension of corresponding efforts, could perhaps also be understood as an expression of repentance—if and precisely insofar as the Church continues to strive theologically to become more conscious of her foundational relationship to Israel and to overcome the after-effects of replacement theology and anti-Judaism.

5. Conclusion

It has become clear that dealing with the phenomenon of Messianic Judaism raises a number of ecclesiological reflections—partly resulting from the question of the ecclesiological significance of Jewish believers in Christ, but also because an examination of Messianic Judaism decisively demands a strengthening of Israel theology in the field of ecclesiology. With respect to the latter, a number of valuable theological approaches do already exist, though they still need to be given a broader ecclesiological reception. Yet one thing becomes clear again and again in the reflections on those questions, namely that the theological, and in particular the ecclesiological conceptual categories are not able to express adequately and unequivocally the *mysterium* of the Church's relationship to Israel and to Christ-believing Jews—a *mysterium* which on the one hand is constitutive for the Church, but on the other hand should not be absorbed or appropriated institutionally: The category "ecumenical" applies, as discussed, to the relationship between Messianic Jews and the non-Jewish Church at most only in a not-unproblematic and terminologically unclear way. And with regard to the relationship between Judaism and Christianity, a comprehensive talk of "ecclesiology" or "Church" seems to prohibit itself (although certain reasons could be given that might justify such terminological usage). This is also the case with a leveling use of the people-of-God concept. After all, there is not only an exclusionary, but also an appropriating form of replacement theology, which does not explicitly deny Israel's lasting salvation-historical significance but seeks to domesticate and integrate it ecclesiologically. This finding, however, considering the epistemological significance of terms and concepts, must be evaluated as a telling expression of an unsatisfactory reflective situation and a lack of theological problem awareness. And even if the indicated terminological problem does not make a precise discussion of the *ecclesia ex circumcisione* and the *ecclesia ex gentibus* totally impossible, it certainly complicates a concise and generally comprehensible theological expression in this field and thus is likely to contribute again to misunderstandings and misinterpretations. In any case, this observation demonstrates that yet more conceptual effort in the discipline of ecclesiology is necessary here.

(Translated by the author herself from the German: "Abkehr vom Substitutionsdenken und Wiederentdeckung der ecclesia ex circumcisione. *Ekklesiologische Reflexionen angesichts des messianischen Judentums")*

Rediscovering the "Church of the Nations" in Light of Messianic Judaism

Response to Ursula Schumacher

James Earle Patrick

THE PRESENT REALITY OF MESSIANIC JUDAISM as a collective expression of Jewish belief in Jesus, whether within or outside the institutional churches, has directed the attention of theologians once more to the bilateral composition and ethnic complementarity of the Church as *ecclesia ex circumcisione* and *ecclesia ex gentibus*—called from the Jews and from the nations to be united in Messiah (Rom 10:11–13; Eph 2:18). Ursula Schumacher's stimulating reflections from a doctrinal and dogmatic perspective address the implications for the Church's theological speech about itself as "the people of God" and as "one, holy, catholic and apostolic" from the Nicene creed. She makes some intriguing proposals about the sacramental and representational role of Jesus-believing Jews both toward "the fullness of nations" and toward "all Israel." And she rightly challenges the value of ecumenical relationships as a model for the Church's approach to the Messianic Jewish phenomenon. All three points deserve detailed engagement from various perspectives, but this response will consider each point (in reverse order) specifically in relation to its implications for the *ecclesia ex gentibus*.

Most believers from the nations fail to recognize this as their own identity, defined in relation to Jewish believers in Jesus (JBJs), and instead assume that they themselves represent the ethnically neutral

"Church" which exists over and against Israel.[1] Knowing their own status as a redeemed member of one of the non-Jewish nations, who all carry their own distinct promises from God in Scripture, will help more gentile believers to celebrate the complementary identity of JBJs and their relation to the nation of Israel.

One preliminary question, to avoid potentially anachronistic interpretations, relates to how we translate *ethnê* in the New Testament. Given how Scripture shaped the authors' worldview, we might be wise to assume unless demonstrably otherwise that the word still preserves a real sense of its corporate meaning "nations" or else "representatives of the nations," corresponding to its consistent use throughout the Septuagint and Hebrew Bible. Paul never used the term for a single "Gentile," but contrasted the singular "Jew/Judaean" with the "Greek" instead (Rom 2:9–10; 10:12; Gal 3:28; Col 3:11). This was no longer the case for later rabbinic writers, who used *goy* (Gentile) for an individual "idolater" regardless of his specific ethnic identity.[2] Yet Paul still envisioned his apostolic task in terms of multiple distinct "nations" (Rom 1:5; 9:25; 15:26–27; 16:26), and Peter is recorded addressing Cornelius and his household not as generic "Gentiles" but as members of certain nations; "in every nation the man who fears him and does what is right is welcome to him" (Acts 10:35).

1. For a clear description of this problematic perspective, see Caroline Johnson Hodge, *If Sons, Then Heirs: A Study of Kinship and Ethnicity in the Letters of Paul* (Oxford: Oxford University Press, 2007), 47.

2. Matthew 18:17 does use *ethnikos* for an individual from the nations, and its plural in 5:47, 6:7 (also 3 John 1:7). Cf. Terrence L. Donaldson, "'Gentile Christianity' as a Category in the Study of Christian Origins," *Harvard Theological Review* 106 (2013): 433–58, at 449–51; James M. Scott, *Paul and the Nations: The Old Testament and Jewish Background of Paul's Mission to the Nations with Special Reference to the Destination of Galatians* (Wissenschaftliche Untersuchungen zum Neuen Testament, 84; Tübingen: Mohr Siebeck, 1995), 121–34, esp. 123. Ishay Rosen-Zvi and Adi Ophir propose in "Paul and the Invention of the Gentiles," *Jewish Quarterly Review* 105 (2015): 1–41, that Paul himself systematized the shift from the biblical meaning "nation" to the Mishna's individualized *"goy"* (cf. Ishay Rosen-Zvi and Adi Ophir, "Goy: Toward a Genealogy," *Dine Israel* 28 (2011): 69–122). Yet it is possible to argue for Paul just as they allow for earlier second-temple writers, that "even in the most privatized usages the biblical meaning is preserved" (p.10 n.33). For Paul, the distinctions between nations were less important theologically than their shared complementary relation with Israel, hence his regular references to the "nations" as a category.

Beginning with Ursula's third topic of ecumenism, Christian history has multiplied divisions of doctrinal confession and institutional structure through the centuries, resulting in numerous denominational differences that cannot and should not simply be "painted over" for the sake of unification. However, the biblical "Jewish"/"of-the-nations" distinction is of a more fundamental nature than sectarian separation, even though it has been viewed for much of Christian history as primarily a difference of religious belief and practice.[3] On the contrary, it is at its core an "ethnic" distinction. During a plenary discussion at the Vienna Symposium on the essence of Jewishness, Étienne Vetö was one of several who offered some tentative pointers toward a definition: Jewishness is genealogical more than biological, salvation-historical more than ontological, along with culture and faith, and Jewish people have various combinations of these realities. Defining Jewishness, however inconclusively, has direct implications for defining Gentileness, and specifically the distinction governs what it means to approach God in our God-given embodied reality, not only as individuals but also within collectives. The believer will belong either to Abraham's genealogical offspring by covenant, or to the groups for whom those offspring are destined to be a blessing—"all the families of the ground" (Gen 12:3), "all the nations of the earth" (Gen 18:18).[4]

3. Hence the historical distinction, to some extent, "between religious anti-Judaism and racist antisemitism" as noted on p.19 of the Church of England's 2019 theological document on Christian–Jewish relations, *God's Unfailing Word* (https://www.chpublishing.co.uk/books/9780715111611/gods-unfailing-word [accessed April 11, 2025]). The former corresponds to Rabbi Lord Sacks' first "mutation" of the antisemitism "virus"—a belief-based Judeophobia—and by extension to the second also—"demonic anti-Judaism"—which effectively attributed Jewish stubbornness against the Christian message to direct Satanic influence. Jonathan Sacks, *Future Tense: A Vision for Jews and Judaism in the Global Culture* (London: Hodder & Stoughton, 2009): 92–98.

4. "For Christians accustomed to thinking of themselves in terms of the church/world paradigm, Paul's words [in Rom 11:13a, 18] are profoundly *decentering*. Gentile Christians are jolted awake with the discovery that they *are*—not just *were*—*Gentile*-Christians, with the discovery that they *are*—and not merely *were*—dependent on God's fidelity to a people *other than themselves*."—R. Kendall Soulen, "'They Are Israelites': The Priority of the Present Tense for Jewish–Christian Relations," in *Between Gospel and Election: Explorations in the Interpretation of Romans 9–11*, ed. Florian Wilk and J. Ross Wagner, with Frank Schleritt (Wissenschaftliche Untersuchungen zum Neuen Testament, 257; Tübingen: Mohr Siebeck, 2010): 497–504, at 502 (emphasis original). Article adapted as ch. 7 of R. Kendall

Our new shared identity in Messiah enables us to accept one another in unity despite our ongoing diversity, which it does not eradicate. The fact that God still values our embodied and societal identity has wider theological and practical implications, relating to distinctions of and relations between male/female, parent/child, and even master/servant, highlighted in the Pauline household codes (*Haustafeln*—Eph 5:22–6:9; Col 3:18–4:1; Rom 14:1–15:13 for the Jew/Gentile relationship) as well as in the situational antitheses (Rom 10:12; 1 Cor 12:13; Gal 3:28; Col 3:11). Even if "there is neither Jew nor Greek," this does not abolish physical and social differences. Rather, it emphasizes that these are not conditions for baptism and participation in Messiah, even if they were for circumcision. Sexual and social and ethnic differentiation continues for believers, just as one body has many members that are different but all equal in value because they belong in the body. "Once in this community, of course, the baptized person must still contend with her or his cultural, economic, and gendered status as well as with the differing status of others."[5]

Some interpreters suggest that these differences will finally be abolished in the eschaton, yet biblical pictures of the coming age still include some such distinctions, most notably the pilgrimage of nations to Messiah in the city of Jerusalem (Mic 4:1–8; Rev 21:22–27). Even when Jesus describes the resurrected as those who "neither marry nor are given in marriage," this dual expression assumes ongoing male/female distinctions. The reason for marriage not happening in that age is not because of abolished sexual differences, but because "they cannot die any more" and thus do not need to reproduce (Luke 20:34–36). Far from downplaying ethnic identity as obsolete, Paul describes the believer's embodied and societal characteristics as a "gift from God," which is why he directs that "Each man must remain in that calling in which he was called" (1 Cor 7:7, 17–27). This applies specifically to the Jewish/Gentile distinction with regard to circumcision, even among believers (1 Cor 7:18).[6] Thus Paul was willing to affirm publicly the ongoing value

Soulen, *Irrevocable: The Name of God and the Unity of the Christian Bible* (Minneapolis, MN: Fortress, 2022): 135–44.

5. Troy W. Martin, "The Covenant of Circumcision (Genesis 17:9–14) and the Situational Antitheses in Galatians 3:28," *Journal of Biblical Literature* 122 (2003): 111–25, at 121.

6. Paula Fredriksen, *Paul, the Pagans' Apostle* (New Haven, CT: Yale University Press): 113–17, see also 73–89.

of circumcision and Torah and customs of the elders for ethnically Jewish believers (Acts 16:1–3; 21:21, 24; 28:17), as long as these outward expressions of Jewish identity do not compromise table fellowship with gentile believers (Gal 2:11–14). Likewise for the *ecclesia ex gentibus*, how far each gentile ethnicity is also still to be celebrated depends upon all of its traditions being submitted to Messiah and to the need for practical unity within the Body (Rom 14:5–6; 15:10).[7]

In his proper concern to emphasize communal Jewish identity, Kinzer has implied that according to Luke–Acts, ethnic characteristics are uniquely important for Jewish believers, whereas Gentiles are addressed as individuals only; "No 'corporate' gentile response from each of the 'nations' is sought or required."[8] However, Paul's sermon in Athens, one of two recorded speeches in Acts before a gentile audience,[9] does affirm that the Creator actively "made . . . every nation of mankind . . . having determined [their] appointed times and the boundaries of their habitation, that they would seek God" (Acts 17:26). There is a distinct and God-given corporate identity for each nation, "made" and maintained by the God of their "one" father Noah, for the express purpose that they might collectively "seek" and "find" their Creator to enjoy a unique relationship with him. The same is implied by the parallel in Ephesians 1:12–14 between "we" Jewish believers and "you" believers of the nations, each of whom receive the Holy Spirit as a pledge of "inheritance" and "redemption of [our] possession" in the age to come. These words have unavoidable connotations of land for a Jewish audience, and thus also for other nations in their own lands

7. Paul sought to define the limits of acceptable gentile ethnic expression in Messiah (1 Cor 5:1; 12:2; 1 Thes 4:3), as explored by Caroline Johnson Hodge, "The Question of Identity: Gentiles as Gentiles—but Also Not—in Pauline Communities," in *Paul Within Judaism: Restoring the First-Century Context to the Apostle*, ed. Mark D. Nanos and Magnus Zetterholm (Minneapolis, MN: Fortress, 2015): 153–73, at 156, 164–67.

8. Mark S. Kinzer, *Jerusalem Crucified, Jerusalem Risen: The Resurrected Messiah, the Jewish People, and the Land of Promise* (Eugene, OR: Cascade, 2018), 140–41. Similarly Fredriksen, *Paul, the Pagans' Apostle* (see note 6), 114—"Paul maintains . . . the distinction between Israel and the nations . . . [but he does] erase the distinctions between and among 'the nations' themselves," citing Rosen-Zvi and Ophir's 2011 and 2015 articles (see note 2). On the contrary, as Hodge points out, Paul's "totalizing language does not de-ethnicize these peoples, but it strategically constructs and highlights a particular facet of their identity, the fact that they are not Jews"—Hodge, *If Sons, Then Heirs* (see note 1), 49.

9. Kinzer, *Jerusalem Crucified, Jerusalem Risen* (see note 8), 130–31.

through Messiah (Acts 20:32; 26:17–18), as the prophets expected (Mic 4:3–4; Zec 8:20–23; 14:16–17).[10] Paul saw the inheritance "of the world" by Abraham or his Seed still in terms of "many nations" (Rom 4:13, 17), just as the "families" to be blessed by Abram (Gen 12:3) had earlier been depicted in Genesis 10, each within their ethnic territory, distinguished variously by land, language, family, or nation. Every people group receives inheritance from God (Deut 2:5, 9, 12, 19).[11]

Consequently, applying this back to the question of ecumenism, we must ask how the multiplicity of denominations can reconceive their local embodied expressions in terms of the biblical vision of "the fullness of the nations" (Rom 11:25). International networks can have value, as Paul's apostolic mission illustrates (1 Cor 7:17; 11:16; 16:1; 2 Cor 8:1, 18–24; 2 Thes 1:4), but unity is manifested by those who can "dwell together," "come together," and "assemble" in person to enact Messiah's authority (Ps 133:1; 1 Cor 11:18; 5:4; Matt 18:17–20). New Testament epistles are addressed to churches defined by their city or region (e.g. 1 Cor 1:2), united despite different apostolic heritages (1 Cor 1:10–13). Perhaps "nations" and similar geographical, ethnolinguistic terms are still the God-ordained expression of diversity within the eschatological Body of Messiah, toward which we ought to strive in our efforts for ecclesial unity-in-diversity (Rev 5:9–10; 7:9–10).

Second, in relation to Ursula's idea of the sacramental or representative function that points ahead to "the fullness of nations," this can be seen as belonging properly to Israel as a whole, not just to Jewish believers in Jesus. Deuteronomy 32:8 seems to interpret God's separation of mankind into seventy nations at the Tower of Babylon (Gen 10; 11:1–9) as a

10. The divine "inheritance" in Eph 1:18, usually read back into 1:14, instead adds another dimension of the term, as paired also in Deut 32:8 and 9. Ephesians hints at this grounded ecclesiology elsewhere too (see also below, note 17). For example, "rule and authority and power and dominion" (1:21; cf. 3:10; 6:12—"world-powers") includes current regional rulers (cf. Col 1:16; Dan 10:13, 20–21 LXX) whose domains will be inherited by the multinational *ekklesia* "in the ages to come" (2:7). Cf. Ernst R. Wendland, "Contextualising the potentates, Principalities and Powers in the Epistle to the Ephesians," *Neotestamentica* 33 (1999): 199–223, at 201 n.5, 218.

11. *Pace* Denys N. McDonald, "'Ex-Pagan Pagans'? Paul, Philo, and Gentile Ethnic Reconfiguration," *Journal for the Study of the New Testament* 45 (2022): 23–50, at 34–35.

prophetic preparation for the representative and salvific role of Israel.[12] Jacob had seventy direct descendants when God took him out of the promised land and into Egypt, effectively sending him into the nations (Gen 46:4, 8–27). This is echoed in Zechariah's prophecy that each language group will take hold of one Jew in order to go up to the LORD in Jerusalem (Zec 8:23; cf. 8:13). Israel in its original formation therefore pointed to God's destiny for all nations, and it continues to bear this sacramental role as God's chosen means of grace for all nations. Yet its fulfillment can only be achieved through Israel's redemption, which is why Paul as a redeemed Jew identified with the missional call upon his nation (Acts 13:45–47). If JBJs are a remnant who represent their nation's calling, the believing remnant of any gentile nation can likewise represent and fulfill their own nation's destiny by assisting with *aliyah* (Isa 11:10–12; 49:22–23; 66:18–20), when they "take hold of the robe of a Jew" who is returning to Jerusalem.[13]

The question of the sacramental or representative function of the Church can therefore be seen in its constituent parts, and not just in the mutual significance of Church and Israel for one another as Kinzer has explored.[14] JBJs are both the remnant of Israel and also the first fruits of their nation's redemption (Rom 11:16; Eph 1:12; James 1:18; Rev 14:4),[15] and their current representational role in weakness and dishonor like their Master will be transformed into one of authority and honor when he is revealed (Matt 19:27–30; Luke 22:28–30).[16] Gen-

12. The Masoretic text "sons of Israel" in this verse is arguably making clearer the intended meaning of the Dead Sea Scrolls reading "sons of God" (4QDt[j]; cf. Deut 32:5–6, 19–20) which had given rise to the misinterpretation "angels" in the Septuagint here. This explanation is overlooked by, e.g., Michael S. Heiser, "Deuteronomy 32:8 and the Sons of God," *Bibliotheca Sacra* 158 (Jan-Mar 2001): 52–74.

13. Paul's financial collection among the churches of the nations (Rom 15:25–28; 1 Cor 16:1-4; 2 Cor 8–9; etc.) would represent a parallel eschatological fulfillment of scriptures such as Isa 60:5, 11.

14. Mark S. Kinzer, *Searching Her Own Mystery:* Nostra Aetate, *the Jewish People, and the Identity of the Church* (Eugene, OR: Cascade, 2015): 168–70.

15. Dan G. Johnson, "The Structure and Meaning of Romans 11," *Catholic Biblical Quarterly* 46 (1984): 91–103, at 98–99.

16. Cf. David L. Turner, "His Glorious Throne: Israel and the Gentiles in Mission and Judgment in the Gospel of Matthew," in *Matthew Within Judaism: Israel and the Nations in the First Gospel*, ed. Anders Runesson and Daniel M. Gurtner (Early Christianity and its Literature, 27; Atlanta, GA: SBL, 2020): 135–68, esp. 149–53. Given the parallels between unending mission to the tribes of Israel and to the nations

tile believers function in precisely the same way in relation to their own nations, as first fruits (e.g., 2 Thes 2:13; Rom 16:5; 1 Cor 16:15) who carry the promise that they too will reign as royal priests on the earth (Rev 5:9–10; 20:4–6), each for their respective nations. In this way, the Church in its fullness will represent all humanity before the throne in a sacramental and intercessory role on behalf of humanity, uniting and perfecting all of its diversity (Rev 7:4–10; 1 Cor 6:2; Eph 3:10).[17]

Finally, speaking of the "apostolic" nature of the Church, the fourth *nota ecclesiae*, Ursula is right to emphasize the Jewishness of the Church's original apostolic dimension, since the twelve Apostles were to represent the twelve tribes of Israel. She then raises the question of a distinct Spirit-governed apostolicity in the Church of the nations, but warns of latent supersessionism unless they also acknowledge continuity with the fundamental and abiding Jewishness of apostolicity. To support this, I suggest it is worth looking more closely at how Luke's Gospel balances the Twelve (Luke 6:13; 9:1) with the Seventy (Luke 10:1). Both groups are "sent" as numerical representatives of the redeemed nation of Israel (Exod 1:2–5), "apostles" of the Lord to bring about his redemption of first the tribes of Israel and then all seventy nations, in "every city and place where He Himself was going to come" (Luke 10:1; Isa 49:3, 5–6).[18]

(Matt 10:5–6; 28:19–20), and between the judgment of Israel and of all the nations when the Son of Man is enthroned (Matt 19:28; 25:31–46), both analyzed in Turner's article (158–65), it is reasonable to see deliberate parallels drawn also between the rulership of the twelve disciples and the "inherit[ance of] the kingship" by the righteous among the nations.

17. *Pace* J. Albert Harrill, "Ethnic Fluidity in Ephesians," *New Testament Studies* 60 (2014): 379–402, who sees in the "one new humanity" ecclesiology of Ephesians an instance of the standard Roman method of creating a new blended (transnational) ethnicity. On the contrary, while believers from the nations are urged to think and act differently from their ethnic groups (Eph 4:17–19), they still remain "of the nations" (2:11; 3:1, 6). In fact, when depicting how the ascended Messiah lays the Church's shared foundation of apostles etc. (2:20; 4:11), the image evoked by the quotation in 4:8 is of Israel's victorious divine King leading in procession first Israelite tribes and then conquered rulers of every other nation (Ps 68:18, 24–32; note female evangelists also in 68:11).

18. Theoretically one might interpret the Seventy as signifying not so much the nations themselves, but the scattered children of Israel among all seventy nations (e.g. Acts 11:19), to be gathered by Messiah (John 7:33–35; 10:16 [= Ezek 37:22–24]; 11:51–52) back into the "fold" of their united "nation" (10:16; 11:50; 18:35). But

Already before Paul's unique call as "apostle to the nations," the Seventy represented Israel's corporate call to go to the nations (Matt 28:19). As such, no nation of the *ecclesia ex gentibus* can claim to have received its gospel blessing unmediated, directly from Jesus, "the Apostle and High Priest of our confession" (Heb 3:1). The apostles of Israel were sent out on his behalf, rightly "entrusted with the oracles of God," so every nation is individually indebted to the Jewish nation for sharing their spiritual riches with the world (Rom 3:2; 15:25–27).

As such, it is right to see the Church/*ecclesia* collectively as the "eschatological people of God," but only in its end-time fullness when both "the fullness of nations" and "all Israel" are included (Rom 11:25–26). On the one hand, the *ecclesia* from every nation is grafted in to participate in Israel's divine election as the "people of God" (1 Pet 2:10). On the other hand, the *ecclesia* from Israel fulfills its original destiny only in bringing salvation to all nations (Rom 11:30–32), who will each in turn become the "people of God" as well (Isa 19:23–25).

I trust that this brief evaluation and development of some of Ursula's proposals, for the sake of an ecclesiology of the *ecclesia ex gentibus*, is a tribute to the quality of her own reflections on the significance of the *ecclesia ex circumcisione* for Christian theology.

---

given that the ingathering of Israel's exiles would not only be accompanied by the ingathering of all nations but also brought about by it (respectively, Isa 56:8; 66:18–20), Messiah himself presumably had both in mind.

Restoration of the Ecclesia ex Circumcisione?

Antoine Lévy, OP

What a difference a question mark makes! I was asked to speak about the restoration of the *ecclesia ex circumcisione*. My only request was to put a question mark at the end of the title of my presentation. Indeed, it is far from granted that this formulation makes sense. In order to speak about restoring an entity, one must not only be sure that one knows about what entity one is talking; one also needs to be certain that such an entity has existed at some point in time.

As is common knowledge, one finds the expression *ecclesia ex circumcisione* on an early fifth-century mosaic of the Basilica di Santa Sabina in Rome. It is personified as a veiled woman with a book in her hand, a representation that is symmetrically contrasted with that of another woman holding a book and wearing the insignia of a Roman matron. The latter is characterized beneath as *ecclesia ex gentibus*. Both figures are parts of a dedicatory inscription that commemorates a priest by the name of Peter of Illyria, the founder of Santa Sabina.

Obviously the two *ecclesiae* evoke the two sources out of which the one Church of Christ was born. Still, this is a composition of fifth-century sacred art. Accordingly, one is entitled to ask whether this late-antiquity artistic representation truly talks about some original—albeit lost—ecclesial entity that would need to be restored in order for the Church to be faithful to her identity and vocation. In my opinion,

(Picture: Antoine Lévy)

conceptual as well as historical precision are of the essence here. I would like to begin the considerations that follow by listing a few meanings of the word "restoration," keeping in mind the theological references with which these meanings correlate. I will then scrutinize the historical substrate of the *ecclesia ex circumcisione*. Finally, I will endeavor to bring forward a new reading of the message conveyed by the mosaic of Santa Sabina.

1. Restoration—what restoration?

Using the *Oxford English Dictionary* as my instrument of reference, I am inclined to ascribe three main meanings to the notion of restoration. Let me shortly review them.

The first is the one that comes to mind whenever we hear a syntagm such as "the restoration of the *ecclesia ex circumcisione*." I quote the OED: "The action of restoring a person to a former state or position; the fact of being restored or reinstated." This meaning can be said to encompass that of returning "something lost or stolen." In the Hebrew Bible, both actions are expressed by the same crucial verb: *lehashiv*. God is the one who leads the nation back to the land promised to Abraham. In Jeremiah 16:15, one reads for instance: ". . . 'As the LORD lives, who brought up the sons of Israel from the land of the north and from all the countries where he had banished them.' For I will restore them to their own land [וַהֲשִׁבֹתִים עַל־אַדְמָתָם / *reducam eos in terram suam*] which I gave to their fathers." In Genesis 20, when God speaks in a dream to Abimelech, the king of Gerar who took the wife of Abraham, He says: "Now therefore, restore the man's wife [הָשֵׁב אֵשֶׁת־הָאִישׁ / *redde uxorem viro suo*], for he is a prophet, and he will pray for you, and you will live." What we have in mind is a concrete point in space and time to which we want to go back. In the language that we speak, this point can be identified with a specific social order. As we read in the *Oxford Dictionary*, "the Restoration" as a self-explanatory substantive has come to designate the re-establishment of the monarchy in England with the return of Charles II in 1660, and in France, that of the Bourbons in 1814. The Protestant world developed a similar pattern with the doctrinal constellation that goes by the name of Restorationism. Classical Reformation is satisfied with putting the Church back on her feet, which it identifies with sound Christian faith. Meanwhile, Restorationism, as a spiritual posture that can be found among early Anabaptists and in different forms among Pentecostals and Mormons, brings forward the original apostolic Church as an ecclesiological model and ideal. In order to remedy the current state of degradation of the Church, true Christians should strive to rediscover the first apostolic community and imitate its way of life.

The second main meaning of "restoration" that one finds in the OED has to do with medical art, first in a technical sense, and then in a much wider one: "reduction of a fracture or dislocation . . . anatomical restoration . . . ," hence "the action of restoring a person to health, consciousness, or vigour; recovery of physical strength." Here there is a complete change of semantic register in the Hebrew Bible, probably because the action at stake is no longer about going back from the present to a point in the past, but about a point in the past somehow resurfacing in the present context. Be that as it may, it is a substantive, *arukha*, that expresses this meaning in Hebrew. In Jeremiah 30:17, one reads: "'For I will restore you to health [כִּי אַעֲלֶה אֲרֻכָה לָךְ / *obducam enim cicatricem tibi*], and I will heal you of your wounds,' declares the LORD." One finds the very same semantic register in the passages of the New Testament that tell about Jesus' miraculous healings. For instance, when Jesus heals the man with the desiccated hand in Mark 3:5, one reads: "And after looking around [at the Pharisees] with anger, grieved at their hardness of heart, [Jesus] said to the man, 'Stretch out your hand,' and he stretched it out, and his hand was restored [ἀποκατεστάθη ἡ χεὶρ αὐτοῦ / *restituta est manus illi*]." I will come back to the Greek verb that is used here, ἀποκαθίστημι, literally to "establish or ordain back again."

I would associate another so to speak "technical" meaning of restoration with this second meaning. Here, the use of the word "restoration" simply shifts from the field of medical science to that of architectural engineering. As a physician restores organs to health, likewise a builder restores houses or walls that were damaged. The OED speaks of "the action of building up again or reconstructing; the process of carrying out alterations and repairs with the idea of restoring a building to something like its original form. . . ." In the Hebrew Bible, it is the same substantive, *arukha*, that renders this meaning of restoration. It immediately evokes the restoration of the Temple after the deportation to Babylon. In 2 Chronicles 24:13, one reads: ". . . the workmen labored, and the repair work progressed in their hands [וַתַּעַל אֲרוּכָה לַמְּלָאכָה בְּיָדָם / *obducebatur parietum cicatrix per manus eorum*], and they restored the house of God according to its specifications and strengthened it." The same formula is applied to the renovation of Jerusalem's walls. In the book of Nehemiah, we read that Persian officials became incensed when they heard that "the repair of the walls of Jerusalem went on [כִּי־עָלְתָה אֲרוּכָה לְחֹמוֹת יְרוּשָׁלַםִ / *quod obducta esset cicatrix muri Hierusalem*]" (Neh 4:7 [*Heb* 4:1]). This understanding of restoration as the action of repairing the damages inflicted to the Temple or to the walls of the city finds a remarkable echo in the Jewish tradition, most especially in the Lurianic *kabbalah*. I have in mind the notion of *tikkun olam*, the task of repairing the cracks that followed God's original act of creation. One could say that *tikkun olam* is the principle that grants meaning and purpose to the whole sphere of *mitzvot* or religious observances within Judaism.

We finally come now to the third main meaning of "restoration." The OED speaks rather vaguely of "the action of bringing back in existence, reestablishment, restitution, renewal." The truth is that no definition can easily capture this meaning of the word "restoration." Its use refers to the notion that we mentioned earlier, that of *apokatastasis*. For the Stoics, *apokatastasis* would designate a radical new beginning of things after a general conflagration in an endless series of cosmic cycles. Leaving aside this pre-Nietzschean concept of eternal return, one comes across this very notion, that of a radical new beginning, in the New Testament. In Matthew 17:11, Jesus declares: "Elijah is coming and will restore all things ['Ηλίας μὲν ἔρχεται πρῶτον, καὶ ἀποκαταστήσει πάντα]." Further, in the Acts of the Apostles, *apokatastasis* is clearly identified with the end of history. Peter urges his fellow Jews to repent so that God might "send Jesus, the Christ appointed for you, whom heaven must receive until the period of restoration of all things [ἄχρι χρόνων ἀποκαταστάσεως πάντων], about which God spoke by the mouth of His holy prophets from ancient time" (Acts 3:21). As is well known, *apokatastasis* as a specific teaching regarding the end of time was later associated with Origen's alleged views on universal salvation, including the salvation of demons, a doctrine formally condemned at the second Council of Constantinople in 553.

Now that we have more or less sorted out the three main meanings of "restoration," we can examine which—if any—of these meanings could or should be associated with the notion of *ecclesia ex circumcisione*. What we need to do first is to examine the configuration of the Church in the apostolic times.

2. *"Salvation is from the Jews" (John 4:22): Ecclesiological implications*

Before assigning any theological significance to the fact that the Church was founded by a Jew and his Jewish disciples, one must underscore that it is a historical fact, just as is the involvement of a relatively great number of so-called Jews in the first communities of disciples of Jesus. The question that we are asking here is whether these facts justify speaking of the early existence of an *ecclesia ex circumcisione*. We already know that, if she ever existed, this *ecclesia ex circumcisione* could never have been identical to the one and only true Church. Of course, before the decision to welcome Gentiles on a par with Jews was taken at the Council of Jerusalem (Acts 15), the disciples were Jews, and these Jews formed the one and only Church. However, did these Jews form the one and only Church because they were disciples of Jesus or because they were Jews? That the first assumption is the correct one became clear with the decision taken at the Council of Jerusalem. According to this decision, the criterion for membership in the one and true Church was identified as discipleship through faith in contrast to ethnicity. Still, did the Jewish disciples within this one and true Church ever form a sub-entity that one could call an *ecclesia ex circumcisione*, just as we speak today of a Latin Church or a Melchite Church within the Catholic Church?

The original community of disciples in Jerusalem, the one associated with the leadership of James, the brother of Jesus, has often been viewed as the proto- and archetype of an *ecclesia ex circumcisione*. Undoubtedly this community had a very special status in the early Church.

The pillars of the Church were established there, as Paul recalls in his epistle to the Galatians (2:9). Notwithstanding, there was something more than the seniority associated with the group of the apostles. It is certainly not a coincidence that the apostles were Jews and that the community of James was established in Jerusalem. The Church in Jerusalem bore witness to the roots of the whole Church; that is, to the fulfillment of the promises made to Abraham and, therefore, to the living legacy of the history of Israel. The inclusion of Gentiles in the Church could only strengthen the calling of James' community to serve as an authorized intermediary between the message of salvation conveyed to the four corners of the world and the bi-millennial Jewish womb out of which it was born. That the community of James found itself connected to the ongoing life of the Jewish nation, in spite of the gap created by the increasingly massive rejection of Jesus' messiahship among the latter, is sufficiently well attested. Ethnically, the community must have remained overwhelmingly Jewish due to the composition of the local population. This is also true religiously. The Acts tell us about the frequentation of the Temple by the disciples (5:12). Hegesippus portrays James as a thoroughly Torah-observant Jew. Yet did these ethnic and religious ties to the Jewish nation make of the community of James a Church within the Church, an ecclesial entity that would by nature be distinct from all other ecclesial entities within the universal Church?

Nowadays, so called *ecclesiae sui juris* base their membership on the adoption of a definite set of customs, rites, and practices. However, what makes an *ecclesia ex circumcisione*—what makes a Church Jewish as it were—could never be anything else than Jewishness itself or the divine election of a specific nation among all the nations of the earth. Now, on what grounds could the very Church community that had seen the proclamation of the decisive equality of Jewish and Gentile disciples of Christ, have prevented Gentile disciples from joining it? Or how could it have asked these Gentiles to convert after affirming that they were part of the Church as Gentiles? Whatever be the percentage of Jews in the Jerusalem community, the formal acceptance of Gentile members *qua* Gentiles would *ipso facto* have turned it into a standard local segment of the universal Church—what would later be called a diocese—which it probably did.

Personally, I do not believe in the structural "otherness" of the Church of James, an "otherness" within the universal Church that would have been the flipside of an almost seamless continuity with the religious institutions of Israel. True, James happened to be the so-called "brother of Christ." But this would have hardly made him a priest in the Jewish sense of the term, since Jesus was not a *kohen* himself. A *metathesis*, to quote the epistle to the Hebrews (7:12), a radical shift affecting the very nature of priesthood, must have taken place in the community of James. It is not a coincidence that the same Torah-observant James depicted by Hegesippus ended up stoned to death by his fellow Jews. The community of James might have been at the center of the Christian world in the early days of the Church, but it has always been at the extreme periphery of Jewish religious orthodoxy.

It is not difficult to synthesize the conundrum with which the early Church wrestled. While there was a general awareness of the significance of an ongoing Jewish presence that would preserve the connection of the Church with the legacy of Israel, the concrete preservation of this Jewish presence would have entailed some degree of separation between Jews and non-Jews, something that the authorities deemed incompatible with the unity of the whole Body of Christ championed by Paul—this great "mystery" according to which "the Gentiles are fellow heirs and fellow members of the body" (Eph 3:6). The impossibility of solving this conundrum led to the disintegration of a living Jewish presence in the Church in the span of a few generations. Jewish disciples being unable to preserve a distinct mode of life and being encouraged to blend into an ever-growing community of Gentile disciples, this disintegration was but a predictable outcome of the leadership's enduring policy.

Accordingly, it is clear—to me at least—that the restoration of the *ecclesia ex circumcisione* cannot be understood in the first sense of the term "restoration" namely, "the action of restoring a person to a former state or position." A Jewish Messianic restorationism in the line of Anabaptist or Mormon restorationism does not make sense, either historically or theologically. At no point in the past, not even at the very beginning of the Church, has there been an autonomous *ecclesia ex circumcisione* that was formally and institutionally defined, either in terms of space, time, practice, or laws. It does not make sense to accuse the Church of having forgotten an entity that never existed, any more than it does to advocate the reestablishment of a type of community that never crystallized into a Church because it was doomed to disintegrate from the start.

Now, if the first meaning of "restoration" found in the OED does not apply to the quest of an *ecclesia ex circumcisione*, can any of the other meanings that we listed earlier make more theological sense? I believe so, and I would like to show this by bringing forward a new reading of the mosaic of Santa Sabina.

3. Apokatastasis *in Santa Sabina*

In a luminous article, Fredric Schlatter—praise given to a Jesuit by a Dominican!—showed that the theme illustrated on the wall of Santa Sabina can hardly have more than one origin.[1] Actually, his article mainly deals with another mosaic, the one that is preserved in the apse of Santa Pudenziana, a mosaic that is about ten to twenty years older than the one in Santa Sabina. The theme of the two mosaics is identical, although the inscription below the two feminine figures of Santa Sabina is missing in Santa Pudenziana. In this other basilica, two women, symmetrically standing on either side of Christ, are holding laurels above the heads of the apostles.

One immediately identifies the allegories of the two Churches, the one originating from the Synagogue and the other from the Gentile world. According to Schlatter, this theme was something of a novelty at the time—it does not follow any established iconographic tradition, nor even any notable patristic line of interpretation. Nevertheless, Schlatter finds the theme repeatedly developed in the commentaries of Saint Jerome on the prophets, commentaries that had been circulating not long before the building of Santa Pudenziana and the creation of its mosaics. For Jerome, the Church of Christ, meaning the present one in contrast to her ancient prototype that he associates with the untainted faith of Israel, stems from two sources, that of the Synagogue and that of Gentility. He often, sometimes acrobatically, sees the two types of Churches allegorically represented by couples of biblical women—for instance, the two women at the judgment of Solomon (Letter 74 to Rufin) or the prostitute and the adulteress that the prophet Hosea is asked by God to marry (Hos 2:1–4; 3:1).

1. Fredric W. Schlatter, SJ, "The Two Women in the Mosaic of Santa Pudenziana," *Journal of Early Christian Studies* 3.1 (1995): 1–24.

(*Picture: Antoine Lévy*)

Following Schlatter's insight, I believe I found the one and only passage of Jerome's commentaries, not mentioned in his article, where the notions of *ecclesia ex circumcisione* and *ecclesia ex gentibus* are explicitly acknowledged and contrasted with each other. In this passage, Jerome comments on the incipit of the book of Haggai where the prophet records that "in the second year of Darius the king, on the first day of the sixth month," those exiled to Babylon got news that the time to rebuild the Temple in Jerusalem had come. Jerome delves into the symbolism of numbers: the sixth month of Darius' reign stands for the sixth day of God's creation, while its second year stands for the number two, symbolizing the restoration, *reparatio,* of the world as well as the *subolis,* the generation of an offspring by two parents: "materia mundi . . . duplicem numerum diligit" ("the matter of which the world is made likes the number two"). What Jerome wants to emphasize is that the timing of the rebuilding of the Temple under Darius says something about the final restoration, the *reparatio* at the end of times of the world as we know it, that is, with its succession of generations. This cosmic *reparatio* must take place right before the Parousia, which Jerome implicitly identifies with the seventh day of creation. Further, playing with the number two and the number twelve, Jerome contemplates the manner in which the *Ecclesia Christi* was or is—that is the ambivalence of the perfect tense in Latin—built, *aedificata est.* Here one comes across the formula that is echoed on the walls of Santa Sabina: ". . . tam ex circumcisione quam *ex gentibus,* Christi Ecclesia prima quae eversa fuerat, aedificata est" / ". . . the primeval Church of Christ, the one that had been overthrown, is rebuilt [literally, is built] from both the circumcision and from the Gentiles."[2] For Jerome, the rebuilding of the Temple under Darius symbolizes the historical beginning of the Christian Church. By establishing the Church, Jewish and Gentile disciples have done something similar to the Jews under Darius: They have rebuilt the Temple of God, a Temple that had been left desolate, not by the Babylonians this time, but by the Jews after their rejection of Christ. In addition, as this very compact passage indicates, Jerome also sees in this restoration of the *Ecclesia Christi* the eschatological plot that must unfold before the Parousia takes place. We therefore have three series of events that fit into one another:

The Jews rebuilt the Temple under Darius upon their return from exile (Hag 1:1).	In the apostolic time, Jews and Gentiles rebuilt the Church, damaged by the infidelity of the Jews.	Together, Jews and Gentiles will re-establish the Church of Christ to her perfect state before the Parousia takes place.

In the light of Jerome's commentary, the iconographic program of the mosaics in Santa Sabina receives a fairly plausible explanation. As one would expect from the dedicatory inscription in which they are framed, this rationale has a very personal dimension. A number of scholars suggested that the ancestral background of Peter of Illyria was Jewish.[3] Otherwise, mentioning that he had been "raised in the halls of Christianity from his childhood," as we read in the inscription, would hardly make sense. Taking into account the fact that Jerome himself originated from Illyria, just as Peter did, illustrating the inscription on the walls of Santa Sabina by these mosaics was a way of saying: "See how Jerome, the glory of my country, the authority of whom is recognized throughout the whole Church, conceives the true *Ecclesia Christi*. This Church stems from Gentiles, but also from Jews who accepted Jesus' messiahship just like me, regardless of life-circumstances that may have played a part. There is therefore no shame in being a priest coming from a Jewish background."

2. Hieronymus, *Commentarium in Haggeu* (Patrologiae Cursus Completus Series Latina; Jacques-Paul Migne, ed.; Paris, 1844–1890), vol. 25, 1401 BC.

3. See, for instance, Geri Parlby, "Images of Conflict: The Art of Anti-Judaism in Fifth-Century Rome," in *The Edinburgh Companion to the Bible and the Arts*, ed. Stephen Prickett (Edinburgh: Edinburgh University Press, 2014), 149–60.

In my opinion, this somewhat anecdotal conjecture conveys a fascinating theological message. Indeed, the passage from Jerome's commentary to which the inscription implicitly refers combines two of the additional meanings of the word "restoration" that one finds in the OED.

Firstly, there is the idea of the restoration of the Temple, the mending of what has been damaged. Secondly, there is the idea of the end of times, the final restoration of all things that correlates with the notion of *apokatastasis.* Accordingly, looking at the mosaics of Santa Sabina, one can discern much more than a historical reference to a point in the past identified with the early beginning of the Church. The mosaic points to the present—there are still people like Peter, people with a Jewish background joining the Church, and these people are contributing to the edification of the House of God on a par with Gentiles. One could say that these people are repairing what has been damaged as a result of the Jewish dismissal of Jesus' Messiahship. They are filling the "empty space" that has upset the inner balance of the Church. Finally, the mosaic points toward the end of times: A moment will come when the *Ecclesia Christi* will be re-established in her perfect state, a state which coincides with an equally valuable influx of Jews and Gentiles at the heart of her communion.

Let me finish with a few considerations on the nature of this apokatastatic re-establishment. What I find interesting about the notion of *apokatastasis* is that it tells of a return to the origin that is quintessentially different from mere repetition. The end of history will be a return to the way it started, but if this return consisted of a mere re-enactment of the beginning, history would lose the meaning that it acquired as a result of the Judeo-Christian revelation. From this perspective, history cannot be the eternal return of the same as in the cosmic cycles theorized by Stoic philosophers. History is a process leading from point A to point B. The *apokatastasis* marking the end of this process does somehow lead back to the point where everything began, but in the mode of a radically new beginning. Pristineness in its most authentic form is not at the beginning of history, but at the end of it—it does not bring with it the simple erasure of sin, but it proclaims Christ's definitive victory over it.

A formally defined, well-established *ecclesia ex circumcisione* never existed, even in the earliest apostolic times. Still, the apostolic Church, with the community of James in Jerusalem and the priority given to the Jewish component of the universal Church, foreshadowed an *ecclesia ex circumcisione*. For fear of going against her own decision to accept Gentiles on a par with Jews, the apostolic Church could not bring herself to establish an exclusively Jewish entity in her midst. However, her teaching, as well as her history, talks about a universal Church that, by virtue of the vibrant witness of Jewish disciples of Christ, is through and through conscious of her roots in the ongoing life of Israel. The overall trajectory of the Catholic Church, as well as that of Orthodox Churches, in the course of almost two thousand years of history, displays a powerful, at times ruthless, tendency to forget this original message stemming from the apostolic times. True, across the centuries, people such as Peter of Illyria tried in more or less explicit ways to spur the Church into remembering this message of old. They did what they could to fix the breaches that disfigured the Temple of God, this *prima Ecclesia Christi* as Jerome would call her. Today, however, some eighty years after the Shoah and the establishment of the State of Israel, the Church stands at a crossroads. In the apostolic times, the leadership of the Church took up the gigantic task, the revolutionary mission of opening the legacy of Israel to the Gentile world. At the point in history where we are, we find ourselves at the other end of this process. It is no longer for the Gentile world that an overwhelmingly Jewish Church needs to make room. On the contrary, it is for segments of the Jewish world that an overwhelmingly Gentile Church should provide a home—that is, for those whom Paul calls the "remnant" of Israel in his epistle to the Romans (11:5), the little but increasingly growing number of Jews that have come to confess Jesus as the true Messiah of Israel. In the apostolic times, the leadership of the Church dismissed a distinction between Jewish and Gentile disciples of Christ that would have been viewed as detrimental to the latter, thus damaging the communion of all the faithful in the one living Body of Christ. Today, drawing the lessons from a history that, since the time of the Apostles, has been nothing short of tragic and sinful, we understand that the perfect accomplishment of communion in the one living Body of Christ requires a distinction without separation, a distinction in a love untainted by envy, between Jewish and Gentile disciples of Christ. The Church of Christ that has turned into an overwhelmingly Gentile entity must find in herself the generosity to give back to Jewish disciples what they actually never enjoyed in the course of history, namely, an established biosphere that will preserve the uniqueness of the nation of Israel in the midst of the universal Church. This is what the restoration of the *ecclesia ex circumcisione* in its most authentic sense, that is its apokatastatic one, is about. As Paul writes in his epistle to the Romans: "For if their rejection be the reconciliation of the world, what will their acceptance be but life from the dead?" (11:15). Until then, we, Jewish disciples of Yeshua, will, with the help of our Gentile friends, continue our endeavor to restore the breaches of the Temple, just as Peter of Illyria did in his own way with the dedicatory inscription on the walls of Santa Sabina.

The Church of Jews and Gentiles

Response to Antoine Lévy, "Restoration of the *Ecclesia ex Circumcisione*?"

David Rudolph

"THE CHURCH IS THE BRIDE OF CHRIST only when it is the church of Jews and Gentiles . . . the existence, building, and growth of the church are identified with the common existence, structure, and growth of Jews and Gentiles."[1] Not a few theologians today would disagree with Markus Barth's theologoumenon, and would consider it counter to Paul's teaching in Galatians, "There is neither Jew nor Greek. . . . For you are all one in Christ Jesus" (Gal 3:28). The notion that the Church ultimately consists of two groups may sound primitive, especially if one thinks of the Church as a *tertium genus* that "superseded its mother religion, Judaism, and left it behind."[2] But if we set aside for a moment our inherited theology of expropriation, and read Paul within Judaism, a compelling case can be made that Barth's evaluation is accurate. Paul, the "circumcised apostle,"[3] viewed the Church as a twofold entity made up of Jews and Gentiles who remained Jews and Gentiles, as I will seek to demonstrate below.

1. Markus Barth, *Israel and the Church: Contributions for a Dialogue Vital for Peace* (Richmond, VA: John Knox, 1969), 90–91.

2. W.D. Davies, "My Odyssey in New Testament Interpretation," *Bible Review* 5:2 (1989): 17–18.

3. Heinrich Graetz, *History of the Jews II* (Philadelphia, PA: The Jewish Publication Society of America, 1893): 367.

1. The ecclesia ex circumcisione *and the two apostolic callings*

In his essay "Restoration of the *Ecclesia ex Circumcisione*?" Fr. Antoine Lévy problematizes the idea of an "autonomous *ecclesia ex circumcisione* that was formally and institutionally defined" in the apostolic period. Nonetheless, in his original paper presented at the symposium, he conceded that, in a broader sense, "there was an *ecclesia ex circumcisione*, to the service of which Peter had been appointed, and an *ecclesia ex gentibus*, the community entrusted to Paul's supervision (Gal 2:7–8)." Paul writes in this passage:

> On the contrary, when they saw that I had been entrusted with the gospel for the uncircumcised, just as Peter had been entrusted with the gospel for the circumcised (for he who worked through Peter making him an apostle to the circumcised also worked through me in sending me to the Gentiles) . . .[4]

(Picture: Avery Library, Columbia University; see note 6)

4. Gal 2:7–8. Note that v. 9 describes Peter's mission as being in conjunction with the ministry of James and John in Jerusalem.

These two apostolic callings[5] are honored in the fifth-century mosaic displayed in the Basilica di Santa Sabina. The original had the figure of Peter above *ecclesia ex circumcisione* and Paul above *ecclesia ex gentibus,*[6] thus connecting the two churches (circumcision and Gentile) with the two missions (Petrine and Pauline).[7]

2. The twofold nature of the Church in Pauline theology

Consistent with Galatians 2:7–8, the Pauline corpus includes a variety of terms and imageries that describe the dyadic nature of the Church and its contours. For example, Paul's letter to the Romans emphasizes that Jews and Gentiles have different callings (Rom 11:28–29). The apostle to the Gentiles divides the world (including the Church) into two groups: Jews and Gentiles (Rom 11:13).[8] Jews are "the circumcised" as distinct from "the uncircumcised" (Rom 3:30; 4:9, 12). Jews are "natural branches" in contrast to "wild olive shoot[s]" (Rom 11:21, 24). Jews are "Israelites" in contrast to "the nations" (Rom 9:4; cf. Rom 10:1; 11:11, 25–26).[9]

In 1 Corinthians 7:17–20, Paul refers to the circumcised and uncircumcised members of his community. His "rule in all the churches" (v. 17) is that the circumcised are "called" to remain circumcised and not to become uncircumcised. "Circumcision" is a metonym for Jewish

5. Cf. Rom 1:1; 1 Cor 1:1.

6. Patricia Krupinski, "*Synagoga* under Erasure: *Ecclesia* and Text in Santa Sabina," *Art Journal* 1.9 (2016): 116–27, at 120, Fig. 5. See Giovanni Ciampini's seventeenth-century drawing of the Santa Sabina inscription mosaic, and the figures above it, in *Vetera Monimenta*, vol. 1 (Rome, 1690): ch. XXI, p. 191, tab. XLVIII. The differences between the Santa Sabina mosaic (422–432) and the apsidal mosaic of Santa Pudenziana (TAQ 417), including the inverted placements of Peter and Paul, are described in Fredric W. Schlatter, "The Two Women in the Mosaic of Santa Pudenziana," *Journal of Early Christian Studies* 3.1 (1995): 1–24, at 4–5. The image of Ciampini's drawing included here is found in Schlatter, "Two Women," p. 13, credited to the Avery Library, Columbia University.

7. Krupinski, "*Synagoga* Under Erasure" (see note 6), 120–21.

8. Cf. Gal 2:15. See David Rudolph, "To the Jew First: Paul's Vision for the Priority of Israel in the Life of the Church," *Kesher: A Journal of Messianic Judaism* 37 (2020): 11–25.

9. David Rudolph, "Zionism in Pauline Literature: Does Paul eliminate particularity for Israel and the land in his portrayal of salvation available for all the world?," in *The New Christian Zionism: Fresh Perspectives on Israel and the Land*, ed. Gerald McDermott (Downers Grove, IL: InterVarsity, 2016): 182–94.

identity and lifestyle.[10] Paul is saying, "If you are Jewish, stay Jewish. Do not stop being Jewish (i.e., do not assimilate)."[11] He similarly states that the uncircumcised are "called" to remain uncircumcised and not to become circumcised. In other words, "If you are Gentile, stay Gentile. Do not stop being Gentile." This is Paul's rule; not just in Corinth but in all of his congregations.

In Ephesians 2–3, there are at least three ways that the writer highlights the continuation of Jewish and Gentile identity in the Church.[12] One is by using "the second person plural pronoun and verb as a way of identifying *Gentiles* in contrast to Jews (Eph 2:11, 12, 13, 17, 19; see also 3:1)."[13] He also uses the first-person plural and *amphoteroi* ("both") to refer to Jews and Gentiles in Messiah who remain Jews and Gentiles:

> ". . . and might reconcile *both groups* to God in one body through the cross, thus putting to death that hostility through it." (Eph 2:16)

> ". . . for through him *both of us* have access in one Spirit to the Father." (Eph 2:18)[14]

10. Paul confirms that circumcision is linked to covenant fidelity and Torah observance when he writes in Rom 2:25, "Circumcision indeed is of value if you obey the law; but if you break the law, your circumcision has become uncircumcision." He makes the same point in more explicit language in Gal 5:3. "Once again I testify to every man who lets himself be circumcised that he is obliged to obey the *entire law.*" Paul's wording in 1 Cor 7:18—"Let him not seek to remove the marks of circumcision"—points back to the Maccabean period when some Hellenistic Jews rejected their Jewish identity, even to the extent of surgically altering their bodies so that they appeared to have a foreskin. 1 Macc 1.11–15 describes Jews who removed the marks of circumcision as "those who abandoned the holy covenant."

11. See David J. Rudolph, "Paul's 'Rule in All the Churches' (1 Cor 7:17–24) and Torah-Defined Ecclesiological Variegation," *Studies in Christian–Jewish Relations* 5 (2010): 1–23; J. Brian Tucker, *"Remain in Your Calling": Paul and the Continuation of Social Identities in 1 Corinthians* (Eugene, OR: Pickwick, 2011): 62–135.

12. This is discussed in David J. Rudolph, "Describing the Church in Relation to Israel: The Language of George Lindbeck and Ephesians 2–3," in *Covenant and the People of God: Essays Presented to Mark S. Kinzer in Honor of His Seventieth Birthday*, ed. Jonathan Kaplan, Jennifer M. Rosner, and David J. Rudolph (Eugene, OR: Pickwick, 2023): 219–32. Cf. Andrew R. Rillera, "Tertium Genus or Dyadic Unity? Investigating Sociopolitical Salvation in Ephesians," *Biblical Research* 66 (2021): 31–51; William S. Campbell, "Unity and Diversity in the Church: Transformed Identities and the Peace of Christ in Ephesians," in *Unity and Diversity in Christ: Interpreting Paul in Context: Collected Essays* (Eugene, OR: Cascade, 2013): 127–45.

13. Mark S. Kinzer, *Searching Her Own Mystery:* Nostra Aetate, *the Jewish People, and the Identity of the Church* (Eugene, OR: Cascade, 2015): 67.

14. Cf. Eph 2:14.

Adding grist to the mill, the verb in Eph 2:18 is present tense, indicating that *both* (*amphoteroi*) Messianic Jews and Gentile believers continue in their respective identities in this new corporate body.

A second way that the writer highlights the dyadic nature of the Church is by using *sun-/sum-* prefixes in Eph 2:19–22, which can be translated as "fellow-," "together with" or "co-." Lionel Windsor explains the significance of these prefixes:

> As several interpreters have observed, the use of three *syn*-compounds indicates a salvation-historical unity-in-diversity. Gentile believers are "fellow-citizens (συμπολῖται) of the saints" (v. 19), every construction is "being joined together" (συναρμολογουμένη, v. 21), and the gentiles are being "built together" (συνοικοδομεῖσθε) into God's dwelling (v. 22). This emphasis on togetherness does not imply that the gentiles have *become* Israel; rather it is a claim that they have become equal sharers *with* Israel in God's blessings. There is a parallel here with vv. 5–6, in which three *syn*-compounds are used to describe believers' relationship to Christ. Believers have been "made alive together" (συνεζωοποίησεν) with Christ, "raised together" (συνήγειρεν) with Christ, and "seated together" (συνεκάθισεν) with Christ (vv. 5–6). While this claim that believers share in the status of the risen Christ is of course remarkable, it is not meant to imply that believers have *become* Christ. Similarly, vv. 19–22 asserts that the gentile believers share in the benefits of Israel. While this too is a remarkable claim, it does not imply that the believers have *become* Israel. In the words of Paula Fredriksen, gentile Christ-believers can be understood as "ex-pagan pagans."[15] In one sense, they are no longer "gentiles," because they have been transformed into being God's people alongside Israel (cf. 4:17); yet in another sense they have a distinct "gentile" identity, albeit one that has been fully transformed in Christ (cf. 3:1, 6).[16]

15. Paula Fredriksen, "Why Should a 'Law-Free' Mission Mean a 'Law-Free' Apostle?," *Journal of Biblical Literature* 134 (2015): 637–50.

16. Lionel Windsor, *Reading Ephesians and Colossians After Supersessionism: Christ's Mission Through Israel to the Nations* (Eugene, OR: Cascade, 2017): 150–51. Cf. Carl B. Hoch, "The Significance of the *Syn*-Compounds for Jew–Gentile Relationships in the Body of Christ," *Journal of the Evangelical Theological Society* 25 (1982): 175–83; Matthew Thiessen, "The Construction of Gentiles in the Letter to the Ephesians," in *The Early Reception of Paul the Second Temple Jew: Text, Narrative and Reception History*, ed. Isaac W. Oliver and Gabriele Boccaccini, with Joshua Scott (London: T&T Clark, 2019): 13–25; Lionel Windsor, "Plural Constructions and Post-supersessionist Possibilities in Ephesians 2:19–22," paper presented at the Annual Meeting of the SBL, Theological Interpretation of Scripture Seminar, San Diego, November 23, 2019, 1–17.

The *sun-/sum-* prefixes also occur in Ephesians 3:6, along with *sus-*, to describe Gentile followers of the Messiah who join Israel's commonwealth as Gentiles. Mark Kinzer translates 3:6 as "the gentiles have become *co-heirs, co-members-of-the-Body,* and *co-sharers* of the promise in Messiah Jesus through the good news."[17] In this passage, as well as in Ephesians 2:19, 21 and 22, the "co-" prefix points back to the antecedent, Israel. In other words, the "co-" prefix clarifies that Gentile believers are closely related to Israel without replacing Israel.

The author of Ephesians did not have to use these prefixes. He could have written that Gentile believers become citizens, heirs, members-of-the-Body, and recipients of the promise in Messiah Jesus. However, he wanted to emphasize that all of these blessings are realized in association with the Jewish people. To put it another way, as Windsor nicely states it, "they were once gentiles *contra* Israel; now they are gentiles *blessed alongside* Israel."[18]

Finally, Ephesians uses marriage imagery to describe the dyadic nature of the Church. Evoking *l'vasar echad* ("one flesh") in Genesis 2:24, the writer portrays the Messiah as having "made both groups into one . . . to create in himself one new man out of two" (2:14–15; cf. 5:31–32). Connubial language in the context of the *sun-/sum-/sus-* prefixes points to a relationship of interdependence between Jew and Gentile. Barth explains:

> Correspondingly, when in Eph 2:15 Christ is called creator and creates a person, then the term "one new man" must mean a person distinct from Christ. No other person can be meant than the "bride of Christ." While this bride is never explicitly named the New Eve, she is identified as the church in 5:23–32. . . . Among the NT books Ephesians alone calls God's covenant partner "one new man" and emphasizes that this man consists of two, that is, of Jews and Gentiles. . . . Above all, the joining of "the two" into "one new" whole reveals that neither of

17. Kinzer, *Searching Her Own Mystery* (see note 13), 80.

18. Windsor, *Reading Ephesians and Colossians After Supersessionism* (see note 16), 226.

> the two can possess salvation, peace, life, without the other. Jews need Gentiles, Gentiles need Jews.[19]

The twofold nature of the Church is highlighted by several Church Fathers in their interpretations of Ephesians 2:14–15.[20] Epiphanius, for example, writes:

> If he has made both one, and has not ended the one in order to establish the other, then he has not changed the former (the Jew) into something else. Nor has he kept the second separate from the first; but he has brought the two together into one. (*Pan.* 42.12.3)[21]

Augustine viewed the relationship between the "two churches" (circumcision and Gentile) as foundational. They were the "two walls" of the *ecclesia*:

> Did not the Lord come for this purpose: to found the church . . . and to make one wall of the circumcision to which another wall from the uncircumcision of the Gentiles would be joined—so that he himself would be the cornerstone of the two walls coming from different directions? . . . If you look closely at the scriptures you will find the two churches signified in many places. For the cornerstone serves this very purpose: to make one out of two. (*Serm.* 137.6)[22]

For Augustine, the Church was a "corner":

19. Markus Barth, *Ephesians 1–3* (Garden City, NY: Doubleday, 1974): 309–11. Cf. Peter Hocken, *The Challenges of the Pentecostal, Charismatic and Messianic Jewish Movements: The Tensions of the Spirit* (Burlington, VT: Ashgate, 2009): 105–106—"The vision of the church as 'the two made one' challenges all our inherited views of the church, whether Catholic, Orthodox or Protestant. . . . There is something dialogical built into the constitution of the church as there is in the eternal 'constitution' of the Trinity. There is the dialogue of the Bridegroom with the Bride (Eph 5:22–33) and there is the dialogue of the 'two made one,' of Jew and Gentile, already on earth."

20. See William Rader, *The Church and Racial Hostility: A History of Interpretation of Ephesians 2:11–22* (Tübingen: Mohr-Siebeck, 1978), 5–53.

21. *Ibid.*, 27.

22. *Ibid.*, 46. Cf. Origen, *Fr. Matt.* 428. It is beyond the scope of this essay to address the tension between Augustine's vision for "two walls" of the Church and his view that Torah-observant Jewish believers in Jesus were heretics (Augustine, *Bapt.* 7.1.1; *Cresc.* 1.31.36; *Epist.* 116.16.1). See Etienne Jodar, "Law-Observance Among Jewish Christians: Benefiting from Augustine's View," *Kesher: A Journal of Messianic Judaism* 41 (2022): 81–91.

> Why is the church a corner? Because to it he has called Jews and Gentiles. Coming like two walls from different locations (*de diverso*) and meeting, he has joined them in himself by the grace of his peace, "For he is our peace who has made both one." (*Serm.* 89.4)[23]

3. *The suppression and restoration of the* ecclesia ex circumcisione

Communities of Torah-observant Messianic Jews existed during Augustine's day.[24] However, in contrast to the apostolic period, there was little in the way of mutual blessing between Jesus-believing Jews and Gentiles. After the First Council of Nicaea (325 CE), and throughout the Middle Ages, Gentile Christian leaders required Jewish believers to renounce their Jewish identity and practice if they wanted to be received as brothers and sisters in the Lord.[25] The Second Council of Nicaea (787 CE), Canon 8, forbade Jewish believers in Jesus from continuing to live as Jews if they wanted to be baptized.[26] All of this led to the suppression

23. Rader, *The Church and Racial Hostility* (see note 20), 47. Cf. Augustine, *Adv. Jud.* 8.11; *Serm.* 88.10; *Serm. Caes. Eccl.* 1.4; *Faust.* 12.24; 22:89; 32:12. See Paula Fredriksen, *Augustine and the Jews: A Christian Defense of Jews and Judaism* (New York: Doubleday, 2008): 255–57.

24. Augustine, *Bapt.* 7.1.1; *Cresc.* 1.31.36; *Faust.* 19.7. See Annette Yoshiko Reed, *Jewish-Christianity and the History of Judaism: Collected Essays* (Texts and Studies in Ancient Judaism, 171; Tübingen: Mohr-Siebeck, 2018): 56; Edwin K. Broadhead, *Jewish Ways of Following Jesus: Redrawing the Religious Map of Antiquity* (Wissenschaftliche Untersuchungen zum Neuen Testament, 266; Tübingen: Mohr-Siebeck, 2010): 181, 186.

25. E.g., the church of Constantinople required Jews to say the following profession of faith in order to be baptized: "I renounce all customs, rites, legalisms, unleavened breads and sacrifices of lambs of the Hebrews, and all the other feasts of the Hebrews, sacrifices, prayers, aspersions, purifications, sanctifications and propitiations, and fasts, and new moons, and Sabbaths, and superstitions, and hymns and chants and observances and synagogues, and the food and drink of the Hebrews; in one word, I renounce absolutely everything Jewish, every law, rite and custom" (Assemani, Cod. Lit. 1:105). See James Parkes, "Appendix 3: Professions of Faith Extracted from Jews on Baptism," in *The Conflict of the Church and the Synagogue: A Study in the Origins of Antisemitism* (New York: Atheneum, 1985): 397.

26. "But if in sincerity of heart and faith any of them convert and confess with his whole heart, divulging their customs and practices in order to refute and correct others, he is to be received and baptized together with his children, and they are to provide a guarantee that they have abandoned Jewish practices. If this is not the case with them, they are not to be received"—Richard Price, trans., *The Acts of the Second Council of Nicaea: Translated with Notes and an Introduction (787)* (Liverpool: Liverpool University Press, 2020): 616.

of Jewish presence in the Church, an unfortunate reality that continues to exist in many parts of the *ecclesia* today.

Can the *ecclesia ex circumcisione* be restored? Lévy answers this question utilizing a relatively narrow definition of *ecclesia ex circumcisione*—an autonomous church that is institutionally defined and well established. Thus, the *ecclesia ex circumcisione* is not something that can be "restored." It is instead something to be explored: the building of "an established biosphere that will preserve the uniqueness of the nation of Israel in the midst of the universal Church." In contradistinction, I have used a broader definition of *ecclesia ex circumcisione*—the community of Jewish followers of Jesus as symbolized by Peter's mission to the circumcised (Gal 2:7–9). From this perspective, the *ecclesia ex circumcisione* is the Jewish wing of the body of Messiah,[27] what Paul called the "remnant" of Israel (Rom 11:5). It was originally composed of the "circumcised" believers in Jerusalem and the Diaspora, who followed in the footsteps of their Jewish Messiah and kept Paul's rule not to assimilate (Acts 15; 16:3; 21:17–26; 24:14; 1 Cor 7:17–24).[28] In Augustinian terms, the church of the circumcision was one of the "two walls" of the Church that existed from the time of the apostles until the fifth century. The *ecclesia ex circumcisione* then disappeared (it would seem) for over a thousand years, mainly due to Gentile Christian supersessionism, and today it has been miraculously restored in the form of a global community of Jewish disciples of Jesus.[29]

As I see it, restoration of the *ecclesia ex circumcisione* directly leads to the restoration of the "one new man" made up of Jews and Gentiles in Messiah who remain Jews and Gentiles (Eph 2:14–15). Restoration of the *ecclesia ex circumcisione* in the modern era includes the re-envisioning

27. See Cardinal Jean-Marie Lustiger, *The Promise* (Grand Rapids, MI: Eerdmans, 2002): 127.

28. Richard Bauckham, "James and the Jerusalem Community," in *Jewish Believers in Jesus: The Early Centuries*, ed. Oskar Skarsaune and Reidar Hvalvik (Peabody, MA: Hendrickson, 2007): 55–95; Reidar Hvalvik, "Named Jewish Believers Connected with the Pauline Mission," in Skarsaune and Hvalvik, eds., *Jewish Believers*, (see above), 154–78; Philip S. Alexander, "Jewish Believers in Early Rabbinic Literature (2d to 5th Centuries)," in Skarsaune and Hvalvik, eds., *Jewish Believers*, (see above), 659–709; Broadhead, *Jewish Ways of Following Jesus* (see note 24), 80–187, 284–300.

29. David Rudolph, "Messianic Judaism in Antiquity and in the Modern Era," in *Introduction to Messianic Judaism: Its Ecclesial Context and Biblical Foundations* (Grand Rapids, MI: Zondervan, 2013): 21–26. See www.yachad-beyeshua.org (accessed April 11, 2025).

of the Church as a twofold community as Barth describes it, characterized by interdependence, mutual blessing, and mutual humbling. It involves Gentile Christians thinking of Jewish believers as their covenant partners,[30] and thinking of themselves as *co*-heirs, *co*-members-of-the-Body, and *co*-sharers of the promise *alongside* Israel. As R. Kendall Soulen puts it, restoration involves "a recovery of the church's basic character as a table fellowship of those who are—and remain—different. . . . The church concerns the Jew as a Jew and the Gentile as a Gentile, not only initially or for the period of a few generations but essentially and at all times."[31]

30. ". . . such a corporate ecclesial body is not simply another national Church or rite. In fact, there is a sense in which such a Jewish ecclesial environment is the complementary partner of the entire Church of the nations, despite the drastic disparity in size distinguishing one from the other. Such an insight is already implicit in a stunning assertion found in the 2015 Vatican document referred to above: 'It is and remains a qualitative definition of the Church of the New Covenant that it consists of Jews and Gentiles, even if the quantitative proportions of Jewish and Gentile Christians may initially give a different impression' [*The Gifts and Calling of God are Irrevocable*, paragraph 43]"—Mark S. Kinzer, "A Messianic Jewish Approach to Jewish Catholicism: Responding to Antoine Lévy's *Jewish Church*," *Pro Ecclesia* 31:3 (2022): 350–88, at 355).

31. R. Kendall Soulen, *The God of Israel and Christian Theology* (Minneapolis, MN: Fortress, 1996): 169–70.

Post-Supersessionist Eschatology

Welcoming Jesus at the Mount of Olives

Mark S. Kinzer

In an article appearing earlier in this volume, I proposed a post-supersessionist Messianology highlighting the ecclesiological implications of the role played by Jewish disciples of Jesus.[1] The article concluded with a brief discussion of the traditional Christian motif of the eschatological "conversion of the Jews."

Most attempts to fashion a post-supersessionist theology have given little attention to the events immediately preceding the second coming of the Messiah, or to the distinctive role of genealogical-Israel within the new age which his coming will inaugurate. There are good reasons for treading warily in this marshy terrain, which has long been inhabited by apocalyptic enthusiasts with little appetite for either theological reflection or engagement with flesh-and-blood Jewish people. But, as with Messianology, there is land here capable of bearing post-supersessionist fruit if properly drained and cultivated.

That is what I sought to do in my 2018 monograph, *Jerusalem Crucified, Jerusalem Risen*.[2] In the present article I will summarize some of the

1. Mark S. Kinzer, "Post-Supersessionist Messianology: The Present and Future Jewish King."

2. Mark S. Kinzer, *Jerusalem Crucified, Jerusalem Risen: The Resurrected Messiah, the Jewish People, and the Land of Promise* (Eugene, OR: Cascade, 2018).

results of that study, which focused on the role of the Jewish people and the land of promise in the eschatological vision of the Gospel of Luke and the Acts of the Apostles. As in *Jerusalem Crucified,* I will consider not only the Lukan teaching, but also historical events of the modern era which might be illumined by that teaching. My aim is to discern in these events the complex workings of divine providence, ever attentive to signs which might contain eschatological import.

1. Post-supersessionism or non-supersessionism

But I will begin with some words concerning the term "post-supersessionist." Kayko Driedger Hesslein prefers the term "non-supersessionist," arguing that the "post" prefix "implies that supersessionism is something that occurred and concluded in the past, and is no longer a concern in the present."[3] But that is not at all how the prefix functions in contemporary English-language discourse. When we speak of postmodern sensibilities, we are not suggesting that modernist perspectives are obsolete and nonexistent. The same can be said for the terms postliberal, postconservative, postcritical, and postmissionary.[4] All of these terms assume that the older intellectual posture (X) transcended by "post-X" continues to exist and to exercise influence.

I prefer the term "post-supersessionist" to "non-supersessionist" because the latter suggests a mere negation of supersessionism. Non-supersessionist could easily be understood to mean anti-supersessionist. And, in fact, the earliest attacks on supersessionism had just such a reactive character.[5] In particular, these early forays into non-supersessionist

3. Kayko D. Hesslein, *Dual Citizenship: Two-Natures Christologies and the Jewish Jesus* (London: T&T Clark, 2015): 11 n.14.

4. On the term "postliberal," see George A. Lindbeck, *The Nature of Doctrine: Religion and Theology in a Postliberal Age* (Philadelphia, PA: Westminster Press, 1984); on the term "postconservative," see Kevin J. Vanhoozer, *The Drama of Doctrine: A Canonical Linguistic Approach to Christian Theology* (Louisville, KY: Westminster John Knox, 2005); on the term "postcritical," see Peter Ochs, *The Return to Scripture in Judaism and Christianity: Essays in Postcritical Scriptural Interpretation* (New York: Paulist Press, 1993); on the term "postmissionary," see Mark S. Kinzer, *Postmissionary Messianic Judaism: Redefining Christian Engagement with the Jewish People* (Grand Rapids, MI: Brazos, 2005).

5. See Rosemary Ruether, *Faith and Fratricide: The Theological Roots of Anti-Semitism* (New York: Seabury Press, 1974); Michael G. Azar, "'Supersessionism': The Political Origins of a Theological Neologism," *Studies in Christian–Jewish Relations* 16.1 (2021): 1–25.

theology often rejected the high Christology of the ecumenical creeds as inherently hostile to Judaism, and sought to build a new theological paradigm on the foundation of that rejection.

In contrast, the "post" prefix suggests a non-reactive posture which has learned from X but now seeks to go beyond it. Thus, postcritical approaches to Scripture accept the validity of historical-critical scholarship and benefit from its achievements, while at the same time adopting canonical or theological modes of reading which offer a different angle of approach to the same texts. In keeping with such usage of the prefix, a post-supersessionist theology would be one which appreciates the wealth of Christian theological tradition and aims to correct its flaws by drawing upon previously untapped resources within the tradition. In particular, post-supersessionist theology—in contrast to early efforts at countering supersessionism—will view the high Christology of the ecumenical creeds as an asset rather than a liability.

2. Eschatology and the "conversion of the Jews"

Those seeking to move beyond supersessionism are rightly troubled by the triumphalist concept of an eschatological "conversion of the Jews." In my previous article in this volume, I offered a perspective on this traditional Christian motif that sought to integrate its high Christology with a post-supersessionist perspective on the historical vocation of the Jewish people—a perspective that summons the Christian Church to its own eschatological "conversion."

Traditional sources have generally based their hopes for an eschatological "conversion of the Jews" on a reading of the eleventh chapter of Paul's letter to the Romans. In *Jerusalem Crucified, Jerusalem Risen* I provide a reading of Luke and Acts which furnishes a wider narrative canvas for considering the historical journey of the Jewish people and their eschatological meeting with "the Messiah appointed for [them]" (Acts 3:20). It is a reading which affirms the universal salvific role of Jesus, while at the same time supporting the covenantal integrity of Jewish life through the ages. It also raises new questions about the theological significance of the city of Jerusalem and the land of Israel.

My exploration of this motif can be summarized through an examination of four key texts in the Gospel of Luke and the Acts of the Apostles. The first of these texts is Luke 13:33–35:

> Yet today, tomorrow, and the next day I must be on my way, because it is impossible for a prophet to be killed outside of Jerusalem. Jerusalem, Jerusalem, the city that kills the prophets and stones those who are sent to it! How often have I desired to gather your children together as a hen gathers her brood under her wings, and you were not willing! See, your house is left to you. And I tell you, you will not see me until the time comes when you say, "Blessed is the one who comes in the name of the Lord." (NRSV)

Still in Galilee, Jesus here anticipates his arrest and execution in Jerusalem, and portrays that event as continuous with Jerusalem's hostile response to a long line of prophetic messengers. He then adopts a prophetic voice, speaking in the first person on behalf of Israel's God who has longed for Jerusalem's obedience, only to be frustrated time and again. In grief over the resistance of his children, God will abandon the city and the temple and render them vulnerable to enemy armies, just as in the destruction of the first temple by the Babylonians—"See, your house is left to you." Nevertheless, as with the prophets Isaiah, Jeremiah, and Ezekiel, the message ends on a more hopeful note with a conditional promise of a divine return to Zion *after the divine departure in 70 CE*: "You [i.e., Jerusalem] will not see me until the time comes when you say, 'Blessed is the one who comes in the name of the Lord!'" God will come in glory to Jerusalem, but only after Jerusalem welcomes the one God sends.

In the second text, Jesus descends from the Mount of Olives (19:29, 37) and rides toward Jerusalem. As in the other Gospels, he is acclaimed by the crowds with the words of Psalm 118 mentioned earlier in the conditional promise of Luke 13: "Blessed is the king who comes in the name of the Lord!" (v. 38). But unlike the other Gospels, Luke states explicitly that the crowds reciting these words are "the whole multitude of the disciples" (Luke 19:37) who are accompanying him on the journey, *not the people of Jerusalem or their leaders.* The condition stipulated in the promise of Luke 13 has not been met, for those words were directed to the people and leaders of the capital. So, Jesus' entry to Jerusalem in Luke 19 does not fulfill God's saving promises to Israel, but only serves as a prophetic sign pointing to an as-yet unrealized hope.

In the third text, the resurrected Jesus converses with his apostles before his ascension. They ask him, "Lord, is this the time [*chronos*] when you will restore [*apo-kathistemi*] the kingdom to Israel?" (Acts

1:6). The verb employed here (*apo-kathistemi*) was a technical term among Greek-speaking Jews, referring to the restoration of Israel's sovereignty in its own land.[6] Jesus tells them that the question cannot be answered because the timing of this restoration is not their business (v. 7). However, contrary to traditional interpretations, Jesus does not correct the underlying assumption that generates their question—namely, the expectation that Jesus will ultimately manifest himself in glory to Israel and rule over them as their king (cf. Luke 1:32–33). After saying these words, Jesus ascends to heaven from the Mount of Olives (vv. 9, 12), and two angelic figures appear, saying, "Men of Galilee, why do you stand looking up toward heaven? This Jesus, who has been taken up from you into heaven, will come in the same way as you saw him go into heaven" (v. 11). Here we have an allusion to the eschatological prophecy of Zechariah 14: "For I will gather all the nations against Jerusalem to battle . . . Then the LORD will go forth and fight against those nations as when he fights on a day of battle. On that day *his feet shall stand on the Mount of Olives,* which lies before Jerusalem on the east; and the Mount of Olives shall be split in two from east to west by a very wide valley. . . . *Then the LORD my God will come,* and all the holy ones with him" (Zec 14:2–5). In other words, what took place in the mode of prophetic sign on Palm Sunday (Luke 19)—the descent of Jesus from the Mount of Olives and his entry to Jerusalem—will occur at the end of the age in the mode of messianic fulfillment. In light of the message of Luke 13 and Luke 19, this implies that the city of Jerusalem and its leaders will in that day welcome the coming Messiah with the words shouted on Palm Sunday only by the disciples: "Blessed is the king who comes in the name of the Lord!"

What remains implicit in Acts 1 becomes explicit in our fourth text, Acts 3:17–21. Here Peter addresses a crowd of Jews in the Jerusalem temple after the healing of a lame beggar:

> Now brothers, I know that you acted in ignorance, just as your leaders did. But what God foretold through the mouth of all His prophets—that His Messiah was to suffer—so He has fulfilled. Repent, therefore, and return—so your sins might be blotted out, so times of relief might come from the presence of *Adonai* and He might send *Yeshua*, the Messiah

6. Kinzer, *Jerusalem Crucified, Jerusalem Risen* (see note 2), 135.

> appointed for you. Heaven must receive Him, until the time [*chronoi*] of the restoration [*apokatastasis*] of all the things that God spoke about long ago through the mouth of His holy prophets. (Acts 3:17–21, TLV)

Peter here interprets for the reader the scene depicted in the first chapter of Acts. Heaven "received" Jesus when he ascended from the Mount of Olives, but God will "send him" back to Jerusalem (via the Mount of Olives), for he is "the Messiah appointed for you" (i.e., for Jerusalem and the Jewish people). The purpose of his return to Jerusalem will be to "restore" the kingdom to Israel—the phrase and technical term (*apokathistemi*) from Acts 1:6 interpreted here in Acts 3 as shorthand for "all the things that God spoke about long ago through the mouth of His holy prophets."[7] This will not happen, however, until Jerusalem and its leaders "repent" and "return"—that is, reverse the negative response to Jesus given in ignorance on Palm Sunday and its aftermath. In other words, Jerusalem will see the Messiah appointed for her when she says "Blessed is the one who comes in the name of the Lord!"

This interlocking set of texts paints a picture of Israel's central role in the divine plan, a role that contrasts starkly with the traditional motif of the eschatological "conversion of the Jews." In the latter, the Church displaces the Jews as the fulcrum of history, and the end-time "conversion" only reinforces that displacement. In Luke and Acts, on the other hand, the Jewish people—and their capital city—retain their privileged place as the center of God's concern. History waits in sustained tension until they are united with the One appointed for them. The eschatological reconciliation of Israel with its king confirms the covenantal status which Israel never forfeited.[8] If the positive response of the Jewish people to the Messiah is a necessary and sufficient condition for his return, then Israel is the hinge on which God's purposes for the world turn.

7. Kinzer, *Jerusalem Crucified, Jerusalem Risen* (see note 2), 35. The noun *apokatastasis* in Acts 3:21 is cognate with the verb *apo-kathistemi* in Acts 1:6.

8. Rabbinic tradition likewise witnesses to the motif that the coming of the Messiah depends upon Israel's repentance. Perhaps the most colorful text in this regard is *b. Sanhedrin* 98a, which tells of Rabbi Joshua ben Levi's encounter with the Messiah at the gates of Rome. At the heart of the story is a messianic midrash on Psalm 95:7 ("Oh that today you would listen to his voice!"), which suggests that the Messiah will come on the "today" when Israel as a whole "listens to his voice." See Dale C. Allison, Jr., "Matt. 23:39 = Luke 13:35b as a Conditional Prophecy," *Journal for the Study of the New Testament* 18 (1983): 75–84.

3. Eschatology and the city of Jerusalem

The eschatological vision of Romans 11 speaks much of Israel but little of Jerusalem. For Luke and Acts, on the other hand, the city of Jerusalem and its leaders represent the Jewish people as a whole, and the judgment or redemption of one is the judgment or redemption of the other. That is why the Mount of Olives plays such a pivotal role in these books. The Messiah is appointed for Jerusalem (and, thereby, for all Israel), and he must return to Jerusalem. However, he will only do so when Jerusalem is ready to welcome him with open arms. As on Palm Sunday, the welcoming party must begin at the Mount of Olives. That site was the earthly launching pad for his ascent to heaven, and it will likewise be the place he lands in order to make his triumphal entry into the city.

We do not know in what way this will be realized at the return of Jesus. The eschatological imagery of Scripture is intentionally elusive, defying literalistic hermeneutical frameworks which attempt to squeeze from the text predictive information that it is reluctant to produce. We can never know exactly how prophetic texts will be fulfilled until the appointed fulfillment is before our eyes. But one thing is unmistakably clear: Luke and Acts view the city of Jerusalem and the land of Israel as intimately bound up with the history and destiny of the Jewish people. Jesus returns to the people of Israel by returning to Jerusalem, and his kingship is established over them by being established in her.

Despite traditional views to the contrary, the geographical structure of Luke and Acts reinforces this thesis.[9] All commentators note the central role of Jerusalem in the Gospel of Luke, which begins in the city, ends in the city, and depicts the intervening drama in the form of Jesus' extended journey to the city. Acts likewise begins in Jerusalem, but from that point on the direction of movement is steadily outward, ending in Rome, the capital of the empire. Commentators have traditionally understood this geographical structure as conveying a supersessionist message: Jerusalem—and the people of Israel whom the city represents—was the past, but Rome—and the Church of the nations which that city represents—is now the present and future.

But this reading of the geographical structure of Acts leaves out a crucial feature: Every time the story takes another step outward, it

9. Kinzer, *Jerusalem Crucified, Jerusalem Risen* (see note 2), 44–53.

concludes that stage of the story by returning to Jerusalem. Paul encounters Jesus on the road to Damascus, *and then returns to Jerusalem* (9:26–29). Peter proclaims Jesus to Cornelius in Caesarea, *and then returns to Jerusalem* (11:2). A congregation arises in Antioch, *and then sends aid to Jerusalem* in a time of famine (11:27–30). Paul and Barnabas journey from Antioch to Asia Minor, *and then return afterward to Jerusalem* for the Jerusalem council (15:2). From Jerusalem, Paul travels with Silas to Greece, *and then returns again to Jerusalem* (18:22).[10] Paul takes his final journey as a free man, *and then returns to Jerusalem*, where he is arrested (21:17–23:11).

For one who senses the dynamic ebb and flow of the narrative, with the ebb continuously expanding outward but always flowing back to its center, the end of the book comes as a shock. The tide has been halted in the middle of its movement. What is the message here? Since Luke and Acts are both likely written after 70 CE, the original readers knew that Jerusalem would be destroyed by Rome not long after Paul's entry to the gentile capital. As a result, Israel—and the Jesus-community, which is inextricably tied to Israel—are in exile, and Rome—the new Babylon—symbolizes that exile. But the story of Israel ends not with exile, but instead with return and restoration. Therefore, the point of this geographical structure is to convey prophetic hope for Israel: The story is not over, but will only reach its conclusion when the tide flows back to its source, the place where it began—Jerusalem, the city of the great king.

The eschatological scenario of Romans 11 is vague, and could be interpreted as anticipating a positive response to Jesus from a large number of individual Jews throughout the world, without any particular geographical focus. The narrative of Luke and Acts, on the other hand, sketches a broad eschatological outline whose contours are clean and legible. The Jewish people will once again have a national presence in the land of Israel, and that presence will be centered in the city of

10. Acts 18:22. "When he goes on to say that *Paul went up and greeted the church*, this is usually understood as a reference to going up to Jerusalem and seeing the church there. . . . If this is a correct assumption, it means that each of Paul's missionary campaigns concluded with a visit to Jerusalem, so that Paul's work began from and ended in Jerusalem in each case"—I. Howard Marshall, *The Acts of the Apostles* (Tyndale New Testament Commentaries, 5; Grand Rapids, MI: Eerdmans, 1980): 301–2.

Jerusalem. The leaders of that city will also be the leaders of the nation. Their response to Jesus will represent and embody the response of "all Israel" throughout the world.

In Luke and Acts, the drama of Jesus' eschatological reconciliation with the Jewish people is enacted on the stage of the land of Israel, with Jerusalem in the spotlight. What might that mean for our theological interpretation of modern history?

4. Discerning divine providence in modern history

As already stated, we can never confidently assert how prophetic texts will be fulfilled until the fulfillment is before our eyes. But in some cases, fulfillment might occur as an extended process rather than a singular event. In such instances, recognition of the fulfillment by disciples of Jesus will likewise be an extended process. From this perspective, the present volume could be considered an early stage within a potentially lengthy period of discernment and recognition.

In *Jerusalem Crucified, Jerusalem Risen* I pointed to two modern historical developments whose synchronicity and formal similarity are striking: the movement to establish an autonomous Jewish presence in the land of Israel, and the movement to establish a corporate Jewish presence in the body of Jesus the Messiah.[11] Both began in the early to mid-nineteenth century, picked up steam at the end of the nineteenth and beginning of the twentieth centuries, and crystallized institutionally in the middle of the twentieth century. Both involved attempts to recover realities lost in the Jewish wars with Rome at the end of the first and beginning of the second centuries. Both featured distorted extremes which dismissed as worthless all that had intervened in Jewish (or Christian) life between the biblical and modern eras. But both have also generated visions of exile and return in which restoration involves the transformation rather than the utter negation of the era of exile, with the redeemed bringing to Jerusalem social, cultural, and spiritual wealth gathered among the nations during the time of dispersion. Of course, these two movements are radically disproportionate in their impact on world affairs. One has gained worldwide attention, while

11. Kinzer, *Jerusalem Crucified, Jerusalem Risen* (see note 2), 240–70.

the other has remained relatively obscure. Nevertheless, the parallels between them are intriguing.

No historical figure displays the connection between these two historical developments more strikingly than Joseph Rabinowitz (1837–1899). In the formative years of Zionism—the 1880s—Rabinowitz was caught up in the intellectual ferment created by the new movement. In 1882, he travelled to Palestine to investigate whether collective immigration to the land might be a solution to the ills plaguing the Jewish people. While gazing on the holy city from the Mount of Olives, Rabinowitz was suddenly convinced that "*Yeshua Achinu*" (Jesus our brother) was the Messiah, and that he alone could save Israel.[12] He returned to Kishinev (Chisinau) in Bessarabia (Moldova), and sought to gather a group of Jewish disciples of Jesus whom he called "Israelites of the New Covenant." This fellowship would circumcise their sons, observe the Sabbath and the Jewish holidays, and guard their autonomy as a Jewish Jesus-believing community. Unable to win governmental authorization, Rabinowitz's group in Kishinev failed to survive his death in 1899. Nevertheless, he gained an international hearing for his program.[13] Following in his footsteps were other like-minded Jewish disciples of Jesus such as Isaac Lichtenstein in Hungary, Mark John Levy in the United States, and Paul Levertoff in Britain. Kai Kjaer-Hansen's biography of Rabinowitz refers to him in its subtitle as "the Herzl of Jewish Christianity," and the moniker points both to his significance within Jewish Christianity, and to the connection between that movement and the Zionist enterprise.[14]

12. Kai Kjaer-Hansen, *Joseph Rabinowitz and the Messianic Movement: The Herzl of Jewish Christianity*, trans. Birger Petterson (Edinburgh: Handsel Press / Grand Rapids, MI: Eerdmans, 1995): 11–22.

13. Rabinowitz traveled to Germany, Hungary, England, Scotland, and the United States, attracting attention wherever he went (cf. Kjaer-Hansen, *Joseph Rabinowitz and the Messianic Movement*, (see note 12), 75–90, 171–78). He even became the subject of an essay by the great Russian philosopher, Vladimir Solovyov, who wrote about Rabinowitz in 1885. Urging the Russian government to grant legal status to the nascent congregation of Kishinev, Solovyov wrote: ". . . on what grounds and interest does our government remove independence from the Jewish commune which attained Christ by its own lawful path, receiving its Messiah on its and His own personal native soil, the soil of a historical, three-thousand-year-long tradition?"—Vladimir Solovyov, *The Burning Bush: Writings on Jews and Judaism*, trans. Gregory Yuri Glazov (Notre Dame, IN: University of Notre Dame Press, 2016): 343.

14. Kjaer-Hansen's subtitle derives from a statement made by Hugh Schonfield in 1936: "The story of Rabinowitz is a remarkable one. He may without unfair

Each of these two movements (and both together) creates conditions among the Jewish people which make possible a scenario of the sort anticipated by the prophetic teaching of Luke and Acts. There is no indication that this scenario will be consummated in either the next year or the next decade. We may be in the early stages of an extended process, or we may be witnessing proleptic signs pointing to an era in the distant future. But, given the message of Luke and Acts, it would be rash to dismiss either of these historical developments as theologically insignificant.

5. Eschatological signs in post-supersessionist perspective

The astonishing dual resurrection in the modern period of (1) a Jewish commonwealth in the land of Israel, and (2) a Jewish expression of the body of the Messiah, challenges Christians to rethink fundamental theological assumptions. These historical phenomena are not minor subplots preparing the way for a narrative climax whose content is unrelated to them. The return of the Messiah is that climax, and the returning Messiah is the King of *the Jews*. He comes to his own city via the Mount of Olives, and his return is contingent upon his being welcomed there by its Jewish leaders and inhabitants. Yes, this is a story about all nations and all creation, and a story about the Church which is their first fruits. But it is a universal story only by virtue of being first a story about a particular people and its land, a people who, like their king, constitute a "stone which the builders rejected." If the eschatological "conversion of the Jews" involves a reversal of the rejection of the stone which is Jesus, the eschatological "conversion of the Christians" involves a reversal of the rejection of the stone which is Israel. And each of these two reversals requires a reassessment of the stone which is the *ecclesia ex circumcisione.*

This is a post-supersessionist eschatology that enriches rather than impoverishes Christology. But it effects that enrichment through its integration with ecclesiology *and* Israelology.

Such an eschatology need not produce new Christian evangelistic missions to the Jews. The Jewish people have their own holy historical

---

comparison be described as the Herzl of Jewish Christianity"—Hugh J. Schonfield, *The History of Jewish Christianity: From the First to the Twentieth Century* (London: Duckworth, 1936): 163.

vocation, which Christians should support rather than undermine. Moreover, just as the hiding of the Messiah's face from Israel was a providential divine act, so the revelation of his face will likewise be a matter of sovereign divine initiative (Rom 11:25–26). As Pope Benedict wrote, "Israel retains its own mission. Israel is in the hands of God, who will save it 'as a whole' at the proper time, when the number of the Gentiles is complete."[15]

However, as already noted, "the proper time" will likely be an extended period rather than a singular moment. Has that period begun? Or is it not at least visible from a distance through proleptic signs? With such a possibility in view, other words from Pope Benedict (uttered when he was still Cardinal Ratzinger) come to mind. Upon meeting privately with a contingent of Messianic Jews in 1997, the prefect of the Congregation for the Doctrine of the Faith reportedly remarked: "If you are whom you say you are, this is an eschatological sign."

Given the eschatological teaching of Luke and Acts, I would propose that the regathering of the Jewish people to the land of Israel, and the emergence of Jewish Christianity and Messianic Judaism, are indeed twin eschatological signs demanding concentrated theological attention. Let us look to the Mount of Olives, and perhaps, like Joseph Rabinowitz, we will meet our brother there.

15. Joseph Ratzinger (Pope Benedict XVI), *Jesus of Nazareth. Part Two: Holy Week, From the Entrance into Jerusalem to the Resurrection* (San Francisco, CA: Ignatius Press, 2011): 46.

Jerusalem and the Mission to the Nations

Response to Mark Kinzer, "Post-Supersessionist Eschatology"

Piotr Oktaba, OP

I FEEL GRATEFUL TO MARK KINZER for opening this conversation on Jerusalem as an eschatological sign. In this discussion, how we conceive eschatology is of the essence. Mark refers to Joseph Ratzinger, which betrays some proximity to the thought of the latter. We are given to understand that God's eschatological design is unfolding even now, right before our eyes. This unfolding happens through actual signs that need to be interpreted in the light of Divine Scriptures. Moreover, we are called to take part in this process of unfolding and interpretation, notwithstanding our limitations and imperfection. We are on a path, and only the second coming of the Lord will usher us to the fullness of our destination.

Jerusalem must be contemplated as such an eschatological sign, a sign given to us as we make our way toward the ultimate fulfillment. I do not only have in mind the Jerusalem that was a long time ago. Neither am I speaking of the one that will sometime be, the "New Jerusalem" which is the final realization of God's promises (cf. Rev 3:12; 21:2). Jerusalem as it now stands is an eschatological gift from God to us. Still, in Jerusalem, just as anywhere else, what should define our participation—or lack thereof—in this process of unfolding remains to be deciphered. Accordingly, how should we read the signs of God's ongoing eschatological manifestation as we think of present-day Jerusalem?

I believe Divine Scriptures provide us with a key element as we strive to answer this question. To my mind, they deliver a criterion to discern the eschatological intent related to Jerusalem.

Mark Kinzer focuses on the role that Jerusalem plays in Luke's writings. Taken together, Luke's Gospel and the Book of Acts offer a coherent vision of the way apostolic preaching developed "in Jerusalem, and in all Judaea, and in Samaria, and unto the uttermost part of the earth" (Acts 1:8). Jerusalem is not merely presented as the starting point of the Christian mission. Acts chapter 15 is central to the structure of the book, and it depicts Jerusalem as the place where those sent to proclaim the gospel meet again. What is at stake at the council of Jerusalem is not only how the gospel should be preached among the Gentiles. It also deals with the fundamental principles that will shape the entire community of Jesus' disciples.

Kinzer's exegesis is balanced and careful. This gives us an additional reason to ponder the conclusions of his inquiry. In my opinion, it is difficult to give a full picture of the role and function of Jerusalem based on Luke's writings only. I suggest combining St. Paul's perspective with that of Luke. Luke's account tells about the point of view of Gentile converts, which complements what Paul, "the Hebrew of Hebrews" (Php 3:5), has to say. Writing about this same council that took place in Jerusalem (Gal 2), Paul singles out the principles that lie at the core of his mission to the Gentiles. In this context, he lays out his position in relation to the mystery of Israel.

The present conference deals with the emergence and development of Messianic Jewish communities worldwide. Many see this phenomenon as a sign from God. They tend to invoke the following statements of St Paul in his Epistle to the Romans: "For I would not, brethren, that ye should be ignorant of this mystery, lest ye should be wise in your own conceits; that blindness in part is happened to Israel until the fulness of the Gentiles be come in" (Rom 11:25 KJV). This particular exegesis sees the emergence of Messianic Jews as fulfilling the expectation of a new era, an era when Israel's "blindness" will finally be healed.

I want to draw your attention to the entirety of the passage from the Epistle quoted here. Paul writes from the point of view of a time when the "fulness of the Gentiles" entering the Church has just begun and is far from being completed. As they read this text in the context of the time we live in, many assume that the situation has changed. The proclamation of the gospel is supposed to have reached all the nations of the earth. To what extent is this assumption valid?

Let me bring forward "signs of the times" of a very different sort. I just arrived at our conference from war-stricken Ukraine. I live in Kyiv, a city that recently went through an encirclement by hostile forces. For a large part, enemy soldiers came from predominantly Buddhist and Muslim ethnicities and nations, all under the command of a country that likes to call itself Christian. A capital city famous for its ancient Christian churches came on the verge of being plundered by troops formed of non-Christian soldiers sent over by a pretended Christian state. One wonders about the success of the Church's age-old "mission to the nations" in this case. If I am not mistaken, the only leader of a religious tradition established in Russia who took a stand against this aggression is Pinchas Goldschmidt, Moscow's chief rabbi. Is this whole discussion really about "Israel's hardening"? Is it not rather about the failure of the Church to properly achieve the "mission to the nations" with which she was entrusted since the time of the Jerusalem council?

Let me ask: How come we are still so far from the moment when the fullness of the nations will enter the Church? It seems as if the course of history contemplated by Paul had stopped at some point. It feels as if both the Church and the Synagogue had gone off the rails that he had described.

A number of texts, both from Luke and Paul himself, tell us about the crucial experience of Paul on the road to Damascus. We can derive even more information from Christian commentaries. However, to what extent do all these sources give us access to the heart of Paul's experience? Something of Paul's fundamental understanding of God and God's relation to his people of Israel must have remained identical before and after Damascus. Otherwise, this series of events would not have produced the sense of profound coherence that guided Paul throughout the rest of his existence.

There is probably one biblical principle that Paul was already familiar with before his conversion and that received particular prominence after his conversion. I have in mind the principle of God's impartiality. There is no way our human considerations could stand in the sight of God. I believe Paul's conversion went together with a fundamental reappraisal of God's impartiality.

Paul refers to this principle when he justifies his mission to the Gentiles:

> But from those who were of high reputation (what they were makes no difference to me; God shows no partiality)—well, those who were of reputation contributed nothing to me. (Gal 2:6 NAS)

The Epistle to the Galatians is meant to speak to the culture of its addressees. The importance of the principle of God's impartiality might not strike us as evident here. Still, it is clear from this passage that Paul refers to this principle as the ultimate argument deciding the issue at stake.

I do not want to discuss Paul's attitude toward those whom he describes as enjoying a "high reputation." I merely wish to point out that, for Paul, the standing of the latter in the Church does not depend on their past achievements but on God's choice. And what dictates God's choice is his impartiality.

As we know, the Jerusalem community was entirely formed of Jewish disciples. Paul has in mind those from among Israel who stood at the head of the community. He writes that God manifested his impartiality when he chose and established them regardless of who they were. As I see it, this attitude testifies to Paul's fundamental understanding of the Church of Jesus Christ. God confirmed the election of Israel through his Messiah, and at the same time, he demonstrated that his election would not derive from any human considerations. All acknowledgement of purely human achievements must definitively be put aside.

From Paul's perspective, the principle of God's impartiality provides a new foundation for Israel's election and uniqueness among the nations. I would venture to interpret the Damascus Road experience of Paul and the beginning of his mission to the nations on this basis. Unfortunately, one needs more than the little time given to me here to fully display what I have in mind here.

Speaking of Luke now, it is fair to claim that he widely developed this theme from the point of view of someone who was called out from the nations. In the Book of Acts, the events that take place at the house of Cornelius are given a central role. It is there that we read the following words:

> And opening his mouth, Peter said, "I most certainly understand now that God is not one to show partiality, but in every nation the man who

> fears Him and does what is right, is welcome to Him." (Acts 10:34–35 NAS)

Acts chapter 10 offers a detailed description of the change in Peter's attitude toward the nations as a result of the new revelation. It is in this context that the principle of God's impartiality recurs. The God of Israel, who has no regard for individuals, looked graciously not only at Peter, but also at Cornelius, and this revelation triggers a fundamental change in Peter's attitude. This comes as a symmetrical echo to what Paul writes about the apostles from among Israel, "those who were of high reputation" on the basis of the very same principle (Gal 2:6). Just as with Gentiles, God holds for nothing any external criteria when dealing with those from Israel. This realization is intimately connected with the change of attitude occurring in Paul.

The God who has no regard for human advantages and social positions is the God who establishes new bonds between human beings as well as between nations. Missions from one nation directed at another nation are the result of this state of things. At the same time, the principle that justifies missions of this type is no longer to be found in the privileged status of a particular nation, but in the choice of God.

According to Luke, the disciple called out from the Gentiles, it is Peter, called out from Israel, who receives the mission to proclaim to Gentiles a God who shows no partiality. In other words, the chosen people only are entitled to announce to the nations that they, too, are given to enter God's chosen family. Meanwhile, according to Paul, the disciple called out from Israel, Messianic Israel itself, as God's special possession, stands on the principle of God's impartiality. That Israel is God's people forever receives a confirmation from the blessing that God has bestowed on its mission to the nations.

The episode that records how Paul took Titus to Jerusalem further corroborates this concept of the mission to the nations:

> Then after an interval of fourteen years I went up again to Jerusalem with Barnabas, taking Titus along also. And it was because of a revelation that I went up; and I submitted to them the gospel which I preached among the Gentiles, but I did so in private to those who were of reputation, for fear that I might be running, or had run, in vain. But not even Titus who was with me, though he was a Greek, was compelled to be circumcised. (Gal 2:1–3 NAS)

Titus' presence was probably not simply due to a desire to present an example of a Christian convert from the Gentiles in Jerusalem. For Paul, Titus was a close associate, a fellow missionary among the Gentiles. Titus was a Greek, and this, from a purely human perspective, could have been seen as conducive to developing the mission among the Greeks: "The Jews are to go to the Jews, the Greeks to the Greeks." Still, had Paul thought exclusively along those lines, he would not have acted as he did. After all, he himself never hid the fact that he was a Jew; on the contrary.

In my opinion, Paul's way of thinking and behaving is much easier to understand when interpreted in a different key. Taking his letters into account, one cannot question Paul's commitment to fostering unity between Jews and non-Jews in all the communities. This emphasis on unity must have had an impact on the way missionary teams came to be conceived. Teams of preachers formed of Jews and Gentiles living in harmony with one another would be sent to the nations. This was a model for missions that Paul may have had in mind when he and Titus discussed this matter with the Apostles in Jerusalem.

I see another confirmation of this concept of mission in a passage from Acts related to the community in Jerusalem. The passage reports a letter sent by the apostolic community in Jerusalem, to disciples from the nations. One cannot overestimate the importance of the letter's beginning: "The apostles and the brethren who are elders, to the brethren in Antioch and Syria and Cilicia who are from the Gentiles, greetings" (Acts 15:23 NAS). To summarize the gist of this address: "We are your brethren, the elder brethren, and you who are from the nations, you are our brethren." A new sign of the accomplishment of God's eschatological design is to call "brothers" those who so far had not been brothers. All are welcome in a home that they will have in common. This process goes back to the events that took place at the house of Cornelius, but it had to be approved in Jerusalem. The community called out from Israel had to manifest this acceptance; without it, all those who stood outside could never have imagined that they would be granted access to the promises made to Israel. The understanding of Jerusalem as an eschatological sign has its foundation here.

Israel's election entrusts this nation with the task of proclaiming a God who has no regard for purely human superiority and social positions. In a very concrete way, Israel comes to the accomplishment of her election when she turns to the nations, as we see with Paul. Conversely, the nations eventually discover their God when they come to recognize the primacy of Israel's election, as we see with Luke. The Church's mission to the Gentiles cannot happen without Israel, but neither can Israel be herself without going beyond herself.

I trust that we see this process unfolding with the emergence of Messianic Jews. The nations in the Church need Messianic Jews, and Messianic Jews need the nations. What happened once in Jerusalem with the first council of the Apostles must happen again reciprocally so that a common blessing might be bestowed on the witness of both parts of the Church.

Mark Kinzer writes about the process that leads Jews to discover that the crucified Jesus is their brother. A similar challenge stands before the nations. They are invited to recognize their brother in Jesus, the King of the Jews. Only thus will the partial hardening of Israel's heart and that of the nations find healing.

The Case for a Catholic Theological Affirmation of Israel[1]

Gavin D'Costa

Introduction

At Vatican II, *Lumen Gentium* (1964) para. 16 and *Nostra Aetate* (1965) para. 4 insisted the Jewish covenant made by God with his people, the Jewish people, is irrevocable. This is what St Paul says in Romans 11:29 about biblical Judaism.[2] In 1980, Pope Saint John Paul II took the further step of identifying the biblical Judaism of *Nostra Aetate* not only with the Church's own roots, but also with post-biblical Rabbinic Judaism, the basis for modern contemporary Judaisms. In doing this, the Pope highlighted that contemporary Judaism is seen as in a covenant relationship with God because the gifts, promises, and callings made by God to the Jews are irrevocable. This does raise a difficult question for Catholicism: Does this underwrite all forms of Judaism—Liberal,

1. A full version of this claim can be found in Gavin D'Costa, *Catholic Doctrines on the Jewish People After Vatican II* (Oxford: Oxford University Press, 2019). Some of the material of this paper draws on Gavin D'Costa, "Catholic Zionism: The Jewish State Is a Sign of God's Fidelity," *First Things* (Jan 2020), 14–19. See also the range of Catholic views on this matter in Gavin D'Costa and Faydra Shapiro (eds.), *Contemporary Catholic Approaches to the People, Land, and State of Israel* (Washington, DC: Catholic University of America Press, 2022).

2. I outline the Council and its teachings in Gavin D'Costa, *Vatican II: Catholic Doctrines on Jews and Muslims* (Oxford: Oxford University Press, 2014).

Reform, Conservative, Orthodox, Atheist, and Secular Judaisms, and of course, Messianic Judaism—the focus of our conference? For the sake of argument, I will presume that the promises were made by God to the "Jewish people," meaning both ethnic and religious Jews, and thus encompass all the groups above—and more.[3]

What does God's irrevocable covenant mean regarding those specific promises and gifts? More precisely, what does this mean regarding the "land promise" to the Jewish nation that saturates what Catholics call the Old Testament and what Jews call the Hebrew Bible?[4] Is that particular gift still valid?

Addressing this question in a tense Middle East is difficult: Muslims, Middle Eastern Catholic Christians and other Christian communities, and of course the Jewish people—all have an investment in the question, and all are dear to Catholics. Given the politics, the theological question might best be avoided at this time in history. Any answer will create new antagonisms. But theology should not be hostage to politics, but to God's revelation. What, if anything, does revelation say to a Catholic on this question?

God's revelation also demands justice and peace, thus in everything that follows please take it for granted that I fully support the Holy See's Fundamental Agreement with Israel of 1993 and its Fundamental Agreement of 2000 with the PLO and the recognition of a Palestinian State by the Holy See in 2015. The Holy See draws upon the 1947 UN partition plan as its starting point for both Israel and Palestine.[5] These political and diplomatic agreements are made by the Secretary of State and are based on international law, as interpreted by the Holy See, and in the interests of the Holy See, and are not always decisions with a theological rationale.

I should also make clear that I hold a theological soft supersessionist viewpoint, by which I mean that Jesus Christ is the Messiah and the

3. See the 2013 Pew Survey which takes a wide approach like my own: https://www.pewresearch.org/religion/2013/10/01/sidebar-who-is-a-jew/ (accessed April 11, 2025). The Catholic Church has not formally attended to this point in her teachings.

4. Admittedly, these are different texts in content, ordering, significance, and hermeneutical reading strategies.

5. George Emile Irani, *The Papacy and the Middle East: The Role of the Holy See in the Arab–Israeli Conflict, 1962–1984* (Notre Dame, IN: University of Notre Dame Press, 1986).

fulfillment of the promises made to Israel; but this does not eradicate the God-given status of the covenant with the Jewish people, or the promises made to them.[6] Aligning these two claims is part of the tightrope walk for post-Conciliar Catholicism.

The case for theologically affirming Israel, with qualifications

My argument has four steps. I of course simplify. First, what does the Old Testament say about the land promise? Second, what does the New Testament say about the land promise? Third, how do these teachings relate to the founding of Israel, starting in 1948? In this brief paper I will only outline the bare bones of a positive answer which would require further defense and argument. Fourth, I will consider the claims made by Messianic Jews.

Step One: Old Testament

The Old Testament is rich with different themes related to the land. Seventy percent of references when covenant is mentioned are linked explicitly to the promise of the land. Amidst this complexity there are three indisputable elements.

The first is God's promise of the land to Abraham and his descendants (Gen 12; 15; 17). The Jewish people are not chosen because of the land. Key figures like Moses never enter the land. They are hardly less Jewish for it. The people existed first. Within the land promises themselves, however, the boundaries of the land are drawn in different ways. Genesis 15:18–21 depicts the largest area. Smaller but varying borders are depicted in Exodus 23:31; Numbers 34:1–15; Deuteronomy 1:7; 11:24; Joshua 1:2–4; and Ezekiel 47:13–20; with 1 Kings 4:7–25 presented not as a promise as such, but as a temporary fulfillment of the promises. Scholars dispute whether these are boundaries "fixed" by God in the narratives or territory related to historical context and existing political conditions to facilitate a home for the people. Regarding boundaries, recall Genesis 13:5–13. A dispute arises between Lot and

6. I agree with David Novak, *Talking with Christians: Musings of a Jewish Theologian* (Grand Rapids, MI: Eerdmans, 2005): 164, who argues that the real problem is "hard" not "soft" supersessionism, for the Christian could not be a Christian without at least soft supersessionism.

Abram over the land. Abram offers Lot first choice of the land so that the dispute may be resolved amicably. Lot chooses the finest portion and Abram is content. Peace and justice, at Abram's cost, have been restored. Likewise with Isaac and the men of Abimelech in Genesis 26:12–33, as an example pertaining to unrelated neighbors within the land.

Second, Israel's gift of the land from God also requires, from his people, a moral and cultic purity (Lev 18:24–28; Num 35:33–34; Deut 28:15–68; Josh 24:14–24). One aspect of moral purity requires treating the stranger justly. The concern for the stranger in the land occurs thirty-six times, often accompanied with the contextual explanation of why this is so important: "you know the feelings of a stranger, for you were strangers in the land of Egypt" (Exod 23:9). I should make clear that I am not thinking of Palestinians in the modern context as "strangers" to the land, but only indicating the importance of this theme. The biblical narrative shows that the people of Israel consistently fall away from this high calling to moral purity. Becoming the people is a process with a lot of messiness and no easy linear trajectory. As Catholics we should have some sympathy given that we are called, by *Lumen Gentium* para. 6, to be the "spotless spouse of the spotless Lamb." The failure of the Catholics to live up to that high standard does not mean we condemn the call and vocation and gift. The same, at the very least, would apply to Israel.

Third, lest the unconditional gift and the process of becoming God's people become a cause for complacency, Leviticus 18:28 contains a stark warning: "if you defile the land, it will vomit you out as it vomited out the nations that were before you." This is key for why Catholics cannot see the modern return of the Jewish people as *the fulfillment* of biblical prophecy regarding the end times. That presumes to make a judgment that only God can make. This in no way negates the promise, but allows for what the promise may further signify in the history of salvation.

I have not touched upon a wide range of issues: the destruction of the inhabitants of the land (*kherem*); the place of the temple; the role of Jerusalem. My initial conclusion, supported by a range of Catholic exegetes, is that the land promise made to Israel is central to the idea of the promises and gifts made by God to his people.[7]

7. See, e.g., the Pontifical Biblical Commission, *The Jewish People and Their Sacred Scriptures in the Christian Bible* (Città del Vaticano, 2002): paras 33, 37, 48, 54, and 65.

Is it possible to avoid a supersessionist reading of the Old Testament while keeping intact the Church's Christological center in the New Testament? Professor Tück also addresses this in his paper in this volume.

Step Two: New Testament

In the New Testament, the Church is never called the "new Israel." In the eighty usages of "Israel," it consistently refers to the Jewish people or their polity or to the land directly.

There are three New Testament themes that are important.

First, Jesus is entirely committed to the land and the Jewish people. Jesus orients his ministry in relation to the land, both at the beginning and the end of his ministry. The birth narratives enact the people's exile in Egypt followed by the holy family's return to the land from Egypt (see Matt 2:13–23). During Jesus' ministry he never leaves the land. He is only concerned with Israel, his people (Matt 15:21–28). Going "to the ends of the earth" is left to the Church gathered around him after the resurrection. This conforms to the expectations regarding the arrival of the Jewish Messiah—who will be a light to the nations. Jesus will make Israel, the people and the land, a light to the nations (Isa 49:6; 60:1–3; Luke 2:32) so that all will worship Israel's God.

Second, many of Jesus' teachings focus on the land. Take for instance: "Blessed are the meek, for they shall inherit the earth" (Matt 5:5). Many biblical scholars argue it is better rendered: "Blessed are the meek, for they shall inherit the *land*." Matthew was drawing on Psalm 37:11. In that psalm, the Hebrew *eretz* refers to the land of Israel, not the "world." Four other verses in Psalm 37 repeat the phrase "inherit the land" with the land of Israel as the clear referent. This would mean that his Jewish disciples would eventually "inherit" the land in the renewal of all things (Matt 19:27–30).

Third, after the resurrection, in Acts 1:6, Jesus responds affirmatively to the question regarding his restoration of the "kingdom to Israel." But he also warns the disciples that the exact timing of this event is "not for you to know." It is the Father's initiative. Any Jewish listener, and all the disciples were Jewish in the narrative, would know this reference is to the land. Mark Kinzer's book *Jerusalem Crucified, Jerusalem Risen* offers a close exegetical reading of the New Testament on this theme, showing that Acts and Luke are centrally structured around the importance of the land.[8]

Fourth, the focus on the land is not confined to Jesus alone. St Paul cites the land gift in Acts 13:19 as part of his recalling of God's mighty acts, culminating (but not finishing) in Jesus Christ. It is the same Paul who also in Romans 9:4 speaks in the present tense of the "promises" belonging to Israel, and in Romans 11:29 says these "gifts" are irrevocable. For any Jewish reader it would be clear that one of these gifts is the land. It is, after all, the secondary focus of the covenantal gift, after the primary one: the creation of a people. All these and many other passages point to one thing: The early followers of Jesus knew that the land was central to the gospel, both in its promise to the Jewish people and its relationship to a messianic restoration.

But the New Testament is complex, as it reconfigures the Old messianically. If the land promise is not consigned to "replacement theology," we must ask whether the restoration of the people to the "land of Israel" (Matt 2:20) should be considered an eschatological sign of Jesus' return? It is difficult to deny that this might be the case. Only God knows. That is not to avoid the important question. It is to answer it saying, we cannot know the hour and must, as Jesus tells us, remain diligent discerning the signs. The creation of Israel in 1948 is a sign that calls for precisely such a discernment, a point that I shall return to shortly.

Finally, what of the New Testament references that seem to move away from the particularity of the land and universalize the kingdom? For example, the location of the transgeographical temple in the risen body of Christ? Jesus says he will rebuild the temple which is his risen body (John 2:19). This universalist movement in the New Testament, leading to the cosmic Christ, remains grounded in the particular, the historical Jesus of Nazareth. The particular is the gate to the universal. The universal does not dematerialize or destroy the particular. Thus one might propose that just as Jesus Christ is the scandal of particularity, so is the land and the Jewish people, both of which constitute his material formation.

8. Mark S. Kinzer, *Jerusalem Crucified, Jerusalem Risen: The Resurrected Messiah, the Jewish People, and the Land of Promise* (Eugene, OR: Cascade, 2018).

When the Pontifical Biblical Commission investigated this question back in 2001, they acknowledged differing traditions regarding the significance of the land in the New Testament for Christians. This question is genuinely not resolved. However, the section treating the New Testament ends: "It should not be forgotten, however, that a specific land was promised by God to Israel and received as a heritage" (para. 57). I am suggesting one way in which we might take that seriously Christologically without de-particularizing the promise of the land, nor slipping into a relativist position (that both Judaism and Christianity are true as they stand—which is not possible to hold).

My tentative conclusions so far are: (a) that the promises to the Jewish people regarding the land can be read as intact—and this is in keeping with the intentions of the Council, that the irrevocability of God's promises should not be denied; (b) that those promises are reconfigured in Jesus Christ, but not in a way that dematerializes the land promise to the Jewish people; and (c) that the land promise to the Jewish people may well be related to eschatology, something that is an open question.

Does any of this apply to Israel in 1948 and following? While all the above may be true and valuable, it is vital to read this sign of the times rightly and address the challenge.

Step Three: Modern Israel

Three qualifications pertain to the phrase "modern Israel": First, I use it to denote the Jewish people living upon the land, not the form of nation state or any particular political party that may run that state, or its prudential judgments. It goes without saying that some form of governance is required for the safety and security of the Jewish people in the land, but I take the *form of governance* to be a contingent factor. The promise by God to the Jewish people is not contingent. Second, I keep with the Holy See's affirmation of the 1947 UN boundaries when speaking about "Israel" and "Palestine," recognizing that this is deeply problematic but is required to advance our reflection on the subject. Third, the Palestinian claims regarding their homeland are intractable, and that should not go out of focus in what follows. The Church's support of modern Israel could not call into question the Church's support for justice for the Palestinian people. Reconciling the two claims is no easy task—which is to be expected when so much blood and tears have been spilled.

My sole question now is whether the biblical promises might relate to Israel from 1948 onward—in terms of people and land, not in support of any government or particular form of governance.

First, if there is an ingathering of Jews to the land—which is certainly the case—this may be God's providential action. Another question: Could modern Israel be the beginning of the end days? Can either of these even be considered when so much darkness and tragedy surrounded the early days of Israel, when murder, destruction, and dispossession are also part of the story? It seems likely that the first question should and can be answered affirmatively, especially given the lead of Pope John Paul II. In his 1991 Pastoral Visit to Brazil, the Pope met with Jewish leaders in Brasilia. In his speech to these leaders, he cited Ezekiel 34:13, employing the Old Testament to read modern history, and employing a passage central to the land promise:

> May our Jewish brothers and sisters, who have been "gathered among other peoples and assembled in other places and taken to their own land," to the land of their ancestors, be able to live there in peace and security, on the "mountains of Israel," guarded by the protection of God, their true shepherd.[9]

If that gathering was the initiative of secular Zionists with the support of evangelical British Christians, it does not seem to matter. That the Pope interprets this ingathering biblically, does matter.

But asserting God's providential care for his people is different logically to the question of whether modern Israel is the beginning of the end days, a sign of the final fulfillment of God's actions in salvation history. Attention to Jesus' teachings requires modesty about confidently declaring this to be the case. Close attention to the biblical promises reinforces reticence: The people may be "vomited out" as we are reminded in Leviticus. It has happened before. We cannot force God's hand or prematurely declare this is *the* fulfillment of Scripture. This is crucial. Please note, I do not rule this out but argue for a considered reticence which is appropriate to the truth of revelation given to us. In

9. https://www.vatican.va/content/john-paul-ii/it/speeches/1991/october/documents/hf_jp-ii_spe_19911015_brasile-comunita-ebraica.html (accessed April 11, 2025). The Ezekiel passage reads: "And I will bring them out from the people, and gather them from the countries, and will bring them to their own land, and feed them upon the mountains of Israel by the rivers, and in all the inhabited places of the country."

conclusion, the ingathering of the Jewish people to the land and their preservation as a people is deeply biblical and cannot be ignored.

Second, justice for the Palestinians is non-negotiable. Justice for all plays a thundering role throughout both the Old and New Testament. Justice is central to Catholic Social Teaching and is grounded in revelation, not modernity's politics. The Catholic Church has a long history of supporting the Palestinian peoples and this must continue. The American and European churches' concerns cannot be played off against those of the Middle Eastern churches. Both Palestinians and Jews have a case—both sides make a demand related to biblical truth—one regarding the land promise, one regarding that justice be exercised. Both claims are a demand on the Church.

Pope Francis, in his speech during the "prayer for peace" visit of Mahmoud Abbas and Shimon Peres to the Vatican in 2014, said: "Peace-making calls for courage, much more so than warfare. It calls for the courage to say yes to encounter and no to conflict, yes to dialogue and no to violence."[10] Whether the result of conversation would be a two-state solution, a single-state bi-national federation agreement, or one of many models floated, is a prudential judgment best reached by the parties involved at the very least.

Third, Catholics in the modern period do not usually affirm "nation-states" per se as God-given, although the relationship of the Catholic Church to different political states is very complex and varied.[11] Some forms of Christian Zionism have often been configured as an underwriting of a nation-state created by God.[12] Some Christian Zionists like Pat Robertson in effect say: "If you oppose Israel, you oppose God." This is to conflate problematically the people, the land, and the modern nation-state of Israel as indivisible. There are two serious objections to this way of construing matters: one historical, the other theological.

The historical objection. Zionism never had a single view of the nation-state, and has encompassed complex relationships between

10. June 8, 2014: http://www.vatican.va/content/francesco/en/speeches/2014/june/documents/papa-francesco_20140608_invocazione-pace.html (accessed April 11, 2025).

11. Paul Christopher Manuel, Lawrence C. Reardon, and Clyde Wilcox, eds., *The Catholic Church and the Nation-State: Comparative Perspectives* (Washington, DC: Georgetown University Press, 2006).

12. See Samuel Goldman, *God's Country. Christian Zionism in America* (Philadelphia, PA: University of Pennsylvania Press, 2018).

people, land, and the state. Dmitry Shumsky's book, *Beyond the Nation-State*,[13] shows how mainstream Zionist leaders also envisioned the future Jewish state in Palestine as either bi-national or part of a larger multi-national framework. This was true of Leon Pinsker, Vladimir Jabotinsky, Theodor Herzl, Ahad Ha'am, and David Ben-Gurion. After 1948, historians wrote a different, more teleological story—and Zionism continued in its many mutations. Further, amongst contemporary Jewish Zionists, many are deeply critical of the actions of the Jewish nation-state. There is no question that there must be some form of governance for people in the land, but it does not mean that the God-given form is the current nation-state.

The theological objection. Emeritus Pope Benedict wrote in 2018 wisely on our topic:

> The question of what to make of the Zionist project was also controversial for the Catholic Church. From the beginning, however, the dominant position was that a theologically-understood acquisition of land (in the sense of a *new political messianism*) was unacceptable. After the establishment of Israel as a country in 1948, a theological doctrine emerged that eventually enabled the political recognition of the State of Israel by the Vatican. At its core is the conviction that a strictly theologically-understood state—a Jewish faith-state [*Glaubensstaat*] that would view itself as the theological and political *fulfillment* of the promises—is unthinkable within history according to Christian faith and contrary to the Christian understanding of the promises.[14]

There are good grounds for Emeritus Pope Benedict's rejection, given the precise specification of what he is rejecting. Note, he is not rejecting the possibility that Pope John Paul affirmed above: that the State of Israel in 1948 and following reflects God's love and care for his people. After the Shoah, they have finally been able to get back to the land of promise. What he is rejecting is a particular Jewish view of the land: one that signifies that a Jewish faith-state is the theological and political fulfillment of the promises. There are many reasons that one

13. Dmitry Shumsky, *Beyond the Nation-State: The Zionist Political Imagination from Pinsker to Ben-Gurion* (New Haven, CT: Yale University Press, 2019).

14. Pope Benedict XVI, "Grace and Vocation Without Remorse: Comments on the Treatise *De Iudaeis*" (Nicholas J. Healey, trans.), *Communio* 45 (2018): 163–84, at 178; original text: Pope Benedict XVI, "Gnade und Berufung ohne Reue. Anmerkungen zum Traktat 'De Judaeis,'" *Communio* 47 (2018): 387–406 (emphasis added).

might wish to say no to such a conception. From a Catholic viewpoint, the theological fulfillment of history comes with Jesus Christ. Even if the return to the land by the Jewish people became part of Catholic consciousness, as I have been urging, it would not signify the fulfillment of the promises as understood by contemporary Judaism. For that fulfillment for Rabbinic Judaism excludes the affirmation that Jesus of Nazereth is the Messiah, the Christ. It is not clear why it is "unthinkable" that such a Jewish state in the land may not pre-figure the *return* of the Jewish Messiah, Jesus Christ, not the first coming of the Messiah, as the latter has happened.

But there are many other conceptions of the land held by Jewish people in and outside Israel and it is not clear whether the one particular conception stated by Benedict exhausts all the many possibilities. Benedict did not probe further in this important essay as to other possible configurations that could be supported by Catholic theology. Above, I have been suggesting one. However, and most importantly, he seems to recognize the point I am making because almost immediately after the quote just cited, he continues: "The Vatican . . . has recognized the State of Israel as a modern constitutional state, and sees it as a legitimate home of the Jewish people, the rationale of which cannot be derived directly from Holy Scripture. Yet, in another sense, *it expresses God's faithfulness to the people of Israel.*"[15]

The final sentence stands in creative tension with the first. How can the State of Israel express "God's faithfulness to his people," yet that very claim not somehow be derived from Scripture? Perhaps one way to resolve the tension would be to see that speaking about an event in 1948 as fulfillment can only be an indirect derivation from Scripture? Scripture gives no dates on the restoration of Israel to the land, and in this sense is indirect, but what can be said directly is precisely what Pope John Paul II affirmed: the State of Israel "expresses God's faithfulness to the people of Israel." And if that much can be said, then it cannot be that the State of Israel can be removed from this configuration of affirmation. Thus I have been recommending a way in which we might affirm the people on the land theologically, without underwriting any Jewish conception of the state's significance. The latter is not done disrespectfully, but indeed, because of an authentically Catholic respect

15. Benedict XVI, "Grace and Vocation" (see note 14), 178 (emphasis added).

whereby Catholics need to listen to what Jews have to say and can only agree or disagree on the basis of Catholic teaching. Hence, if we distinguish, as I have done, the state from the people and the land, might it then make sense to speak of God's faithfulness to the people of Israel? I believe so—and so does Emeritus Pope Benedict.

The way forward through this genuine tension is surely to decouple the people and land (indirectly affirmed in the Bible) from the nation state (which is not). Admittedly, some form of positive affirmation of the need of governance for people must be conceded, but not granted theological status in itself. Catholic theology cannot underwrite which form of governance is best, although it is able to criticize various forms based on its Social Doctrine.

Step Four: Messianic Jews?

Before concluding, let me now turn to the status of Messianic Jews in relation to the conclusion I have drawn.

I wish to distinguish between three types of "Messianic Jews," although this is hardly a comprehensive classification: (a) those who are not so concerned with the gentile churches since they have excluded and done harm to Jewish followers of Jesus and have sinned grievously against the Jewish people;[16] (b) those who are concerned to establish a bilateral ecclesiology with gentile followers of Jesus to establish a bridge and find solidarity with both gentile followers of Jesus and with the Jewish people (e.g., Mark Kinzer);[17] and (c) those Jewish followers of Christ who have become part of the Catholic Church and are variously represented in the current volume, especially Antoine Lévy who has paid most attention to this question.[18] All three groups are inheritors of the promise, and in my view all three groups rightly make claims about Israel, Kinzer more strongly than I have, and Lévy more strongly than I have, but less strongly than Kinzer.[19]

16. Found in the writing of Daniel C. Gruber, *The Separation of Church and Faith, vol. 1: Copernicus and the Jews* (Hanover, NH: Elijah Publishing, 2016).

17. See Mark S. Kinzer, *Postmissionary Messianic Judaism: Redefining Christian Engagement with the Jewish People* (Grand Rapids, MI: Brazos, 2005).

18. In what follows I draw most on Antoine Lévy, *Jewish Church. A Catholic Approach to Messianic Judaism* (Lanham, MD: Lexington Books, 2021).

19. Kinzer, *Jerusalem Crucified, Jerusalem Risen* (see note 8); and Antoine Lévy, "*Tractatio Theologico-Politica*: Palestinian Suffering and the Official Catholic Teaching

This leads to two important points on which I would like to conclude. If the arguments advanced are persuasive to Catholics, then gentile Catholics and Jewish Catholics are impacted by them in different ways. For gentile Catholics, critical support of Israel is very important as a theological datum deriving from revelation. For Jewish Catholics, the same is true, while they themselves have a claim regarding the right of return (*aliyah*) to the land promised by God. This relates to the important Israeli Supreme Court decision regarding Oswald Rufeisen, the Catholic friar sometimes known as Brother Daniel, who was born into a Jewish family, helped Jews escape the Nazis, and was celebrated in Yad Vashem, and who converted to Catholicism. Nevertheless, after his living in Israel he claimed *aliyah* and was denied it on the social-cultural grounds that he had converted to another religion.[20] This issue has been revived by Antoine Lévy in an op-ed in the *Times of Israel*,[21] and of course, the thinking about Jewish identity is very fluid and the Supreme Court have more recently taken the simple path of a broader category of the definition of who is a Jew.

The Supreme Court after the Rufeisen case also extended the judgment to Messianic Jews in 1989 in the famous Beresford case.[22] However, that judgment was overthrown in 2008 regarding Messianic Jews, with further relevant developments in 2021 when Reform and Conservative Jews were recognized as "Jews" and not as "converts."[23] It may well be the case that soon Catholic Jews could qualify for *aliyah*.

The second point I would wish to make is that from a Catholic ecclesiological standpoint, Antoine Lévy's position is (one might say, obviously) more coherent and attractive as it takes seriously the question

---

on the State of Israel" in *Contemporary Catholic Approaches*, ed. D'Costa & Shapiro (see note 1), 191–218.

20. The Supreme Court ruling can be read in full at: https://openscholar.huji.ac.il/sites/default/files/hebrewlaw/files/rsvvld_rvpyzn_ngd_shrhpnym_bgts_ms_72-62.pdf (accessed April 11, 2025). The English translation of the judgement can be found in *Selected Judgments of the Supreme Court of Israel*, ed. Asher Felix Landau (Jerusalem: Ministry of Justice, 1971): 1–77.

21. See: https://blogs.timesofisrael.com/im-a-catholic-friar-and-also-a-jew-the-law-of-return-should-work-for-me/ (accessed April 11, 2025).

22. Linda Alexander, *The Unpromised Land: The Struggle of Messianic Jews, Gary & Shirley Beresford* (Baltimore, MD: Messianic Jewish Publishers, 1994).

23. See: https://www.bloomberg.com/opinion/articles/2021-03-02/israel-expands-its-right-of-return-and-sparks-a-debate (accessed April 11, 2025).

of what constitutes "unity" of the Jewish and gentile *ecclesiae*, whereas Kinzer's bilateral ecclesiology fails to define "unity" in a way that would make sense to Catholic sensibilities. Of course, since Kinzer does not operate on the same premises as Lévy, there is a slight deadlock in the discussion about how to move forward regarding "unity" or bilateral ecclesiology. However, this is not important for the debate on the land and can be left to one side for the moment.

Conclusion

On a personal note, I confess that until my research began some fifteen years ago, I was a strong supporter of the Palestinians and viewed Israel as a colonialist power with no legitimacy in the region. Theology has pushed me to reconsider and change my view, but without undermining my support for the Palestinian people.

Catholics are called to attend to revelation, first and foremost. By not addressing the question of the land, the Catholic Church will not be attentive to revelation. Her silence should not replicate previous silences regarding the matter of the Jewish people.

Response to Gavin D'Costa, "The Case for a Catholic Theological Affirmation of Israel"

Jennifer M. Rosner

It is an honor to respond to my friend and colleague, Gavin D'Costa, whose rigorous and innovative work on this topic deserves due consideration. D'Costa's perspective is nuanced and provocative in the best possible ways, particularly his balanced and even-handed assessment of the land and its ongoing theological significance. In what follows, let me offer four points in response to D'Costa's case for a Catholic theological affirmation of Israel.

1. Gratitude and appreciation

First, I would like to offer a simple word of gratitude for D'Costa's important and constructive work and thinking on these issues. What I find most compelling about D'Costa's perspective is his commitment to taking the biblical text seriously, and—within this commitment—his willingness to soberly reckon with the theological significance of the modern state of Israel, retaining a certain reticence to presume too much in doing so.

There is a restraint in D'Costa's work that reveals his refusal to, as he puts it, hold theology hostage to politics. This aspect of D'Costa's work is honest, hopeful, and refreshingly conducive to constructive engagement. D'Costa's work has a prophetic and urgent ring to it, as he poignantly invokes the Catholic Church's "previous silences regarding the matter of the Jewish people," beseeching Catholics not to replicate this mistake. In this way, there is a strong resonance between D'Costa's perspective and that of Mark Kinzer, in that both attempt to "provide a set of theological parameters within which advocates of the right, left, and center can all take their stand."[1] More on this in point number 4 below.

2. On "moral and cultic purity"

In his discussion of the land in the Old Testament, D'Costa mentions God's requirement of moral and cultic purity among the people of Israel, and he mentions multiple times the reality that God has (and very well could once more) vomit the people out of the land on account of their failure in this regard. This haunting thread of the biblical narrative animates and largely funds the land theology of thinkers such as Walter Brueggemann and Gary Burge; for them, the politics of the modern nation-state serve *only* to call into question any appeal to continuity between biblical promises and current possession of the land. As Burge states unequivocally, *"if Israel makes a biblical claim to the Holy Land, then Israel must adhere to biblical standards of national righteousness."*[2]

Here I would like to draw our attention to a key observation made by Kinzer, namely that there are "two distinct strands of prophetic teaching about Israel's return from exile." The Deuteronomistic strand, exclusively emphasized by Burge and others, "requires Israel's repentance as a condition for its national restoration." However, the primary note sounded in the prophetic texts tells a different story.

> For example, in Ezekiel 36 God restores Israel "for the sake of my holy name," and "not for your sake, O house of Israel" (vss. 21–23; 32). God acts not because Israel has fulfilled a covenantal condition, but because God's name is irrevocably tied to Israel, and because Israel's desolate state brings dishonor to God's name. This act of divine restoration

1. Mark S. Kinzer, *Jerusalem Crucified, Jerusalem Risen: The Resurrected Messiah, the Jewish People, and the Land of Promise* (Eugene, OR: Cascade, 2018): 264.

2. Gary Burge, *Whose Land? Whose Promise? What Christians Are Not Being Told About Israel and the Palestinians* (Cleveland, OH: Pilgrim, 2003): 13 (italics original). See also Walter Brueggemann, *Chosen? Reading the Bible Amid the Israeli–Palestinian Conflict* (Atlanta, GA: Westminster, 2015).

> involves *first* a return to the land (vs. 24), and *then* an internal transformation that enables Israel to obey God's statutes and ordinances (vss. 25–27) and to abide in a renewed covenant relationship (vs. 28). Here Israel's repentance (vs. 31) is a *result* of God's restorative work rather than its *condition*. Moreover, Israel's repentance *follows* rather than precedes its return to the land. A similar eschatological scenario appears in Isaiah 40–66.[3]

To acknowledge *both* strands in the Old Testament allows for a much more creative reading of the modern state of Israel from a biblical perspective. Again, I find D'Costa's restraint in drawing firm conclusions to be wise; but that restraint must go in both ways. Just as we cannot be sure that the modern state of Israel straightforwardly warrants some kind of divine sanction, so too we cannot rule out the possibility that it is part and parcel of God's faithfulness to the people of Israel and reflects God's unyielding commitment to sanctifying his covenant people.

3. *Reconfiguration and "soft supersessionism"*

D'Costa describes his position as a form of "soft supersessionism,"[4] whereby "Jesus Christ is the Messiah and the fulfillment of the promises made to Israel," though in such a way as to not "eradicate the God-given status of the covenant with the Jewish people, or the promises made to them." His reflections on the land flow from this position, such that God's promises "are reconfigured in Jesus Christ, but not in a way that dematerializes the land promise to the Jewish people." D'Costa admits that holding these commitments in tension is "part of the tightrope walk for post-Conciliar Catholicism." Nonetheless, more clarity in *how* to affirm simultaneously both sides of this theological puzzle is necessary, as this particular expression of "soft supersessionism" seems to lie at the heart of the issue.

3. Kinzer, *Jerusalem Crucified, Jerusalem Risen* (see note 1), 253–54. Isaiah 44:22 reads, "I have swept away your transgressions like a cloud, and your sins like mist; return to me, for I have redeemed you." Kinzer (254 n.36) notes that "here the demonstration of divine forgiveness and redemption serves as the motive for Israel's repentance, rather than its result."

4. For a discussion and critique of the term "soft supersessionism," see R. Kendall Soulen, *Irrevocable: The Name of God and the Unity of the Christian Bible* (Minneapolis, MN: Fortress, 2022): 175 n.2.

What does it look like for God to uphold his promises to the Jewish people, particularly regarding the land, *and* for those very promises to be reconfigured in Jesus Christ? It is quite clear how we can wholly uphold either side of this tension; positions exist that read Jesus as merely underwriting God's land promises or, alternately, as doing away with them all together in some kind of hand-waving universalization and spiritualization of God's covenant with Israel. The contours of these two extremes are easy to discern; what is more difficult to tease out is precisely how to hold the two in a kind of creative and prophetic (not to mention, biblically sound) tension. This issue is closely related to the tension between fulfillment and supersessionism, a topic which D'Costa has addressed elsewhere.[5]

4. Decoupling the people and land of Israel from the modern state of Israel

One of the most helpful theological moves that D'Costa makes (again, similar to Kinzer) is to decouple the *people* and *land* of Israel from the modern *state* of Israel. This move creates much-needed breathing room for discussing and reflecting upon God's faithfulness to his covenant and what that means in our day, amidst contemporary human history. D'Costa critiques classic Christian Zionism on this very point: As a theological position, it "conflate[s] problematically the people, the land, and the modern nation-state of Israel as indivisible." In other words, to read profound theological significance into the Jewish people's return to their biblical homeland does not require unwavering and uncritical support of the modern state of Israel as the current mode of human political governance of that homeland.

To decouple land and people from state cuts both ways: It allows us to declare with D'Costa that "the ingathering of the Jewish people to the land and their preservation as a people is deeply biblical and cannot be ignored." And yet, it allows us simultaneously to regard the modern state of Israel as we would any other modern nation-state; it is not endowed with any particular divine sanction, and it cannot be immune from legitimate critique and censure. This decoupling implies

5. Gavin D'Costa, *Catholic Doctrines on the Jewish People After Vatican II* (Oxford: Oxford University Press, 2019): esp. 21–26.

that, while anti-Zionism *may* in some cases be a form of antisemitism, it is not necessarily so. As evidenced by the wide range of Jewish views on the Zionist enterprise, criticizing the modern state of Israel can actually be to uphold the core values that have always stood at the heart of Judaism. Here I find Fr. David Neuhaus' language to be jarringly apt:

> . . . criticizing Zionist ideology, the politics and practices of the State of Israel, its military or state organisms and acting against them do not constitute Antisemitism per se. It is true that there is a fine line to be drawn here to prevent legitimate criticism from becoming racist diatribe but the line must be drawn. . . . Ultimately, this can only be done coherently and with moral integrity when the struggle against all forms of racism, injustice and human rights abuses includes an awareness of both the pernicious traces of continuing Antisemitism and the myriad forms of anti-Palestinian and anti-Arab sentiment, Islamophobia and the brutal whitewashing of occupation and discrimination in Israel-Palestine today.[6]

I would like to conclude with another important observation made by Neuhaus. He notes that, "theology is a discipline profoundly marked by the situation of the theologian. A study of the discipline reveals how much the socio-political context, intellectual formation and personal commitments of the theologian influence his or her perspectives."[7] This key acknowledgment is especially relevant to the current topic at hand, in which each of us brings a unique (and often charged) set of identity markers, convictions, experiences, and perspectives to our theologizing.

I count it a great gift to have D'Costa, Kinzer, and Neuhaus (among others!) as dialogue partners on this topic, for their contrasting views prevent us from formulating theology in cozy, siloed echo chambers in

6. David M. Neuhaus, SJ, "Antisemitism and the Question of Palestine," *Cornerstone* 84 (Spring 2022): 15. For a critique of the term "occupation" from the vantage point of international law, see Eugene Kontorovich, "Pompeo Busts the 'Occupation Myth,'" *Wall Street Journal*, November 19, 2019. https://www.wsj.com/articles/pompeo-busts-the-occupation-myth-11574207220 (accessed October 23, 2022); Abraham Bell and Eugene Kontorovich, "Palestine, *Uti Possidetis Juris*, and the Borders of Israel," *Arizona Law Review* 58.3 (2016): 633–92. https://arizonalawreview.org/palestine-uti-possidetis-juris-and-the-borders-of-israel/ (accessed October 23, 2022).

7. David M. Neuhaus, SJ, "A Catholic Perspective on the People, Land, and State of Israel," in *Contemporary Catholic Approaches to the People, Land, and State of Israel*, ed. Gavin D'Costa and Faydra Shapiro (Washington, DC: The Catholic University of America Press, 2022): 169–90, at 169.

which our views are not adequately challenged or critiqued. Finally, may our discussion of this topic never be detached from a keen awareness of the daily lived reality of the diverse peoples who call this land home, and, amidst our varying positions, may we "be united in a common prayer for peace and for the wellbeing of all who live there."[8]

8. David M. Neuhaus, SJ, "People of Israel, Land of Israel, State of Israel," *La Civiltà Cattolica* (English edn) 4.10 (2020): art. 5, 1020. https://www.laciviltacattolica.com/people-of-israel-land-of-israel-state-of-israel/.

Parousia, Land, and Thousand-Year Kingdom of Peace

Does Augustine's Domestication of Chiliasm Need to Be Revised?

Jan-Heiner Tück

As diverse as the Messianic Jewish movement is internally, so diverse are the eschatological ideas that have developed within the movement. For the majority of Messianic Jews in the United States premillennial ideas dominate, which are influenced by evangelical end-times ideas and show a proximity to *dispensationalism* (Arnold Fruchtenbaum).[1] In a literal interpretation of Scripture, a certain sequence of end-time events is assumed: rapture, tribulation, Parousia of Christ and thousand-year kingdom of peace, release of Satan, general resurrection of the dead, judgment with dual outcome, and consummation.[2] At the same time, a special role is ascribed to the Messianic Jews as the holy remnant of Israel in this scenario. In a certain proximity to this, postmillennial ideas are also represented in the Jewish Messianic movement (David H. Stern, Daniel C. Juster), and at the same time there are amillennial or agnostic positions (Rich Nichol, Baruch Maoz), which

1. Arnold Fruchtenbaum, *Israelology: The Missing Link in Systematic Theology* (Tustin, CA: Ariel Ministries, 1993); Arnold Fruchtenbaum, "Eschatology and Messianic Jews: A Theological Perspective," in *Voices of Messianic Judaism: Confronting Critical Issues Facing a Maturing Movement*, ed. Dan Cohn-Sherbok (Baltimore, MD: Messianic Jewish Publishers, 2001): 211–19.

2. Cf. Richard Harvey, *Mapping Messianic Jewish Theology: A Constructive Approach* (Milton Keynes: Paternoster, 2009): 232–61.

avoid a chronology of end-time events and direct the eschatological hope toward Jesus Christ. Whatever the finer points of the eschatology look like, all variants agree in ascribing theological importance to the land of Israel and the city of Jerusalem and in supporting Zionism. The return of many Jews to Israel, the founding of the state in 1948 three years after the Shoah, and yet also the growing number of Jesus-believing Jews since the late 1960s, are interpreted as signs pointing to the imminent Parousia. Indeed, the believing response of part of Israel is viewed as a prerequisite for the Parousia, which at the same time will restore the kingdom to Israel (Mark Kinzer).[3]

This presents a challenge for Christian eschatology as it is represented by the majority in the sphere of the Catholic Church. In it, apart from a few recent exceptions,[4] no importance is attached to the biblical promise of land and the city of Jerusalem. This *Israel-theological blank space* in eschatology is significant. Even the Parousia expectation has largely faded in the Catholic Church. One is rather skeptical about the scenario of the Second Coming, as it is presented in the Synoptic apocalypses (Mark 13:26–27; Matt 24:30–31; Luke 21:27) and the New Testament epistles (1 Thes 4:15–17; 2 Thes 2:1, 8; Col 3:1; 1 Tim 6:14; 1 Pet 4:13; James 5:7). Under modern conditions, the Parousia expectation has given way to a form of consummation hope that is largely individualized and spiritualized. Karl Rahner, who repeatedly warned against reading apocalyptic ideas as anticipatory reporting of end-time events, expressed this change of Parousia expectation in the statement that Christ "'comes again' insofar as everyone arrives at him."[5] Other

3. Mark S. Kinzer and Russell L. Resnik, *Besorah: The Resurrection of Jerusalem and the Healing of a Fractured Gospel* (Oregon: Cascade, 2021): 89: "The return of Jesus will initiate the restoration of Israel's kingdom . . . the return of Jesus will occur only after, and as a consequence of, the faithful response by his own flesh and blood to his words and person." In the background stand texts like Luke 21:24 and Acts 1:6–7; 3:19–21.

4. Cf. the works of Helmut Hoping, Rudolf Pesch, Christian Rutishauser SJ, and Gavin D'Costa.

5. "'wiederkommt,' insofern alle bei ihm ankommen"—Karl Rahner, "Kirche und Parusie Christi," in Karl Rahner, *Schriften zur Theologie*, vol. 6 (Einsiedeln / Zürich: Benziger, 1965): 348–67, at 348. Cf. Karl Rahner, "Parusie," *Lexikon für Theologie und Kirche* 8 (2nd edn 1963): 123–24, at 124—"who returns, insofar as through his deed all arrive with him at their consummation in salvation or perdition" ["der wiederkehrt, insofern durch seine Tat alle bei ihm zu ihrer Vollendung in Heil oder Verlorenheit ankommen"].

Catholic theologians, such as Walter Kasper,[6] Medard Kehl,[7] and Joseph Ratzinger,[8] also reject the idea that Christ will come in glory at some futuristic Point "X" on the time axis, at some specific location, and stress the incommensurability of time with consummation. From Christ, the risen crucified one, one must read off what is to be expected; everything else is said to be dispensable, time-conditioned, apocalyptic clothing. In universal eschatology, the Parousia motif is focused on the view that the history of the world cannot reach consummation through human efforts, but only through God and his Christ. The reference to God as consummator stands here against secularized chiliasms that want to establish a "kingdom of God without God" (Ernst Bloch).[9]

Here the expectations in the Messianic Jewish movement set clearly contrasting emphases. Against the fading of Parousia expectation in the Church they set the hope that the Messiah will come as King of the Jews. They counter the individualization and spiritualization with collective-historical expectations pertaining to Israel and the nations. And to the abstract hope that Christ comes in that we arrive at him, they give a concrete note by tying the Parousia to the topography of Jerusalem. Jesus will come again as King of the Jews from the Mount of Olives (cf. Zec 14:4; Acts 1:6–12). Messianic Jewish eschatology thus confronts Catholic theology with a segment of its own tradition that was believed to have been overcome—a subtle chiliasm that was advocated by some theologians in the early Church. This raises the question of whether the domestication of chiliasm that Augustine carried out in his work *De civitate Dei*, when he identified the Church age with the thousand-year kingdom, is in need of revision.

To deal with this question, I would like, in a first step, to recall voices of patristic theology that expected a messianic kingdom of peace

6. Walter Kasper, "Die Hoffnung auf die endgültige Ankunft Jesu Christi in Herrlichkeit," *Internationale katholische Zeitschrift – Communio* 14 (1985): 1–14.

7. Cf. Medard Kehl, "'Bis du kommst in Herrlichkeit . . .' Neuere theologische Deutungen der 'Parusie Jesu,'" in *Hoffnung über den Tod hinaus: Antworten auf Fragen der Eschatologie*, ed. Josef Pfammatter and Eduard Christen (Theologische Berichte XIX; Zürich: Benziger, 1990): 95–137.

8. Joseph Ratzinger, *Eschatologie – Tod und ewiges Leben* (Regensburg: Pustet, 2006).

9. "Reich Gottes ohne Gott"—Ernst Bloch, *Das Prinzip Hoffnung* (Frankfurt a. M.: Suhrkamp, 1959): 1413.

and connected Israel-theological references with it. In a second step, I will go into the ecclesiological domestication of chiliasm by Augustine, who, in his writing *De civitate Dei*, identified Christ's thousand-year kingdom of peace with the Church age, a setting of the course that has shaped Catholic theology to this day. In a third step, I would like to deal with the Parousia of Christ, the land of Israel, and chiliasm—three productive irritations that result from the dialogue with Messianic Jewish theology.

1. Voices of patristic theology on the thousand-year reign of Christ

The destruction of Jerusalem in AD 70 and the expulsion of the Jews from Judaea after the Bar Kochba revolt (AD 132–135) were a deep historic caesura that had to be processed theologically. The emergence of rabbinic Judaism can be interpreted as the answer to the ending of the temple cult. At the same time, the destruction of Jerusalem and the expulsion of the Jews from Palestine gave the boost of hope in Jewish-Christian circles that very soon the Messianic kingdom of peace would be established. In the theology of Asia Minor, this hope becomes literarily tangible in Cerinthus, who links the Messianic intermediate kingdom with the concrete expectation that the bodies of the righteous would indulge in sensual pleasures in Jerusalem and that the sacrificial cult would be resumed in Jerusalem.[10] The eschatological sensualism may be alienating, but what is significant is that the expectation of a thousand-year "joyful wedding celebration" is topographically tied to the city of Jerusalem. In Papias of Hierapolis, this earthly chiliasm is further elaborated and linked to the expectation of paradisiacal fruitfulness.[11] Justin Martyr also ascribes historical-theological meaning to the destruction of Jerusalem and the dispersal of the Jews. He regards these historical events as the precondition for the Christians to be able to take over the "new Jerusalem" as an inheritance. In his *Dialogue with Trypho* the Jew, he advocates that the Jews convert to Christ and through baptism receive the spiritual circumcision so that they too can

10. Eusebius of Caesarea, *Ecclesiastical History* III.28.2–6, IV.14.6.

11. Eusebius of Caesarea, *Ecclesiastical History* III.39.11–13; Irenaeus, *Against Heresies* V.33.3–4. Cf. Stefan Heid, *Chiliasmus und Antichrist-Mythos. Eine frühchristliche Kontroverse um das Heilige Land* (Hereditas, 6; Bonn: Borengässer, 1993).

obtain a portion in the inheritance of the new Jerusalem. Justin supposes that with the Parousia of Christ, the Christians can liberate the land of Israel from Roman occupation. He assumes a thousand-year kingdom "in a Jerusalem built up and adorned and enlarged."[12] Here Christians will live together with the righteous of the old covenant, practice agriculture, and continue to multiply through procreation. Justin disputes the Jews' claim to the Holy City, which is said to have passed over to the Christians as the "true . . . Israel."[13]

> But they who persecuted Christ, and still persecute Him, and do not repent, shall not inherit anything in the holy mountain. While the nations that have believed on Him [i.e., Christ], and have repented for all the sins they have committed—they shall inherit, with all the patriarchs and the prophets and the righteous men that have been born of Israel. Even though they do not keep sabbath nor are circumcised nor keep the festivals, they shall certainly inherit the holy inheritance of God.[14]

Stefan Heid comments: "The Jews are expelled from their land—the Christians stake a claim to it!"[15] The continuity of salvation history is secured by chiliasm, insofar as God fulfills the promises he once made. This is a counterpoint to Marcion, who differentiates between the dark, evil Creator God and the good Redeemer God, and who excises from his canon of Holy Scripture the writings of what was later called the Old Testament as well as the Revelation of John. Marcion views chiliasm as an outdated Jewish idea that, after the destruction and expulsion of the Jews from Jerusalem, looks to a warlike Messiah who will reconquer the city and make possible its reconstruction. For him, chiliasm is a regression into a pre-Christian form of hope that acts as if Christ had not already come.

12. Justin, *Dialogue with Trypho* 80.5—A. Lukyn Williams, trans., *Justin Martyr, The Dialogue with Trypho: Translation, Introduction, and Notes* (London: SPCK / New York / Toronto: Macmillan, 1930): 171.

13. Cf. Justin, *Dialogue* 11.5; 123.9 and 135.3—*Ibid.*: 24, 256–57, 278.

14. Justin, *Dialogue* 26.1—*Ibid.*: 52.

15. "Die Juden sind aus ihrem Land vertrieben – die Christen erheben Anspruch darauf!"—Heid, *Chiliasmus und Antichrist-Mythos* (see note 11), 232. Justin "objects regarding the messianic hope of the Jews: The soon resurrection of Israel will not benefit you if you do not convert to Christ" ["wendet gegenüber der messianischen Hoffnung der Juden ein: Die baldige Resurrektion Israels wird euch nicht zugute kommen, wenn ihr euch nicht zu Christus bekehrt"]—*Ibid.*, 47.

Tertullian contradicts him but accommodates Marcion's criticism by toning down the realism and relinquishing a coarsely sensual depiction of the chiliastic hope.[16] Lactantius[17] and Irenaeus of Lyon also hold fast to the expectation of a thousand-year kingdom of peace. Irenaeus, who in his work *Adversus haereses* engages critically with the gnostic currents but also with Marcion, defends not only the unity of the Creator and Redeemer God but also the continuity of salvation history. It is notable that within the framework of his salvation-pedagogical theology, he develops the idea of a recapitulation, into which he integrates chiliasm as an intermediate phase of acclimatization to the final consummation. In the fifth book of *Adversus haereses*, which is devoted to eschatological questions, the following passage is found:

> . . . by means of which kingdom those who shall be worthy are accustomed gradually to partake of the divine nature (*capere Deum*; [Or, "gradually to comprehend God."]); and it is necessary to tell them respecting those things, that it behoves the righteous first to receive the promise of the inheritance which God promised to the fathers, and to reign in it, when they rise again to behold God [*ad apparitionem Domini*] in this creation which is renovated, and that the judgment [*omnium iudicium*] should take place afterwards. For it is just that in that very creation in which they [i.e. the righteous] toiled or were afflicted, being proved in every way by suffering [*probati per sufferentiam*], they should receive the reward of their suffering; and that in the creation in which they were slain because of their love to God, in that they should be revived again; and that in the creation in which they endured servitude, in that they should reign. For God is rich in all things, and all things are His. It is fitting, therefore, that the creation itself, being restored to its primeval condition, should without restraint be under the dominion of the righteous . . .[18]

16. Tertullian, *Against Marcion* III.25—"But we do confess that a kingdom is promised to us upon the earth, although before heaven, only in another state of existence [*alio statu*]; inasmuch as it will be after the resurrection for a thousand years in the divinely-built city of Jerusalem, 'let down from heaven,' (Rev. xxi. 2)." Peter Holmes, trans., *The Five Books of Quintus Sept. Flor. Tertullianus Against Marcion* (Ante-Nicene Christian Library, VII; Edinburgh: T&T Clark, 1878): 170.

17. Lactantius, *Divine Institutes* VII.19–26.

18. Irenaeus of Lyon, *Against Heresies* V.32.1—Alexander Roberts and W.H. Rambaut, trans., *The Writings of Irenæus, vol. II* (Ante-Nicene Christian Library, IX, pp. 1–208; Edinburgh: T&T Clark, 1871): 141–42.

Crucial elements of the chiliastic scenario are found in this passage. With the Parousia of Christ, first the righteous will be resurrected bodily. The emphasis on the *resurrectio carnalis* has an anti-gnostic thrust. They will receive the promised inheritance. Faithfulness to the Old Testament promises that pertain to the renewal of this earth prohibits a spiritualization of the Christian hope. Moreover, the talk of "reward of their suffering" indicates that Irenaeus has martyrs in view, who were killed for their faith. This corresponds to the situation of the Christians in the time before the Constantinian turn, who time and again were exposed to religio-political pressure. The argument aims at a continuity of the topography: The martyrs are to receive their reward in the very world in which they had suffered. Enjoying the fruits and drinking anew from the vine of this earth—but they can only do if they are truly resurrected. Thus, a place beyond the heavens where no wine can grow is just as surely rejected as the gnostic idea of a bodiless resurrection. After the resurrection of the righteous and their thousand-year reign with Christ, there follows the general judgment with a dual outcome.

As witnesses for chiliasm, Irenaeus refers, alongside the oral tradition of presbyters, to the authority of Papias of Hierapolis, who is identified as "hearer of John" and "companion of Polycarp," and yet also to the testimony of the prophets who foretell the kingdom of peace. Isaiah's visions are enlisted, of wolf and lamb grazing together, of the suckling putting his hand in the hole of the asp without it doing anything to him (cf. Isa 11:6–9; 65:25). Both quotations refer to Jerusalem with their mention of Mount Zion. According to Irenaeus, along with peace, there will be prosperity in abundance, of wheat and wine, and yet there will be no lack of herbs either. It is depicted vividly. In the background stands the anti-Marcionite argument about the unity of salvation history. The promises made in the old covenant are redeemed in the new covenant. After the destruction of Jerusalem and the expulsion of the Jews from the Holy Land, there will come a real restitution (cf. Ezek 28:25–26; Isa 65:18–22). Irenaeus explicitly rejects an allegorical interpretation of the prophetic promises.[19] He gives the eschatology an anti-spiritualizing note, which Hans Urs von Balthasar described

19. Cf. *Against Heresies* V.35.2 (*Ibid.*, 154–55)—"and nothing is capable of being allegorized, but all things are stedfast [sic], and true, and substantial, having been made by God for righteous men's enjoyment."

as "heartening."[20] After the end of the chiliastic interregnum, the new heaven and the new earth will come, where the eternal wedding feast of the Lord with the righteous will take place.

In Alexandrine theology, chiliasm comes up against some reservations. The interpretation of the Bible is rejected here as too literal, too "Jewish." Origen expressly advocates a "deterritorialization" of the eschatological expectations. He sets himself apart from chiliasts, "who reduce 'the heavenly Jerusalem, which is the mother of us all' (Cf. Gal 4:26; Heb 12:22.), understanding the prophetic words with unworthy meaning to the condition of one of the earthly cities."[21] He reads spiritually the passages in Isaiah that refer to a kingdom of peace (cf. Isa 55; 65). The Christian hope is not directed toward Israel or Jerusalem but toward the eternal home in heaven.[22]

In the West, chiliasm lost its prominence after the Constantinian turn. With the imperial legal recognition of Christianity by Emperor Theodosius, the interpretation of Rome as the "whore of Babylon" and of the emperor as the "Antichrist" became obsolete. Ambrose leaves out millenarianism, Jerome rejects it, Augustine domesticates it.

2. The ecclesiological domestication of chiliasm by Augustine

According to Augustine, the thousand-year kingdom has already begun with the Church age. Before I go into more detail about his explanations, I would like to note three things in advance:

(1) *Augustine opposes a de-Judaizing of Christianity and defends the Old Testament.* In dispute with the Manichaeans, who take offence at the "horrid" sacrifices and "ridiculous" stories of the Old Testament and therefore remove them from the canon, Augustine defends the unity of Holy Scripture in the duality of Old and New Testaments. He retains the

20. Hans Urs von Balthasar, *The Glory of the Lord: A Theological Aesthetics*, vol. II, ed. John Riches; trans. Andrew Louth, Francis McDonagh, and Brian McNeil (San Francisco, CA: Ignatius Press, 1984), 93; Original German: Hans Urs von Balthasar, *Herrlichkeit. Eine theologische Ästhetik*, vol. II/1 (Einsiedeln: Johannesverlag, 1963), 92—"wohltuend."

21. Origen, *Homilies on Leviticus* 11.3—Gary Wayne Barkley, trans., *Origen, Homilies on Leviticus 1–16* (The Fathers of the Church, 83; Washington, DC: Catholic University of America Press, 1990): 216-17.

22. Cf. Origen, *On the First Principles* II.11.2.

inheritance of Israel, albeit through a biblical hermeneutic that reads it as originating from Christ and oriented toward Christ. According to Augustine, however, the true meaning of their own Scriptures remains closed to the Jews, because they read these *secundum carnem* ["according to the flesh"].[23]

(2) *With the incarnation Augustine also defends the Jewish origin of Jesus.* The Manichaeans represent a Docetic Christology that attributes to Jesus an illusory body.[24] In contrast, Augustine emphasizes that Jesus was born in Bethlehem of Mary, a *virgo israelitica,* and was circumcised on the eighth day (Luke 2:21). In a dispute with Faustus the Manichean, he points out that Christ is a descendant of David "according to the flesh" (cf. Rom 1:3). But the Jews themselves according to Augustine failed to recognize their Messiah and crucified him, which happened due to blindness and obduracy.[25]

(3) *Augustine teaches that the Church is the "novus Israel"* and advocates the salvation-economy form of supersessionism. At the same time, however, he ascribes to the Jews an enduring role in salvation history! He compares them to Cain who murdered his brother Abel.[26] Just as Cain does not wear his mark as a sign of punishment but of protection, so the Jews also remain protected by God throughout history in that they differentiate themselves from other peoples by distinguishing marks such as circumcision, the Sabbath commandment, and the purity regulations. The sons and daughters of the people of Israel, dispersed in all lands, are, without knowing it, witnesses to the truth, in that they keep present the Law and the Prophets, which have been fulfilled in Christ.

> But the Jews, who killed him and would not believe in him, because he must needs die and rise again, were ravaged still more miserably by the Romans, and were utterly uprooted from their kingdom, where they had already been ruled by foreign-born rulers; and they were scattered throughout the lands,—for indeed there is no place where they are not found,—*and so by means of their own Scriptures they bear witness on our behalf that we have not forged the prophecies about Christ.* . . . Therefore, when

23. Augustine, *On Christian Doctrine* III.5, 9.
24. Augustine, *Against Faustus* 3.1.
25. Augustine, *Against Faustus* 16.21; *Tractates on the Gospel of John* 4.4.
26. Cf. Lisa A. Unterseher, *The Mark of Cain and the Jews. Augustine's Theology of Jews and Judaism* (Piscataway, NJ: Gorgias, 2014).

> they do not believe in our Scriptures, their own Scriptures, to which they are blind when they read, are fulfilled in them. Unless indeed anyone says that the Christians forged the prophecies about Christ that are quoted under the name of a Sibyl or of others, if there be any, which have no connection with the Jewish people. For us, to be sure, those suffice which are quoted from the books of our enemies, for we see and know that it is in order to bear this witness,—which they involuntarily supply on our behalf by possessing and preserving these same books,—that they themselves are scattered among all peoples, in whatever direction the church of Christ expands. For a prophecy about this thing was given in advance, in the Psalms which they, too, read, where it is written: "My God, his mercy shall go before me; my God has shown me concerning my enemies, that you are not to slay them, lest they some day forget your law; scatter them by your might." (Psalms 59.10, 11)[27]

Augustine now provides in his work *De Civitate Dei* a theological refutation of chiliasm. He relates the idea of the kingdom of peace within history to the Church age between ascension and Parousia. With this *ecclesiological* interpretation, he sidelines, on the one hand, the chiliasm that expects a salvation-historical *novum* in history with the establishment of a thousand-year kingdom of peace. On the other hand, Augustine does not advocate an ecclesiological triumphalism, since he emphasizes that the Church, under the conditions of history, is a *corpus permixtum*, in which the righteous and sinners live together until the judgment. But fundamentally Christ has already triumphed over the power of evil and has established his rule with the faithful in the Church.[28]

Augustine further develops his teaching of the two *civitates* that determine the course of history: *civitas Dei* ["city of God"] and *civitas terrena* ["earthly city"]. Origin and goal transcend history. The history in between is an interim that begins with Cain and Abel, continues through different periods of the history of Israel, and culminates with Christ in the Church age. But even the Church age stands under the banner of the pilgrimage in a foreign place (*peregrinatio*). Then follow

27. Augustine, *On the City of God* 18.46—William Chase Greene, trans., *Saint Augustine, The City of God Against the Pagans*, in seven volumes, vol. VI, (Loeb Classical Library; Cambridge, MA: Harvard University Press / London: William Heinemann, 1960): 49, 51, emphasis added; cf. Augustine, *Against Faustus* 12.23. Cf. Paula Fredriksen, *Augustine and the Jews: A Christian Defense of Jews and Judaism* (Yale, CT: Yale University Press, 2010).

28. Cf. Augustine, *City of God* 20.6–9.

judgment and consummation in the *civitas caelestis* ["heavenly city"]. Augustine's thinking about the two citizenships should neither be narrowly interpreted politically nor misunderstood in an idealistic way. A theocratic interpretation that sees "the spiritual foundation for the Holy Roman Empire of the Middle Ages" laid with Augustine's City of God (Jacob Taubes),[29] is just as misguided as an idealistic interpretation that believes one can recognize in the *civitas Dei* a purely invisible hidden entity (Adolf von Harnack, Heinrich Scholz, and others). *Civitas Dei* is rather the people from among the peoples, whom God is gathering in the world, the community of the Church, which, on account of her sacraments, also has a visibly institutional structure. In the distinction between the two citizenships, the concern is with the question: What are the ultimate determinations that guide people in their actions in history? On the one side there is the posture of turning away from God and turning toward oneself—this is the maxim on which is based the behavior of angels and men who are united in the *civitas terrena*. On the other side there is the posture of turning to God and turning away from self-centered thinking—that is the maxim on which is based the behavior of angels and men who are united within the *civitas Dei*. The drama of history consists in the fact that the two *civitates* run next to each other and man is called to turn away from the *civitas terrena* and to the *civitas Dei*.

The *civitas Dei* finds its visible form in the Church but is not coextensive with her. Augustine knows from the conflict with the Donatists how problematic it is to demand a Church free of sinners. Church is, for Augustine, a *corpus permixtum* in which sinners and the righteous are journeying together until the last judgment, as the parable of the wheat and tares makes clear (Matt 13:34–40). The question is when the harvest will take place, in which the tares will be separated from the wheat—in history, as the chiliasts claim, or in connection with the consummation of history at the last judgment? Augustine clearly opts for the latter, as can be inferred from his Book XX about the last judgment, in which he presents a commentary on the descriptions of the thousand-year kingdom of peace in John's Apocalypse (cf. Rev 20:1–6;

29. "das geistige Fundament für das Heilige Römische Reich des Mittelalters"—Jacob Taubes, *Abendländische Eschatologie. Mit einem Anhang* (Munich: Matthes & Seitz, 1991): 79.

cf. Ps 90:4; Dan 9). Augustine criticizes the idea that after six thousand years of history a thousand-year Sabbath rest begins for the holy ones who are worthy of the first resurrection. Augustine regards the chiliasts' idea that this Sabbath rest is associated with bodily table-delights and indulgences as a "ridiculous fable," and himself advocates a spiritual interpretation. He understands the talk of the first resurrection to mean that the transition from death to life is already taking place in a spiritual way (cf. Rom 7:22; Eph 3:16). Whoever makes this transition in faith and through baptism will be preserved from the second death, damnation. But the second resurrection means the resurrection of bodies in connection with the last judgment at the end of time. Augustine interprets the scenario of the Apocalypse in such a way that the binding of Satan has taken place and the Church already reigns with Christ. In the dramatic finale, Satan is briefly released once more to gather the deceived peoples for war against the Church. But the elect—Augustine is convinced of this—will, despite the tribulation, not fall away from the faith but rather will prove themselves in suffering and through the onslaught from without will be strengthened in their holiness (XX.8). The judgment, which will carry out the separation of wheat from tares, brings the eschatological transformation: The Church as *corpus permixtum,* which gathers the righteous and sinners equally, will be transformed into the true *civitas Dei* of the holy ones (XX.9). The devil is thrown "into the lake of fire" so that the *civitas terrena* no longer has any power. Only now does the kingdom of Christ become fully a reality (XX.14).

The meaning of *De Civitate Dei* lies in the fact that here the promise of the kingdom of God is connected to a concrete historical bearer, the Church. The "thousand-year" kingdom of Christ has already dawned in the Church; it does not have to be awaited or brought about by an appropriate pious practice. In this theology of history, Israel comes into view initially as Church before the Church. After Christ, however, the dispersed children of the house of Israel still have the salvation-historical significance of keeping present throughout the world the truth of the scriptures that point to Christ. In the end, a portion of them will come to the knowledge of Christ and find entrance into the *civitas Dei.*

Can one hold on to the domestication of chiliasm by Augustine—and at the same time develop an eschatology that is sensitive in terms of Israel theology, one that takes seriously the renaissance of chiliasm in the Messianic Jewish movement as an impetus?

3. Does the domestication of chiliasm need to be revised? Parousia, land promise, and thousand-year kingdom of peace as productive irritation

The Augustinian taming of chiliasm was adopted by Thomas Aquinas[30] and the Reformers.[31] It shapes the amillennial theology of the Catholic Church to this day. However, Augustine's legacy brought with it a certain atrophy of the Church's *historical-theological sensory processor*. The Church age, as an interim between the first and the second coming of Christ, knows no fundamental crises and innovations. The shock of the Shoah, but also the return of many Jews to Israel and the emergence of the Jewish Messianic movement, cannot be interpreted more closely using Augustine's historical-theological narrative. Now, on the basis of *Nostra Aetate*, the Catholic Church has begun to work self-critically through anti-Jewish burdens in catechesis, liturgy, and theology. Neither can she uphold the teaching that God has rejected his chosen people because they rejected the Messiah—that would be the punitive variety of supersessionism. Nor can she maintain the teaching of the Church as "new Israel"—that would debase the theological dignity of post-biblical Jewry. To connect the turning away from anti-Judaism with positive impulses, the Jewish identity of Jesus has been newly emphasized in Christology, and the salvation-historical dignity of Israel as the "apple of God's eye" has been highlighted.[32] Nevertheless, the structural significance of Israel for the history of the Church and for eschatology has not yet been adequately worked out. Does this have something to do with Augustine's amillennial setting of the course?

The ecclesiological domestication of chiliasm has left the Catholic Church susceptible to triumphalist self-descriptions, in which the

30. *Summa Theologica* III, Supplement, Q. 77, art. 1–4; *Summa contra Gentiles* III.27 and IV.83. Here the Three Ages doctrine of Joachim of Fiore is repudiated.

31. Cf. *Augsburg Confession* 17 and *Second Helvetic Confession* 11.

32. On the Jewish re-dimensioning of Christology, cf. Helmut Hoping, *Jesus aus Galiläa – Messias und Gottes Sohn* (Freiburg i. Br.: Herder, 2019); on the salvation-historical dignity of Israel, cf. Jan-Heiner Tück, *Gottes Augapfel. Bruchstücke zu einer Theologie nach Auschwitz* (Freiburg i. Br.: Herder, 2016).

Jewish people only had a place as blindfolded *Synagoga*, against whom the *Ecclesia* was made to shine brightly. The promise surplus of the Old Testament prophecies (cf. Isa 2; Mic 4 and others) was hardly noticed. The Church's eschatological sensory processor has also been stunted; she has hardly anything to say about the Parousia of Christ and the eschatological signs of the time. The abstract and individualistic reduction of eschatology, as expressed in Rahner's reinterpretation of the Parousia, stands at odds with the return of chiliastic ideas in the Messianic Jewish movement. There it is assumed that God will fulfill his promises first to Israel and then to the nations. In this, the topography of Israel plays a significant role. The spiritualization and the "de-territorialization" of eschatology, in the footsteps of Augustine's theology of history, is here productively irritated!

In closing, I would like briefly to highlight three such productive irritations:

Parousia Christi

The expectation of the early Christians that the Son of Man would come again on the clouds of heaven was soon dampened and is today largely extinguished. This is connected not only with the ongoing history of the Church, but also with tectonic shifts in cosmology.[33] The geocentric worldview that is presupposed by the biblical authors was superseded by the Copernican turn in the modern period; indeed, the heliocentric worldview itself has become obsolete due to the newer cosmology, which assumes a multiverse with innumerable solar systems.[34] To this can be added the eschatological reservation, which calls to mind the finite and perspective-bound nature of theology when it warns against painting an overly concrete idea of the time, place, and circumstances of the Parousia.[35]

33. Cf. Hans Blumenberg, *Die Genesis der kopernikanischen Welt*, 3 vols. (Frankfurt a. M.: Suhrkamp, 1981).

34. Tom Siegfried, *The Number of the Heavens: A History of the Multiverse and the Quest to Understand the Cosmos* (Harvard, MA: Harvard University Press, 2019).

35. Cf. Christian Stoll, "Der eschatologische Vorbehalt. Zum dialektischen Ursprung einer theologischen Denkfigur," *Internationale katholische Zeitschrift – Communio* 45 (2016): 539–59.

Nevertheless, the Church's Parousia hope, which is preserved in the Apostles' Creed and Niceno-Constantinopolitan Creeds, never entirely faded. The Christ who will come to judge the living and the dead is none other than the one who has already come. In the process, the *Jewish identity of Jesus* has long been forgotten or denied. If one takes seriously the fact that Jesus of Nazareth was not only born of a Jewish mother and circumcised on the eighth day according to the Torah (Luke 2:21) but also will be enduringly recognizable as a Jew and Messiah of Israel, then an impetus from the Messianic-Jewish movement can be taken up here. This not only challenges the expectation fatigue of many Christians today and contradicts voices in liberal Jewish theology who think they should assert that the Messiah is no longer expected by Jews.[36] Messianic Jewish theology also gives the Parousia hope an Israel-theological concreteness. The exalted Christ may have remained unrecognized by the majority of Jews in history, but in the context of the Parousia he will also and first reveal himself as "King of the Jews" and thereby finally establish his kingdom. Jewish Messiah expectation and Christian Parousia hope then come together when "all Israel" acknowledges its Messiah (cf. Rom 11:26).[37] But the gentile Christian Church will be convicted by the Parousia Christ of having forgotten Israel. In a reversal of the image of the blindfolded *Synagoga*, which is attached to the portals of a number of medieval cathedrals as a contrast to the resplendent *Ecclesia*, one could say: The blindfold is removed from the eyes of the *ecclesia ex gentibus* when she recognizes Jesus as "King of the Jews" and is ashamed to discover that in history she has often been guilty in relation to the brothers and sisters of Jesus and has marginalized and eliminated the *ecclesia ex circumcisione*. Artists like Marc Chagall or poets such as Paul Celan have seen in the Jewish suffering story of the twentieth century a picture of the Passion of Jesus.[38] However, the growing number of Jesus-believing Jews not only raises fresh awareness of the *ecclesia ex circumcisione*; it can also be interpreted as an "eschatological sign."

36. Cf. Walter Homolka, Juni Hoppe, and Daniel Krochmalnik, *Der Messias kommt nicht. Abschied vom jüdischen Erlöser* (Freiburg i. Br.: Herder, 2022).

37. Cf. on this the further statements of Cardinal Walter Kasper in this volume.

38. Cf. the poems *Tenebrae* and *Benedicta*. On this: Jan-Heiner Tück, *Gelobt seist du, Niemand. Paul Celans Dichtung – eine theologische Provokation* (Freiburg i. Br.: Herder, 2021): 170–93.

The land of Israel

The spiritual reading of the biblical promise of land has led to a deterritorialization and de-historicization of the consummation hope: "Our home is in heaven" (Phil 3:20). "For here we have no lasting city, but we seek the future one" (Heb 13:14). But if the land promise is part of the unrevoked covenant that God made with Israel, then Catholic theology is called to think afresh about the land.[39] The return of the Jews to the land of their fathers after almost two thousand years of Diaspora is a noteworthy event; the founding of the State of Israel in 1948 after the Shoah is an event in need of interpretation. Shalom Ben-Chorin saw the "finger of God" at work in the terrors of Auschwitz, interpreting the Shoah as a punitive judgment and the founding of the State as "fleshly resurrection of Israel."[40] Christian theology is, with good reason, more reticent to interpret momentous dates of Jewish history with Christian categories. With respect to the founding of the State of Israel, Benedict XVI remarked that the Catholic Church acknowledged the State of Israel as an independent and sovereign constitutional state in 1993, but that "a theologically-understood acquisition of land in the sense of a new political messianism" is to be rejected.[41] That is an

39. Gavin D'Costa, *Catholic Doctrines on the Jewish People After Vatican II* (Oxford University Press, 2019): chs. 3 and 4.

40. "fleischliche Auferstehung Israels"—Julius H. Schoeps, ed., *Auf der Suche nach einer jüdischen Theologie. Der Briefwechsel zwischen Schalom Ben-Chorin und Hans-Joachim Schoeps* (Frankfurt a. M.: Suhrkamp, 1989): 49–50. After an almost two-thousand-year diaspora and statelessness of the Jewish people, the ingathering of the dispersed from all lands of the earth has begun. The Hebrew language, which for centuries was still used only in synagogue services and in the teaching conversations of the rabbis and was otherwise a dead language, has become a living language again through the impetus of Eliezer Ben Jehuda (1858–1922). Although his project of reviving the Hebrew language was initially opposed by orthodox Jews as a desecration of the holy language, it prevailed. Palestine, which Mark Twain had described in his travel diary *The Innocents Abroad, or The New Pilgrim's Progress* (1869) as "a hopeless, dreary, heart-broken land," this desolate land has since the Jewish resettlement—between 1882 and 1940, first by buying land (cf. Jer 23:44), then by rebuilding cities, and finally by planting vineyards and orchards (cf. Amos 9:14–15; Isa 17:10)—become a flourishing landscape (cf. Ezek 36:34–35). The founding of the State of Israel was able to be carried out in 1948 despite threats of annihilation by the Arab states. Even if one views a literal hermeneutic of the biblical writings with reservations, these are nevertheless events that demand an interpretation.

41. Joseph Ratzinger / Benedict XVI, "Grace and Vocation Without Remorse: Comments on the Treatise *De Iudaeis*," *International Catholic Journal – Communio* 45 (2018): 163–84, 178.

orientation mark. A religious legitimation of the politics of the State of Israel or even extreme forms of Zionism leads astray—already because the rights of the Palestinians are not to be respected any less.[42]

At the same time, in correspondence with Vienna's chief rabbi Arie Folger, Benedict admitted that the return of many Jews to Israel could be interpreted as "a sign of God's faithfulness" to his chosen people.[43] The use of the concept of a sign invites one to understand the return of many Jews to the land of their fathers as a sacramental reality and, in doing so, to make recourse analogously to the threefold distinction of Thomas Aquinas.[44] As a *signum rememorativum*, the gathering of the dispersed children of the house of Israel is a reminder of the manifold land promises of the old covenant. As a *signum demonstrativum*, the homecoming of the exiles to the land is at the same time the initial redemption of the promise and thus a sign of God's covenant faithfulness to Israel. Finally, a *signum prognosticum* can also be recognized in this noteworthy historical event, if in fact an eschatological surplus is connected with this initial realization of the land promise. This surplus has the heavenly home as its vanishing point (cf. Heb 4:1–11; 6:13–20; 11:8–10) and gives a clear justification to the spiritualization and metaphorization of the land motif, which already begins in Hellenistic Judaism and then becomes dominant in the Christian tradition. The return of many Jews to Israel and the founding of their own state are a productive irritation for Catholic eschatology, since they can glimpse in it a "sign of God's faithfulness" to his chosen people—an impetus to cautiously break open their historical-theological agnosticism.[45] Open questions in the debate about the land, which has only just begun in Catholic theology, are, according to Gavin D'Costa, the borders of Israel,

42. However, it must resolutely be criticized that the Palestinian Authority has published maps that "provide in the Holy Land only space for a Palestinian state, but not for a Jewish state called Israel." (Correspondence of July 21, 2022 from Pastor Martin Rösch, Schopfheim).

43. "Zeichen der Treue Gottes"—Benedict XVI, "Briefwechsel mit Rabbi Arie Folger," *Internationale katholische Zeitschrift – Communio* 47 (2018): 613.

44. Cf. *Summa Theologica* III, Q. 60 art. 3. Cardinal Walter Kasper has rightly emphasized that, with this analogy, despite all the similarity one should note the "greater dissimilarity" (*maior dissimilitudo*) in the sense of the Fourth Lateran Council.

45. Similarly, Benedict XVI, in his correspondence with Rabbi Arie Folger (see note 43), 613.

the form of government, and the political status of the Palestinians in the State of Israel.[46]

Christ's thousand-year kingdom of peace?

In contrast to chiliastic theologies, which interpret Revelation 20 literally and let the roadmap for the events of the end times begin with the founding of the state of Israel, the eschatological conceptions in the German-speaking sphere move in the amillennial paths of Augustine. Paul Althaus, Walter Kreck, and Wolfhart Pannenberg on the Protestant side,[47] and Karl Rahner, Joseph Ratzinger, and Medard Kehl on the Catholic side,[48] clearly reject chiliasm. However, they see the justified element of chiliasm in the fact that it brings the history-changing power of Christian hope to bear against flight from the world and consolation in the hereafter. Within the spectrum of current systematic theology, a positive appreciation is offered by Jürgen Moltmann, who differentiates between "historical chiliasm" and "eschatological chiliasm" in his book *The Coming of God*. He rejects the first because it is, in his view, susceptible to a religious legitimation of political power and easily takes on repressive traits. The second he advocates as a "picture of hope in resistance, in suffering, and in the exiles of this world."[49] In his view, eschatological chiliasm marks a transition between historical time and the new creation. It is about a Messianic kingdom of Jews and Christians.

46. Gavin D'Costa, "Catholic Zionism: The Jewish State Is a Sign of God's Fidelity," *First Things* (Jan 2020).

47. Paul Althaus, *Die letzten Dinge. Eschatologie* (Gütersloh: Bertelsmann, 4th edn 1933): 318; Walter Kreck, *Die Zukunft des Gekommenen* (Munich: Kaiser, 1961): 188; Wolfhart Pannenberg, *Systematische Theologie*, vol. 3 (Göttingen: Vandenhoeck & Ruprecht, 1992).

48. Rahner, "Kirche und Parusie Christi" (see note 5); Rahner, "Parusie" (see note 5); Kasper, "Die Hoffnung" (see note 6); Medard Kehl, *Eschatologie* (Würzburg: Echter, 1986).

49. Jürgen Moltmann, *The Coming of God: Christian Eschatology*, trans. Margaret Kohl (Minneapolis, MN: Fortress, 1996): 192. In this context, Moltmann (p. 193) quotes Karl Barth: "Ethics can no more exist without millenarianism, without at least some minute degree of it, than without the idea of a moral personality. The man who claims he is happily free from this *judaica opinio* has either not yet learned or has forgotten what the ethical problem really is"—Karl Barth, "The Problem of Ethics Today" (1922), in Karl Barth, *The Word of God and the Word of Man*, trans. Douglas Horton (New York, NY: Harper & Row, 1957): 136–82, at 158.

It is noteworthy that Moltmann also mentions the importance of the land here: "If the chosen and 'sealed' Christians are joined together with the chosen and 'sealed' Jews, together with them becoming the messianic people of the messianic kingdom, then it is not impossible also to think . . . of Jerusalem and the land of Israel: 'the central people' and 'the land of the first fruits.'"[50] The expectation that before the new heaven and the new earth there will be an interim period of transition, in which Jews and Christians with Christ will establish the kingdom of peace, is for Catholic theology a productive irritation. It would have to partially revise the Augustinian narrative of the Church age as the thousand-year kingdom if it wanted to advocate an eschatological chiliasm in the footsteps of Moltmann, which connects to the early Church Fathers before Augustine and comes into a conversation with the expectations of many Messianic Jews that God has begun to work anew in history.

(Translated by John David Martin, James Earle Patrick, and Wayne Coppins from the German: "Parusie, Land und 1000jähriges Friedensreich. Muss die Domestizierung des Chiliasmus durch Augustinus revidiert werden?")

50. Moltmann, *The Coming of God* (see note 49), 198–99; quoting Johann T. Beck, *Die Vollendung des Reiches Gottes. Separatabdruck aus der Christlichen Glaubenslehre* (Gütersloh, 1887): 63–64.

Response to Jan-Heiner Tück, "Parousia, Land, and Thousand-Year Kingdom of Peace"

Ulrich Laepple

PROFESSOR TÜCK, writing from a Catholic perspective, has made Augustine the starting point for his reflections on eschatology and presented him as the antithesis to the Jewish eschatological tradition. Since it is not far from Augustine to Martin Luther, the Church Father of the Protestants, I am complementing Professor Tück's comments from a Protestant perspective. I shall do this in three steps, followed by a fourth with two problem indicators that result for me from Tück's presentation.

1. From Augustine to Luther

Luther was a monk of the Augustinian order. Therefore, he lived in and with the Augustinian tradition and theology. These great figures of Church history, Augustine and Luther, both had one thing above all in common: a profound *personal faith experience*. Augustine depicts his conversion experience impressively in his *Confessions*. Martin Luther also relates his "conversion experience" which, against the background of his monastery experiences, led, in the struggle for the certainty of faith, to the breakthrough of trust in the gracious God.[1] This experience was

1. Cf. the preface to vol. 1 of the complete edition of his Latin writings, 1545 (Weimarer Ausgabe 54, 185).

decisive for his later doctrine of justification: The fundamental question, *"How do I obtain a gracious God?"* found its answer in the *"sola gratia"* ["only by grace"] of the gospel.

Even if this question which was so central for Luther and the Reformation should not be missing from any ecumenical theology, it is too narrow as a hermeneutic key for the Bible.[2] For the theological concentration on the existential question of a gracious God runs the risk of becoming blind to the greater dimensions of the promise-historical threads of the Bible, above all those applying to Israel as the chosen people. Luther's wonderful explications of Old Testament texts in particular, which spiritualize God's tidings to Israel, have their limitations against the background of this theological hermeneutic. For example, he applied the statements about the new covenant from Jeremiah 31 in a traditional spiritualizing way to the Church, and thus disinherited Israel, its past and its future. He could no longer interpret election and justification in the context of Israel as Paul does in the Epistle to the Romans, but could only relate both to the individual person and their faith.[3] Under this premise, he repeatedly accused the Judaism of his time of remaining stuck in the worldly and earthly, because it expected an earthly Messiah and placed its hope in an earthly kingdom in the land of the fathers.

What I want to say with this first reflection is that with respect to the de-Israelizing, spiritualizing, and individualizing of the biblical message, Catholics and Protestants, for all the differences in detail, are sitting in *the same* boat, together with the entire Western theological tradition.

2. *Renewing the Church—with the help of the Jews!*

How might one regain the lost connection to the real Old Testament Jewish (and that means, biblical) history of hope, and get out of the

2. Karl Barth viewed this anthropological narrowing in Luther's theology (especially the young Luther) critically as an attempt "to make the history of Jesus Christ coincident with that of the believer, and *vice versa*"—*Church Dogmatics* IV.1, trans. Geoffrey Bromiley (Edinburgh: T&T Clark, 1956): 767 (XIV, §63.2).

3. For this, cf. Bertold Klappert, "Erwählung und Rechtfertigung. Martin Luther und die Juden," in *Miterben der Verheißung. Beiträge zum jüdisch–christlichen Dialog*, ed. Bertold Klappert (Neukirchen-Vluyn: Neukirchener, 2000): 105–147.

Israel-forgetting Western boat? *Nostra Aetate* took an impressive lead in 1965 with its critique of replacement theology. On the Protestant side, the necessary far-reaching change only became possible because the Church in humility and willingness to repent had asked Jews to help it renew itself on the basis of the Bible. What an irony of history: Christians, after almost two thousand years of anti-Jewish history, are asking the Jews to help them understand their own, Christian message anew. The fact that Jews have said yes to this is the miracle of the Christian–Jewish dialogue, especially in Germany.

This dialogue was fruitful because through the generations Judaism has preserved biblical truths that the Church since the second century has successively removed and lost from its faith content.[4] The Church could therefore regain them only from Jewish hands. The task of Christian theology must therefore be to bring to the fore anew the biblical horizons preserved in Judaism, which are not revoked but rather confirmed in the New Testament with Jesus Christ, its center, through the encounter with Judaism.

3. Return to the land of Israel—a "sign of God's faithfulness"?

In his reflections on chiliasm, Tück devoted special attention to the "land of Israel." Rightly so. For the question of the land determines whether we are serious about the theological reversal of our traditional anti-Jewish theology. The geographical land of Israel is not an idea, nor is it a theological construct. Even after the catastrophe of the Jewish War in the first century, it has remained a living hope of Israel, which—in the Zionism of the twentieth century and with the founding of the State of Israel in 1948—has led to a renewed historical-political fact. The Synodal Declaration of the Protestant Church in the Rhineland has therefore dared to formulate that it professes the "insight that the enduring existence of the Jewish people, its homecoming to the

4. An outstanding and at the same time moving example of this experience is the way the synodal resolution of the Protestant Church in the Rhineland came into being in the dialogue between Christian theologians and Jewish scholars: cf. Yehuda Aschkenasy, "Mein Weg nach Bad Neuenahr," in *Umkehr und Erneuerung. Erläuterungen zum Synodalbeschluss der Rheinischen Landessynode 1980 "Zur Erneuerung des Verhältnisses von Christen und Juden,"* ed. Bertold Klappert and Helmut Starck (Neukirchen-Vluyn: Neukirchener, 1980): 1–4.

land of promise, and also the establishment of the state of Israel are *signs of God's faithfulness* to his people."[5]

But what does "signs of God's faithfulness" mean? In later commentary it is specified: It does not mean *"eschatological* signs." The formulation does not want to give the impression that "the homecoming of Israel to its land and the founding of the state of Israel" can be read off God's world clock, so to speak. The formulation affirms only the faithfulness of God in the continuity of Israel's history. It wants neither to glorify Israeli politics nor encourage a prophetic-enthusiastic fantasy.[6]

4. Two questions following Professor Tück's presentation

(1) On Catholic "land theology"

In the conclusion of his presentation, Tück calls the "return of the Jews to Palestine" a "noteworthy event from a [theology-of-]history perspective" and an "event in need of interpretation."[7] That is a very cautious formulation and sounds as if a commitment is meant to be avoided. Since, however, "the land promise is part of the unrevoked covenant," Tück nonetheless sees "Catholic theology . . . called to think afresh about the land."[8]

I have asked myself if there is a specifically "Catholic" inhibition with regard to an Israel-theological assessment of the land. In 1965, *Nostra Aetate* remained silent on the "question of the land." In contrast, a French synod of bishops demanded with recognizable impatience a further step vis-à-vis *Nostra Aetate*:

5. ". . . Einsicht, dass die fortdauernde Existenz des jüdischen Volkes, seine Heimkehr in das Land der Verheißung und auch die Errichtung des Staates Israel *Zeichen der Treue Gottes* gegenüber seinem Volk sind"—Cited according to Bertold Klappert, "Zeichen der Treue Gottes," in *Umkehr und Erneuerung* (see note 4), 73–88, at 73.

6. *Ibid.*, 81ff.

7. Tück's original text had "a noteworthy event from a theology-of-history perspective" ["ein geschichtstheologisch denkwürdiger Vorgang"], now revised to "a noteworthy event" ["ein denkwürdiger Vorgang"]" with an additional mention of "this noteworthy historical event" ["diesem denkwürdigen historischen Vorgang"] later in the same section, p. 376.

8. See p. 375 in this volume.

> Christians must take into account the interpretation given by Jews to their ingathering around Jerusalem, which, according to their faith, is considered a blessing. . . . It is an essential question . . . whether or not the ingathering of the dispersed Jewish people . . . will despite so many tragic events prove to be one of the final ways of God's justice for the Jewish people and at the same time for all the nations of the earth. How could Christians remain indifferent to what is now being decided in that land?[9]

Here, in impassioned language, solidarity with Israel is underlined through the reference to the eschatological significance of the land. That which is "now" happening "around Jerusalem" is placed in the horizon of the eschatological consummation.

(2) On Messianic Judaism

In his presentation on the theme of "eschatology and land," Tück collectively uses "Messianic Judaism" as a dialogue partner, aware of its diversity.

My question is whether the dialogue with the still relatively new movement of Messianic Judaism is really suitable for, to some extent, upsetting the apple cart of the Western Israel-forgetting tradition. In Messianic Judaism—worldwide and also in Israel itself—a lot is still very much in flux. Secondly, Messianic Judaism does not always live up to its name, because it often does not represent Judaism convincingly; in fact, it sometimes thinks it has to distinguish itself sharply from it.

9. Statement by the French Bishops' Committee for Relations with Jews (April 16, 1973): section 5, § e. English translation cited according to https://ccjr.us/dialogika-resources/documents-and-statements/roman-catholic/other-conferences-of-catholic-bishops/cefr1973 (accessed May 1, 2025). ["Ils [i.e. les Chrétiens] doivent tenir compte de l'interprétation que donnent de leur rassemblement autour de Jérusalem les Juifs qui, au nom de leur foi, le considèrent comme une bénédiction. . . . C'est une question essentielle . . . de savoir si le rassemblement des dispersés du peuple juif, . . . sera finalement ou non, malgré tant de drames, une des voies de la justice de Dieu pour le peuple juif et, en même temps que pour lui, pour tous les peuples de la terre. Comment les Chrétiens resteraient-ils indifférents à ce qui se décide actuellement sur cette terre?"]—Conférence épiscopale française, "L'attitude des chrétiens à l'égard du judaïsme. Orientations pastorales du Comité épiscopal pour les relations avec le judaïsme" (Documents Épiscopat; Bulletin de la Conférence épiscopale française, n.10, April 1973): section 5, § e. https://eglise.catholique.fr/wp-content/uploads/sites/2/2017/02/1973_Eglise-de-France-%E2%80%93-Orientations-pastorales.pdf (accessed May 1, 2025).

Not infrequently it appears as a Jewishly inculturated Christianity in the evangelical mold. Also, as Tück himself says, the eschatology of Messianic Jews is bewilderingly diverse (p. 360). This is why I think that the dialogue with Messianic Judaism cannot and must not replace the dialogue with the non-messianic, majority Judaism.

Quite a few friends of Christian–Jewish dialogue from the churches are hoping from the Messianic Jewish movement that its representatives will develop a theology that is in lively dialogue with Judaism and is therefore both "Messianic" and also "Jewish." I see in Mark Kinzer's books how his Messianic Jewish theology has been developed in constant conversation with names like Buber, Rosenzweig, Heschel, or Wyschogrod and many others from the rabbinic tradition, and has thereby been enriched.[10] By the way, this applies also to Christian theology: Tück rightly points to Jürgen Moltmann's eschatology, which would be unthinkable without the dialogue with Judaism.[11] And the eschatology of Friedrich-Wilhelm Marquardt is determined by the dialogue with Judaism to an even greater extent.[12]

Please allow me to underscore this last reflection with a citation from a Jewish scholar who attempts to put biblical eschatology into words. The sentences come from Jewish scholar Michael Wyschogrod, who passed away in 2015. He uses the expression "Jewish messianism" to express the total transformation of the world—with Israel as the center of God's presence:

> Jewish messianism makes it possible for the Jew to hope when otherwise there would seem to be no hope. . . . Because there waits in the future a transformation of the human condition, such as has never been known before, the past has only limited significance as a guide to the future. The saving acts of God will be unexpected, revising much of our previously held wisdom, bringing into being a new heaven and a new earth in which not only the body of Israel will be circumcised but also its heart.

10. Cf. Mark S. Kinzer, *Jerusalem Crucified, Jerusalem Risen: The Resurrected Messiah, the Jewish People, and the Land of Promise* (Eugene, OR: Cascade, 2018).

11. Jürgen Moltmann, *The Coming of God: Christian Eschatology*, trans. Margaret Kohl (Minneapolis, MN: Fortress, 1996). Cf. on this, but partly critical: Bertold Klappert, *Worauf wir hoffen. Das Kommen Gottes und der Weg Jesu Christi. Mit einer Antwort von Jürgen Moltmann* (Munich: Kaiser, 1997).

12. Friedrich-Wilhelm Marquardt, *Was dürfen wir hoffen, wenn wir hoffen dürften. Eine Eschatologie*, 3 vols., ed. Hartmut Spenner (Munich: Kaiser, 1993–1996).

> The circumcised body of Israel is the dark, carnal presence through which the redemption makes its way in history. Salvation is of the Jews because the flesh of Israel is the abode of the divine presence in the world. It is the carnal anchor that God has sunk into the soil of creation.[13]

For the Messianic Jewish movement, it should be welcome and instructive that, as with Wyschogrod's eschatological "Jewish Messianism," there are more than just connections to an inner-Jewish conversation. This is true despite the different answers to the Messiah question.[14]

No ecclesiastical Christian theology should attempt to "domesticate" this Jewish-Messianic and biblical-eschatological knowledge, either in an Augustinian-Catholic nor Augustinian-Lutheran way. Rather, as a Church, we must recover it anew.[15]

(Translated by John David Martin, James Earle Patrick, and Wayne Coppins from the German: "Antwort auf Jan-Heiner Tück")

13. Michael Wyschogrod, *The Body of Faith. Judaism as Corporeal Election* (New York: Seabury Press, 1983): 256.

14. Here again the books by Mark Kinzer should be referred to, in which this inner-Jewish conversation is conducted impressively.

15. In contrast, the question of chiliasm in the narrower sense, as presented above all in dispensationalist conceptions, should be of secondary importance.

List of Contributors

Bakker, Henk holds the James Wm. McClendon Chair in Baptist and Evangelical Theologies at the Vrije Universiteit Amsterdam, and was formerly Professor of Baptist History, Identity and Theologies there from 2013–2017.

Bockmuehl, Markus has been Professor of Biblical Exegesis at the University of Oxford since 2014 and Fellow of Keble College, Oxford, since 2007.

D'Costa, Gavin is emeritus Professor of Catholic Theology at the University of Bristol and Professor of Interreligious Dialogue, Pontifical University of St Thomas Aquinas, Rome. He is also a consultant on interreligious dialogue and theology for the Catholic Church in England and Wales and the Anglican Church.

Fichtenbauer, Johannes serves as head deacon in the Roman Catholic Archdiocese of Vienna under Cardinal Christoph Schönborn, and is responsible for training permanent deacons. He is also Director of Towards Jerusalem Council II (TJCII) in Europe.

Harvey, Richard is an associate lecturer at All Nations Christian College, UK, where he was previously academic dean. He was a founding member of the London Messianic Congregation and is a past president of the International Messianic Jewish Alliance.

Hoping, Helmut is Professor of Dogmatics and Liturgical Studies at the Albert Ludwigs University of Freiburg i. Br., after having held the Chair of Dogmatics at the Faculty of Theology of the University of Lucerne from 1997 to 2000.

Kasper, Walter was Professor of Dogmatics in Münster and Tübingen from 1964–1989. In 1989 he was appointed Bishop of Rottenburg-Stuttgart. From 1999–2010 he headed the Council for Promoting Christian Unity, and was created a cardinal in 2001.

Kinzer, Mark is moderator of the international ecumenical fellowship Yachad BeYeshua, Rabbi emeritus of Congregation Zera Avraham in Ann Arbor, Michigan, and President emeritus of Messianic Jewish Theological Institute.

Laepple, Ulrich was a member of the Christian–Jewish Committee of the Regional Synod of the Protestant Church in the Rhineland and a member of the Missionary Services Working Group of the EKD (Protestant Church in Germany).

Lévy OP, Antoine is a professor at the University of Helsinki / University of Eastern Finland. In addition to several memberships in theological dialogue groups, he has been a member of the dialogue group between the Catholic Church and Messianic Jews since 2011.

Mallmann, Bernard is an assistant (post doc) at the Institute for Dogmatics and Dogma History at the Faculty of Catholic Theology of the University of Vienna.

Neuhaus SJ, David was vicar of the Latin Patriarchate of Jerusalem for Hebrew-speaking Catholics from 2009–2017. His academic posts to date have been at Bethlehem University, the Latin Patriarchate Seminary in Beit Jala, and as a research fellow at the Shalom Hartman Institute, Jerusalem.

Oktaba OP, Piotr teaches Biblical Theology at the Superior Institute of Religious Studies of St Thomas Aquinas in Kyiv.

Patrick, James Earle is the theological coordinator of TJCII-Europe, a member and former officer of the Society for Old Testament Study, secretary of the Love Never Fails coalition in the UK, and has served as a theologian to the NewFrontiers family of churches.

Rosik, Mariusz has been a professor at the Pontifical Faculty of Theology in Wrocław (Breslau), Poland, since 2006. He is a member of the Studiorum Novi Testamenti Societas (Cambridge).

Rosner, Jennifer is Assistant Professor of Systematic Theology at Fuller Theological Seminary, and also teaches at The King's University, Azusa Pacific University, and the Messianic Jewish Theological Institute.

Rucks, Hanna is a pastor of the Reformed Church Bern-Jura-Solothurn (Switzerland). She studied theology in Basel and Göttingen and one year of Jewish Studies at the Hebrew University in Jerusalem. Currently, she is working alongside her profession on a third-party funded project of the University of Tübingen on the topic of the integration of converts from Islam into Christian congregations in Germany.

Rudolph, David is Professor of New Testament and Jewish Studies and Director of Messianic Jewish Studies at The King's University in Southlake, Texas.

Rutishauser SJ, Christian is Delegate for Schools and Universities of the Central European Province of the Jesuit Order. He completed his doctoral studies in Jewish Studies in Jerusalem, New York, and Lucerne. He has been a delegation member of the Vatican Commission for Religious Relations with Judaism since 2004 and a permanent advisor to the Holy See in the same capacity since 2014.

Schönborn, Christoph is a member of the Dominican Order. He was Professor of Dogmatics and Eastern Church Theology at Fribourg in Switzerland. In 1991 he was appointed Auxiliary Bishop of the Archdiocese of Vienna, in 1995 became Archbishop of Vienna, and was created a cardinal in 1998.

Schumacher, Thomas has been Professor of New Testament Exegesis at the University of Freiburg i. Üe. (Switzerland) since 2015.

Schumacher, Ursula has held the Chair of Dogmatics at the University of Lucerne since 2022, and was formerly Professor of Catholic Theology and Religious Education at the High School of Education at Karlsruhe.

Schwienhorst-Schönberger, Ludger held the Chair of Old Testament Exegesis at the Catholic Theological Faculty of the University of Vienna from 2007–2022. He is co-editor of the commentary series *Herders Theologischer Kommentar zum Alten Testament* (Freiburg i. Br.).

Soulen, R. Kendall is Professor of Systematic Theology and Chair of the Institute for Theological Studies in the Laney Graduate Division of Religion at Emory University. He currently serves as president of The Society for Post-Supersessionist Theology.

Theobald, Michael was Professor of Biblical Theology at the Free University of Berlin from 1985–1989 and Professor of New Testament at Eberhard Karls University Tübingen from 1989–2016.

Tiwald, Markus has been Professor of New Testament Exegesis at the University of Vienna since 2019.

Tück, Jan-Heiner has been Professor of Dogmatics and Dogma History at the University of Vienna since 2010. He has been editor of the *International Catholic Journal: Communio* since 2006.

Vetö ICN, Étienne has been an associate professor at the Pontifical Gregorian University in Rome since 2014. In 2017 he became director of the Cardinal Bea Centre for Jewish Studies, and in 2023 he was appointed Auxiliary Bishop of the Archdiocese of Reims.

Index